Insurance Law in Hungary

Insurance Law in Hungary

Edit Antal Ujvári
Judit Barta

This book was originally published as a monograph in the International Encyclopaedia of Laws/Insurance Law.

Founding Editor: Roger Blanpain
General Editor: Frank Hendrickx
Volume Editor: Herman Cousy

Wolters Kluwer

Published by:
Kluwer Law International B.V.
PO Box 316
2400 AH Alphen aan den Rijn
The Netherlands
E-mail: lrs-sales@wolterskluwer.com
Website: www.wolterskluwer.com/en/solutions/kluwerlawinternational

Sold and distributed by:
Wolters Kluwer Legal & Regulatory U.S.
920 Links Avenue
Landisville, PA 17538
United States of America
E-mail: customer.service@wolterskluwer.com

ISBN 978-94-035-2298-2

e-Book: ISBN 978-94-035-2308-8
web-PDF: ISBN 978-94-035-2318-7

The Authors

Judit Barta was born on December 18, 1969. She obtained her law degree in 1993. She has professional experience in the field of insurance law. In 2001, she obtained her PhD degree. She obtained a Master of Laws (LLM) as an insurance law specialist in 1996. The title of her PhD dissertation was "The System of the Hungarian Private Pension Fund." Between 2005 and 2010, she was the stately recognized professor and member of the examination board of the (dependent and independent) insurance intermediary higher education established by the Ministry of Justice. She represented insurers as an attorney from 1996 to 2002. Since 1997, she has been the legal representative of the Association of Architects of Borsod-Abaúj-Zemplén County, and she was also a legal expert of the Chamber of Hungarian Architects between 2009 and 2013. Her research topic covers the field of company law, private insurance systems, commercial contracts, copyright, and hunter's right. She gives lectures at the University of Miskolc and at other Universities as well. Within the framework of the doctorate course at the University of Miskolc, she gives special courses in various topics, such as supplementary pension system, life insurance, and liability insurance in the European Union (EU).

Currently, she is a professor and the Head of the Department of Commercial Law, Institute of Civil Sciences, Faculty of Law, at the University of Miskolc. Since 2022, half-time professor Department of Civil Studies, Faculty of Public Governance and International Studies, at the National University of Public Service.

The Authors

Edit Antal Ujvári was born on January 13, 1954. She obtained her in Law in 1982. She obtained a Master of Laws (LLM) as an insurance law specialist in 1996. Since 1988, she has worked at the Department of Commercial Law, Institute of Civil Sciences, Faculty of Law at the University of Miskolc, currently as an honorary associate professor. She gives civil law, commercial contract law, company law, competition law, bankruptcy law, commercial papers, and consumer law lectures for full-and part-time graduate law, engineering, and economics students. Since 1990, she has been an attorney-at-law at the Law Firm No. 10 of Miskolc. She is most experienced in insurance law, commercial contracts, company law, and consumer law. She was a company solicitor at the State Building Company and at the State Insurance Company between 1982 and 1986, and she was an attorney at law at the Generali Insurance Company in 1987 and between 1990 and 2017. Her research topics include tort law, company law (corporate governance), commercial contract law (especially insurance law, commercial agency law, franchising, factoring, and e-commerce), and consumer law. She has been a member of the Bar Association of Borsod-Abaúj-Zemplén County since 1990 and of the Association of Civil Law Professors since 2009.

Translators
Dr. Edit Sápi.
Dr. Bence Udvarhelyi.

Table of Contents

List of Abbreviations

AHIC	Association of Hungarian Insurance Companies
Arb.	Act LX of 2017 on Arbitration
BIns.	Act LXXXVIII of 2014 on the Business of Insurance
CC	Act V of 2013 on the Civil Code
CCP	Act CXXX of 2016 on the Code of Civil Procedure
CDP	Curia Decisions on Principle
cDP	Court Decisions on Principle
CHIS	Act LXXXIII of 1997 on the Services of the Compulsory Health Insurance System
CJD	Collection of Judicial Decisions
CP	Act CLV of 1997 on Consumer Protection
DCA	Decisions of Courts of Appeal
EEA	European Economic Area
EEC	European Economic Community
EIOPA	European Insurance and Occupational Pensions Authority
EU	European Union
FAB	Financial Arbitration Board
HACP	Hungarian Authority for Consumer Protection
HCA	The Hungarian Competition Authority
HCSO	Hungarian Central Statistical Office
HFSA	Hungarian Financial Supervisory Authority
IAIS	International Association of Insurance Supervisors
IDD	Insurance Distribution Directive
JD	Judicial Decisions
KID	Key Information Document
MND	Ministry of National Development
MVI	Act LXII of 2009 on Insurance Against Civil Liability in Respect of the Use of Motor Vehicles
NBHA	Act CXXXIX of 2013 on the National Bank of Hungary
NBH	National Bank of Hungary

List of Abbreviations

NTCA	National Tax and Customs Administration
OAC	Act CLXI of 2011 on the Organization and Administration of the Courts
PIT	Act CXVII of 1995 on Personal Income Tax
PPF	Act LXXXII of 1997 on Private Pensions and Private Pension Funds
PRICL	Principles of Reinsurance Contract Law
PUBC	Act XLVII of 2008 on the Prohibition of Unfair Business-to-Consumer Commercial Practices
PUTP	Act LVII of 1996 on the Prohibition of Unfair Trading Practices and Unfair Competition
TCC	Total Costs Charged
UD	Uniformity Decisions
VMIF	Act XCVI of 1993 on Voluntary Mutual Insurance Funds

General Introduction

Chapter 1. General Background Information

Judit Barta

§1. Political System

1. Hungary is an independent, democratic, and constitutional state governed by the rule of law.

The form of Government of Hungary is a unitary, parliamentary, representative democratic republic.

Hungary's constitutional arrangement is a parliamentary democracy. The supreme legislative body is the National Assembly, and the supreme executive power is the Government, while the judiciary is exercised by the courts.

Hungary's legal system is based on the Fundamental Law. The Fundamental Law and other laws shall be binding on everyone.

The President of the Republic of Hungary is the main dignitary who is the guardian of the role of the democratic operation of the state laid down by the constitution, and he embodies the unity of the nation.

Hungary's supreme body of popular representation is the Parliament. Its main task is the legislation and the control of the executive branch. The National Assembly consists of representatives elected by the citizens for a term of four years.

The head of the executive branch is the Government which consists of the Prime Minister and the ministers. The Government is led by the Prime Minister whose main task is to determine the general direction of the Government's policy. The ministers are responsible for the direction of a special area.

Before 2014, Hungary's (blended) electoral system was among the most complicated in Europe; it saw the election of Members of the National Assembly six times as of 1990. The system was reformed by Act CCIII of 2011 on the Election of Members of the National Assembly, with provisions first implemented during the 2014 general elections. That spring, Hungarian citizens elected 199 Members of Parliament to a four-year term, voting directly by secret ballot based on universal and equal suffrage. The 2018 parliamentary elections were also held in this electoral system for the 2018–2022 parliamentary cycle.

At the 2022 national elections, Fidesz-KDNP won an outstanding victory which won 135 mandates, resulting in a two-thirds majority in the 199-member Parliament. Prime Minister Orbán's fifth government took office on May 24, 2022.

The Constitutional Court, which operates independently from the normal judicial body, has eleven members. Its main task is the protection of the constitution.

In Hungary, it is the duty of the judiciary, the prosecution, and the law enforcement bodies to ensure the protection of citizens' rights, to protect the constitutional order, and to fight against the perpetrators of criminal offenses. The organs of the judiciary are independent.

§2. Commerce and Industry

I. The Hungarian Economy

2. The privatization process of Hungary's economy started in 1990. The process was accelerated by the significant involvement of foreign capital which has gained considerable weight in the construction, telecommunications, energy, and banking sectors in Hungary. By 1997, as a consequence of the privatization, the proportion of public assets decreased to 30% while the proportion of private ownership augmented to 70%. Thanks to the emergence of multinational corporations in many industries—e.g., the automobile industry and electronics industry—world-class production facilities have settled in Hungary. While foreign companies are employing a disproportionately small share of the domestic labor force, small- and medium-sized enterprises are the mass employers in Hungary. The largest employer in Hungary is the Hungarian State Railways group of companies.

The performance of the Hungarian economy started to increase dynamically in 2013, which continued in 2015. The most important sectors of Hungary's economy in 2020 were industry (23.5%), wholesale and retail trade, transport, accommodation and food services (17.7%), and public administration, defense, education, human health and social work activities (17.5%).

Intra-EU trade accounts for 78% of Hungary's exports (Germany 28%, Romania, Slovakia, Austria and Italy all 5%), outside the EU, 3% go to the United States and 3% to the United Kingdom.

In terms of imports, 71% come from EU Member States (Germany 24%, Austria 6%, and Poland and the Netherlands 5%), while outside the EU, 9% come from China and 4% from the Republic of Korea.

II. Agriculture

3. The market economy has forced the private ownership of land, especially agricultural land. Natural persons own 87.7% of the outer areas of arable land and 83% of the agricultural land. The percentage of state-owned forest areas is high. The cropping structure of the domestic arable land production shows a relatively consistent picture in recent years. According to the data of the Hungarian Central Statistical Office (HCSO), more than two-thirds of the sown area is utilized for cereals, ranging on an average of around 70%. Within this, the two dominant plants are wheat and corn. The harvested area of commercial crops like sugar beet has not changed in recent years. This was definitely caused by the measures of the European Union (EU) aiming at reducing the overproduction of sugar; therefore, the acreage of the sector has decreased significantly since 2008. Since our accession to the Union, continuous expansion of oilseed production can be observed. One reason for this is the demand for the production of biofuel feedstock.

In recent years, the structure of the gross output of the agricultural industry has changed significantly. At the beginning of the last decade, crop and livestock production contributed nearly 50%–50% to the gross output of agriculture, counted at current prices. In recent years, the percentage of crop production has increased every year. In 2011, the percentage share of the two main activities was 66%–34% in relation to each other. By 2021, the proportion of crop cultivation continued to increase at the expense of livestock production.

The plant grown in the largest area is corn.

Since 2010, the number of cattle with respect to livestock has continuously increased and reached 902,000 by 2021.

The largest stock is chickens (32,114 thousand), followed by pigs (2,726 thousand) and sheep.[1]

III. Industry

4. Between 2013 and 2019, the volume of industrial production increased by 35%, but in 2020, it decreased by 6.0% due to the pandemic situation. In 2021, compared to the relatively low base of the previous year, the output increased by 9.6% and exceeded the pre-pandemic level of 2019 by 3.0%.

Among the national economic branches of industry, the most significant is the manufacturing industry (over 90%), followed by the energy industry and mining, which represent a small weight.[2]

Among the sub-sectors of the manufacturing industry, the most significant are vehicle manufacturing, the electronics industry, and the food industry.

As in the previous two years, the production of electrical equipment expanded most dynamically, which resulted from the growth in the production of electric motors and batteries.

The six companies with the largest gross sales revenue in Hungary in 2021 are Hungarian Oil Plc. (MOL), Audi Hungária Plc., Magyar Villamosművek Plc., Robert Bosch Group, Mercedes-Benz Hungary Manufacturing Ltd., Samsung Electronics Hungarian Plc.

IV. Commerce

5. Due to the moderate level of domestic demand, foreign trade of goods and services has become one of the most important drivers of Hungary's economy in

1. https://www.bkmkik.hu/attachments/article/5512/Magyarország%20számokban_2021.pdf.
2. *Ibid.*

recent decades. After the accession to the EU, new foreign markets opened. The dynamically expanding foreign trade has become the main pillar of economic growth for Hungary.

In 2015, the volume of foreign trade—according to preliminary data—increased by 7.9% in exports and 7.0% in imports compared to 2014.

The balance of the foreign trade has shown a surplus since 2009; the amount of surplus varied between EUR 6 and 7 billion during 2012–2014, and its size was unprecedented in 2015.

In 2021, both the volume and the value of our foreign trade turnover in euros reached a level never seen before. Compared to the low base of the previous year, there was a significant increase in both traffic directions, but the traffic also exceeded the record values of the previous two years.[3]

The products exported with the highest value are, e.g., cars, car components, electric batteries, and TV sets.

The products imported with the highest value are phone components, electricity, and natural gas.

Since 2013, the purchasing intention of the population has increased; the volume of retail sales increased by 1.8% in 2013 and 5.2% in 2014 compared to the previous year. This was due to the improving labor market conditions and moderate inflation environment as well as a more optimistic outlook for households, the increase in real wages, and the measures of the Government aiming at the enhancement of the transparency of the retail trade, such as the mandatory use of the online cash registers directly connected to the tax office.[4]

In 2021, the total value of domestic retail trade was close to HUF 14.1 thousand billion; its volume was 3.4% higher than the year before.[5]

§3. Financial Institutions

6. The Hungarian financial market can be divided into two major areas: there are, on the one hand, the financial institutions and, on the other, insurance companies, insurance brokers, health and pension funds, etc.

I. Financial Institutions

7. The Hungarian financial institutions operate under strong supervision, which is guaranteed by the highest level of law.

According to Act CCXXXVII of 2013 on Credit Institutions and Financial Enterprises, credit institutions and financial enterprises are recognized as financial institutions.

Credit institution means a financial institution whose business, *inter alia*, includes taking deposits or other repayable funds from the public (not including the issue of

3. *Ibid.*
4. *Ibid.*
5. *Ibid.*

bonds to the public as specified in the relevant legislation) and granting credits and loans. The following activities may be pursued by credit institutions only:

(a) taking deposits and other repayable funds from the public in excess of their own funds, without a guarantee or without any surety facilities provided by a credit institution or the state for guaranteeing repayment;
(b) currency exchange services.

Credit institutions may be banks, specialized credit institutions, or credit institutions set up as cooperative societies. A credit institution set up as a cooperative society may operate in the form of a savings and loan or credit union.

8. By the end of 2015, forty of the forty-five private limited company credit institutions (banks) which operated in 2014 still worked. Thanks to the decrease of the bank tax in Hungary and the beginning of bank lending, a slow construction phase started in the banking sector. In the first half of 2016 (according to IFRS), all major banks became profitable.

Based on profit after tax, the largest banks in 2021 were OTP Group, K&H Bank Plc., ERSTE Bank Hungary Plc., UniCredit Bank Plc., Raiffeisen Bank Plc., CIB Bank Plc.[6]

At the end of 2021, the number of banks was twenty-nine, of which nine were bank groups, twelve were independent banks and eight were branches.[7]

Due to legislative regulation, the cooperative credit institutions went through integration in 2013. The integration consists of 121 independent, privately owned cooperative credit institutions. The credit unions have their own separate supervisory body.

The Hungarian Savings Bank is the Central Bank of the integrated cooperative credit institutions; its primary role is the coordination of the business cooperation of the cooperative credit institutions and the insurance of competitive and prudent management. On the one hand, the Savings Bank regulates and provides the common banking business of the credit institutions participating in the integration and coordination of their business development, on the other hand, it provides advanced products and services to the cooperative credit institutions.

In addition to its function as the Central Bank, Savings Bank Plc. is an independent commercial bank, which provides a full range of financial services to domestic and international medium and large companies and investment services to corporate and retail customers.

The integration of savings cooperatives began in 2016 and ended in October 2019. All savings cooperatives merged into Savings Bank Plc., which became a universal commercial bank.

Act XXX of 1997 on Mortgage Loan Companies and on Mortgage Bonds applies to mortgage credit institutions as a specialized type of credit institution.

---

6. https://www.portfolio.hu/bank/20220601/itt-a-friss-banki-rangsor-lat-valaki-extraprofitot-548293.
7. A_hitelintezetek_prudencialis_adatai_202206.xlsx (live.com).
https://view.officeapps.live.com/op/view.aspx?src=https%3A%2F%2Fstatisztika.mnb.hu%2Ftimeseries%2FA_hitelintezetek_prudencialis_adatai_202206.xlsx&wdOrigin.

A mortgage credit institution is a specialized financial institution which provides loans secured by mortgaged properties located in the territory of Hungary or another Member State of the European Economic Area (EEA) (hereinafter EEA Member State) to which the sources are collected by issuing mortgage bonds (securities). Only mortgage credit institutions are entitled to issue mortgage bonds.

In 2022, four mortgage credit institutions operated on the Hungarian market: OTP Mortgage Bank Plc., UniCredit Mortgage Bank Plc., ERSTE Mortgage Bank Plc., Takarék Mortgage Bank Public Lc.[8]

In 2016, the National Bank of Hungary (NBH) issued a regulation which stipulated that all Hungarian banks carrying out mortgage lending are required to finance at least 15% of their loan portfolio with mortgage bonds from October 1, 2016. A mortgage bond is a covered bond with more than a hundred years of history in our country and abroad.

According to the Act CXIII of 1996 on Home Savings and Loan Associations, the Home Savings and Loan Association is a specialized financial institution which is exclusively authorized to take deposits and lending. It collects deposits from savers (individuals, condominiums, housing associations) for residential purposes and, with respect to this amount, provides low-interest housing loans if requested. The savings amount and preferential loans can be used only for housing purposes as defined by the law (reconstruction, modernization, purchase of a house, replacement of an existing, lower-rate home loan, etc.). Home savings are encouraged by state aid; the amount of the annual payable amount maximized by law is complemented by an additional 30% from the state. Since October 2018, state support has ceased.

In 2022, three Home Savings Banks operated: Erste Home Savings Plc., OTP Home Savings Plc. and Fundamenta Home Savings.

In 2022, a total of forty-one credit institutions operated on the Hungarian market.[9]

II. Institutions of the Financial Market Outside the Banking Sector

9. Outside the banking sector, other institutions of the financial market are insurance companies, insurance brokers, health funds, and pension funds.

The number of voluntary pension funds is thirty-one, and the number of private pension funds is four.

The funds play a strong role in financing the economy, and a crucial part of their wealth is still held in Hungarian Government securities.

A significant sales channel of the insurance market is composed of independent insurance agents and multiple agents.

At the end of 2021, according to the data of the NBH, 353 insurance brokers and forty insurance multiple agents sold insurance products. (data refer to companies).

8. https://view.officeapps.live.com/op/view.aspx?src=https%3A%2F%2Fstatisztika.mnb.hu%2Ftimeseries%2Fhit-int-reszletes-2022-03-31.xls&wdOrigin.
9. *Ibid.*

According to the data published by the NBH, the total number of registered insurance intermediaries on 30.06.2023 is 361 thousand (324 insurance brokers and 37 insurance multiple agents).[10]

§4. Currency Legislation and Monetary Regulations

I. The Regulation of Cash Transfer

10. The definition of payment service provider is stipulated in the Act LXXXV of 2009 on the Pursuit of the Business of Payment Services, according to which it shall mean credit institutions, electronic money institutions, the institution operating the Postal Clearing Center, financial institutions, the NBH, and the Treasury, whose business includes the provision of payment services.

The definition of money transmission service can be found in the Act CCXXXVII of 2013 on Credit Institutions and Financial Enterprises:

(a) services enabling cash to be placed on a payment account, as well as all the operations required for operating a payment account;
(b) services enabling cash withdrawals from a payment account, as well as all the operations required for operating a payment account;
(c) execution of payment transactions between payment accounts;
(d) execution of the payment transactions referred to in (c), where the funds are covered by a credit line for a payment service user;
(e) issuing and accepting cash-substitute payment instruments, excluding checks and electronic money;
(f) money remittance;
(g) execution of payment transactions where the consent of the payer to execute a payment transaction is given by means of any telecommunication, digital, or IT device, and the payment is made to the telecommunication, IT system, or network operator, acting only as an intermediary between the payment service user and the supplier of the goods and services.

The regulations of the two abovementioned Acts define the frameworks of money transmission services, activities which are controlled by the NBH.

II. Monetary Regulation

11. Act CXXXIX of 2013 on the NBH contains the monetary regulations.

The NBH is the Central Bank of Hungary and controls the banking system, insurance, money transmission services, pension funds, and the monetary market.

10. https://statisztika.mnb.hu/statistical-topics/supervisory-statistics/iii_-insurance-sector/insurance-intermediaries.

The NBH is a member of the European System of Central Banks and the European System of Financial Supervisors. Stemming from its membership in the European System of Financial Supervisors, the NBH shall carry out the tasks delegated from the competencies of the European Banking Authority, the European Insurance and Occupational Pensions Authority (EIOPA), the European Securities and Markets Authority, and the European Systemic Risk Board upon the NBH.

The primary objective of the NBH shall be to achieve and maintain price stability.

The NBH shall define and implement monetary policy.

The NBH shall be entitled to issue banknotes and coins in the official currency of Hungary (forint). Banknotes and coins—including commemorative banknotes and coins—issued by the NBH in the official currency of Hungary shall be legal tender in Hungary.

The NBH shall hold and manage official foreign exchange and gold reserves in order to preserve the external stability of the Hungarian economy.

The NBH shall execute foreign exchange operations in relation to the management of foreign exchange reserves and the implementation of exchange rate policy. The NBH shall oversee payment and settlement systems and securities settlement systems and, within this framework, shall oversee the operations of the system and the operations of the organization performing the activity of the central counterparty in order to ensure the sound and efficient functioning of these systems and the uninterrupted completion of cash transactions.

12. With regard to the monetary tasks of the NBH, the Monetary Council is the supreme decision-making body of the NBH. The Monetary Council shall consist of at least five and, at most, nine members.

The members of the Monetary Council are:

(a) the Governor of the NBH, as the Chairman of the Monetary Council;
(b) the Deputy Governors of the NBH; and
(c) other members elected by Parliament for six years.

13. In the interest of achieving its monetary policy and primary objective, the NBH shall influence the supply of and demand for money and credit.

The NBH shall independently define the monetary policy and the instruments for implementing such policy within the framework laid down by the law.

As instruments of its monetary policy, the NBH shall:

(a) accept deposits in relation to its account management activity and provide credit based on adequate collateral;
(b) buy and sell securities, as well as act as securities intermediary in the spot and derivative markets within the framework of open market operations and repurchase agreements;
(c) issue securities;
(d) set exchange rates and interest rates and exercise influence in the setting thereof;
(e) discount (rediscount) securities;

(f) regulate minimum reserves; and
(g) introduce other Central Bank instruments.

14. The NBH shall determine the Central Bank base rate as a benchmark interest rate. The level of the base rate is decided by the Monetary Council. The Governor of the NBH shall establish the level of the base rate by way of a decree.

The NBH shall quote and publish the official exchange rates for the conversion of foreign currency into forint and vice versa. The Government shall determine the exchange rate regime and all the features thereof in agreement with the NBH.

§5. Insurance Business, General Organization and Special Features

I. Features of the Insurance Financial Market and Data[11]

15. Since the beginning of the 1990s, the features of the insurance market have changed fundamentally by the inflow of foreign capital. The foreign investors obtained, first, the minority, then the majority, and finally, the exclusive right of ownership in the newly established insurance companies; therefore, in 1992, the privatization of the insurance market became complete with the privatization of the state insurance.

The premium income of the insurance market has been continuously growing since 2012. The number of continuous-premium life insurance contracts also began to grow, which is primarily due to the state tax-supported pension funds. The level of savings of Hungarian households corresponds to the region's average rate but remains significantly lower than the average of the EU. Savings allocated to life insurance and pension funds are significantly low compared to those of other EU countries.

The source of profits of the insurance companies basically consists of cost results, mortality results, fund management fees, and the yield of invested equity. The income derived from insurance activities makes up a significant portion: 70% is the result of insurance technology, and only a small proportion, 30%, is attributable to the activities arising from investments.

As of 2017, the market had two main drivers: (1) the development of the pension insurance market (which forms the fifth of the regular premium life insurance); and (2) the dynamic growth of the motor vehicle insurance market.[12] Until 2022, the most spectacularly growing portfolio is that of state-subsidized pension insurance.

The cumulative after-tax profit of insurance companies was HUF 80.2 billion in 2021 and HUF 82.3 billion in 2020.

---

11. Veronika Varga & Zoltán Madari, *The Hungarian Insurance Market Structure: An Empirical Analysis.* Central European Journal of Operations Research (2023) 31: 927–940, https://doi.org/10.1007/s10100-023-00842-8.
    https://link.springer.com/article/10.1007/s10100-023-00842-8.
12. https://www.portfolio.hu/finanszirozas/biztositok-penztarak/eletbiztositasba-tenned-a-penzed-nagy-segitseg-erkezett.272867.html.

In 2021, the premium income of the Hungarian insurance market increased by 10.4% to HUF 1,330 billion. Life insurances increased by 13.7%, and their premium income was HUF 603 billion, while non-life insurances increased by 7.9%, and their premium income was HUF 727 billion.[13]

In 2022, a total of thirty-three insurance companies and insurance associations supervised by the NBH operate, of which twenty-two insurance companies fall under the scope of Solvency II. Twenty-one insurance companies operate in the market as joint-stock companies, two as large associations and ten as small associations.

Among the twenty-two insurance companies covered by Solvency II, there are four life, nine non-life and nine composite insurance companies.

In 2022, thirteen insurance branches operated in the Hungarian market.[14]

In 2015, the five largest insurance companies operating in the insurance market, from the point of view of their premium income, were: (1) Generali Insurance Plc. (2) Allianz Hungaria Plc. (3) Groupama Insurance Plc. (4) AEGON Hungary General Insurance Plc. (5) NN Insurance Plc. (former ING) which solely deals with personal insurance.[15]

In 2021, the five largest insurance companies operating in the insurance market, from the point of view of their premium income, were: (1) Allianz Hungaria Plc. (2) Generali Insurance Plc. (3) AEGON Hungary General Insurance Plc. (4) Groupama Insurance Plc. (5) UNION Vienna Insurance Group Plc.[16]

II. Reserves, Investments, Results

16. At the end of 2020, the size of the insurance companies' net technical reserves was HUF 2,475,437 million.

17. The insurers and the pension funds still have a strong state financing role, and government securities play a dominant role in their investments. Their investment share exceeded 47% in 2020. This is followed by other securities; the proportion of shares is around 2%.

---

13. https://www.portfolio.hu/uzlet/20220304/fityiszt-mutattak-a-valsagnak-a-magyar-biztositok-14-eve-nem-szarnyaltak-ennyire-az-eletbiztositasok-531019.
    Hungarian Insurers' Yearbook 2022. (Includes data for 2021).
    https://mabisz.hu/wp-content/uploads/evkonyv/mabisz-evkonyv-2022-en.pdf.
    Hungarian Insurers' Yearbook 2021. (Includes data for 2020).
    https://mabisz.hu/wp-content/uploads/evkonyv/mabisz-evkonyv-2021-V6j4-EN.pdf.
    Flora Medve. *Market Share of Insurance Companies in Hungary in 2021*, by gross premiums written, 15. 08. 2023. (online).
    https://www.statista.com/statistics/1264417/hungary-insurance-companies-market-share-by-gross-premiums-written/.
14. https://www.mnb.hu/letoltes/kocka-zati-jelente-s-2022-hun-0825.pdf.
15. http://www.portfolio.hu/finanszirozas/biztositok_penztarak/letaszitottak_tronjarol_magyarorszag_legnagyobb_biztositojat.228445.html.
16. https://mabisz.hu/wp-content/uploads/2021/09/mabisz-evkonyv-2021-V6j3-HU.pdf.

18. The proportion of loans granted to life insurance bond holders in the investment portfolio is still negligible, below 0.1%.[17]

Fixed assets behind the reserves have not changed decisively in recent years: behind the reserves of the unit-linked products (*see* Part V Chapter 5 Life Insurance), there are mainly investment units,[18] while behind the mathematical reserves, there are mainly Government securities. Life insurance liabilities are primarily long-term, and the expiration of the portfolio behind them also orientates to this. Therefore, long-term Government securities are bought by insurers.

17. *Ibid.*
18. Act XVI of 2014 on Collective Investment Trusts and Their Managers, and on the Amendment of Financial Regulations:

> Section 4
>
> 21. investment unit shall mean transferable securities issued as part of a series and offered by an investment fund—subject to the form and content requirements laid down in this Act—as representing the claim and other rights of participants in the assets of such an investment fund, as specified in the investment fund's management policy.

Chapter 2. Historical Background of Insurance and Insurance Legislation

Edit Antal Ujvári

§1. The First Period of the History of Insurance

19. In Hungary, the first insurance-like institution was the first domestic guild charter from 1307. The guilds collected the payments of its members in "companion chests," from which they provided aid for the indigent members of the guild. The guilds flourished in the sixteenth century.

Due to the underdevelopment of the country's economy, the insurance business evolved very slowly and did not obtain larger dimensions. Concerning this period, it has to be emphasized that, for the management of the risks associated with safe transportation, the Royal and Imperial Company of Rév-Komárom for the Encouragement of Shipping was founded in 1807, while the Generali of Trieste opened its representation in Budapest in 1832 (Trieste General Insurance Association). The first company founded in Hungary was the Hungarian Mutual Insurance Association against Hail (1843), while the establishment of the First Hungarian General Insurance Company was a major turning point in the history of Hungarian insurance (1857). Thanks to the prosperities of the 1860s, dozens of insurance companies operated in our country at the turn of the century. It is also worth mentioning that the Farmers Insurance Cooperative was formed in 1899 and was established by landowners in the area of agricultural insurance.[19]

Until the outbreak of the First World War, the economic conditions had a beneficial effect on the development of the Hungarian insurance business, although it was common that Hungarian companies were pushed into the background by the strong competition from foreign capital which forced them to deal with the less profitable insurance businesses with higher damage proportion. During the First World War, the insurance business declined.

In the early 1920s, an important step was the creation of the state supervision of insurers, whose task was the authorization of the operation of the new companies and the financial supervision of the existing companies. At the time of the outbreak of the Second World War, sixty-eight insurance public limited companies and more than one hundred insurance associations, organized on a regional, professional, or on a risk basis, and self-help organizations operated in the country.

The legal regulation of insurance evolved under the strong influence of Austrian and German law in this period. The Commercial Code[20] regulated the details of the insurance contract law's special law applied to certain questions relating to the payment of insurance premiums, to the state supervision of insurance, and to the insurance agents.

---

19. Tamás Gábor, *A biztosításügy története Magyarországon a kezdetektől 1857-ig* [History of Insurance in Hungary from the Beginnings to 1857] Sangrey Ltd. (2013), Solymár.
20. Sections 543–514 of Act XXXVII of 1875.

§2. The Main Events in the History of the Hungarian Insurance Between 1945 and 1989

20. After the Second World War, the assets of the German-owned companies operating in our country became the Hungarian interest of the Soviet state insurance according to the Potsdam Agreement.

In 1948, the nationalization and concentration of insurance companies began. The Soviet Union handed over the assets of the insurers with Soviet ownership (Eastern European Insurance Plc., European Goods and Luggage Insurance Plc.) to the Hungarian state; their administration was taken over by the State Insurance National Company, which began its operation on June 20, 1949. This step basically completed the socialist state insurance monopoly.

During the forty years of the state monopoly, the insurance market progressed slowly, which was influenced by the fact that the state-owned insurance ban lasted until 1968, so only the cooperative property and modest private property could have been ensured. Because of the small scattering of property and financial conditions, the low-premium insurance models were common (e.g., home insurance, group life and accident insurance). After the removal of the ban on state property insurance, the small- and medium-sized companies concluded the insurance of properties, and the major state-owned companies engaged in the support of the budget in cases of damage. During the 1970s–1980s, voluntary vehicle insurance and compulsory motor vehicle liability insurance were the coverage for traffic risks. The different types of individual life insurances slowly played an increasing role. In the early 1980s, fundamental changes started in the area of Hungarian insurance policy. In 1986, the State Insurance was divided into two ways: the Hungária Insurance Company and the (new) State Insurance Company were founded, and then in 1990, both companies transformed into public limited-liability companies. In 1987, two other Hungarian insurance companies were established, the Garancia Insurance Plc. and in 1988 Atlas Travel Plc. which specialized in travel insurance.

The political changes in the country had a positive impact on the development of the Hungarian insurance policy.

In 1988, the Hungarian Government and the World Bank concluded a new loan contract, which facilitated the transformation of the ownership structure of the country, the dismantling of public property, the freedom of enterprise, and the development of economic competition.

These processes led to the change of regime and, in the end, to the proclamation of the Republic of Hungary, which happened on October 23, 1989, and the former state arrangements definitively ceased to exist.

§3. From the Change of Regime to the Accession

21. Changes in the state supervision of insurance happened in multiple steps. In 2000, the supervision of insurance merged into a single financial supervisory system, which was called the Hungarian Financial Supervisory Authority (HFSA). In 2013, another significant change occurred in the monitoring system: since then, the

NBH has carried out the state supervision of insurance.[21] Between 1990 and 1992, more and more establishment took place. Foreign-owned insurance companies have been founded and at the end of 1992 already thirteen insurance companies operated as a result of the growing competition. The institutional reform created a free choice of insurance in most areas.

Hungary pursued Western (European) integration after the change of regime and the establishment of diplomatic relations between Hungary and the European Community. The tasks related to the Community's internal market were launched by a Government Decision for the first time, and it was also decided that the Hungarian legislation shall take into account the relevant Community rules.

The international legal basis for voluntary alignment was laid down in the European Agreement which concluded in 1991 and entered into force on February 1, 1994. It was promulgated by Act I of 1994 on the "Accession Agreement between the Republic of Hungary and the European Communities and their Member States undersigned in Brussels on 16 December 1991." (Hereinafter: "Accession Agreement"). One of the functions of the Accession Agreement was to prepare Hungary for membership. In Article 67, the Contracting Parties recognized that one of the essential preconditions of Hungary's economic integration into the Community is that the country's legislation shall be harmonized with Community law "as much as possible" (so-called soft harmonization, which means that harmonization is desirable but not compulsory until the accession). The National Assembly demanded the Government to provide an annual report on the implementation and harmonization process.

22. Chapter III of Title V of the European Agreement includes regulations about the legal harmonization, and Article 68 provides an indicative list of the areas which are covered by the legal harmonization, such as the area of financial services.

Hungary submitted an application for membership to the EU on March 31, 1994. In June 1995, the Cannes Summit of the European Council adopted the so-called White Paper, which describes, in detail, the most important tasks required for the accession and the proposals for the harmonization of national legal and institutional systems to the EU law.

In accordance with this, the national program on the adoption of EU legislation has been developed.[22]

23. During the accession process, the European Commission made a national report which examined how Hungary could fulfill the Copenhagen criteria. On March 30, 1998, the accession negotiations started. Hungary became a member of

21. It means that the expression of Authority and the NBH have the same content.

22. Decision No. 2403/1995. (XII.12.) on the "National Program on the implementation of the acquis communautaire" defined the legal harmonization obligation.

Decision No. 2174/1995. (VI.15.) on the "five years legal harmonization program" and Decision No. 2282/1996. (X.25.) "Modification and consolidation of the harmonization and internal market integration programs preparing for accession to the European Union" regulated comprehensively the Hungarian legal harmonization program in accordance with the EU Agreement and the White Book from 1995. It followed the system of the White Book and defined the four stages of the program (3rd stage—among other insurance to 1998).

the EU on May 1, 2004, and on December 21, 2007, Hungary joined the Schengen area, which enabled the free movement of persons (the airport border controls only stopped from March 30, 2008).

§4. The Effects of the Processes on the Legal Regulation of the Insurance Market until the Accession

24. The first code after the change of regime was Act XCVI of 1995 on Insurance Institutions and the Insurance Business.[23] According to the justification of the original text of the Act, it has taken into account the so-called first-generation directives of the European Community, which have been amended several times because other directives in the field of insurance shall be applied at a higher level in the process of accession to the EU.

Within the EU, the directives on the single insurance market have three “generations.” In the first stage, the directives (“non-life”[24] and “life” activity[25]) tried to harmonize the foundation rules of insurance companies. The directives of the second stage[26] reflect the higher level of integration because the aim is to provide the freedom of services, which was realized only by the third-generation directives and by the internal insurance market.[27]

However, the Hungarian regulation exceeds the provisions of the two directives in certain areas because the Act has to be applied to the insurance intermediaries as well. The original text of the law does not contain “the freedom of establishment”; therefore, it regulated, in detail, the Hungarian representation of foreign insurers and the foreign activity of Hungarian insurers.

The legal basis of the insurance system was in accordance with the basic requirements of the European institutions.

According to the regulations, only an insurance company can carry out insurance activity, and—besides exemptions defined by law—other activity directly connected to it (e.g., management, investment of the insurer’s own funds).

Insurance companies can perform the activities in the form of private limited companies, cooperatives, and associations. The amount of capital required for the establishment of the insurance company is determined depending on the specific organizational forms. The first generation of directives—legislation of which is maintained by the further directives—list the two–five legal forms of certain countries which can be accepted and in which the insurance activity can be continued,

23. Act CXLVIII of 1997 made a significant modification, because it allowed the establishment of branch offices of foreign insurance companies.
24. First Council Directive 73/239/EEC of Jul. 24, 1973 on the coordination of laws, regulations, and administrative provisions relating to the taking up and pursuit of the business of direct insurance other than life assurance (OJ 1973 L 228/3).
25. First Council Directive 79/267/EEC of Mar. 5, 1979 on the coordination of laws, regulations and administrative provisions relating to taking up and pursuit of the business of direct life assurance (OJ 1979 L 63/1).
26. Second (non-life) Council Directive: 88/357/EEC (OJ 1988 L 172/01); and (life) Council Directive 90/619/EEC (OJ 1990 L 330/50).
27. Third (non-life) Council Directive: 92/49/EEC (OJ 1992 L228/1); and (life) Council Directive 92/96/EEC (OJ 1992 L 360/1).

but the directives add that "any corporate form adopted by public law" can be accepted. In most of the countries of the Community, the basic forms of insurance companies are private limited companies, cooperatives, and associations. According to the directives, the regulation has already separated, organizationally, the sectors of life and non-life insurances, which meant the restructuring of the internal organization and operation of insurance companies in which the two branches of insurance can be sustainable with regard to the previous commitments. Since the Insurance Act entered into force, composite insurance companies, which means the combination of the life and non-life insurance branches, cannot be created.

The monitoring and control system was fundamentally transformed because the role of financial control increased, and the role of the former material-type control decreased. This was also expressed in the fact that, in general, non-life insurance products should not be authorized, but only the insurance supervision had to be informed after the introduction of the certain product. The law, therefore, exceeded the possibility prescribed by the second-generation directives as it provided the product authorization not only to the "large risk" but also to every branch of property insurance, and at the same time, it switched to the "ex post" control corresponding the third-generation directive. The system of compulsory licensing survived in two areas in the context of the original text of the law: within the framework of the life insurances and the compulsory insurances. Originally, the authorization obligation of life insurance products remained in force until December 31, 1998, while in the case of compulsory insurances (in general liability insurances), the authorization obligation remained for a long time.

An important provision of the law is that insurance contract obligation can only be established by the law after January 1, 1998.

Requirements for the operating conditions of insurance companies (determination and training of technical provisions, regulations on the calculation, principles and ingredients of solvency and safety capital, provisions on bailout plan, investment rules, accountancy, requirements for annual reports, etc.) basically correspond to the directions of the EC legislation, but in some places, they are slightly milder, while others are more restrictive.

Amendment of regulations on the insurance business and the legal regulations on the transfer of insurance portfolio also follows the EC's instructions. The rules of special types of insurances (legal expenses insurance,[28] compulsory insurance) are in full conformity with the relevant EC directives.

The European Commission reviewed the situation of the legal harmonization of the Hungarian insurance market within the framework of the chapter on the free movement of services in 1999. The Government committed that the Hungarian legal system will comply with all EU rules by the date of accession. Accordingly, at the first stage, we took over the regulations which helped us prepare for the single market. During the second phase, legal acts were adopted which were aimed at achieving full harmonization with the EU acquis, namely the establishment of free movement of services in the Hungarian insurance market. Taking attention to this, the Hungarian Parliament adopted—and repealed the earlier—the Act LX of 2003

28. Council Directive 87/344/EEC on the coordination of laws, regulations and administrative provisions relating to legal expenses insurance (OJ 1987 L 185/77).

on insurance companies and insurance activity, which entered into force on the date of entry into force of the Act on the promulgation of the international treaty on the accession to the EU.

Chapter 3. Sources of Insurance Law

§1. Legislation

Judit Barta

25. The performance of the insurance business is affected by several important acts directly or indirectly, which all will be described later.

The most important acts which directly affect the insurance business:

- Act V of 2013 on the Civil Code[29] (CC), which contains the rules regarding insurance contracts, furthermore the relevant rules on consumer protection, and rules on tort law, inheritance law, company law, etc.
- Act LXXXVIII of 2014 on the Business of Insurance (BIns.).
- Act LXII of 2009 on Insurance Against Civil Liability in Respect of the Use of Motor Vehicles (MVI), which contains the general rules on compulsory motor vehicle insurance.
- The rules regarding the control of the insurance business and the mediation are regulated by the Act CXXXIX of 2013 on the National Bank of Hungary (NBHA).
- Act CII of 2012 on Insurance Tax.

The most important acts which indirectly affect the insurance business:

- The CC shall be applied for insurers in relation to their organizational structure, which also contains the rules regarding companies, associations and cooperative societies.
- Insurance business is also affected by the act on accounting with regard to their business activity (Act C of 2000 on Accounting), by the act on corporate tax (Act LXXXI of 1996 on Corporate Tax and Dividend Tax), and by the act on the rules of taxation (Act XCII of 2003 on the Rules of Taxation).

§2. Governmental Regulations

Judit Barta

26. The *Government* authorizes by decree:

(a) the detailed provisions relating to the own funds and technical provisions of insurance companies and reinsurance companies;
(b) the detailed regulations relating to the protection of the IT system of insurance or reinsurance companies;

29. The official identification of Hungarian legislation is as follows: The year of adoption of the act, the number of the act in Roman numerals and the title of the act.

(c) the detailed rules relating to the minimum content requirements for the liability insurance policies of multiple agents and brokers;
(d) the detailed rules relating to the contents and means of publication of solvency and financial condition reports connected to insurance and reinsurance activities.

The minister in charge of the money, capital, and insurance markets is entitled to authorize by decree the following detailed rules:

(a) relating to the form and content requirements regarding the information to be supplied to clients in connection with unit-linked life insurance policies;
(b) on the accounting of profit or loss of insurance companies from compulsory motor vehicle liability insurance policies;
(c) for the method of the segregation of insurance branches;
(d) for the official training and examination of insurance intermediaries, and the requirements for obtaining a certificate for the pursuit of insurance mediation activities, whether as tied agents or independent insurance intermediaries, the amount of the examination fee, the terms of payment, and the conditions for refund.

§3. Regulation by Governmental Agencies

Judit Barta

27. The *Governor of the NBH* is authorized, acting within its function as the supervisory authority of the financial intermediary system, to decree:

(a) the detailed regulations concerning the procedure for providing information to clients before the conclusion of a contract, during and upon the termination of the contractual relationship for handling client complaints, and the form in which to provide it;
(b) the detailed regulations relating to the contents and the means of statistical information on cross-border activities;
(c) the detailed rules for and contents of the internal data disclosure of insurance companies;
(d) the detailed rules for the reports to be filed by multiple agents and brokers;
(e) the detailed provisions on the notification for the registration of insurance intermediaries by the insurance company, multiple agents, or broker;
(f) the detailed rules on the reporting obligation relating to compulsory motor vehicle liability insurance products;
(g) the detailed rules on the contents list of the life insurance questionnaire;
(h) the detailed rules relating to the calculation and publication of the total costs charged (TCC);
(i) the detailed rules on the highest permissible technical interest rate;

(j) the detailed provisions concerning the supervisory reporting obligation defined by BIns., in accordance with the provisions of the Solvency II Directive relating to information to be provided for supervisory purposes.

28. Beyond the laws affecting the activity of the insurance sector supervised by the NBH, certain monitoring tools are required which can help and orient the supervised institutions in relation to the interpretation and application of the legal regulations. To ensure this, the NBH applies more monitoring instruments. The monitoring instruments are not binding (they have no legislative power), and their compliance cannot be forced, but their application is examined and assessed by the NBH.

29. The instruments which concern the supervised institutions and their leaders and communicates the NBH's legal interpretation and expectation are the following:

- *recommendation;*[30]
- *chief circular;* and
- methodological manuals.

30. Model policies and model informative issued by the NBH also help to respect the legal rules, which can be introduced to the regulations of the insurer.

The *informative* is made for those who are interested in priority topics and they can provide useful information to market participants, including customers.

31. The *Financial Stability Board*[31] can also issue recommendations according to Point (i) of subsection 2 of section 13 of the NBHA, which are instruments helping judicial practice but don't have binding force, and the tools of the implementation of guidelines and recommendations of the European Supervisory Authorities (e.g., EBA, EIOPA). The recommendations aim to increase the predictability of the law, promote the uniform application of relevant EU and national legislation, and describe the principles suggested to be applied by the NBH.

§4. Private International Law

Edit Antal Ujvári

32. The Rome Agreement on the law applicable to contractual obligations adopted by the Member States of the European Communities contained regulations on insurance activity only in a narrow circle. According to Article 1, section 3, the regulations didn't have to be applied to the insurance contracts which covered the

30. Recommendation from 2016, for example, Recommendation No. NBH 8/2016. (VI.30.) of the NBH on the application of prudential and consumer protection principles relating to unit-linked life insurance.
31. One of the bodies of the NBH (The bodies of the NBH are: The Financial Stability Board; etc.).

risks in the territory of the European Economic Community (EEC), with the exception of property insurance contracts. In the process of the establishment of the single internal insurance market, the Member States didn't achieve success in the field of harmonization of insurance contracts, but the freedom of services raised some issues. The second generation of the directives contained detailed provisions with regard to the applicable law[32] both in the field of non-life and life insurances.

The Act XLVIII of 2004 enacted the rules in accordance with the directives of the Hungarian law. The issues regulated in Decree-Law 13 of 1979 on private international law cannot be applied.[33]

The BIns.[34] repealed these regulations on December 25, 2014. One of the obvious reasons for this is that the Rome I. Regulation[35] governs the law applicable to contractual obligations as the unified collision law of the Member States. The provisions of the regulation cover all of the insurance contracts, with the exception of the insurances provided by companies and professional organizations to their employees. It was also fixed that regulations of insurance contracts usually prevail over the provisions of other sectoral insurance regulations (Article 23).

33. In case of the so-called insurance contract covering a large risk, the applicable law does not depend on whether the risks occurred in one of the Member States. In other cases, the regulation defines the applicable law only if the risks covered in the insurance contract occurred in the territory of the Member States. The regulation stipulates detailed provisions for the determination of applicable law regarding insurance contracts:

(a) Reinsurance contracts: Article 7 shall not apply to reinsurance contracts, so according to the general rules in Articles 3 and 4, the law chosen by the parties, in the lack of the parties' choice, the law which is most closely connected to the situation shall be applied (Article 7, section 1, second sentence).
(b) Insurance contract covering a large risk: It shall be governed by the law chosen by the parties, to the extent that the applicable law has not been chosen by the parties, the insurance contract shall be governed by the law of the country where the insurer has his/her habitual residence (Article 7, section 2, first and second sentences). Where it is clear from all the circumstances of the case that the contract is manifestly more closely connected with another country, the law of that other country shall apply (Article 7, section 2, third sentence).

32. Second (non-life) Directive: 88/357/EEC (OJ 1988 L 172/01); (life) Directive 90/619/EEC (OJ 1990 L 330/50) (Art. 7); and European Parliament and of the Council Directive 2002/83/EC concerning life assurance (OJ L 345/19), (Art. 32).
33. With Government Decree No. 1337/2015. (V.27.) the Government ordered the modernization of the Decree-Law 13 of 1979 on international private law. The purpose of the review is to create a new, international private law regulation in line with the rules of private international law at the EU and international level. Act XXVIII of 2017 on the international private law was adopted on the Apr. 14, 2017.
34. Act LXXXVIII of 2014.
35. Regulation (EC) No. 593/2008 of the European Parliament and of the Council of Jun. 17, 2008 on the law applicable to contractual obligations (Rome I).

(c) Other mass contracts: The hereinafter detailed provisions of the regulation shall be applied if the risks are situated in a Member State. In other cases, the general provisions (Articles 3–4) or the regulations on consumer contracts (Article 6) shall be applied. Primarily, the applicable law chosen by the parties shall be applied to the contracts listed in Article 7. Article 7, section 3 restricts the choice of law for the law of certain states, e.g., the law of the state where the risk occurred, the law of the country where the policyholder has his/her habitual residence, or in the case of life assurance, the law of the Member State in which the policyholder is a national. To the extent that the law applicable has not been chosen by the parties in accordance with this paragraph, such a contract shall be governed by the law of the Member State in which the risk is situated at the time of the conclusion of the contract (Article 7, section 3, last sentence).

(d) Compulsory insurance contracts: The abovementioned regulations shall be applied to compulsory insurance contracts, too, which shall be determined on whether it is an insurance contract covering a large risk (Article 7, section 2) or an insurance contract covering limited value, mass contract (Article 7, section 3). Nevertheless, Member States can provide that the law of the Member State imposing compulsory insurance shall be applied to contracts on compulsory insurance. In case of a compulsory insurance, if the law of the Member State where the risk occurred, and the law of the Member State imposing insurance obligation are in collision with each other, the latter shall be applied.

§5. Jurisdiction

Judit Barta

I. The Hungarian Judicial System

34. In Hungary, jurisdiction is performed by courts in a four-grade system in accordance with the rules of the Fundamental Law[36] and the Act CLXI of 2011 on the Organization and Administration of the Courts (OAC):

(1) district courts in towns;
(2) general courts in counties;
(3) five Courts of Appeal; and
(4) the Curia as the highest judicial authority.

35. The Curia is the highest judicial authority. The former name, the Highest Court, was modified to Curia by the Fundamental Law on January 1, 2012.

The Curia shall hear the appeals filed against decisions of the general courts and the Courts of Appeal in cases specified by law. This activity is performed by the chambers of the Curia.

36. Fundamental Law of Hungary (Apr. 25, 2011).

Besides the judicial activity, the other important task of the Curia is to develop a uniform and coherent judicial practice. This important task is performed by the *adoption* of the so-called uniformity decisions (UD).

The UD are binding upon all courts of law and has normative power because it affects the parties at the judicial law enforcement. The UD can be considered a legal source: a legal norm but not an act.[37] The decisions shall be published in the Hungarian Gazette, on the Curia website, and in the *Collection of Judicial Decisions (CJD)* as well.

The Curia has adjudication chambers, chambers passing UD, chambers issuing decisions on principle (criminal, civil, and administrative-labor colleges), as well as working groups examining judicial practice.

If the adjudication chamber of the Curia has adopted a decision on the issues of principle in a case that concerns the majority of the population or that is of the utmost importance with respect to the general public, the presiding judge shall, after the decision is executed in writing, forthwith notify the head of the college affected. The head of college shall submit the decision to the chamber issuing the decisions in principle which shall decide to have it published as Curia decisions on principle (CDP) if deemed justified.

For the selection and publishing of the CDP and Court decisions on principle (cDP), criminal, civil, economic, and administrative-labor chambers operate. The CDP and cDP selected by the chambers shall be published on the Curia website and in some special journals as well.

The working group examining judicial practice shall analyze judicial practices. Examination targets shall be defined on an annual basis by the President of the Curia, following consultation with the colleges of the Curia. The working group examining judicial practice shall sum up its opinion and findings in an executive summary. The college of the Curia of competence for the subject shall debate the executive summary, and if in agreement, the head of the group shall publish its conclusions on the Curia website.

36. The five Courts of Appeal[38] are between the general courts and the Curia; the aim of their establishment was to relieve the Curia. Courts of Appeal shall hear the appeals filed against decisions of the general courts.

General courts are under the Courts of Appeal. They shall precede the cases in two ways:

(1) if one or both parties appeal against the decision of the district courts; and
(2) if there are such cases as, e.g., of greater value, complicated sues, in which the general courts shall hear in the first instance.

37. Petrétei József, *Magyarország alkotmányjoga. 1. köt. Alapvetés, alkotmányos intézmények* [Constitutional Law of Hungary. Vol.1. Basics, Constitutional Institutions]. Pécs: Kodifikátor Foundation, 2013. 161.
38. In Budapest, Debrecen, Pécs, Győr, and in Szeged.

II. Judicial Decisions in Law Enforcement

37. In Hungary, judicial decisions (JD) are not binding upon the courts, with only one exception. According to subsection 1 of section 42 of the OAC, UD shall be published in the *Hungarian Gazette*[39] and on the central website and the website of the Curia, and they shall be binding upon the courts from the time of publication in the Hungarian Gazette.

III. Officially Promulgated Sources of the Legal Practice

38. The JD, which has an orienting effect on judicial practice, are published in professional legal journals of prestigious publishers.

Legal journals which have high importance in the field of insurance law are the following:

- The *"Curia decisions,"* the Official Journal of the Curia, Hungary's highest judicial forum, which bears this name since January 1, 2013; before, its title was *"Judicial decisions."* The most significant judgments of the Curia are published in it, which are chosen by a special editorial board. The decisions appear with the abbreviation "JD" (in Hungarian, it is BH, the abbreviation of "bírósági határozat"), in that way, followed by the year and then by the publication number of the decision, which is renumbered from the start annually, e.g., JD2002. 102 or JD/2002. 102.

  UD are also published in the periodical. UD are (re)numbered annually and they include the year and the abbreviation of the name of the uniformity council which brought the decision. For example, the indication for the number four civil law uniformity decision of 2013 will be 4/2013. CUD (in Hungarian 4/2013 PJE).
- The journal of the CJD contains civil and business law decisions in principle of the five Courts of Appeal and other significant decisions of individual cases, but the important decisions of the general courts in counties can also be found in the journal. All of the decisions are edited, and the key ascertainments of the decision are highlighted, but the decision contains the relevant elements and legal background of the case anonymized. The indication for the published decisions is the abbreviation of the title of the periodical (CJD, in Hungarian, it is BDT), followed by the year and the continuous number of the case, hence the appearance, e.g., CJD 2013. 2899 (in Hungarian BDT 2013.2899).
- The aim of the periodical of the "*Decisions of Courts of Appeal*" (DCA) is to publish the most important decisions of the five Courts of Appeal selected by the editorial board in edited form. The indication for the published decisions is the abbreviation of the title of the periodical (DCA, in Hungarian, it is ÍH), followed by the year and the annually restarting number of the case, e.g., DCA 2010. 105 (in Hungarian ÍH 2010.105).

39. The Official Journal of Hungary is the Hungarian Gazette. Laws shall be published in the Hungarian Gazette, with the exception of municipality regulations.

39. In order to secure the publicity of the JD, section 163 of the OAC stipulates that the Curia shall publish the UD, CDP, cDP, and its decisions adopted on the substance of a matter, while the Court of Appeal shall publish its decisions adopted on the substance of a matter in the Register of Court Decisions, in digital form.

The decision shall be published in the Register of Court Decisions by the President of the adopting court within thirty days after the decision is executed in writing. The designation of the published decisions shall contain the description of the court and the relevant field of law, the year when the decision was adopted, and the number of the decision. The court, having adopted the decision, shall specify, at the time of publication, the specific rules of the statutes on the basis of which the decision was adopted. The Register of Court Decisions contains the decisions in digital form. The collection is available in the *Anonym Register of Court Decisions*. In principle, all of the personal data of the parties shall be deleted from the decision (anonym decision). Decisions made in certain procedures shall not be published; these are listed in the Act.

Chapter 4. Dispute Settlement and Arbitration

Judit Barta

§1. The Financial Arbitration Board

40. The NBHA contains regulations concerning the Financial Arbitration Board (FAB), which is a platform for alternative dispute settlement. The powers of the FAB shall cover disputes between consumers and insurers—in connection with the services supplied—relating to the conclusion and performance of contracts (hereinafter referred to as: "*consumer dispute of a financial nature*") with a view to reaching an out-of-court settlement. For this purpose, the FAB shall attempt to reach a conciliation agreement or, failing this, to adopt a decision in the case to enforce consumer rights simply, efficiently, and practically and under the principle of cost-efficiency.

The FAB is an independent body operated by the NBH. The Board shall not be instructed in their decision-making process in relation to consumer disputes.

Members of the Arbitration Board must have a law degree or a university diploma in economics and must clear a bar exam.

The FAB proceeds in a council of three (hereinafter mentioned as: "council"), except in less complicated consumer cases where the amount in dispute is below HUF 50,000 and petitions for special consideration that can be handled by a single board member. The condition for the proceedings in the FAB is that the consumer has attempted to settle the case directly with the insurer.

The insurer can file a standard statement of submission to the FAB in writing, which remains in effect until further notice, in which he/she undertakes to be bound by the proceedings of the Arbitration Board and to the decision adopted in the absence of a negotiated settlement.

If the consumer can prove that he/she concluded the insurance contract because the insurer has claimed in its commercial communication to abide by the proceedings of the Arbitration Board and to the decision adopted by the Arbitration Board in the absence of a negotiated settlement, the insurer shall be bound to his/her statement even if he/she didn't file a standard statement of submission. The procedure of the FAB is started upon the consumer's request.

The request shall be submitted to the FAB in writing, using the prescribed form, with the exception of requests for special consideration.

If the jurisdiction of FAB is established, the Board shall notify the parties and shall set a hearing date within seventy-five days of the opening of the proceedings. In the notice, the FAB communicates to the parties the names of those appointed to the competent council or the name of the sole board member acting alone in a given case.

The insurer shall be duty-bound to cooperate in the procedure of the FAB; due to this obligation, he/she shall send the response to the complaint to the FAB with the content and within the time limit provided by the Act.

The parties can be represented in the proceedings by an authorized representative.

In the proceedings, the chairman of the council shall attempt to negotiate an agreement between the parties. If the negotiation is in conformity with the relevant legislation, the council shall approve it.

During the proceedings, the council shall afford equal treatment to the parties and shall provide all parties with an opportunity to present their case and table any motions they may have. If necessary, the chairman of the council shall inform the consumer of his/her rights and obligations. The proceeding is closed unless both parties have consented to have the proceedings held publicly.

The council shall decide on the merits of the case by a simple majority. The council shall conclude the proceedings within ninety days of the time of opening, but in justified cases, the Chairman of the FAB can extend this time limit by a maximum of thirty days.

In the absence of a negotiated settlement, the council shall:

(a) adopt a binding decision if the request is found substantiated and the insurer has undertaken to be bound by the decision of the FAB in a standard statement of submission, in its commercial communication, or in a statement filed at the time of the opening of the proceedings or, at the latest, before the decision is adopted;[40] or
(b) make a recommendation if the request is found substantiated, but the insurer has refused to be bound by the decision of the council in a statement filed at the time of the opening of the proceedings or did not declare its position concerning the decision of the council in the terms of submission.

In the absence of a negotiated settlement, the council can also adopt a binding decision if the insurer did not file a statement of submission, but the request is found substantiated, and the consumer's claim shown in the request does not exceed HUF 1 million at the time the binding decision is adopted.[41]

In the binding decision, the costs of the proceedings and the party who shall pay the costs shall also be specified. The costs of the proceedings shall be borne by the party against whom the decision was passed.

In respect of the fulfillment of the obligation established in the decision, a time limit of at least fifteen days shall be set from the next day of the delivery of the decision.

---

40. Submission is a written statement by the insurer in which it undertakes to submit itself to the decision made in such a procedure, in the absence of the procedure and agreement of the FAB. There are two types of submissions:

    (1) *General Submission Statement.* The financial service provider submits itself to the binding decision of the FAB in the absence of agreement, without the knowledge of the specific case. In the general submission the insurer's obligation can be limited by scope, value, timing, etc. The FAB keeps a record of the submissions.
    (2) *Case-by-case Submission Statement.* The insurer submits itself to the binding decision of the FAB in the absence of agreement in the knowledge of the concrete case.

41. Section 113 of NBHA.

The FAB can publish a brief description of the dispute and the outcome of the proceedings without indicating the names of the parties.

The decision of the council is adopted without prejudice to the consumer's right to have its claim enforced in the court of law. Within fifteen days of receipt of the binding decision, the insurer is entitled to bring an action against the decision. If the action is filed within the stipulated time, the opposition is transformed into a legal action. If the FAB does not dismiss the statement of opposition, it shall send the documents submitted for the case, the resolution, and the statement of opposition itself to the court within fifteen days from the date of submission of the statement of opposition.

41. If the binding decision is challenged by way of a statement of opposition within the time limit, the resolution shall be abolished, provided that the FAB does not dismiss the opposition.

If the FAB does not dismiss the statement of opposition, it shall deliver the statement of opposition to the consumer within eight days and shall advise the consumer to simultaneously lodge a petition submitted to the court:

(a) containing a plea for a specific court decision (statement of claim);
(b) showing the cause of action, including a description of the circumstances invoked as the basis of the claim and a description of the evidence supporting the claim; and
(c) pay the court fees.

In the event of a customer's failure to comply with what is contained in the notice, the court shall dismiss the action.

42. If the insurer does not execute the binding decision or the negotiated settlement approved by resolution within the time limit, the consumer is entitled to request the court to append an enforcement clause to the said decision.

43. Between 2014 and 2021, the majority of insurance cases received by the Board arose from legal disputes over home insurance. The typical dispute areas were storm and other natural (elemental) damage, fire and blast damage, and burglary damage; therefore, a majority of compromises were born in these insurance branches as well. The basis of the disputes was the question of whether the damage that occurred, which was reported by the consumer, could be regarded as an insurance event. In many instances, special questions arose which required technical or other experts. If, during the proceeding of the Board, there is no possibility for the appointment or the application of an expert, the Board cannot make a final decision in these cases.

In numerous cases, the injured person turned to the Board in connection with compulsory motor vehicle liability insurance. The two main types of cases in connection with indemnity liability relating to motor vehicles (CASCO) were the damage caused by the party's own failure and the damage that occurred by theft of the motor vehicle. The basis of the disputes in most of the cases brought to the Board was the amount of the insurance service. In lots of cases, the final decisions couldn't be made because the amount of damage to the motor vehicle or the determination of the value of the stolen motor vehicle was a technical (expert) issue.

In case of accident and health insurances, the subject of the dispute was, in most cases, the amount of the health damage resulting from an accident (loss of capacity). Several legal disputes occur in connection with the typical damage settling practice where the medical expert requested by the insurer makes the decision to reject the insurance service according to the medical papers attached by the insured person without the personal hearing of the insured person. The Board cannot make a decision in medical cases.[42]

§2. Procedure of Arbitration

44. According to the *Act LX of 2017 on Arbitration (Arb.)*, arbitration means the resolution of disputes arising from a commercial legal relation instead of state court litigation proceedings in the proceedings chosen by the parties, conducted either by an ad hoc or permanent arbitration institution.

The arbitration court contract is the parties' agreement under which they submit all disputes or a specifically defined dispute having arisen or arising in the future between them, resulting from their determined legal relation, whether contractual or not, to arbitration. The arbitration court contract may be a part of another contract (hereinafter referred to as "arbitration court stipulation") or an independent contract. The arbitration court contract shall be set in writing.

An agreement that was made through electronic communication without an electronic signature shall also be regarded as an arbitration court contract concluded in writing if the data set out in the electronic communication are accessible to the other party and are suitable for making reference to them later on. Electronic communication shall be any announcement of the parties that is mediated by data transfer. Data transfer means the production, sending, receipt or storage of the information in an electronic, magnetic, optical or similar manner, in particular through electronic data exchange, electronic mail (email), telegram, telex or fax.

The arbitration court contract shall also be regarded as a contract concluded in writing when in his statement for referral to an arbitration court or in the pleadings of his petition of claim the party asserts the existence of the arbitration court contract and the other party does not dispute it.

Reference made in a contract concluded in writing to a document that contains an arbitration court stipulation shall be deemed as an arbitration court contract concluded in writing, provided that the stipulation as set out there in constitutes a part of the contract.

45. According to the Arb., an arbitration clause requires at least one of the parties to be professionally engaged in economic activity. Insurance activity shall be regarded as such an activity. Application of arbitration isn't prohibited by the CC or

42. https:// www.mnb.hu/letoltes/pbt-eves-jelentes-2021.pdf.

by the OAC, so all of the legal disputes or certain legal disputes arising from insurance contracts can be settled within the framework of arbitration. In the case of an arbitration clause, parties shall exclude the court settlement of their dispute.

Although arbitration clauses are common among the institutions operating in the financial market, especially among credit institutions and leasing companies, insurance companies do not use this opportunity. These clauses can be found in the field of reinsurance and, occasionally, in the contractual clauses applied by foreign reinsurers.

In Hungary, the following Arbitrational Tribunals operate:

(1) The Hungarian Chamber of Commerce and Industry Arbitrational Tribunal (legal disputes arising from insurance contracts shall be settled in this Tribunal).
(2) National Chamber of Agricultural Economics Arbitrational Tribunal.
(3) Sport Arbitration Tribunal.

§3. The Advantages and Disadvantages of Arbitrational Tribunals Compared to Ordinary Court Proceedings

46. Advantages of arbitration:

- The judge is selected by the parties, which method provides the specific expertise.
- The procedure can be conducted quickly, which is provided mainly by the single level of the procedure because legal remedies cannot be found in the arbitration procedure. According to statistics, most of the cases will be settled in one year.
- The total exclusion of the public from the procedure and decision is also an advantage.

47. Disadvantages of arbitration:

- Fees and costs of the arbitrational procedure are generally higher than the procedural duties and charges, which can be compensated due to the single-level procedure and the shorter procedure time.
- It is a disadvantage that there are no remedies against the decisions of Arbitrational Tribunals; consequently, decisions are final, and the mistakes of the decision can't be repaired or the possibilities of remedies are limited. The party who is affected by the judgment may file for action within sixty days of the date of delivery of the decision of the Arbitration Tribunal at the court of law to have the decision overturned, but only in the cases which are exhaustedly stipulated by the section 47 of the Arb.
- It can also be mentioned as a disadvantage that a lot of procedural questions are doubtful and problematic, which are obviously settled in civil law actions by the Act CXXX of 2016 on the Code of Civil Procedure (CCP).

The decision of an Arbitration tribunal is equal to the decision of an ordinary court. Section 53 of the Arb. stipulates that "the decision of an arbitrational tribunal shall have the same effect as that of a binding court decision, and its implementation shall be governed by the regulations on judicial enforcement." The decision of the Arbitrational Tribunal has the same effect of substantive judgment as the final decision of the court.

§4. Arbitration Clause in Consumer Contracts

48. Several lawsuits began in the higher courts, which led to the formulation of the question of whether an arbitration clause is unfair in consumer contracts which contain standard contract terms. The courts made various decisions in regard to this question, and the Curia made a UD about the unfairness of arbitration clauses. According to the Civil Law Uniformity Decision No. 3/2013., arbitration clauses shall be regarded as unfair in consumer contracts, in standard contract terms, or in the contents of a contract term which has not been individually negotiated.

49. The Government Decree No. *18/1999. (II.5.),* which has been annulled because of incorrectness, implemented the EU Directive on the unfair contractual terms in consumer contracts, and it said that a contract term shall be regarded unfair if it excludes or limits the consumers' enforcement claim, which is derived from an act or from the parties' contract, unless the claim can be substituted by another dispute settlement method. This was interpreted, in most cases, as that an arbitration clause is not unfair according to this provision because the effect of this clause is that the parties exclude the right to access the courts, but they substitute it with another manner of dispute settlement.

The following provision was integrated into the CC as the proper interpretation of the Directive:

> Point i) of Subsection 1 of Section 6:104 exclude or hinder the consumer's right to take legal action or exercise any other legal remedy, particularly by requiring the consumer to take disputes exclusively to an arbitration system not foreseen generally in legal provisions, restrict the evidence available to the consumer or impose on the consumer a burden of proof which should legally lie with the other party.

50. With regard to the cited provision of the CC, insurance companies probably will not apply arbitration clauses in their standard contract terms, especially in those products where the contract can be concluded by consumers as well.

Chapter 5. Consumer Protection (In General and with Regard to Insurance)

Edit Antal Ujvári

§1. The Institutional System

I. State Institutional System

51. Before 1989, in Hungary, consumer protection meant the protection of quality, the guarantee of the security of supply, and the protection against the disparity derived from the contractual relationship between the seller and the buyer.

In the 1990s, after the change of regime, the vulnerability of consumers intensified because of the significant increase in supply, so the overall regulation in the area of consumer protection became necessary. Our accession to the EU on May 1, 2004, had a crucial impact on the legislation and building up of an institutional system.

Hungary had to ensure, as far as possible, that the future laws shall be compatible with the law of the Community. The so-called White Paper which was adopted in 1995, provided assistance in this. The White Paper served as a guide for the implementation, and Chapter 23 summarized the requirements for the harmonization of the law of consumer protection.[43]

In 1991, authoritative organizations (Consumer Protection Authority and local authorities) were created as the first step in building up the institutional system for consumers

After this, a comprehensive law was enacted with the *Act CLV of 1997 on Consumer Protection (CP),* which was based on five principles of consumer protection:

(1) protection of consumers' health and safety;

43. *See* the details about the development of the Hungarian consumer protection Dr. Fazekas Judit, *Fogyasztóvédelmi jog* [Law of Consumer Protection]. Budapest (Complex Publisher 2007), 37–90, 137–153.

Furthermore Dr. Fazekas Judit, *A fogyasztóvédelmi acquis átvételének jogi és szervezeti kérdései. Csatlakozás-Jogközelítés* [Legal and Organisational Question on the Reception of Consumer Protection Acquis]. Budapest (KJK KERSZÖV Publisher 2013), 153–193.

Lévayné Fazekas Judit, *A magánjog kihívásai a XXI. században* [The Challenges of Private Law in the XXI. century], [online] in Jog-Állam-Politika, *Jog- és politikatudományi folyóirat*, 2020, XII. évf. Különszám, A Széchenyi István Egyetem Deák Ferenc Állam- és Jogtudományi Karának tudományos kiadványa, Győr, 131–144.

https://jap.sze.hu/images/lapsz%C3%A1mok/2020/K%C3%BCl%C3%B6nsz%C3%A1m/JAP_2020_KOLONSZAM.pdf.

Lévayné Fazekas Judit & Lévay Miklós, *A fogyasztóvédelem alkotmányossági kérdéseiről és a magyar fogyasztóvédelmi intézményrendszer változásairól* [On the constitutional issues of Consumer Protection and Changes in the Hungarian Consumer Protection Institutional System], in Homicskó Árpád Olivér & Szuchy Róbert (szerk.), *De Iuris Peritorum Meritis 11. 60 Studia In Honorem Péter Miskolczi-Bodnár.* Károli Gáspár Református Egyetem Állam- és Jogtudományi Kar, Budapest, 2017, 373–389.

Fazekas Judit, *Fogyasztóvédelmi jog 2.0* [Consumer Protection Law 2.0] Gondolat Kiadó, Budapest, 2022.

(2) protection of consumers' economic interest;
(3) right to enforcement of consumer claims;
(4) right to information (information and education of consumers);
(5) representation of consumers (right to be heard and right to enforcement the interests).[44]

Act LXI of 2022 on the amendment of certain laws necessary for effective consumer protection amended the CP Act. Although the scope of the law does not extend to the activities of organizations and persons supervised by the Hungarian National Bank, as a result of the amendment effective from June 25, 2023, the scope of the law also extends to the financial sector and to the representative actions initiated due to a violation by a company that affects the collective interests of consumers adversely or is presumed to be detrimental in accordance with Directive (EU) 2020/1828 of the European Parliament ad of the Council of November 25, 2020 on representative actions for the protection of the collective interests of consumers and repealing Directive 2009/22/EC.

Consumers are increasingly buying goods and using services in the digital space. In order to ensure a high level of consumer protection, it is necessary that, in relation to representative claims, the scope of the Act on consumer protection, after the amendment, extend beyond the general consumer protection law to areas such as data protection, financial services, travel and tourism. Since there is an increased consumer demand for financial and investment services, it is particularly important to improve the enforcement of consumer protection law in the mentioned areas.

Collective interests of consumers shall mean the general interest of consumers and, in particular, for the purposes of redress measures, the interests of a group of consumers. (Point 15 of section 2 of CP Act)

---

44. This Act shall not apply to the activities supervised by the NBH, acting within its function as supervisory authority of the financial intermediary system, of organizations and persons engaged in activities which are supervised by the NBH (hereinafter referred to as "financial service activities").

According to the Act, "consumer" shall mean any natural person who is acting for purposes of purchasing, ordering, receiving and using goods or services which are outside his trade, business or profession, or who is the target of any representation or commercial communication directly connected with a product. In the application of the provisions on arbitration boards—excluding Regulation (EU) No. 524/2013 of the European Parliament and of the Council of May 21, 2013 on online dispute resolution for consumer disputes and amending Regulation (EC) No. 2006/2004 and Directive 2009/22/EC—consumer shall also mean—in addition to what is contained above—any civil society organization, ecclesiastical legal entity, condominium association, housing cooperative, micro, small and medium-size enterprise acting for purposes of purchasing, ordering, receiving and using goods or services which can be regarded as outside its trade, business or profession, or that is the target of any representation or commercial communication directly connected with a product. Furthermore, for the purposes of Regulation (EU) 2018/302 of the European Parliament and of the Council of Feb. 28, 2018 on addressing unjustified geo-blocking and other forms of discrimination based on customers' nationality, place of residence or place of establishment within the internal market and amending Regulations (EC) No. 2006/2004 and (EU) 2017/2394 and Directive 2009/22/EC (hereinafter referred to as "Regulation 2018/302/EU") any company that qualifies as a customer under Regulation 2018/302/EU shall also be treated as a consumer.

Representative action shall mean an action for the protection of the collective interests of consumers that is brought by a qualified entity as a claimant party on behalf of consumers to seek an injunctive measure, a redress measure, or both. (Point 25 of section 2 of CP Act)

The structure of the Act:

I. Part One: General Provisions and Consumer Protection Provisions
   Chapter I General Provisions
   Chapter II (Repealed)
   Chapter III (Repealed)
   Chapter IV Specific Requirements Relating to the Supply of Goods and Services
   Chapter IV/A Specific Requirements Relating to Protection of Children and Juveniles Chapter IV/B Prohibition of Organizing Consumer Groups
   Chapter V Consumer education, Chapter VI *Enforcement of consumer rights*
   - Costumer Assistance and Complaint Handling sections 17/A–17/C
   - Consumer Relations Officer section 17/D
   - Arbitration board, sections 18-37/A
   - Consumer Protection Platform for Household Overhead Section 37/B
   - Legal recourse in the Public Interest Section 38 (from 25 June 2023, it was replaced by the subchapter entitled representative actions for the protection of the collective interests of consumers; the detailed provisions are regulated in Sections 38/A-38/G
   - Bringing Action in the Public Interest Section 39

II. Part Two: Consumer Protection Schemes Sponsored by the state, local governments and nongovernmental organizations
   Chapter VII Government Scheme for the Protection of Consumers Interests
   Chapter VIII The role of local governments, and communities
   Chapter IX Associations for the Protection of Consumers
   Chapter X Proceedings of the Consumer Protection Authority

III. Part three: Closing provisions.

Domestic representative actions and cross-border representative actions may be brought by a qualified entity that complies with the criteria defined by the Act. The decision to designate an entity as a qualified entity for the purpose of bringing action lies with the minister in charge of consumer protection. Designation as a qualified entity is not required for the following entities for the purpose of bringing domestic representative actions:

(a) the consumer protection authority;
(b) the public prosecutor;

(c) the Magyar Nemzeti Bank (National Bank of Hungary); and
(d) all administration bodies of the central government, autonomous government bodies and autonomous regulatory agencies whose tasks consist of the protection of consumer rights based on the provisions of Union laws specified in Annex I to Directive 2020/1828/EU and other statutory provisions.

The Fundamental Law of Hungary meant a big promotion toward this goal because it stipulated the protection of the rights of consumers and set tasks for the state. Article (M) declares the following:

(1) The economy of Hungary shall be based on work which creates value, and on freedom of enterprise.
(2) Hungary shall ensure the conditions of fair economic competition. Hungary shall act against any abuse of a dominant position, and shall protect the rights of consumers.

52. According to the Hungarian laws, in line with the regulations of the EU, a consumer shall mean any natural person acting for purposes which are outside his/her trade, business, or profession.[45]

The institutional system for consumer protection incorporates the institutional system of the state, the local Government, and the civil societies and associations representing the consumers' interests. The Consumer Protection Committee was established at the inaugural meeting of the National Assembly in the new parliamentary term of 2010. The Consumer Protection Committee took part in the activity of the National Assembly as an advisory, initiating, and proposing body and it took part in the control of the Government's activity. Its members could only be members of the Parliament. Later and still at present, consumer protection falls under the remit of the Economic Committee as a standing committee of the Parliament.[46]

According to the current legislation, consumer protection falls within the responsibility of the Ministry of Justice at the government level.[47] Prior to this, it was the responsibility of the Ministry for Innovation and Technology, previously the Ministry of National Development (MND).[48]

Within the framework of its responsibility for consumer protection, the Minister:

– prepares legal acts on the prohibition of unfair commercial practices towards consumers, on consumer protection and on economic advertising activities;

---

45. According to the Act IV of 1959 which entered into force before Mar. 15, 2014, a consumer shall mean not only a natural person but also any person who is a party to a contract concluded for reasons other than economic or professional activities.
46. The Parliament on the establishment of the committees of the Parliament and the election of their members and officials.
47. Section 127 of Government Decree No. 182/2022. (V.24.) on the duties and powers of the members of the Government.
48. Until Jan. 1, 2017 the HACP acted at the central level and consumer protection inspectorates acted beside the Government offices at the local level. As a result of the organizational change, the MND and the Pest County Government Office became the general successor of the former National Consumer Protection Authority (hereinafter referred to as "NCPA").

- develops the concept of consumer protection policy, action and professional programs related to consumer protection and general product safety and monitors their implementation;
- defines the institutional system of market supervision;
- supports the establishment and operation of alternative dispute resolution forums for consumer legal disputes, in the framework of which it performs organizational, regulatory, support and development tasks related to consumer protection civil organizations and arbitration bodies, as well as government tasks related to the organization appointed to the Network of European Consumer Centers;
- with the involvement of the relevant member of the Government, takes and initiates measures for the protection and enforcement of consumer rights;
- carries out institutional development tasks with regard to the safety and conformity of goods and services.[49]

On July 21, 2022, the Minister of Justice submitted to the Government the objectives of the consumer protection policy, which the Government adopted with its Government Decision No. 1353/2022. (VII.21.). The new policy program declares the Government's commitment to "protect the rights of Hungarian people and Hungarian families, take action against consumer protection violations, and promote voluntary legal compliance."

At the suggestion of the Minister of Justice, a new body, the Consumer Protection Roundtable, supports the work of the existing Consumer Protection Council by discussing current problems and developing concrete solutions.

The Ministry operates the Consumer Protection Council,[50] which has the right to consult, make legal opinions, and make proposals in connection with consumer protection.

Consumer protection authorities play a prominent role in the institutional system of state consumer protection. First-instance consumer protection responsibilities appear in 197 districts; therefore, consumers can make their complaints primarily before the regionally competent district offices from January 1, 2017. In the Government Decree No. 387/2016. (XII.2.), the Government designated the consumer protection authorities, with the exception of matters falling within the scope of responsibilities related to the supervision of the financial intermediation system, as the supervision of the financial intermediation system is still carried out by the NBH.

Until January 1, 2017, the Hungarian Authority for Consumer Protection (HACP) acted at the central level, and consumer protection inspectorates acted beside the Government offices at the local level.[51]

53. Other organizations also carry out tasks in relation to consumer protection.[52]

---

49. Section 127 of Government Decree No. 182/2022. (V.24.) on the duties and powers of the members of the Government.
50. According to the Government Decree No. 1259/2011. (VII.27.) on the Consumer Protection Council, its members are the representatives of the governmental, social, and professional side.
51. The HACP was a body with general competence and did not have any powers to deal with specific consumer protection duties and powers granted to other public authorities in other legislations.
52. https://ec.europa.eu/info/sites/default/files/national-consumer-organisations_hungary-en_0.pdf.

The main task of the Competition Authority is to guard the purity of the market, and only a secondary task is to protect consumers through these activities.

The Hungarian Competition Authority (HCA) shall act in such situations which affect the competition in merit, especially in cases where somebody is engaged in unfair trade practices.[53]

In the case of the organizations supervised by the HCA under the relevant legislation, the NBH is entitled to respond to the rights of such consumers who use financial services and to help find the responsibility and decency of the service providers.

54. The Consumer Protection Act shall not apply to the activities, supervised by the NBH, acting within its function as the supervisory authority of the financial intermediary system, of organizations and persons engaged in activities which are supervised by the NBH.

II. Local Governments

55. The role of the local Government is significant in consumer protection. The representative bodies of local Governments may promote the formation of independent consumer associations, may support the activities of associations for the protection of consumers' interests at the local level, and may operate consumer protection consulting offices, depending on consumer demand.

III. Associations for the Protection of Consumers

56. The civil organizations, and especially the consumer associations within them, are important members of the system of consumer protection.

In their specific competences defined by law, they can act in the interest of consumers (e.g., monitor the standard contractual conditions applied with regard to consumers, bring action in the public interest, request proceedings, inquiries, or measures in the interest of protecting the rights and interests of consumers), can represent consumers in reconciliation forums and bodies, can participate in the legislation in such a way that they can assess legislative bills concerning to consumers, can participate in the drafting of consumer protection policies, and can monitor the implementation of such policies. In the proceedings of the consumer protection authority, client rights shall be conferred to the associations for the protection of consumers, with respect to the consumer interest they protect and to the qualified entities established under the laws of any EEA Member State that are included in

53. *See,* for example, JD2019. 182. The commercial communication can be considered as misleading and therefore illegal, which suggests that by paying HUF 100 per day you can get an insurance amount of up to HUF 3.5 million with life insurance (although this is excluded by the insurance scheme).

the list published in the Official Journal of the European Communities. In other proceedings, client rights shall be conferred upon the associations for the protection of consumers' interests only if the infringement investigated concerns a broad range of consumers.

They can achieve significant results in the development of consumer awareness through information and education of the consumers.[54]

Furthermore, Consumer Counseling Offices and Financial Consulting Offices[55] can also help consumers learn about their rights and the enforcement of their claims by providing free services.

IV. Promoting the Consumer Tasks of Business Entities: Consumer Relations Officer

57. The legal basis of consumer protection in Hungary puts emphasis on the fact that both consumers and business entities shall be aware of their rights. A consumer relations officer is a relatively new legal institution who shall be employed by small and medium enterprises governed by law.[56]

The responsibilities of the consumer relations officer shall include the monitoring of the business entity's activities affecting consumers, arranging training on a regular basis for the business entity's employees on the enhancement of a new approach in consumer protection, and improving employees' education relating to consumer protection rules. The consumer relations officer shall maintain contact with the consumer protection authority, Arbitration Boards, and other public entities tasked with consumer protection duties, among other responsibilities.

§2. Consumer Protection Legal Institutions in Consumer Contracts

58. Because of the special nature of insurance relationships, we review the area of consumer protection legal institutions, which generally concern consumer contracts.

I. Standard Contract Terms: Unfair Contract Terms

59. The Act V of 1959 on the Civil Code was modified in 1977, the amendment of which introduced the regulations concerning standard contract terms and the voidability of unfair contract terms (section 209). After this, another modification occurred in 1997, the primary objective of which was to create consistency with

54. *See*: Hungarian Association of Consumer Protectors (Fogyasztóvédők Magyarországi Egyesülete—FOME). http://www.fome.hu.
55. http://fogyasztovedelem-gte.hu/penzugyi-fogyasztovedelmi-tanacsado-irodak/.
56. The regulations relating to the consumer relations officer is contained by the CP.

community law,[57] but the implementation was not fully realized. Another modification was necessary, which happened in 2006.[58]

The CC regulates the definition of a standard contract term, how it can become part of a contract (section 6:77–6:81), and when it shall be regarded as unfair. (section 6:102).[59]

A standard contract term shall be considered unfair if, contrary to the requirement of good faith and fair dealing, it causes a significant and unjustified imbalance in contractual rights and obligations to the detriment of the party entering into a contract with the person imposing such contract term. The unfair nature of a standard contract term shall be assessed, taking into account the nature of the services for which the contract was concluded and by referring, at the time of conclusion of the contract, to all the circumstances leading to the conclusion of the contract and to all the other terms of the contract or of another contract on which it is dependent. The provisions relating to unfair standard contract terms shall not apply to the definition of the main subject matter specified in the contract or to the ratio between the price determined, on the one hand, and the services provided in exchange, on the other, insofar as these terms are in plain, intelligible language. The standard contract terms defined by legislation, or established in accordance with the provisions of the relevant legislation, shall not be deemed unfair. Any unfair contract term that has been incorporated into the contract as a standard contract term may be contested by the injured party.

In consumer contracts, the provisions relating to standard contract terms shall also apply to the contract terms which have been drafted in advance by the business party and which have not been individually negotiated. The burden of proof to verify that a contract term has been individually negotiated lies with the business party. According to the rules of the CC, contracts which involve a consumer and a business party, where a standard contract term or any contract term which has been

---

57. Council Directive 93/13/EEC of Apr. 5, 1993 on unfair terms in consumer contracts.
58. *See* in details: Dr. Fazekas Judit, *Hungarian Contract Law*. International Encylopaedia of Laws, General Editor Prof. Dr. R. Blanpain, Vols. 31, 32 (Kluwer Law International Pub. Co., 2003), Dr. Fazekas Judit, *Fogyasztóvédelmi jog* [Consumer Protection Law].Budapest (Complex Publisher 2007), 137–153, Dr. Miskolczi Bodnár Péter & Dr. Sándor István, *A fogyasztóvédelmi jog magyar szabályozása* [Hungarian Regulations on the Law of Consumer Protection]. (Patrocinium Publisher 2010), 97–104.

    Miskolczi Bodnár Péter, *Fogyasztói szerződések* [Consumer Contracts]. Budapest (Patrocinium 2015).

    Harsányi Gyöngyi, *Reflexiók a fogyasztó és a befektető, mint jogi fogalom megjelenéséről a magyar magánjogban* [Reflections on the Appearance of Consumer and Investor as Legal Concepts in Hungarian Private Law]. In *Ünnepi tanulmányok Fazekas Judit tiszteletére* Keserű Barna Arnold, Szoboszlai-Kiss Katalin (szerk.), 227–241. ISBN 978-615-6491-12-1 DOI: 10.59199/salusvocalis.2023 Kiadó: UNIVERSITAS-Győr Nonprofit Kft.

    Miskolczi Bodnár Péter, *A kógens és klaudikálóan kógens fogyasztói szabályok gyökerei* [The Roots of Cogent and Claudically Cogent Consumer Rules]. In *Ünnepi tanulmányok Fazekas Judit tiszteletére,* Keserű Barna Arnold, Szoboszlai-Kiss Katalin (szerk.), 523–537. ISBN 978-615-6491-12-1 DOI: 10.59199/salusvocalis.2023 Kiadó: UNIVERSITAS-Győr Nonprofit Kft.
59. The aim of this legal regulations was to comply with the legal harmonization obligation relating to the Council Directive 93/13/EEC of Apr. 5, 1993 on unfair terms in consumer contracts.

drafted in advance by the business party and which has not been individually negotiated, shall be regarded as unfair if they are not drafted in plain and clearly understandable language, solely on that basis.

Any unfair contract term that has been incorporated into a contract that involves a consumer and a business party shall be null and void. Nullity may be invoked in favor of the consumer.

The CC gives an exemplificative list of the clauses applied in consumer contract, which shall be regarded as unfair and, therefore, null and void.

The other group of clauses is the terms which shall be considered unfair until proven otherwise.

The persons entitled by the CC can bring a public interest action in which the court shall establish the annulment of an unfair contract term in favor of all of the parties with which the party imposing the condition has a contractual relationship and shall order the party who applied the contract term in question to take measures for having a public notice declaring the contract term unfair published at their own cost. Moreover, an action may be brought, in the public interest, requesting to have a standard contract term or condition, that has been defined for consumer contracts and made available to the general public, declared unfair, regardless of whether the term or condition in question had, in fact, been applied or not. If the court finds the contested standard contract term unfair, the court ruling may also contain a clause banning the party who made it available to the public from the further use of such.

The lawsuit may be brought against any party who publicly recommends the use of any unfair standard contract term or condition that has been defined for consumer contracts and made available to the general public. If the court finds the standard contract term unfair, it shall be declared null and void for future purposes, banning any further recommendation for use.

II. Interpretation of Contracts, Unilateral Cogency, Nullity of Abandonment

60. The CC stipulates various regulations in relation to the interpretation of contracts. According to the general rule which appears in subsection 1 of section 6:86 of the CC, contract terms and statements are to be interpreted in accordance with the contract as a whole. If the party applies standard contract terms in the conclusion of the contract and its terms or the contents of the contract term, which has not been individually negotiated, cannot be clearly established by the application of the general provisions for the interpretation of the legal statement, the interpretation that is more favorable to the party entering into a contract with the person imposing such contract term shall prevail. In connection with a contract that involves a consumer and a business party, this provision shall also apply to the interpretation of any contract term.

§3. Consumer Protection Relating to Electronic Commerce

61. The European Parliament and the Council of the European Union adopted Directive 97/7/EC (distance selling[60]) with regard to changed selling methods from the point of view of consumer protection, which doesn't apply to financial services. After a lengthy preparation, Directive 2002/65/EC[61] was born in this area. The Directive puts emphasis on the regulations of information requirements and the consumer's right of withdrawal.

62. In trade and in the field of insurance, the classical contracting formulas are replaced by contracts concluded by modern IT tools, which resulted in the reevaluation of the form of writing as well. The EU adopted Directive 2000/31/EC on electronic commerce for the sake of ensuring the legal framework relating to the free movement of IT services between the Member States. For the development of the electronic business, credibility is essential, which means that the messages and legal statements between partners in different locations shall be reliable. This need was recognized by the EU when it created Directive 1999/93/EC for electronic signatures (Directive on e-signatures).[62]

63. Hungary accepted—according to the obligation undertaken based on the Association Agreement—the Decree on the contracts concluded by parties at a distance,[63] later implemented the Directive 2002/65/EC by the adoption of the Act XXV. of 2005 on the Financial Service Sector Contracts Concluded by Distance Selling, and Directive 2000/31/EC was implemented by the Act CVIII of 2001 on the Electronic Commerce and on Information Society Services.

64. For the sake of the uniformity of legal regulations, the EU repealed the "distance selling" Directive and amended the Unfair Contract Directive (93/13/EEC) with the new Consumer Rights Directive (2011/83/EU). The Government Decree No. 45/2014. (II.26.) on the detailed regulations of contracts concluded by consumer and business company, which repealed the former rules.

65. The CC takes into consideration the provisions of consumer protection, which are built into the Code to a higher extent than the previous rules.

We have already mentioned the regulations relating to unfair contract terms, where consumer protection is of great importance, but we can find the rules relating to the process of concluding the contract by electronic means as a new provision in

60. Directive 97/7/EC of the European Parliament and of the Council of May 1997 on the protection of consumers in respect of distance contracts.
61. Directive 2002/65/EC of the European Parliament and of the Council of Sep. 23, 2002 concerning distance marketing of consumer financial services and amending Council Directive 90/619/EEC and Directives 97/7/EC and 98/27 EC.
62. New Regulation: Regulation (EU) No 910/2014 of The European Parliament and the Council of Jul. 23, 2014 on electronic identification and trust services for electronic transactions in the internal market and repealing Directive 1999/93/EC.
63. Government Decree No. 17/1999. (II.5.).

the CC. The CC contains regulations on the information obligation of the party providing the electronic means for concluding the contract, on the obligation of correcting the errors, on the effectiveness of the contract statement made by way of electronic means, the confirmation of the legal statement, and the termination of the binding period. These rules are all cogent in connection with a contract which involves a consumer and a business party (section 6:82–6:85 of the CC).

66. The CC settles the question of when the legal statement made by electronic means can fulfill the condition of writing. In this respect, the law requires the same conditions for the former technical possibilities of legal statements (telegraph, telex, telefax) and for legal statements made through electronic means. A legal statement shall be construed to have been made in writing if executed in a form with facilities for retrieving the information contained in the legal statement unaltered, for identifying the person making the legal statement and the time when it was made.

§4. Consumer Protection: Unfair Commercial Practice[64]

67. In the field of consumer protection, the comprehensive act is the Unfair Commercial Practice (UCP) Directive (2005/29/EC) on *the unfair business-to-consumer commercial practices*. The Directive was harmonized by Act XLVII of 2008 on the Prohibition of Unfair Business-to-Consumer Commercial Practices (PUBC).[65] The Directive and the Hungarian Act in line with the Directive determine the insurance practice in Annex 1, which shall be regarded as unfair practice according to the law.[66]

§5. EU Documents Defining Consumer Protection Policy Currently and Their Implementation into the Hungarian Law

68. In 2015, the European Commission published its Communication on the European Digital Single Market Strategy, which laid down the foundations for the

64. Barta Judit, *A pszichés nyomásgyakorlás, mint tisztességtelen kereskedelmi gyakorlat* [Psychological Pressure as an Unfair Commercial Practice]. In *Ünnepi tanulmányok Fazekas Judit tiszteletére,* Keserű Barna Arnold, Szoboszlai-Kiss Katalin (szerk.), 33–49. ISBN 978-615-6491-12-1 DOI: 10.59199/salusvocalis.2023 Kiadó: UNIVERSITAS-Győr Nonprofit Kft.
65. The directive seeks to a so-called maximum harmonization, i.e., it intends to unify the legal regulations of the Member States.
66. Schedule to Act XLVII of 2008: Unfair Commercial Practices:

> 27. Requiring a consumer who wishes to claim on an insurance policy to produce documents which could not reasonably be considered relevant as to whether the claim was valid, or failing systematically to respond to pertinent correspondence, in order to dissuade a consumer from exercising his contractual rights.

development of the Digital Single Market.[67] The aim of the digital single market strategy is to ensure that the economy, industry, and society of the EU can take full advantage of the benefits associated with the new digital era. This affects, among others, the establishment of common European data protection rules, the reform of telecommunications rules, and the development of rules on copyright and taxation. The modernization of consumer protection rules for online and digital purchases and the provision of access to digital goods and digital content were also included.

The basic aim of the consumer protection program for the period 2014–2020[68] is to ensure a high level of consumer protection in the EU's internal consumer market. The cornerstone of the consumer protection program is a document from 2018 entitled "New Deal Consumers."[69] In this context, the directive adopted for the more effective implementation and modernization of the EU consumer protection rules, which also amended previous directives, should be highlighted.[70]

In Hungary, the Directive was implemented by Act CXXXVI of 2020 on the amendment of certain acts related to consumer protection and Government Decree No. 712/2020. (XII.30.), which amended several government decrees related to consumer protection, which entered into force on May 28, 2022.

In order to increase the trust of consumers and, thereby, the cross-border e-commerce, two more new directives were adopted: on certain aspects concerning contracts for the sale of goods and on certain aspects concerning contracts for the supply of digital content and digital services.[71] Both directives are considered a primary step in the adaption of European private law to the requirements of the digital economy.[72] 373/2021 on the detailed rules of contracts for the sale and purchase of

67. Communication from the Commission to the European Parliament, the Council, the European Economic and Social Committee and the Committee of the Regions. A Digital Single Market Strategy for Europe (COM(2015) 192 final, 6.5.2015).
68. Regulation (EU) No. 254/2014 of the European Parliament and the Council of Feb. 26, 2014 on a multiannual consumer program for the years 2014–20 and repealing Decision No. 1926/2006/EC (Official Journal of the European Union, L 84/42, 20.3.2014).
69. Communication from the Commission to the European Parliament, the Council and the European Economic and Social Committee A New Deal for Consumers (COM (2018) 183 final), (Brussels, 11.4.2018).
70. Directive (EU) 2019/2161 of the European Parliament and of the Council of Nov. 27, 2019 amending Council Directive 93/13/EEC and Directives 98/6/EC, 2005/29/EC and 2011/83/EU of the European Parliament and of the Council as regards the better enforcement and modernisation of Union consumer protection rules (Official Journal of the European Union, L 328/7, 18.12.2019).
71. Directive (EU) 2019/771 of the European Parliament and of the Council of the Council of 20 May 2019 on certain aspects concerning contracts for the sale of goods, amending Regulation (EU) 2017/2394 and Directive 2009/22/EC, and repealing Directive 1999/44/EC (Official Journal of the European Union, L 136/28, 22.5.2019).

    Directive (EU) 2019/770 of the European Parliament and of the Council of the Council of May 20, 2019, on certain aspects concerning contracts for the supply of digital content and digital services Official Journal of the European Union, L 136/1, 22.5.2019).
72. For the directives *see*: prof. Hugh Beale, *Digital Content Directive and Rules for Contracts on Continuous Supply*. Journal of Intellectual Property, Information Technology and Electronic Commerce Law, Vol. 12, Issue 2 (April 2021), 96–111. https://www.jipitec.eu/issues/jipitec-12-2-2021/5286, Prof. Martin Ebers, *Liability For Artificial Intelligence And EU Consumer Law*. Journal of Intellectual Property, Information Technology and Electronic Commerce Law. Vol. 12, Issue 2 (April 2021), 204–220.

    https://www.jipitec.eu/issues/jipitec-12-2-2021/5289.

goods and the provision of digital content and digital services between a consumer and a business in order to transpose these laws into Hungarian law (VI.30.). It took place by government decree.

These legal acts were implemented into the Hungarian legal system by Government Decree No. 373/2021. (VI.30.) on the detailed rules of the contracts between the consumer and the business for the sale and purchase of goods, as well as the provision of digital content and the provision of digital services.[73]

The EU consumer protection policy action program for the next period is based on the new consumer strategy adopted on November 13, 2020,[74] which outlines the vision for EU consumer protection policy for the period 2020–2025. The strategy covers five priority areas, of which the creation of a safer digital space for consumers should be highlighted.[75]

§6. NBH and Consumer Protection

69. The NBH annually publishes its reports on consumer protection online and in printed form since 2016.

The power of the NBH extends beyond the authoritative and mediatory tasks and, especially, covers the following:

- *actio popularis*;
- issuance of legal regulations and other acts which are not compulsory;

Barta Judit, *Az EU által meghirdetett digitális forradalom hatása a kereskedelmi jog egyes területein: szerződések, fogyasztóvédelem, gazdasági verseny, gazdasági társaságok* [The Impact of the Digital Revolution Announced by the EU in Certain Areas of Commercial Law: Contracts, Consumer Protection, Economic Competition, Business Companies].

https://www.mjsz.uni-miskolc.hu/files/13820/4_bartajudit_t%C3%B6rdelt.pdf.

73. The database in the website http://www.jogsertowebaruhazak.kormany.hu/ lists the online stores, which have been committed a so-called serious violation of the law defined in a separate government decree.
74. European Commission Communication from the Commission to the European Parliament and the Council New Consumer Agenda Strengthening consumer resilience for sustainable recovery Brussels, 13.11.2020, COM/2020/696 final.
75. In order to improve the functioning of the internal market, the EU seeks to strengthen cyber security by updating Directive 2016/1148 concerning measures for a high common level of security of network and information systems across the Union (NIS Directive). Within the framework of the Union's new cyber security strategy, the European Commission presented the draft legislation for the modernization of the NIS Directive ("NIS2 Directive") on Dec. 16, 2020, which was announced in the Official Journal of the European Union on Dec. 27, 2022 and entered into force on Jan. 16, 2023. *See*: Directive (EU) 2022/2555 of the European Parliament and of the Council of Dec. 14, 2022 on measures for a high common level of cybersecurity across the Union, amending Regulation (EU) No. 910/2014 and Directive (EU) 2018/1972, and repealing Directive (EU) 2016/1148 (NIS 2 Directive).

In 2021, the NBH also conducted a survey on the digitalization level of domestic insurance companies, which provides an up-to-date picture of the preparedness and commitment of the sector, as well as the level of digitalization of insurance products and background processes. According to the survey, the initiation and the customer notifications are mostly digitalized in connection with residential property insurances, but the digitization of notifications related to company products has also begun.

Fintech And Digitalization Report of the NBH, June 2022.

- submission of legislative proposals;
- operation of customer service and consulting networks;
- participation in the international organizations on consumer protection.

The NBH annually prepares a Report on Insurance, Funds, Capital Market Risks and Consumer Protection.[76] The NBH shall prepare a prudential and consumer risk report each year on the activities of the bodies and persons covered by the acts and on the functioning of the financial markets and the financial intermediary system.

70. The tasks of the NBH can be emphasized by the following:

The NBH shall supervise the financial intermediary system with a view to:

(a) ensuring the smooth, transparent and efficient functioning of the financial intermediary system;
(b) facilitating the prudent operation of the persons and organizations comprising the financial intermediary system and overseeing the prudent exercise of owners' rights;
(c) discovering undesirable business and economic risks threatening individual financial organizations or individual sectors of financial organizations, mitigating or eliminating existing individual or sector-related risks, and taking preventive measures with a view to ensuring the prudent operation of individual financial organizations;
(d) protecting the interests of parties using the services rendered by financial organizations and strengthening public confidence in the financial intermediary system.

The NBH shall, within the framework of its responsibilities, supervise the bodies and persons and the activities covered by, *inter alia*, the Act on Insurance Institutions and the Insurance Business;

71. The NBH shall provide for the implementation of Regulation (EC) No. 2006/2004 of the European Parliament and of the Council of October 27, 2004, on the cooperation between national authorities responsible for the enforcement of consumer protection laws with regard to any infringement within any EEA Member State of national laws on the transposition of:

(a) Council Directive 93/13/EEC of April 5, 1993, on unfair terms in consumer contracts.
(b) Directive 2002/65/EC of the European Parliament and of the Council of September 23, 2002, concerning the distance marketing of consumer financial services and amending Council Directive 90/619/EEC and Directives 97/7/EC and 98/27/EC.

76. MNB: Report on Insurance, Funds, Capital Market Risks and Consumer Protection 2022. https://mnb.hu/letoltes/kockazati-jelentes-2022-hun-0613-2.pdf.

(c) Directive 2005/29/EC of the European Parliament and of the Council of May 11, 2005, concerning unfair business-to-consumer commercial practices in the internal market and amending Council Directive 84/450/EEC, Directives 97/7/EC, 98/27/EC and 2002/65/EC of the European Parliament and of the Council and Regulation (EC) No. 2006/2004 of the European Parliament and of the Council with respect to the commercial practices connected to the activities within its scope of supervision.

For the purposes of this Act:

(a) "consumer" shall mean any natural person who is acting for purposes which are outside his trade, business or profession;
(b) "service contract" shall mean any contract other than a service contract provided for in the Consumer Protection Act under which the body or person covered by the acts enumerated in section 39 supplies or undertakes to supply a service to the consumer, and the consumer pays or undertakes to pay the price thereof;
(c) "online service contract" shall mean a sales or service contract where the body or person covered by the acts enumerated in section 39, or the intermediary thereof, has offered goods or services on a website or by other electronic means, and the consumer has conveyed his intention to access such goods or services on that website or by other electronic means.

Act LXI of 2022 on the amendment of certain laws necessary for effective consumer protection modified the Act on NBH. According to subsection 1 of section 82, in a consumer protection procedure, the rights of the client also apply to those authorized entities established under the law of any other EEA state with reference to the violation of the provisions transposing the directives defined in the law, which can be found in the list published in the Official Journal of the European Union in accordance with Article 5(1) of Directive (EU) 2020/1828 of the European Parliament ad of the Council of November 25, 2020, on representative actions for the protection of the collective interests of consumers and repealing Directive 2009/22/EC.

72. The NBH shall control, upon request or on its own motion:

- the ensuring of compliance with the rules of the behavior of the supervised entities against consumers who impress the services of such entities (regulations on consumer protection, e.g., provisions relating to the prohibition of unfair competition practice against consumers, to commercial advertising, to the electronic commerce services); and
- the obligations, in relation to financial consumer disputes, of ensuring compliance with the procedural rules of consumer protection.

73. The consumer can initiate the consumer protection process after the complaint was proposed to the organization in accordance with the form set by the law but didn't get a response to the complaint, or the justification of the complaint was not made in line with the law, or the consumer presumes other circumstances, which harm the consumer rights stipulated by the laws.

In the proceedings for the protection of consumers' interests, client rights shall be conferred upon the qualified entities established under the laws of any EEA Member State with respect to the consumer interests they protect—that are included in the list published in the Official Journal of the European Communities pursuant to Article 4(3) of Directive 2009/22/EC of the European Parliament and of the Council of April 23, 2009, on injunctions for the protection of consumers' interests with respect to any violation of the legal provisions on the transposition of the directives mentioned before.

74. The NBH is entitled to supervise the compliance of the provisions relating to the transaction by testing transactions within the framework of consumer protection procedures.

The NBH shall have powers to conduct:

(a) direct inquiries;
(b) thematic investigations; or
(c) follow-up inspections.

On the bodies or persons for the purpose of consumer protection.

75. If the NBH finds any infringement of the relevant consumer regulations or its resolution adopted in proceedings for the protection of consumers' interests, the NBH may impose the following sanctions:

- issue a warning for taking the measures necessary for compliance with the relevant legal provisions;
- issue a warning for eliminating the discrepancies detected;
- order the cessation of the infringement;
- prohibit any further infringement;
- ban or impose conditions regarding the pursuit of the activity or the supply of services involved in the infringement until the infringement is eliminated; and
- impose a consumer protection fine.

Additional sanctions may be laid down in the legislation containing provisions for the protection of consumers for any violation of the provisions prescribed therein.

According to the report of the NBH for the first half of 2021, it concluded three comprehensive investigations and one target investigation for insurance companies, and two prudential investigations for insurance intermediaries. In case of procedures launched in 2021, the full implementation of the new insurance sales directive (Insurance Distribution Directive (IDD))[77] regulations affecting the insurance

77. IDD Insurance Distribution Directive—Directive (EU) 2016/97 of the European Parliament and of the Council of Jan. 20, 2016 on insurance distribution.

sector, especially the regulations regarding the product supervision and management system, as well as the examination of Key Information Document (KID) documents, continued to be of particular importance.[78]

76. In 2011, the Authority engaged in the workflow of the development of consumer protection standards at the European level. In 2011, three sector-oriented European Supervisory Authorities were established within the framework of the new European System of Financial Supervisors, with major consumer protection powers and objectives. The objective of the EIOPA is to secure the trust and confidence in the financial system and the protection of consumers. The tasks of the authorities are the analysis of consumer trends and the monitoring of Member States' initiatives in connection with financial education.

The NBH is a member of the International Association of Insurance Supervisors (IAIS), established in 1994. This is a voluntary membership organization of insurance supervisors and regulators from more than two hundred jurisdictions, constituting 97% of the world's insurance fees. It is an international standard-setting body responsible for developing and assisting in the implementation of principles, standards and other supporting material for the supervision of the insurance sector. The IAIS also provides a forum for Members to share their experiences and understanding of insurance supervision and insurance markets. In recognition of its collective expertise, the IAIS is routinely called upon by the G20 leaders and other international standard-setting bodies.

I. System of Financial Arbitration

77. The FAB was established by the Act on the HFSA. It was a professionally independent body within the HFSA and was directly under the President of the HFSA. Until the establishment of the FAB, the consumers could bring their financial case to the Arbitration Board, which had general jurisdiction and was competent according to the place of residence, if they didn't want to go to court. Financial cases are usually complicated, long, and costly, while arbitration is free; economists and financial jurists are involved and try to make an arrangement between the parties.

The operation of the FAB didn't change with the modification by which the NBH became the supervisory body. The FAB performs its task in accordance with the operational principles declared by the Recommendation of the Commission of 98/257/EC. Its principles of operation appear in the NBHA as concrete legal rules.[79]

The FAB can provide a cheaper and faster solution for the legal disputes between consumers and the financial service providers than the courts. The powers and competence of the FAB shall cover disputes between consumers and the bodies and persons covered by the acts relating to the conclusion and performance of contracts in

78. https://www.mnb.hu/letoltes/fe-leves-jelente-s-2021-hun-0927.pdf.
79. Independence, transparency, adversarial procedure, efficiency, legality, freedom, possibility of representation.

connection with the services supplied (hereinafter referred to as "consumer dispute of a financial nature") with a view to reaching on an out-of-court settlement. To this end, the FAB shall attempt to reach a conciliation agreement or, failing this, adopt a decision in the case to enforce consumer rights simply, efficiently, and practically and under the principle of cost-efficiency. In the absence of a negotiated settlement, the council may also adopt a binding decision if the body or person falling within the scope of the acts enumerated in section 39 did not make a statement of submission, and the request is found well-established, and the consumer's claim shown in the request does not exceed HUF 1 million at the time of the request and the adoption of the binding decision.

78. The FAB is entitled to proceed in cross-border consumer disputes if the service provider submits to the procedure of the FAB in the concrete legal dispute and if it recognizes the decision of the FAB as compulsory.[80] If the proceedings cannot be opened, the FAB shall inform the consumer of any alternate means available for the settlement of disputes, that is to say, the competent bodies established in other EEA Member States, which are also members of the FIN-Net. The FAB shall discharge the duties set out in the bylaws of the Financial Services Complaints Network (hereinafter referred to as "FIN-Net"), offering alternate means for the settlement of disputes of a financial nature.

Since January 1, 2012, the FAB has been a member of the INFO Network as well, which compacts the ombudsmen of the world and has more than fifty member associations from five continents. The main purpose of the INFO Network is to coordinate the mechanisms of alternative dispute settlement in the financial sector and to draw up a comprehensive system. The members of the organization created four regions: Eurasia, Africa, America, and Australia. It works by the six basic principles adopted by the members: independence, impartiality, efficiency, equity, transparency, and accountability.

II. Legal Recourse in the Public Interest

79. The NBH may bring civil actions on behalf of consumers against persons engaged in any violation of the provisions of the acts and the legislation adopted for the implementation of such acts or the provisions, furthermore, against those who are allegedly engaged in the use of any unfair standard contract term covered by the Civil Code in connection with their activities, where such illegal action affects a wide range of consumers whose identity can be established relying on the circumstances of the infringement.

The NBH may bring civil actions on behalf of consumers against persons engaged in any violation of the provisions of the acts listed and the legislation adopted for the implementation of such acts or the provisions of the Act on unfair commercial practice, furthermore, against those who are allegedly engaged in the

80. In 2015, forty-two such new cases were received, thirty-eight cases were closed of which six cases were filed against an insurer.
https://www.mnb.hu/letoltes/mnb-eves-jelentes-2015.pdf.

use of any unfair standard contract term covered by the Civil Code in connection with their activities, where such illegal action affects a wide range of consumers whose identity can be established relying on the circumstances of the infringement.

No action may be brought after three years following the time of the commission of the aforementioned infringement. Where, with respect to the consumers affected by the infringement, the legal grounds for the claim and the amount of damages and the amount of restitution demanded, or the overall contents of the claim in the case of other claims, can be clearly established irrespective of the individual circumstances of the consumers affected by the infringement, the NBH may request the court to award such claims and order the body or persons determined by the Act to satisfy these claims. The decision can be executed in the case of nonperformance. Otherwise, it can request the court to declare the facts of the infringement with effect for all consumers. In such cases, the consumer affected by the infringement, in the case of a claim for damages, shall prove the amount of damage and the causal link between the breach and the damage in the lawsuit which was brought against the organization. The facts also have an important role in that the court may authorize the NBH to publish the court's decision in a national daily newspaper at the infringer's expense or to make it available to the general public by means consistent with the nature of the infringement. The recourse exercised by the NBH is without prejudice to the consumers' right to bring civil action independently against the infringer.

The entitlement to file for legal action shall be afforded not just to the NBH but to the associations for the protection of consumers' interests and, furthermore, to all qualified entities established under the laws of any EEA Member State—with respect to the consumer interest they protect—that are included in the list published in the Official Journal of the European Communities pursuant to Article 4(3) of Directive 2009/22/EC of the European Parliament and of the Council on injunctions for the protection of consumers' interests, provided that the claim for which the action is filed pertains to any infringement of the legal provisions on the transposition of the directives.

§7. Consumer Protection Regulations Relating to Insurance Relationship

I. Consumer Protection Regulations in the Law of Insurance in the CC

80. In the general rules of consumer protection, we detailed the consumer protection rules relating to the law of insurance contracts and insurance commercial practice.

The general rules of the CC and the rules relating to the insurance contract are usually dispositive, although the protection of the consumer has great importance—because of its specialty—in the insurance relationship. It also realizes the fact that there are different rules relating to insurance contracts if the contracting party is a consumer. The rules of the CC contain unilaterally cogent rules only in connection with the consumer[81] insurance contracts.

If the contract is concluded by a consumer, the contract can deviate from the general rules of the insurance contract only for the benefit of the contracting party, the insured person, and the beneficiary in the fields defined in the CC.

II. The Regulations of the BIns. Relating to the Consumer Protection in the Insurance Relationship

81. In order to protect the consumer, the EU rules put great emphasis on ensuring the prudent and solvent operation of insurance companies. An important means for the protection of consumers in contractual relations is the obligation of insurance service providers to provide information. Solvency II Directive[82] regulates the information obligation imposed on the insurers in the field of both life and non-life insurance contracts. Intermediaries are important participants in the insurance market and the contracting process, for whom even the public law regulations[83] contain increasingly strict requirements.

The PRIIPs regulation[84] and the already mentioned IDD directive set out clear rules for insurance products. The former contains regulations for information before concluding a contract, while the latter sets out rules for sales and information.

In the insurance legal relationship, the obligation to provide information is extremely complex because it is necessary to pay attention to the general and special rules of the Civil Code, to the public law norms appearing at several levels, to the rules of the BIns., to the directly applicable EU standards, to the PRIIPs regulation, and to the rules regarding special contract conclusion methods. Furthermore, it also has to be taken into consideration whether the person wishing to conclude a contract is considered a consumer or a client (retail investor) based on these laws.

The definition of the consumer in the BIns. (Article 4.33) is not exactly the same as the concept defined in the Civil Code, while the concept of client is much broader.

According to Point 3 of Article 8:1 of the CC, *consumer* shall mean any natural person acting for purposes which are outside his trade, business or profession.

According to the BIns., consumer shall mean any natural person who is acting for purposes which are outside his trade, business or profession, while client shall

81. According to Point 3 of Art. 8:1.§ of the CC *consumer* shall mean any natural person acting for purposes which are outside his trade, business or profession.
82. Directive 2009/138/EC (Solvency II). *See*: Dr. Szedlák Katalin Viktória, *A biztosítási tevékenységről szóló 2014. évi LXXXVIII. törvény bemutatása a Szolvencia II. tükrében* [Presentation of Act LXXXVIII of 2014 on Insurance Activity in the Mirror of the Solvency II]. *Biztosítás és Kockázat*, II/1, 12–19.
83. Directive (EU) 2016/97 of the European Parliament and of the Council of Jan. 20, 2016 on insurance distribution (recast) (Official Journal of the European Union, L 26/19, 2.2.2016.).
84. Regulation (EU) No. 1286/2014 of the European Parliament and of the Council of Nov. 26, 2014 on KIDs for packaged retail and insurance-based investment products (PRIIPs) (Official Journal of the European Union, L 352/1, 9.12.2014).

mean the policyholder, the insured person, the beneficiary, the injured party, any other person who makes a contractual offer to the insurance company and who is entitled to receive benefits from the insurance company, furthermore, in the case of independent insurance intermediaries, any person who enters into a contract with an independent insurance intermediary for the purpose of brokering.

Insurance companies shall always act honestly, fairly and professionally in accordance with the best interests of their clients. Insurance companies shall not make any arrangement—in particular by way of remuneration—that could provide an incentive to insurance distributors to recommend a particular insurance product to a client when the insurance distributor could offer a different insurance product which would better meet the client's needs.[85]

82. During the analysis of the law of contracts, we have already discussed that the BIns. has an important specialty in that it regulates both the public and the private (contractual) law regulations relating to insurance relationships. These regulations protect not only the consumer but also the client. Nevertheless, we consider it important to mention the most important regulations in connection with consumer protection as the regulations of consumer–client protection rules in a wide sense:

- Information obligation of insurance companies (sections 152–158/C of the BIns.), insurance intermediaries (section 378 of the BIns.), and persons who carry on the activity of ancillary insurance mediation (section 368 of the BIns.) in line with the provision of the IDD Directive.
- Determination of the content of the information (Annex 4 of the BIns.).
- The ascertainment of the needs and requirements of the client by the broker before the conclusion of the contract (subsection 6 of section 398 of the BIns.).
- Minimal content of the insurance contract (section 121 of the BIns.).
- Obligations relating to the fixation of the documents to be presented to the insurer in the contract and to performance (sections 123–124 of the BIns.).
- Regulations on the amendments of the contract (section 122/A of the BIns.).
- Nondiscrimination on the basis of sex (section 134 of the BIns.), which needs to be taken into account during the performance of the fees and services according to Council Directive 2004/113/EC of December 13, 2004, implementing the principle of equal treatment between men and women in the access to and supply of goods and services.
- The marketing of insurance products (sections 130–131/A of the BIns.).
- Regulations on the suspending and prohibiting of the marketing of an insurance product (sections 130–131, section 300 of the BIns.).
- Insurance obligation (section 129 of the BIns.).
- Regulations relating to the insurance secrets in connection with the insurer (sections 135–143 of the BIns.) and the insurance agent (sections 379–381 of the BIns.).
- Rules relating to the complaints handling of the insurer (section 159 of the BIns.) and the agent (section 382 of the BIns.).

85. Section 130/A of the BIns. (in force from Feb. 28, 2018).

- Data disclosures made for the purpose of the protection of risk groups (sections 149–151 of the BIns.).
- Provisions relating to the satisfying of claims relating to the insurance contract during the liquidation process and to the ordering of it (sections 183–188 of the BIns.), which prefers the liabilities in connection with personal injury, accident, or sickness.

From June 26, 2021, the insurance companies shall prepare claims handling information for losses listed under Part *A)* of Annex 1—covering all products or for a single product or a group of products—and shall make it available on its website at all times.

The claims handling information shall, in particular, contain the following: *(a)* claims reporting procedures available; *(b)* settlement rules and deadlines; *(c)* potential ways of settlement of claims and loss adjustment, including where a settlement is reached by agreement.

Chapter 6. Compulsory Insurance

Edit Antal Ujvári

83. Compulsory insurance means the limitation of the freedom of contract because it restricts the party in respect of the conclusion of the contract. The party isn't restricted in the question of which insurance company will be selected by him/her. Article 129 of the BIns. declares that the obligation to obtain insurance cover can be prescribed in cases provided for by the highest laws, so, by Act or by Government decree, upon the authorization of an Act. Obligation of compulsory insurance refers to the non-life insurance contracts which are determined in Annex 1 Part A of the BIns.[86]

The minister responsible for drafting the Act on the obligation to obtain insurance cover shall notify the Authority of the contents and on the entry into force of the legislation on the obligation to obtain insurance cover.

An insurance contract may be accepted if it meets the conditions set out in the Act on the obligation to obtain insurance cover and in the Government decree adopted by the authorization of such an Act pertaining to compulsory insurance cover.

If the insurance contract is terminated, the insurance company is required to notify—by way of the means and within the time limit specified in the Act or in the relevant Government decree—the authority of competence and jurisdiction to monitor the policyholders' obligation to obtain insurance cover.

One part of the law regulates the essential elements of the content of the concludable contract, but most of the law only prescribes the obligation of insurance. It doesn't prescribe the minimum amount covered by the insurance contract or the maximum amount of excess.

In some cases, the obligor can fulfill his/her obligation imposed by law by the rendering of other financial guarantees. The compulsory motor vehicle liability insurance shall be emphasized within the area of compulsory insurance contracts because its content is regulated by law, in detail, in line with the European standards, and, in certain situations, the freedom of choice of partner is also restricted for the contractor.

The law also necessitates the content requirements of the insurance contract for the independent financial service intermediaries and for the liability insurance contracts concluded by the person carrying out property assessments.

84. Insurance obligation relating to liability of nuclear damage shall also be mentioned. The Act[87] stipulates the amount and conditions for the insurance of financial coverage of liability for nuclear damage.

---

86. Obligation of compulsory insurance are prescribed by legal acts, *inter alia*, in the following areas: car operation, health care, medical services, lawyer activities, multiple brokerage and brokerage activities, etc.
87. Act CXVI. of 1996 on Atomic Energy, and Government Decree No. 227/1997. (XII.10.).

A legal act[88] entered into force on January 1, 2017, requires the conclusion of liability insurance for the subjects defined in the act in the case of the construction of new residential buildings with a total useful floor area of no more than 300 square meters

88. Government Decree No. 155 of 2016 (VI.13.) on the simple notification of the construction of the residential building.

Part I. The Insurance Company Chapter

Chapter 1. The Insurance Company: Its Form

Edit Antal Ujvári

§1. MUTUAL INSURANCE, REINSURANCE, OTHER

85. The BIns. shall be applied to all insurance activities and reinsurance activities as well, so, the separate Act relating to reinsurance became ineffective. According to the authority of the Act, the regulations of a separate Act[89] shall be applied to the technical provisions and solvency of insurance and reinsurance companies.[90]

86. Insurance services shall mean underwriting insurance in a commitment that is based on an insurance contract whereby the insurance company undertakes to designate a group of persons deemed to be exposed to the same risk or similar perils (risk group) in order to assess the risks that can be insured and measured by mathematical and statistical means, establish and collect a consideration (premium) for the commitment, set up specific reserves, assume the risks stipulated, and provide services as contracted, including the pursuit of activities for the provision of annuity benefits carried out on a commercial basis, irrespective of whether consideration for the commitment represents payment of a specific sum of money (premium) or any other form of remuneration. (Point 11 of section 4 of the BIns.)

89. Government Decree No. 43/2015. (III.12).
90. This Government Decree ensures compliance with:
    (a) Directive 2009/138/EC of the European Parliament and of the Council of Nov. 25, 2009 on the taking-up and pursuit of the business of Insurance and Reinsurance (Solvency II).
    (b) Directive 2014/51/EU of the European Parliament and of the Council of Apr. 16, 2014 amending Directives 2003/71/EC and 2009/138/EC and Regulations (EC) No. 1060/2009, (EU) No. 1094/2010 and (EU) No. 1095/2010 in respect of the powers of the European Supervisory Authority (EIOPA) and the European Supervisory Authority (European Securities and Markets Authority).
    (c) Directive (EU) 2019/2177 of the European Parliament and of the Council of Dec. 18, 2019 amending Directive 2009/138/EC on the taking-up and pursuit of the business of Insurance and Reinsurance (Solvency II), Directive 2014/65/EU on markets in financial instruments and Directive (EU) 2015/849 on the prevention of the use of the financial system for the purposes of money-laundering or terrorist financing.

87. Insurance companies can be established in the forms of a Hungarian insurance company, a European Public Limited-Liability Company, cooperative societies, associations, Hungarian branches of insurance companies in other Member States, or Hungarian branches of third-country insurance companies, while reinsurance companies can be established in the forms of a public limited-liability, a European Public Limited-Liability Company, cooperative societies, Hungarian branches of reinsurance company established in other Member States, or Hungarian branches of third-country reinsurance companies.

88. According to the Act (Point 112 of section 4), reinsurance activity shall mean the activity consisting in accepting risks ceded by an insurance company or a reinsurance company, or third-country insurance or reinsurance companies, in whole or in part, in return for a fee, under contract; in the case of the association of underwriters known as Lloyd's, the activity consisting in accepting risks, ceded by any member of Lloyd's, by an insurance or reinsurance company other than the association of underwriters known as Lloyd's; or the provision of cover by a reinsurance company to an institution for occupational retirement provision.[91]

The BIns. contains different rules relating to small insurance companies (sections 204–236 of the BIns.).

89. The regulations of the following Acts shall be applied with the differences included in BIns.:

(a) for insurance and reinsurance public limited-liability companies, the CC shall be applied;
(b) for European Public Limited-Liability Insurance and Reinsurance Companies, the provisions of the Act on European Public Limited-Liability Companies[92] shall be applied;
(c) for insurance and reinsurance cooperatives, the regulations on cooperatives of the CC shall be applied;
(d) for mutual insurance associations, the regulations of CC and the Act on the Freedom of Association, on Public-Benefit Status and on the Activities of and Support for Civil Society Organizations[93] shall be applied; and
(e) in the case of branch offices, the provisions of the Act on Hungarian Branch Offices and Commercial Representative Offices of Foreign-Registered Companies[94] shall be applied.

In 2021, there are still a total of thirty-three supervised insurance companies and insurance unions, twenty-two of which fall within the scope of Solvency II (S2). As regards the institutional form of the insurance companies twenty-two of them operate in the market as joint-stock company, two institutions as large insurance unions and ten as small insurance unions. There are also thirteen insurance branch offices

91. Established by s. 161 of the Act CXXVI of 2018, in force from Jan. 13, 2019.
92. Act XLV of 2004 on European Public Limited-Liability Companies.
93. Act CLXXV of 2011.
94. Act CXXXII of 1997.

operating in the Hungarian market. In respect to those the NBH has competence only in respect to consumer protection. Due to their size or activity one insurance joint-stock company and the ten small insurance unions fall outside the scope of S2. From the twenty-two institutions that fall within the scope S2, there are four life insurers, nine non-life insurers and nine composite insurers, based on the insurance segments. In 2021, premium income at the sector level was HUF 1,330 billion, representing a year-on-year growth of 10.4%. The life segment and the non-life segment contributed to this in a proportion of 42–58%.[95]

Insurance and reinsurance companies shall keep internal registers on their contributors and managers responsible for distributions for the purpose of facilitating the registration and supervision of managers responsible for insurance or reinsurance distribution operations and contributors of insurance or reinsurance distribution activities. The internal registers shall comprise the internal records of managers responsible for insurance or reinsurance distribution operations and the internal records of contributors to insurance or reinsurance distribution activities.[96]

I. Insurance and Reinsurance Public Limited-Liability Companies

90. According to the rules of the CC, limited companies[97] are business associations founded with a share capital consisting of shares of a predetermined number and nominal value, where the obligation of shareholders to the limited company extends to the provision of funds covering the nominal value or the accounting par value of shares. Unless otherwise provided for in this Act, shareholders shall not be held liable for the limited company's obligations (Article 3:210 of the CC).

Limited insurance companies shall be allowed to provide the full spectrum of insurance services within the branch and class of insurance for which they are authorized, and they are allowed to take up the business of reinsurance in the authorized classes of insurance without special authorization. Limited reinsurance companies shall be allowed to perform the full spectrum of life reinsurance or non-life reinsurance activities, or both, in possession of the relevant authorization.

At the time of taking up the business of insurance or reinsurance, the share capital of limited insurance or reinsurance companies, the capital of cooperative insurance or reinsurance companies, the initial capital of mutual associations, and the endowment capital of the Hungarian branches of third-country insurance or reinsurance companies must be sufficient to cover:

(a) the implementation of an appropriate system of governance required for the commencement of operations, including personnel conditions in respect of management and the employees, and the material conditions for operations; and

95. MNB: Report on Insurance, Funds, Capital Market Risks and Consumer Protection, 2022, 18. https://www.mnb.hu/letoltes/kocka-zati-jelente-s-2022-hun-0825.pdf.

96. Section 48/A of the BIns, in force from Feb. 23, 2018.

97. Dr. Papp Tekla, *International Encyclopaedia of Law—Corporations and Partnerships Suppl. 81 Hungary Wolters Kluwer*. Alphen aan den Rijn, (Kluwer Law International 2015), 139–188; ISBN 978-90-654-4946-7.

(b) the minimum guarantee fund.

91. The minimum amount of funds required to cover the costs of setting up a department for carrying out administrative services and business operations is:

(a) HUF 100 million for limited insurance and reinsurance companies and for branches of third-country insurance companies (within this, the minimum amount of cash capital contribution is 70%, and immaterial assets of accountancy rules cannot be part of the non-cash capital contribution[98]).
(b) HUF 50 million for cooperative insurance and reinsurance companies (within this, the minimum amount of cash capital contribution is 70%, and immaterial assets of accountancy rules cannot be part of the non-cash capital contribution).
(c) HUF 1 million for mutual associations (within this, the minimum amount of cash capital contribution is 70%).

A limited insurance and reinsurance company may be registered in the register of companies only if, prior to the submission of the application for registration, cash contributions have been paid up in full.

II. Cooperative Insurance and Reinsurance Companies

92. According to the rules of the CC, cooperative society means a legal person established with a capital made up of the members' contributions; it operates under the principle of open membership and variable capital with the objective of lending assistance to its members so as to satisfy their economic and societal needs, where the obligation of its members toward the cooperative society covers the provision of capital contribution and their personal involvement as provided for in its statutes. Members shall not bear liability for the cooperative society's obligations. (subsection 1 of section 3:325 of the CC)

93. Cooperative insurance companies shall be allowed to provide the full spectrum of insurance services within the branch and class of insurance for which they are authorized, and they are allowed to take up the business of reinsurance in the authorized classes of insurance without special authorization.

Cooperative reinsurance companies shall be allowed to perform the full spectrum of life reinsurance or non-life reinsurance activities, or both, in possession of the

98. Intangible assets:

(1) Activated value of foundation reorganization.
(2) Activated value of experimental development.
(3) Property rights.
(4) Intellectual Products.
(5) Business value.
(6) Advances on Intangible Assets.
(7) Value adjustment of intangible assets.

relevant authorization. A cooperative insurance company and cooperative reinsurance company can be founded by ten members.

Cooperative insurance and reinsurance companies can be registered in the register of companies only if, prior to the submission of the application for registration, cash contributions have been paid up in full.

Cooperative insurance or reinsurance companies can be transformed into limited insurance and reinsurance companies.

III. Mutual Associations

94. According to the rules of the CC:

(a) Associations are legal persons with registered members created for the purposes defined in their statutes in order to achieve their common objectives on a continuous basis.
(b) Associations may not be formed with the objective of performing economic activities, and they are authorized to perform economic activities only if they are directly related to the achievement of the association's goals.
(c) Associations shall use their assets in accordance with their objective; they shall not be allowed to distribute their assets among their members and may not pay dividends to their members. (section 3:63 of the CC).

95. Mutual associations are mutual-type associations established to provide predetermined services for a premium exclusively to its members under insurance contract—other than reinsurance cessions—upon the occurrence of insured events. The perils covered and the technical principles are defined in the terms and conditions of insurance. An insurance contract shall be concluded as a precondition for admission into a mutual association. If the legal conditions are met, upon the termination of the insurance contract membership shall not be terminated unless the statutes of the association provide otherwise.

A mutual association shall receive authorization for the taking up of operations only if all of the cash contributions of the initial capital are paid up in full. Mutual associations must clearly indicate, in their corporate name, the fact that they are set up as mutual associations. Mutual associations are allowed to provide the full spectrum of insurance services within the branch and class of insurance for which they are authorized, and they are allowed to take up the business of reinsurance in the authorized classes of insurance without special authorization.

IV. Hungarian Branches of Third-Country Insurance and Reinsurance Companies

96. The branches of third-country insurance companies pursuing insurance activities in Hungary shall be allowed to provide the full spectrum of services within the branch and class of insurance for which they are authorized. The branches of third-country reinsurance companies pursuing reinsurance activities in Hungary shall be allowed to perform the full spectrum of life reinsurance or non-life reinsurance activities, or both, in possession of the Authority's authorization for the pursuit of such activity. Branches of third-country insurance companies and the branches of third-country reinsurance companies may apply for authorization to engage in the branch of insurance or for the pursuit of reinsurance activities for which the parent third-country insurance company or the parent reinsurance company is licensed in the country where established.

V. Hungarian Branches of Insurance Companies and Reinsurance Companies Established in Other Member States

97. The branches of insurance companies established in other Member States pursuing insurance activities in Hungary shall be allowed to provide the full spectrum of insurance services within the branch and class of insurance for which they are authorized by the supervisory authority of the home Member State.

VI. Activities of Insurance Companies and Reinsurance Companies Established in Other Member States Performed in Hungary in the Form of Cross-Border Services

98. Insurance and reinsurance companies established in other Member States can pursue insurance or reinsurance activities in Hungary in the form of cross-border services within the branch and class of insurance for which they are authorized by the supervisory authority of the home Member State.

VII. Principle of the Exclusivity of Insurance and Reinsurance Activities

99. Apart from insurance and reinsurance activities and the activities involved in or closely related to insurance, insurance companies are not allowed to pursue any other business activities; moreover, the business of insurance may be pursued by insurance companies only. For instance, mediation of financial services, securities lending and securities borrowing, recruitment services, etc., provided under the Act on Voluntary Mutual Insurance Funds are such activities.

Apart from reinsurance activities and the activities involved in or closely related to reinsurance, reinsurance companies are not allowed to pursue any other business activities; moreover, the business of reinsurance may be pursued by insurance and reinsurance companies only. For example, the functions and activities of holding companies, with the exception of the regulations relating to insurance companies, shall apply to reinsurance companies; the provision of statistical or actuarial advice, risk analysis, or research connected to insurance or reinsurance.

VIII. Group Supervision of Insurers and Reinsurers

100. The legislation on the group supervision of insurance and reinsurance companies[99] serves the compliance with the following European standards:

- Directive 2009/138/EC of the European Parliament and of the Council of November 25, 2009, on the launching and conducting of insurance and reinsurance activities (Solvency II).
- Directives 2003/71/EC and 2009/138/EC as well as directives 2014/51/EU of the European Parliament and of the Council of April 16, 2014 on the amendment of regulations 1060/2009/EC, 1094/2010/EU and 1095/2010/EU concerning the competences of the European Supervisory Authority (European Insurance and Occupational Pensions Authority) and the European Supervisory Authority (European Securities and Markets Authority).
- Directive 2009/138/EC on launching and conducting insurance and reinsurance businesses (Solvency II), directive 2014/65/EU on the market of financial instruments, as well as directive 2019/2177/EU of the European Parliament and of the Council of December 18, 2019 on the prevention of the use of financial systems for the purpose of money laundering or terrorism financing.

§2. Public or Private Nature

101. Furthermore, insurance has at least two legal aspects. On the one hand, we can speak about the insurance business, which is regulated by public law, and on the other hand, we can speak about insurance contracts, which are regulated by private law.

I. Insurance Business

102. Regulations for the establishment of insurance companies and the comprehensive ruling for the control of insurance activities can be found within the framework of public law, which appears in the BIns. in a unified legal background. Nevertheless, these public law regulations have connecting points to other private law areas.

European processes have an effect on the overall system of insurance activity. According to the "first-generation directives," aiming at the freedom of establishment, the persons applying for authorization had to confirm the appropriate organizational form. The Directives list the types of organizations in which insurance

99. Government Decree No. 436 of 2016 (XII.16.).

activities can be carried out, which the regulations are maintained by further directives and the present effective directive too,[100] adopted by countries in which insurance activity can be operated, but add that "any corporate form adopted by the common good" can be accepted.

The Directives determine the form of organisation of insurance activities by country, but Member States may be set up, where appropriate, undertakings under any form of known public law provided that such institutions have as their object insurance operations in conditions equivalent to those undertakings under private law.

The BIns. declares only the special regulations relating to the particularly important questions of our topic, but the norms of private law shall be applied as underlying rules, which can be found in the CC. In the case of mutual insurance associations or branches, the abovementioned special acts shall be taken into consideration.

Competition rules[101] shall be taken into consideration during the establishment, the operational link and the activities of insurance companies. For situations of bankruptcy and insolvency of the insurers, the BIns. contains special rules, but in addition to these rules, this process falls within the scope of bankruptcy law.[102]

In the course of the insurance company's activities, the insurance company comes into possession of a number of data relating to the personal circumstances, the state of health, property and income situation of its customers. The handling, use, and transmission of these data fall within the regulatory scope of insurance secrecy. The Act on the Right of Informational Self-Determination and on Freedom of Information[103] and the BIns. contains the data protection rules that apply to the activities and cooperation of insurance companies.

The Act on the Prevention and Combating of Money Laundering and Terrorist Financing[104] obliges insurance companies and independent insurance brokers to prepare internal rules in order to fulfill their statutory reporting obligations and recognize unusual cases where money laundering is suspected.

In addition to insurance companies, the Association of Hungarian Insurance Companies (AHIC) has to be highlighted, which was founded in 1990 by eight insurance companies. It is the professional interest protection organization of insurance companies and other institutions engaged in insurance activities in Hungary. Its main objective is to represent and protect the interests of the Hungarian insurance profession. Until now, the Hungarian insurance companies, insurance associations and the majority of Hungarian branches of EU Member States' insurers joined AHIC. The activities of AHIC are divided into two main areas: the professional advocacy activities of the association and the tasks related to third-party insurance.

100. Directive 2009/138/EC of the European Parliament and of the Council of Nov. 25, 2009 on the taking up and pursuit of the business of Insurance and Reinsurance (Solvency II).
101. Act LVII of 1996 on the Prohibition of Unfair Trading Practices and Unfair Competition.
102. Act XLIX of 1991 on Bankruptcy Proceedings and Liquidation Proceedings.
103. Act CXII of 2011 on the Right of Informational Self-Determination and on Freedom of Information.
The National Authority for Data Protection and Freedom of Information verifies the compliance with the Data Protection Act and other legislation on data management.
104. Act LIII of 2017 on the Prevention and Combating of Money Laundering and Terrorist Financing.

A Separate Organizational Unit of AHIC (ESZE) carries out a number of tasks delegated to it by law in connection with the mandatory motor vehicle liability insurance.

II. Insurance Contract

103. Public law provisions concerning the law of insurance contracts can be found in the BIns., in the laws in the field of consumer protection, and in the regulations which impose insurance obligations. Consumer protection has great relevance in the area of insurance law, and the legal effect of the relevant acts covers the parties of the insurance contract, especially for insurance companies.[105] The CC applies unilaterally cogent provisions only to consumer contracts; the regulation is usually dispositive.

The insurance contract provisions of the CC do not make any distinctions according to the forms of the insurer; moreover, it expands the effect of regulations of insurance contract[106] since it declares that the provisions shall also be applied to insurance relationships on the basis of association membership.[107]

Contract freedom is restricted by the norms imposing insurance obligations, but this public law intervention is happening for the interest of the potentially injured parties. This public law intervention can be based on the highest level norms: section 129 of the BIns. imposes that the obligation of insurance can be set out in the Act or by the authorization of such an Act in Government decrees. The obligation to obtain insurance cover can be prescribed in cases provided for by law, with regard to insurance contracts under classes of non-life insurance provided for in Part A of Annex 1, to persons prescribed by law as policyholders.

105. Insurance companies shall take into consideration the regulations of the Act XLVII. of 2008 on the Prohibition of Unfair Business-to-Consumer Commercial Practices during carrying out the activities.

106. Section 6:439–6:490 of the CC.

107. Section 6:457 of the CC.

Chapter 2. Access to Business: Authorization—Requirements and Procedures

Judit Barta

§1. Foundation Authorization

104. The Authority's authorization shall be required for the foundation of insurance and reinsurance companies.[108]

The application for the foundation shall be filed to the NBH, the supervisory body.[109] The required annexes of the application are listed in section 238 of the BIns.

In possession of the foundation permit, the insurance or reinsurance company may begin to make preparations for its insurance activity and activities involved in, or closely related to, insurance.[110]

§2. Activity Authorization

105. The Authority's authorization shall be required *to start up* the business of insurance and reinsurance.[111]

In Hungary, insurance and reinsurance activities and, for the commencement of, activities involved in, or closely related to, insurance and reinsurance activities can be performed only by the authorization of the NBH.

I. Performance of Activity Authorized by Other Member State

106. If the activities are carried out in the form of cross-border services or through a branch, the activities can be performed by the authorization of the supervisory authority of the home Member State.

II. Activity of Third-Country Insurance Companies

107. Third-country insurance companies (not EU Member State) may take up and pursue activities in the territory of Hungary through a branch authorized by the Authority. Third-country reinsurance companies may take up and pursue the business of reinsurance in the territory of Hungary through a Hungarian branch under an international agreement without having to set up a branch.[112]

108. Point a) of sub. 1 of s. 237 of the BIns.
109. Section 238 of the BIns.
110. Section 242 BIns.
111. Point b) of sub. 1 of s. 237 of the BIns.
112. Section 41 of the BIns.

III. Territorial Scope of the Authorization

108. In terms of territorial scope, the activity license issued by the Authority shall cover all Member States and shall constitute an entitlement for the insurance company or reinsurance company to pursue activities in the territory of any Member State in the form of cross-border services or through a branch. As regards the Hungarian branches of third-country insurance or reinsurance companies, the territorial scope of the activity license issued by the Authority shall cover the territory of Hungary and the activities may be pursued on the territory of Hungary only.[113]

IV. Material Scope of the Authorization[114]

109. The Authority issues the activity license for *line of insurances*[115] and for *class of insurances.*[116]

The activity license covers the whole area of the insurance class, except if the insurer intends to insure only certain risks or risk groups within the insurance class in line with the business plan.

Insurance companies and the Hungarian branches of third-country insurance companies shall not be authorized to transact both non-life and life insurance business concurrently, with the exceptions set out in the law. The exceptions are the followings:

- The Authority may authorize an insurance company licensed to pursue the business of life insurance to pursue the classes of accident and sickness with the proviso that the insurance company shall not be authorized to pursue other classes in the non-life insurance branch.
- The Authority may authorize an insurance company licensed to pursue activities exclusively in the classes of accident and sickness to pursue life insurance activities.

The Authority shall issue an activity license to a reinsurance company for non-life reinsurance activities, life reinsurance activities, or the full spectrum of reinsurance activities.

---

113. Section 42 of the BIns.
114. Sections 43–44 of the BIns.
115. *Line of insurance:* shall mean the two main groups of insurance distinguished on the basis of risk criteria, specifically, non-life insurance or life insurance.
116. *Class of insurance:* shall mean a subgroup within a line of insurance consisting of services covering the same or similar perils. In non-life insurance sector, e.g., insurance of accident, illness, vehicle, consignment, damage caused by fire and natural disaster, etc. In life insurance sector, e.g., life insurance, matrimony insurance, birth insurance, etc.

§3. CONDITIONS OF LICENSING THE ACTIVITY

110. Upon receipt of the Authority's authorization of establishment, the insurance or reinsurance company shall be required to submit another application to the Authority within ninety days for authorization for taking up the pursuit of the business of insurance or reinsurance.[117]

The Authority withdraws the activity license if the application fails to meet the time limit. The BIns. lists the required annexes of the application.[118]

The activity license has personal, material, and financial conditions. The applicant shall apply a real business plan and shall have proof that the insurance or reinsurance company possesses the eligible basic funds to cover the absolute floor of the minimum capital requirement, the appropriate leaders and professionals, the appropriate system of governance, and the required material conditions.

I. Capital Requirements[119]

111. At the time of taking up the business of insurance or reinsurance, the share capital of limited insurance or reinsurance companies, the capital of cooperative insurance or reinsurance companies, the initial capital of mutual associations, and the endowment capital of the Hungarian branches of third-country insurance or reinsurance companies must be sufficient to cover:

(a) the implementation of an appropriate system of governance required for the commencement of operations, including personnel conditions, in respect of management and the employees, and the material conditions for operations; and
(b) the minimum guarantee fund.

112. The minimum amount of funds required to cover the costs of setting up a department for carrying out administrative services and business operations is:

(a) HUF 100 million for limited insurance and reinsurance companies and for branches of third-country insurance companies.
(b) HUF 50 million for cooperative insurance and reinsurance companies.
(c) HUF 1 million for mutual associations.

II. The Scheme of Operation[120]

113. The scheme of operations shall specify the scope of the insurance or reinsurance activities and the important facts and information from the perspective of performing the commitments undertaken in the insurance or reinsurance contract, particularly:

117. Subsection 1 of s. 243 of the BIns.
118. Subsection 1 of s. 244 of the BIns.
119. Section 93 of the BIns.
120. Section 95 of the BIns.

(a) descriptions of the branch and class of insurance and the risk groups within the various classes, and descriptions of the class of reinsurance and the risk factors within the various classes;
(b) definition of the field of operation;
(c) the basic own-fund items covering the absolute floor of the minimum capital requirement;
(d) the estimated costs of setting up the administrative services and the organization for securing business and the means of financing; if the insurance company plans to provide assistance services, a description of the financial resources and other assets at the insurance company's disposal for performing such assistance services;
(e) the kinds of reinsurance arrangements which the reinsurance company proposes to make with ceding companies;
(f) the guiding principles of retrocession.

In addition, the scheme shall include the following for the first three financial years of the insurance or reinsurance company's operations:

(a) a forecast balance sheet;
(b) estimates of the future solvency capital requirement on the basis of the forecast balance sheet, as well as the calculation method used to derive those estimates;
(c) estimates of the future minimum capital requirement on the basis of the forecast balance sheet, as well as the calculation method used to derive those estimates;
(d) estimates of the financial resources intended to cover technical provisions, the minimum capital requirement, and the solvency capital requirement;
(e) in regards to non-life insurance:
  - estimates of management expenses, in particular, acquisition costs, current general expenses, and commissions;
  - estimates of premiums and claims.
(f) in regards to life insurance, also a plan setting out detailed estimates of premiums and claims arising out of, or in connection with, insurance contracts; in regards to life insurance and to reinsurance acceptances and reinsurance cessions, both.

In addition, the scheme of operations shall specify any plans pertaining to reinsurance, showing separately the estimated proceeds and expenses regarding reinsurance.

114. The Act stipulates differential rules relating to small insurance companies and small insurance associations. If an insurance company intends to introduce legal expenses insurance, its application for authorization for the commencement of operations shall contain a statement indicating its choice from among the types of legal expenses for the sake of avoiding the conflict of interest between the insurance and the client.

The BIns. stipulates the cases in which the authorization application shall be refused.[121]

Obviously, in the case of branches of third-country insurance or reinsurance companies, the application for activity is sufficient.

§4. The Authorization Procedure for Application of Foundation and Operation

115. The application shall be applied by submitting an electronic form.

For the issuing of the license, the applicant shall submit the application previously, which means before the registration of the insurance company or association, or before the start of the activity. Without license, insurance activities cannot be started.

The applicant must declare that it has disclosed to the NBH all important facts, data, and information required for the authorization.[122]

For the authoritative proceedings of the NBH, the Act CXL of 2004 on the General Rules of Administrative Proceedings and Services *shall be applied with the exceptions listed in the NBHA.*

116. In the foundation and authorization proceedings, the official language is Hungarian; the client shall provide the certified Hungarian translation of the documents.[123] The administrative time limit shall be reckoned from the day following the date of delivery of the petition,[124] and the administrative time limit in the proceedings for the authorization of the foundation shall be three months, which may be extended on one occasion by up to another three months.[125]

If an insurance or reinsurance company uses an internal model to calculate the eligible basic own funds to cover the solvency capital requirement, the administrative time limit for granting the activity license shall be six months.[126]

If the application the client has submitted for the foundation or licensing proceedings referred to is incomplete, the NBH shall advise the applicant, within thirty days, to supply a remedy for such deficiencies.[127] If the complete application and its enclosures do not meet the requirements set out in the relevant legislation, if they contain impracticable or unreasonable stipulations, the NBH shall, within thirty days of receiving the complete application, request the client to supplement or

121. Subsection 1 of s. 245 of the BIns.
122. Subsection 2 of s. 59 of NBHA.
123. Section 50 of NBHA.
124. APS. 33. §(5).
125. Subsections 1–2 of s. 61 of NBHA.
126. Section 246 of the BIns.
127. Subsection 6 of s. 61 of NBHA.

revise the application or its enclosure, within the prescribed time limit.[128] The applicant shall submit a statement, in a private document of full probative value,[129] in which he/she entitles the NBH to determine the truthfulness of the submitted documents.

According to the NBH Decree No. 14/2015. (V.13.), a certain amount of administrative service fee is payable by the foundation that is starting the activity.

128. Subsection 7 of s. 61 of NBHA.
129. *See*: Act CXXX of 2016 on the Code of Civil Procedure s. 325.

Chapter 3. Supervision

§1. Solvency Control

Judit Barta

I. About the Supervision in General

117. Supervision is provided by the NBH based on the rules of the NBHA.

Unless otherwise provided for by law, the NBH shall, within the framework of its responsibilities set out in subsection 9 of section 4, supervise the bodies and persons and the activities covered by *the Act on Insurance Institutions and the Insurance Business.*

II. Control of Solvency

118. The supervision has taken on a risk-based approach; its main aim is to provide the appropriate protection of clients, and furthermore, the financial stability, efficient operation, and monitoring trials have been confirmed. So, supervision is based on a forward-looking and risk-oriented approach. Within the framework of the supervisory review process, the authority reviews and evaluates the strategies, the internal processes, and the reporting process of the insurances, which are established for the sake of compliance with the relevant rules. Furthermore, it reviews the risks which are undertaken by the company and the company's ability to assess and settle the risks. The Authority can take the necessary measures in time as the result of the assessment of the abovementioned circumstances becomes available for the sake of the proper functioning.

The calculation of the solvency capital necessity is possible on the basis of two models: the so-called standard model does not require authorization, and the application of the full or partial internal model requires the authorization of the Authority.

If the available solvency is below the minimum solvency, the Authority can suspend or revoke the operating license of the insurer.

If the value of the available solvency exceeds the minimum solvency capital necessity but does not reach the solvency capital necessity, the Authority can take actions defined by law in order to improve the situation.

Optimally, the available solvency exceeds the value of the required solvency.

Insurance companies have started the preparation for supervisory reporting in relation to Solvency II—at reduced data content—since 2014, with regard to the changes in 2016.

The solvency capital requirement of the insurance sector shows a 97% increase compared to Solvency I. In the Solvency II system, the insurer needs to form a significant amount of capital for lots of risks, which do not appear explicitly in the current rules relating to the calculation of the solvency capital necessity, and they are not proportional to the input data calculations of the current capital requirement (e.g., reserve holdings, premium income, reinsurance rates). In the insurance sector, the major part of the solvency capital requirement under Solvency II is based on three risk modules: life and non-life insurance and market risks.

The capital recharge of the insurance sector at the end of 2014 was 217% upon Solvency II and 169% upon Solvency I.

In addition to the 100% capital adequacy required by the EU, the NBH recommends a stricter 150% compliance.

At the sector level, capital adequacy was 196% at the end of 2021. This level is stable after the introduction of the Solvency II framework in 2016. In recent years, the solvency capital requirement and the solvency capital have also increased continuously, therefore, the sector holds capital in line with the increase in risks. The capital adequacy of 196% meets the strict requirements of the NBH. Individual capital requirements differ among insurance companies. At the end of 2021, all insurance companies have already met the minimum capital requirement of 150% required by the NBH. With this, he also met the legally required level of 100%.[130]

A. *General Obligation to Notify Regarding the Insurance Solvency*[131]

119. Insurance and reinsurance companies shall inform the Authority *within two working days*:

(a) if unable to meet their payment obligations due to lack of financial cover;
(b) if their technical provisions—including technical provisions of accountancy—are below the amount required at the time when determined, or if the cover for technical provisions of accountancy is insufficient; furthermore, in the case of insurance or reinsurance companies using the matching adjustment, if they are no longer able to meet the conditions for using the matching adjustment;
(c) if they observe that the solvency capital requirement is no longer complied with or where there is a risk of noncompliance in the following three months;
(d) if they observe that the minimum capital requirement is no longer complied with or where there is a risk of noncompliance in the following three months;
(e) if it acquires a share in the capital of another company in excess of 10% of its own subscribed capital;
(f) regarding the appointment, employment, or delegation of any senior executive or nonmanagement officer, including when such appointment, employment, or delegation is terminated;
(g) upon the relocation of their headquarters;
(h) regarding the appointment of an auditor, including when such appointment is terminated;
(i) if their credit liabilities have exceeded 5% of the subscribed capital;
(j) in the event of any changes in the internal records of insurance intermediaries;

130. https://www.mnb.hu/letoltes/kocka-zati-jelente-s-2022-hun-0825.pdf.
131. Subsection 1 of s. 267 of the BIns.

(k) on transferring eligible own funds available in one class of insurance for covering the solvency capital requirement of the other class of insurance.

B. Certain Notification Obligations Regarding Solvency[132]

120. Insurance and reinsurance companies shall notify the Authority within thirty days:

(a) the result of the recalculated solvency capital if the risk profile of the insurance or reinsurance company deviates significantly from the assumptions underlying the last reported solvency capital requirement;
(b) the reason if the minimum capital requirement[133] is determined by the limit provided for in section 102, subsection 1 of the BIns.

C. Reporting Obligation to the Authority[134]

121. Insurance and reinsurance companies shall report to the Authority in accordance with the NBH Act.

Insurance and reinsurance companies shall send to the Authority:

(a) a supervisory report once a year, in addition to the annual account;[135]
(b) a quarterly report concerning the key characteristics of the insurance or reinsurance company's operations, as well as a report covering large exposures and the estimated figures for the solvency margin, own funds, and technical provisions;
(c) the outcome of the calculation of the solvency capital requirement once a year;
(d) the outcome of the calculation of the minimum capital requirement quarterly.

D. Authority Control and Authority Rights Concerning Solvency

122. Within the framework of its control procedures, the Authority shall review and evaluate the strategies, processes, and reporting procedures which are established by the insurance and reinsurance companies to comply with the conditions provided by the BIns. or other regulations and administrative provisions adopted relative to insurance activities and in supervisory decisions.[136]

This review and evaluation shall comprise the assessment of the qualitative requirements relating to the system of governance, the assessment of the risks which

132. Subsection 1 of s. 268 of the BIns.
133. According to sub. 1 of s. 102 of the BIns., the minimum capital requirement shall neither fall below 25% nor exceed 45% of the insurance or reinsurance company's solvency capital requirement.
134. Subsections 1–2 of s. 269 of the BIns.
135. The supervisory reporting obligation of the insurers and reinsurers are determined in a Degree by the President of the NBH.
136. Subsection 1 of s. 276 of the BIns.

the insurance or reinsurance companies concerned face or may face, and the assessment of the ability of those insurance or reinsurance companies to assess those risks, taking into account the environment in which the companies are operating.[137]

The Authority shall, in particular, review and evaluate the technical provisions provided for in the Government Decree No. 43/2015. (III.12.) on the Own Funds and Technical Provisions of Insurance Companies and Reinsurance Companies (henceforward: 43/2015. Government Decree), the quality and quantity of own funds, solvency margin requirements, and the ongoing compliance with the requirements for full and partial internal models.[138] The 43/2015. Government Decree includes the detailed regulations of authority supervision:

> During the supervision, the Authority shall examine the continuing compliance with these requirements:
>
> (a) the technical provisions determined by the Decree;
> (b) the capital requirements determined by the Decree;
> (c) the amount and quality of the solvency determined by the Decree; and
> (d) if the insurance or reinsurance company applies a full or partial internal model, the provisions regarding the full or partial internal model are determined by the Decree.[139]

123. In order to ensure solvency, the Authority is entitled to take the following action:

> Advise the insurance or reinsurance company:
>
> – to recalculate the solvency margin requirement; and
> – to maintain the solvency margin as appropriate.[140]

E. The Authority's Imposition on Additional Capital Requirement

124. According to subsection 1 of section 59 of the Government Decree No. 43/2015. the Authority is entitled to impose additional capital requirements for the insurance and reinsurance company if the following can be stated during the supervision procedure:

(a) the risk profile of the insurance and reinsurance company significantly differs from the assumptions, which are the basis of the solvency needs and are counted with the standard formula; and

137. Subsection 2 of s. 276 of the BIns.
138. Point b) of sub. 3 of s. 276 of the BIns.
139. Section 58 of Government Decree No. 43/2015.
140. Point c) of sub. 1 of s. 291 of the BIns.

(i) the imposition for the application of the internal model is inadequate or ineffective; or

(ii) the elaboration of a partial or full internal model is being processed.

(b) the risk profile of the insurance and reinsurance company significantly differs from the assumptions, which are the basis of the solvency needs and are counted with the standard formula, because certain quantifiable risks are captured insufficiently, and the model has not been adjusted to the specific risk profile within the reasonable period of time;

(c) the management system of the insurance or the reinsurance company significantly differs from the rules of the BIns., and the deviations obstruct the insurance or reinsurance company from being able to properly identify, measure, monitor, manage, and report the risks which threaten or can threaten the insurer or reinsurer, and the use of other measures in itself is not likely to be able to remedy the deficiencies within a reasonable period of time; and

(d) the risk profile of the insurance and reinsurance companies significantly differs from the conditions stipulated in the Government Decree.

The Authority shall check the measures which are taken to eliminate the deficiencies in relation to the additional capital requirement of the insurance or reinsurance companies, at least once a year.[141]

III. Regulations Relating to the Capital Requirement

125. The BIns. stipulates the rules relating to the technical provisions, to the solvency capital, and to the minimum capital requirement. It has to be emphasized that these rules shall be considered framework rules, and the detailed rules can be found in *Government Decree No. 43/2015.* and in the Solvency II. Directive, which shall be applied together.

A. Most Important Regulations Concerning the Capital Requirements

126. According to the provisions of the BIns. the quantitative-based capital adequacy of the Solvency I. system will be replaced by the risk-based economy system of Solvency II, which is based on the economic evaluations, introducing the *system of standard or internal model.* The *capital calculation* will act upon the insurance, market, operational, and other risks.

Especially the capital requirements can reflect the specific risk profile of the insurance companies. The new regulation establishes two capital levels: *the solvency capital requirements* and the *minimum capital requirements.*

Insurance and reinsurance companies shall hold eligible own funds covering the solvency capital requirement.[142]

141. Section 60 of Government Decree No. 43/2015.

142. Section 99 of the BIns.

According to section 27 of the Government Decree No. 43/2015., the insurance or reinsurance company shall count the solvency capital requirements, at least once a year, and report the result to the Authority.

127. The insurance or reinsurance company shall maintain enough solvency capital for the last reported solvency capital requirement. The insurance or reinsurance company shall continuously monitor the amount of the considerable solvency capital and the solvency capital requirements. If the risk profile of the insurance and reinsurance company significantly differs from the assumptions which are the basis of the last reported solvency needs, the insurance or reinsurance company shall recount the solvency capital requirements within thirty days and report it to the Authority. If there are grounds for believing that the risk profile of the insurance or reinsurance company has changed significantly since the solvency capital requirement was reported to the Authority, the Authority can require the insurance and reinsurance company for the recalculation of the solvency capital requirement and the formulation of sufficient amount of solvency capital requirement.[143]

128. Insurance and reinsurance companies shall hold eligible basic own funds covering the minimum capital requirement.[144]

The minimum capital requirement shall correspond to an amount of eligible basic own funds below which the performance of insurance and reinsurance obligations arising out of, or in connection with, insurance or reinsurance contracts may be exposed to an unacceptable level of risk.

The minimum capital requirement shall neither fall below 25% nor exceed 45% of the insurance or reinsurance company's solvency capital requirement.[145]

The insurance and reinsurance company shall calculate the minimum capital requirements, at least once quarterly, and report the result of the calculation to the NBH.[146]

129. The insurance or reinsurance company can *use a full or partial internal model* for the calculation of the solvency capital requirement with the permission of the NBH.[147]

If the insurance or reinsurance company use a full or partial internal model for the calculation of the solvency capital requirement, only in duly justified cases and with the permission of the NBH, it can define the whole or any part of the solvency capital requirement under the standard form.[148]

130. The calculations are based on two principles: the approach of economic risk (especially in line with the counting of solvency capital and supervision) and the market-based assessment. The Solvency II system takes into consideration some part of the basic accounting data, which are the basis of the calculation, in a form

143. Section 27 of Government Decree No. 43/2015.
144. Section 101 of the BIns.
145. Section 102 of the BIns.
146. Subsection 4 of s. 43 of Government Decree No. 43/2015. Kr. 43. §(4).
147. Section 41 of Government Decree No. 43/2015.
148. Section 43 of Government Decree No. 43/2015.

of market value which is not in line with the book values which are based on the accounting rules of the relevant European standards.

The provisions of the International Accounting Standards (IAS/IFRS) contain some of the determinations which are used during the evolving of the market value. The application of the Solvency II system supposes that insurers shall also perform a parallel market evaluation in order to account for the Solvency II balance. This evaluation shall not be transferred to the accounting administration since the solvency balance serves the official and prudential observation.

131. The scope of the framework of Solvency II only affects the large-scale operation insurers.

The so-called small insurance companies are excluded from the scope of the Directive (their gross premium income is below EUR 5 million, and the total of the undertaking's technical provision does not exceed EUR 25 million, furthermore their business does not include insurance or reinsurance activities covering liability, credit, and suretyship insurance risks) and the simplified requirements of the Solvency I. system are maintained.

An important new regulation is the rules relating to the small insurance associations whose premium income and revenues from membership fees for a year do not reach HUF 300 million in three consecutive years and who provide insurance services in connection with agricultural activity.

132. The most important part of the new Insurance Act is the implementation of the new European rules of Solvency II; the most relevant changes concern the capital adequacy system and the establishment of technical provisions of the insurers and the reinsurers. The new Act replaces the quantitative-based capital adequacy system of Solvency I with an economic evaluation principle and risk-based system, introducing the standard and internal models. The new system specifies the value of the technical provisions as the sum of the best estimate and the risk margin which correspond to the amount which would be required by another insurance or reinsurance undertaking to take over the underlying insurance and reinsurance obligations. The so-called small insurance companies are out of the scope of Solvency II, so they continue their operations under the simplified provisions of Solvency I.

§2. Supervision of Tariffs and Insurance Conditions

Edit Antal Ujvári

133. In the Hungarian insurance market, insurers can distribute insurance products only with the prior permission of the supervisory authority since the entry into force of Act VIII of 1923, which established the Insurance Supervisory Authority, which is an independent institution.

The justification for the introduction and maintenance of the prior authorization was especially the moving of the imbalance situation between the contracting party and the insurance in favor of the consumer.

The Hungarian legislation had to help prepare for the accession to the EU in the 1990s. Prior authorization has been terminated by the third generation of Directives of the Community.[149] These Directives aimed at the free movement of services, which would be obstructed if any of the Member States imposed a prior authorization in the field of life and non-life insurance.

According to the law on the state insurance supervision, insurance companies were obliged to authorize all insurance products before distribution before December 31, 1995. The first Act after the change of regime (1989) was the Act XCVI of 1995 on the insurance institutions and insurance activity. According to the justification of the original text of the Act, the law has taken into consideration the so-called first-generation Directives of the European Community, namely Directive 73/239/EEC and 79/267/EEC,[150] which were amended several times.

With this law, the supervisory and monitoring systems are transforming as the role of financial control is increasing and the former material type of control is decreasing.

The pre-modality authorization of the Authority went into the background because of the demand for maximum adaptation to the European Directives. Prior authorization will be terminated because of the legal harmonization.

According to the original rules of the Act, the authorization of non-life insurance products is not required, but the Authority shall be informed about the introduction of the product.

134. The law exceeded this possibility, which is regulated by the second generation Directives, in that it dropped the product licensing not just in the "large risk" insurance branches but in all of the insurance branches and changed to the "post" authorization in line with the third-generation directives.

According to the original text of the Act, the system of compulsory licensing was maintained in two areas: in the area of the life insurances and the compulsory insurances; then, prior authorization was terminated by December 31, 1998, in compliance with the requirements of the EU Directives. The compulsory motor vehicle liability insurance product was an exception because the Act stipulated different rules in relation to it.

It has to be mentioned that although the prior control of the insurance products is terminated, the insurer is required to take into account the legal provisions during the formulation of the product, for example, the determination of the minimum content of the contract terms, or the supervision is entitled to suspend the distribution of the product within the framework of the post controls, or the supervision can prohibit the distribution of the product, if the product or the distribution violates the law or the interests of the insured person.

135. The current BIns. still contains regulations in relation to the minimum conditions of insurance contract. Insurance relationships are affected by the rules as

149. Third Council Directive: (non-life) 92/49/EEC (OJ 1992 L228/1) and (life) Council Directive 92/96/EEC (OJ 1992 L 360/1).
150. First Council Directive: (non-life) 73/239/EEC (OJ 1973 L 228/3) and (life) 79/267/EEC (OJ 1979 L 63/1).

well, which declare the expectations relating to the performance of the insurance company and the nondiscrimination on the basis of sex. Regulations concerning the information of clients (sections 152–158 of the BIns.) have great importance in the process of concluding the insurance contract and in relation to the protection of the contracting party as well.

136. No special license is required for the marketing of insurance products (section 131 of the BIns.), but the BIns. prohibit employing any method in the course of offering insurance products:

(a) whereby any special advantage is promised to the deficit of other persons in exchange for having the insured or the contracting party pursue others to conclude the same or a similar insurance contract;
(b) that involves an investment on the part of the insured person or the contracting party that is to be recovered, in part or in full, from other persons targeted to conclude the same or a similar insurance contract; or
(c) that renders the purchase of the insurance product conditional upon entering a distribution scheme for remuneration.

Insurance companies which develop and offer any insurance product for sale to clients shall maintain and operate a process for the approval of each insurance product internally before it is marketed or distributed to clients, or for the review of existing insurance products already sold, and shall review it on a continuous basis and at least annually.

During the approval process, a product distribution strategy and an identified target market for each product shall be specified, and it shall be ensured that all relevant risks are assessed. In that context, it shall be ensured that the intended distribution strategy is consistent with the identified target market, and reasonable steps shall be taken to ensure that the insurance product is distributed to the identified target market. The review has to be carried out regularly but at least annually, during which any event has to be taken into consideration that could materially affect the potential risk to the identified target market, hence to assess at least whether the product remains consistent with the needs of the identified target market and whether the intended distribution strategy remains appropriate. Insurance companies which develop insurance products shall make available to insurance distributors all appropriate information on the insurance product and the product approval and review process, which are required for the insurance distribution activities, including information on the identified target market of the insurance product.

Where an insurance distributor advises on or proposes insurance products which it does not develop, it shall be done in accordance with the information provided by law and shall obtain such information from the insurance company.

This section shall not apply to high-risk insurance products.[151]

151. Section 131/A of the BIns., effective in force from Feb. 28, 2018. These provisions shall be applied in conjunction with the provisions adopted by the European Commission within the meaning of Art. 25(2) of Directive 2016/97/EU of the European Parliament and of the Council.

These violations may result in public penalties used by the Authority.

137. The current legislation provides power to the Authority in the same way as the former regulations in relation to Suspending and prohibiting the marketing of an insurance product (sections 300–301 of the BIns.).

It has to be mentioned that the compulsory motor vehicle liability insurance is specific from this viewpoint, too, because the contract terms are defined by the relevant law, but the other important elements of the product (e.g., insurance fee) can be determined freely. Insurance companies shall publish the applied insurance fee in accordance with the law. Insurance companies shall calculate the premium based on the premium tariff rate published for each individual insurance policy, with effect from the first day of the period or term, and—unless otherwise provided for by law—shall not make any changes during the period of insurance cover to which it pertains, with the exception where the premium shown in the contract differs from the one to be calculated based on the premium tariff rate due to the policyholder operator's breach of the obligation of disclosure or cooperation at the time of conclusion of the contract.

Chapter 4. Technical Reserves and Investments

Judit Barta

§1. Technical Reserves

138. During the counting of the technical provisions, the insurance and reinsurance company shall apply regulations issued by the Commission according to the regulations of the BIns., the Government Decree No. 43/2015., and the Solvency II Decree together.

Insurance and reinsurance companies shall establish technical provisions with respect to all of their insurance and reinsurance obligations arising out of, or in connection with, insurance or reinsurance contracts. The calculation of technical provisions shall make use of and be consistent with information provided by the financial markets and generally available data on underwriting risks. Insurance and reinsurance companies shall segment their insurance and reinsurance obligations into risk groups when calculating their technical provisions.[152]

The value of technical provisions of insurance companies and reinsurance companies corresponds to the current amount insurance and reinsurance companies would have to pay if they were to transfer their insurance and reinsurance obligations immediately to another insurance or reinsurance company. Technical provisions shall be calculated in a prudent, reliable and objective manner.[153]

On the request of the NBH, the insurance and reinsurance company shall justify the appropriateness of the level of the technical provisions and the appropriateness of the used statistical data within the framework of the extraordinary data disclosure stipulated by the NBHA.

If the technical provisions of insurance and reinsurance companies do not fulfill the requirements imposed by the NBH, according to the authorization of the *BIns.*,[154] the insurance and reinsurance company can be obliged to form a sufficient amount of the technical provisions.[155]

§2. Investment

139. Under the freedom of investment, insurance or reinsurance companies shall be entitled to invest in any asset. Insurance or reinsurance companies are free to make investment decisions without any restrictions. Those decisions shall not be subject to any kind of prior approval by any supervisory authority, and the NBH

152. Subsections 1–4 of s. 97 of the BIns.
153. Subsections 2–4 of s. 4 of Government Decree No. 43/2015.
154. Point l(b) of sub. 1 of s. 291 of the BIns.
155. Subsection 1 of s. 16 of Government Decree No. 43/2015.

may not prescribe systematic notification requirements relating to such decisions. Investments shall be made with a high standard of care in a safe and prudent manner.[156]

With respect to the whole portfolio of assets, insurance and reinsurance companies shall invest in assets and financial instruments whose risks the company concerned can properly identify, measure, monitor, manage, control, and report. All assets shall be invested in such a manner as to ensure the security, quality, liquidity, and profitability of the portfolio as a whole; moreover, those assets shall be invested in such a manner as to ensure their availability to the insurance company. Assets held to cover the technical provisions shall also be invested in a manner appropriate to the nature and duration of the insurance and reinsurance liabilities.

Assets held to cover the technical provisions shall be invested in the best interest of all clients, taking into account any investment objective disclosed in the investment policy.[157]

The assets of an insurance or reinsurance company can be managed—in part or in whole—by the company itself, but only if the special personal requirements imposed by the BIns. are provided.[158]

Investments and assets which are not admitted to trading on a regulated financial market shall be kept to prudent levels. Assets shall be properly diversified in such a way as to avoid excessive reliance on any particular asset, issuer or group of companies, or geographical area, and excessive accumulation of risk in the portfolio as a whole. Investments in assets issued by the same issuer, or by issuers belonging to the same group shall not expose the insurance companies to excessive risk concentration.[159]

In connection with the investment and management of the assets held as a cover for the reserves of unit-linked life insurance policies, special rules shall be applied which can also be found in the Act.

156. Subsections 1–3 of s. 103 of the BIns.
157. Subsections 1–5 of s. 104 of the BIns.
158. Section 104/A of the BIns.
159. Subsections 2–4 of s. 106 of the BIns.

Chapter 5. Accountancy

Judit Barta

§1. In General about the Accountancy

140. The application of the Solvency II system supposes that insurers shall also perform a parallel market evaluation in order to account for the Solvency II balance. This evaluation shall not be transferred to the accounting administration since the solvency balance serves the official and prudential observation.

141. It was also mentioned that calculations of the Solvency II system are based on two principles: the approach of economic risk (especially in line with the counting of solvency capital and supervision) and the market-based assessment. The Solvency II system takes into consideration some part of the basic accounting data, which are the basis of the calculation, in a form of market value which is not in line with the book values which are based on the accounting rules of the relevant European standards. The provisions of the International Accounting Standards (IAS/IFRS) contain some of the definitions which are used during the evolving of the market value. The parallel market evaluation which is required by the accounting of the Solvency II balance shall not be transferred to the accounting administration since the solvency balance serves the official and prudential observation.

Because of these reasons the generally applicable accountancy rules and the special accountancy provisions determined by the Government Decree shall be applied together to insurance companies. The Government Decree regulates the determination of the technical provisions which are required for the annual report. These regulations shall be applied to small insurers and also to the insurers which are under the effect of Solvency II. Special regulations can be found for the determination of elements of the solvency in relation to the small insurers and the insurers which are under the effect of Solvency II.

§2. Rules of BIns. Connecting to Accountancy[160]

142. Insurance and reinsurance companies shall keep their business records in Hungarian, in due compliance with the provisions of the laws and regulations on accounting, with facilities permitting inspection at any given time. Insurance companies shall dissociate the accounting records for the costs and technical provisions of accountancy connected to compulsory motor vehicle liability insurance policies from all other insurance products. The *rules for the accounting records of the compulsory motor vehicle liability insurance* branch of insurance companies shall be decreed by the minister in charge of the money, capital, and insurance markets.[161]

160. Sections 111–115 of the BIns.

161. Decree No. 45/2011. (XII.21.) of the Minister for National Economy on the accrual accounting of the compulsory motor vehicle insurance products.

Insurance and reinsurance companies shall, within 150 days of the balance sheet date, *send to the NBH* a copy of their annual account—as approved by the general meeting containing an audit certificate—as well as their annual report, the minutes of the general meeting, and the resolutions adopted. If required, the insurance and reinsurance companies shall *file a consolidated annual account* and send it to the NBH, together with the connecting documents, within 180 days of the balance sheet date.

Insurance and reinsurance companies shall be required to file financial reports annually on the reinsurance and retrocession contracts they conclude with foreign companies, including their results, and shall *send such reports to the NBH* together with the annual account.

Insurance and reinsurance companies *shall send to the Authority* the contract concluded with the auditor—for auditing the annual account—and all of the reports prepared by the auditor regarding the annual account.

§3. The Accounting Act and Special Rules on Accounting Relating to Insurance Companies

143. The regulations of Act C of 2000 on Accounting concern all taxpaying companies, so it concerns insurance companies as well. Due to the authorization of the Act, the Government is entitled to define the special *accounting* rules for insurance companies by decree.[162] These are stipulated by the Article 114 of the BIns. when it declares that the special aspects of the annual reporting and accounting obligation of insurance companies shall be decreed by the Government.

The *Government Decree No. 192/2000. (XI.24.) on the special aspects of the annual reporting and accounting obligation of insurance* was enacted on the basis of this authorization.

144. According to the Government Decree No. 192/2000. insurance companies shall prepare an annual report based on double entry. The annual report of the insurance company consists of a balance, income statement, and supplementary attachments. The insurance company shall also prepare a business report at the same time as the annual report.[163]

162. Section 178 of Act C of 2000 on Accounting:

(1) The Government is hereby authorized to decree:

b) the special regulations concerning the annual accounts and accounting obligations of the Magyar Nemzeti Bank, credit institutions, financial firms, investment firms, *insurance companies* (including reinsurance companies), the stock exchange, bodies pursuing central securities depository and central counterparty activities, investment funds and other funds, institutions for occupational retirement provision, and health insurance funds following consultation with the Magyar Nemzeti Bank;

c) the special regulations concerning the annual accounts and accounting obligations of entities defined in Point 4 of subsection (1) of section 3, other than those mentioned in Paragraph b).

163. Section 2 of Government Decree No. 192/2000.

Insurance associations which have their income defined by the Government Decree No. 192/2000. can prepare an abridged annual report. According to the Accounting Act, insurance companies shall employ an auditor; this rule is completed by Government Decree No. 192/2000. stating that the Hungarian branches of foreign-based companies operating insurance activities shall also be subject to audit obligations.[164]

164. Section 16/A of Government Decree No. 192/2000.

Chapter 6. Taxation of the Company

Judit Barta

§1. The Corporate Tax[165]

145. The companies which are operating business activities in associated forms and have separate assets from the owners, such as insurance companies, shall pay tax as per the Corporate Tax Act. The Act LXXXI of 1996 on Corporate Tax and Dividend Tax sets out the rules of tax liability, determination of tax base, tax rate, tax exemption, tax allowance, and the prepayment and payment of tax.

According to the Act, the corporate tax shall be 10% of the positive tax base up to HUF 500 million and shall be 19% of the positive tax base exceeding this amount.[166]

§2. The Insurance Tax[167]

146. The newly introduced insurance tax assisted in keeping the budget deficit aim of the Government. In 2012, it could be seen that the aim was reachable with additional measures, such as tax revenue. One of the instruments for increasing the tax incomes is the new insurance tax which burdened the insurers, introduced by Act CII of 2012 on Insurance Tax.[168]

Although it is a direct tax, it has a turnover tax feature. Insurance tax replaced three rates and taxes paid by insurers:

(1) special tax for financial institutions imposed on insurers;
(2) accident tax;
(3) fire prevention contributions.

It shall be emphasized that insurance tax doesn't burden life insurance and health insurance, so it doesn't have a negative effect on savings.

The Act relates to taxable transactions on insurance services and classifies here the compulsory motor vehicle liability insurance, comprehensive insurance, property insurance, and accident insurance. The Act imposes a tax on supplementary accident insurance connecting to life insurance.

165. The amount of corporate tax paid by insurers in 2014 was app. HUF 2.6 billion.
166. Section 19 of Act LXXXI of 1996 on Corporate Tax and Dividend Tax.
167. Three years have passed until the insurers could recover from the effects of insurance tax. Insurers have not yet transferred, or have only partly transferred, the insurance tax to the consumers; therefore, according to the data of the NBH, the insurance technical result of the non-life insurance sector was negative in 2013 and 2014 and was still not too strong in the last year. In the first half of 2016, non-life insurance branch returned to the previous state, and the technical result exceeded HUF 15.5 billion.
168. The Act entered into force on Jan. 1, 2013.

The provision of insurance services shall be subject to taxation if the risk is situated in Hungary.

According to the Act, the tax shall be based on the gross premium accounted by the insurer upon the accounting rules. According to the Act, *premium* shall mean the gross fee charged by an insurance company for insurance services provided, shown in the records according to accounting regulations, including the sums not shown as gross premium according to accounting regulations, which, however, are treated as cover for insurance services in consideration for insurance services, but not including the gross premium charged for agricultural insurance and the premium income received from other insurance companies for reinsurance acceptances—shown as gross premium income. If the insurance company provides more than one of the insurance services within the framework of a single insurance relationship or provides either of the insurance services together with another insurance service, premium shall mean the premium charged separately for each insurance service.

The tax rate varies with the type of insurance services.

In accordance with this, it shall be 15% of the tax base for comprehensive insurance policies, 10% of the tax base for property and accident insurance policies, 23% of the tax base in connection with compulsory motor vehicle liability insurance policies, not exceeding HUF eighty-three/motor vehicle for each calendar day of the period of risk coverage provided by the insurance company.[169]

As regards any taxpayer whose consolidated tax base on taxable insurance services mentioned in paragraphs a) and b) of subsection (1) for the tax year immediately preceding the month of tax assessment is below HUF 8 billion, the amount of tax calculated:

- shall be 25% of the tax payable on taxable insurance services under subsection (1) not exceeding HUF 100 million of the tax base on taxable insurance services mentioned in paragraphs a) and b) of subsection (1);
- shall be 50% of the tax payable on taxable insurance services under subsection (1) between HUF 100 million and 700 million of the tax base on taxable insurance services mentioned in paragraphs a) and b) of subsection (1);
- shall be the tax payable on taxable insurance services under subsection (1) above HUF 700 million of the tax base on taxable insurance services mentioned in paragraphs a) and b) of subsection (1).[170]

The tax is a self-assessment tax. In connection with this, the Act stipulates that the insurance companies shall assess the tax on all premium payments received during a month, by the twentieth day of the following month, and shall declare and pay it using the form prescribed by the state tax authority.

169. Subsection 1 of s. 5 of Act CII of 2012 on Insurance Tax.
170. Subsection 2 of s. 5 of Act CII of 2012 on Insurance Tax.

Part II. The Insurance Contract: General

Chapter 1. Generalities[171]

Edit Antal Ujvári

147. The general regulations of insurance contract can be found in section 6:439–6:490 of the CC, although the content of the legal relationship is also governed by provisions in the BIns:

> Under an insurance contract the insurer undertakes to provide coverage for the risk specified in the contract, and to provide settlement or benefits for loss arising upon the occurrence of a specific future event after the starting date of risk coverage, and the insured person undertakes to pay an insurance premium agreed upon.[172]

148. The CC does not contain a list of the possible insured events; it has to be stipulated in the contract by the parties.

The most important differences between the insurance contracts in the CC and the general rules of contracts can be summarized as follows:

(a) "The freedom of contract" substantially prevails, although in the establishment of the legal relationship, limitations of the freedom of contract can be observed; for example, the law may oblige the contracting parties to establish an insurance contract, for example, in case of insurance against civil liability in respect of the use of motor vehicles or in case of professional liability insurance.
(b) The "freedom of content" is strongly restricted in case of consumer contracts where unilateral cogency prevails.

---

171. *See* further: Ujváriné Dr. Antal Edit, *Biztosítási szerződés* [Insurance Contract] In Majoros Tünde (ed.), *Kereskedelmi szerződések alapvető szabályai* [General Rules on Commercial Contracts]. Budapest, (Patrocinium Publisher 2015), 219–273.
Dr. Zavodnyik József, *A biztosítási szerződési jog alapjai* [Basis of Insurance Contract Law]. Budapest, BOI, 2004; Dr. Zavodnyik József, *A biztosítási szerződések* [Insurance Contracts]. In Osztovics András (ed.), *A Polgári Törvénykönyvről szóló 2013. évi V. törvény és a kapcsolódó jogszabályok nagykommentárja, III. kötet* [General Commentary of the Act V of 2013 on the Civil Code and of the Relating Legal Acts—Vol. 3.] Budapest, Opten Ltd. (2014), 1106–1270.

172. Subsection 1 of s. 6:439. of the CC.

(c) The CC specifies only here the possibility of the implicit creation of a contract according to which if an insurance contract can be regarded as a consumer contract, the implied behavior of the insurer may also lead to the conclusion of the contract.

(d) The obligation of cooperation is not only a general principle of the CC and a special principle of the law of contracts, but it also occupies a prominent rule in the creation of insurance relationship and during its existence. The BIns. also emphasizes the information requirements of the insurer and the insurance intermediary, which exists not only for the characteristics of the contract but the contracting party also has to be informed about the major data of the insurer taking the risk. These rules are in line with the European standards, i.e.,—with the Act CXLV of 2017 modifying the BIns.—with the PRIIPs Regulation,[173] and with the IDD Directive. Both directives contain important regulations in connection with the insurance products—the former in connection with the pre-contractual information obligation while the latter in connection with the sales and information rules.[174] However, both the contracting party and insured party have reported and change notification obligations. (*See*, in more detail, in the creation of the contract.).

(e) The BIns. strengthens the position of the contracting persons (insured persons) and determines the mandatory elements of the contract.

(f) The insurance relationship may be established by means of individual contracts, but still, the use of standard contract terms[175] is typical, which means that the insurer develops the contractual terms in advance, according to which it plans to conclude mass transactions.

(g) In the insurance relationship, it is typical that the date of the contract and the date of commencement of risk differ fundamentally based on the agreement by the parties.

(h) According to the tortuous liability system of the CC, a person can be held liable for an infringement if his/her behavior was not generally expected, i.e., his/her conduct was actionable. The content of consciousness (intentional, reckless) of the tortfeasor does not concern the liability.

---

173. Regulation (EU) No. 1286/2014 of the European Parliament and of the Council of Nov. 26, 2014 on KIDs for packaged retail and insurance-based investment products (PRIIPs).

174. In connection with the relationship of these legal acts *see*: Lencsés Katalin & Paál Zoltán, *Több vagy jobb minőségű tájékoztatás a befektetési termékek piacán? Az Európai PRIIPS szabályozás státusza és kihívásai* [More or Better Information on the Investment Product Market? Status and Challenges of the European PRIIPS Regulation]. Biztosítás és Kockázat, Vol. 3(2015), 12–29, Lencsés Katalin, *Bevezetés az új európai biztosítási értékesítési (IDD) irányelvbe* [Introduction to the New IDD Directive]. Biztosítás és Kockázat, Vol. 3 (2015), 16–31.

175. *See* Dr. Fazekas Judit, *Az általános szerződési feltételek—tisztességtelen kikötések* [Standard Contract Terms—Unfair Terms] In Csehi Zoltán et al. (ed.), *(L)ex Cathedra et Praxis. Ünnepi kötet Lábady Tamás 70. születésnapja alkalmából* [(L)ex Cathedra et Praxis—Festive Volume on the 70th Anniversary of Lábady Tamás]. Budapest, (Pázmány Press, 2014), 269–285; Dr. Fazekas Judit, *General Contract Terms and Unfair Contractual Provisions in Hungarian Civil Law*. In Peter Vojcik & Ján Husár (ed.) Posobeni *práva v. 21. storoci Sukromné právo v súcastnosti a perspektive. Košice, Univerzita Pavla Jozefa Safárika v Kosiciach*, (2013), 58–72.

In case of insurance contracts, subjective elements sometimes also have importance; for example, the insurance company shall be exempt from its payment obligation if it is able to prove that damages have been caused unlawfully, either willfully or by gross negligence by:

(i) the insured person or the contracting party;

(ii) any family member living in their household, any managing partner or any employee, member or agent working in a position specified in the standard contract terms; or

(iii) any executive officer of the insured legal person specified in the standard contract terms or any member, employee or agent of such insured legal person authorized to manage the insured property.

(i) The protection of the consumers increasingly appears in the insurance relationship; different rules apply to insurance contracts where a consumer wishes to enter into a contract. The CC only contains unilaterally cogent rules in case of the consumer insurance contracts, otherwise, the regulation is dispositive. If the contracting party is a consumer, the contract shall be allowed to derogate from the general provisions of the insurance contracts only to the benefit of the contracting party, the insured person, and the beneficiary, where such provision pertains:

(i) to the insurance company's implicit conduct in a consumer contract;
(ii) to any considerable increase in insurance risk;
(iii) to the consequences for nonpayment of premiums;
(iv) to maintain the amount of insurance cover;
(v) to the obligation to prevent and mitigate damage;
(vi) to the obligation of disclosure and notification of changes and the obligation of reporting the occurrence of an insured event;
(vii) to any composition between the insured person and the injured party;
(viii) to premium payment obligation when the contract is terminated;
(ix) to the insurance company's exemption from settlement obligation; and
(x) to claims for compensation.

If the contracting party is a consumer, the contract shall be allowed to derogate from the exclusion of derogation only to the benefit of the contracting party, the insured person, and the beneficiary with respect to fixed-sum and health insurance policies.

(j) It is more and more common to conclude insurance contracts by organized distance sales and electronic means. A special law applies to these contracts, which contains further rules for the protection of the consumers due to the special method of contracting.

(k) Section 6:457 of the CC prescribes the extension of the application of provisions on insurance contracts, according to which the provisions shall also apply to insurance relationships on the basis of association membership.

Chapter 2. Insurable Risk

Edit Antal Ujvári

149. The general rules relating to insurance contracts are regulated in the CC as follows:

(a) General Provisions (Chapter LXII. General Provisions on Insurance Contracts (section 6:439–6:457)).
(b) Indemnity Insurance (Chapter LXIII. Indemnity Insurance Contracts. (1) General provisions on indemnity insurance contracts (section 6:458–6:469), (2) Liability insurance policies (section 6:470–6:474)).
(c) Fixed-sum Policies (Chapter LXIV. Fixed-sum Policies (1) General provisions on fixed-sum policies (section 6:475–6:476), (2) Life assurance policies (section 6:477–6:484), (3) Accident insurance policies (section 6:485).
(d) Health Insurance (Chapter LXV Health Insurance Contracts (section 6:487–6:490)).

150. Indemnity Insurance: the insurance interest is the preservation of the insured property; the insurance risks and its rate assumed by the insurer (the limitation) are determined in the standard contract terms and in the individual contract.

Liability Insurance: the insured party shall be entitled, under a liability insurance policy, to request the insurance company to exempt him/her, in the manner and up to the limit specified in the policy, from paying for damages, or paying restitution, for which he is legally liable. The way and extent of the liability of the insurer is specified in the insurance contract. In these contracts, it is typical to determine the duration of the contract, which is relevant for the liability of the insurer, and to set up an upper limit (limitation) of the liability of the insurer as well.

Fixed-sum Policies: the main obligation of the insurer is the payment of a sum specified in the contract (insurance amount).

Fixed-sum Policies are:

(a) Life insurance—meaning a type of policy which connects to a specific event in the life of the insured person (death, attainment of a certain age, marriage, childbirth, retirement). In case of the event determined in the standard contract terms and in the individual contract, the insurer is obliged to pay a specific sum of money to the other person fixed in the contract.
(b) Accident insurance—meaning a type of policy where the insurer is obliged to pay a specific sum of money in case of an accident suffered by the insured person determined in the contract.

Health Insurance: has the specialty that the concrete insurance contract can be regarded either as indemnity insurance or as fixed-sum insurance, depending on the definition of the service in the contract. Therefore, it cannot be classified into indemnity insurance or fixed-sum insurance; the concrete legal relationship determines whether the rules relating to the contract of indemnity insurance or to the fixed-sum insurance can be applied in the concrete case.

The BIns. follows the EU Directives on insurance activities, which regulate life and non-life insurance businesses separately, and determines the following two main insurance businesses based on their insurance risk:

– non-life insurance business; and
– life insurance business.

In order to protect the insured people, an insurer cannot carry out life and non-life insurance business at the same time, which is excluded according to the Directives. The distinction is primarily based on public law rules because in certain sectors, the rules on capital requirements, on reserves, and on supervision are different.

The history of the legal expenses insurance[176] regulated in the BIns. is relatively short, although it is now more and more significant. This type of insurance is regulated in EU law and Hungarian law as a self-insurance activity and as a type of contract.

The assistance activity regulated in the BIns. shall mean the insurance activity which consists of assistance provided against prior payment of a premium, comprising the provider of assistance to make aid immediately available in the form of money or other means (including the use of the service provider's own staff or equipment) to the beneficiary under an assistance contract where that person is in difficulty while traveling, following the occurrence of a chance event, in the cases and under the conditions set out in the contract; assistance, however, shall not cover servicing, maintenance, after-sales service, or the mere indication or provision of aid as an intermediary.[177]

The terms and conditions of the insurance contract determine the concept of the insured event; however, its interpretation has caused a number of legal disputes before the courts.

176. Point 48 of sub. 1 of s. 4 of BIns., ss. 16–166 of BIns.
177. Point 87 of sub. 1 of s. 4 of BIns.

Chapter 3. Formation of the Insurance Contract[178]

Edit Antal Ujvári

§1. The Process of the Formation of the Insurance Contract

I. Obligation of Providing Information and Cooperation[179]

151. In connection with the obligation to provide information, the general and special regulations of the Civil Code, several public law norms at different levels,

178. Ujváriné Dr. Antal Edit, *Az új Polgári Törvénykönyv biztosítási szerződéssel kapcsolatos szabályai különös tekintettel a szerződés létrejöttére és hatályosulására a jogharmonizáció tükrében* [Regulation of the New Civil Code Relating to the Insurance Contract, with Particular Emphasis on the Conclusion and the Effectiveness of the Contract in Light of the Legal Harmonization]. *In Miskolci Konferenciák 2010. Kodifikációs Tanulmányok a Polgári jog és a Polgári Eljárásjog témakörében* [Conferences in Miskolc 2010. Codification studies on Civil Law and Civil Procedure Law]. Miskolc (Novotni Publisher 2011), 160–179; Ujváriné Dr. Antal Edit, *A biztosítási szerződési jog változásai az európai jogfejlődés áramában* [The Changes of the Insurance Contract Law in the Light of the European Legal Development]. In Európai Tükör Vol. XV/10, (2010); Ujváriné Dr. Antal Edit, *A biztosítási szerződési jog sajátosságai és változásai Novotni Zoltán szellemi hagyatékának tükrében* [The Specialities and Changes of the Insurance Contract Law in the Light of the Intellectual Heritage of Novotni Zoltán]. In *Emlékkönyv—In memoriam Novotni Zoltán* [Memory book—In memoriam Novotni Zoltán]. Miskolc (Novotni Publisher 2003), 235–269.

Ujváriné Dr. Antal Edit, *Tanulmány "A biztosítási szerződés létrejötte, hatályosulása (Ptk. Kodifikációs Bizottság 'Kártérítés és Biztosítás' Munkabizottság részére készített tanulmány az Igazságügyi Minisztérium Közigazgatási Államtitkárának megbízása alapján [The conclusion and effectiveness of the insurance contract* (Study for the "Compensation and Insurance" Working Committee of the Civil Code Codification Committee on the mandate of the State Secretary of Public Administration of the Ministry of Justice], 2000. (Manuscript); Ujváriné Dr. *Antal Edit: Impact of the European Union Law on Hungarian Insurance Law.* In PRAWO CCLXXII Current Problems of English and European Law and reforms. In Central Europe (Poland, Hungary) Edited by Konrad Nowachky, (Wroclaw 2000), Wydawnictwo Uniwersytetu Wroclawskiego, 551–563; Ujváriné Dr. Antal Edit: *Approximation of Laws on the Field of Hungarian Insurance Law*. In Sectio Juridica Et Politica TOMUS XIV. (Miskolc University Press 1997). 39–51; Ujváriné dr. Antal Edit, *A biztosítási törvény és a polgári jog kapcsolódási pontjai* [Linking Points Between the BIns. and the Civil Law]. In, Jogtudományi Közlöny, 1996/6., 236–245; Ujváriné dr. Antal Edit, *Jogharmonizációs törekvések a magyar biztosítási jogban* [Legal Harmonization Efforts in the Hungarian Insurance Law]. Sectio Juridica et Politice. Tomus, Vol. 14 (Publicationes Universitatis Miscolcinensis 1997), 39–51.

179. Barta Judit examines the Hungarian regulation of notification in light of the compliance with EU law. Dr. BARTA Judit, *A biztosító tájékoztatási kötelezettsége a szerződéskötés folyamatában, különös tekintettel az EU vonatkozó irányelveire* [The Notification Obligation of the Insurer During the Conclusion of the Contract with Particular Emphasis on the Relevant EU Directive]. In *Az UNIO-s csatlakozás hatása a letelepedés és a szolgáltatások szabad áramlása körében Tanulmánykötet* [The Effects of the Accession to the EU from the Point of View of the Freedom of Establishment and Services]. Miskolc (Novotni Publisher 2005), 28–49.

See further: Ujváriné dr. Antal Edit, *Az általános szerződési feltételek alkalmazása és a tájékoztatási kötelezettség a biztosítási szerződési jogban* [The Use of Standard Contract Terms and the Notification Obligation in the Insurance Contract Law]. In Sectio Juridica Et Politica Tomus XVI. (Miskolc University Press 1999),. 311–322.

and the rules of the BIns. directly applicable EU norms, the PRIIPs Regulation,[180] as well as the rules relating to the special contracting methods have to be taken into account. Furthermore, it is also important whether the person intending to conclude a contract can be considered a consumer or a client (retail investor) under these legislations.

There is a significant difference between the public and private law norms: the general rules, as well as the regulations relating to the insurance contracts of the Civil Code, are basically dispositive. The CC only contains unilaterally cogent rules in connection with the consumer insurance contracts.

In accordance with European norms, the definition of marketing of insurance products in the BIns. covers insurance sales and insurance intermediation as well. In the future, insurance companies which develop and offer any insurance product for sale to clients shall maintain and operate a process for the approval of each insurance product internally before it is marketed or distributed to clients, or for the review of existing insurance products already sold, and shall review it on a continuous basis, at least annually. Insurance companies which develop insurance products shall make available to insurance distributors all appropriate information on the insurance product and the product approval and review process, which are required for the insurance distribution activities, including information on the identified target market of the insurance product (section 131/A of the BIns.).

In connection with the obligation to provide information, it is important to take into account whether the obligation is subject to an insurer or an insurance intermediary (dependent or independent insurance intermediary); whether there is a life (including those with investment elements or not) or non-life insurance contract; whether it is associated with counseling or not; whether there is a cross-selling (i.e., the insurance product is offered with an additional product or service, or conversely, the insurance is the ancillary product) taking place or not.

Infringement of the obligation to provide information regulated by public law may involve public law sanctions, but in connection with a contractual relationship, civil law consequences (tort liability) may also occur.

In connection with insurance-based investment products, the PRIIPs Regulation prescribes the transfer of the KID to the consumer. According to the rules of the BIns., the seller of non-life insurance products is also required to compile a product brochure in accordance with European regulations, which must be transferred to the customer when the product is sold.[181]

According to sections 152–158 of the BIns., the insurer or the insurance agent (section 378) is obliged to provide the prospective policyholder in due time with easily intelligible, clearly written, accurate, not misleading, fair, and detailed information free of charge, that is verifiable and documented, about the main data of the insurer and about the characteristics of the insurance contract before an insurance contract is concluded. Furthermore, the information shall be sufficient to focus attention on the conditions under which the insurance company is released from

180. The BIns. goes beyond the EU minimum rules by requiring mandatory advice for the investment products.

181. Commission Implementing Regulation (EU) 2017/1469 of Aug. 11, 2017 laying down a standardized presentation format for the insurance product information document.

liability; on the conditions under which the insurance company is entitled to limit its services; on the exclusions stipulated in the insurance contract; and on all other terms and conditions that differ substantially from common contractual practice, contracting regulations, or any contract clause previously accepted by the parties.[182] *In case of the exclusion of risk, the insurance contract does not cover the defined insured event; they shall not become part of the contract. (CDP2010. 2221, JD153. 2006)*

Before the conclusion of the life insurance contract, the insurer has other obligations stipulated in BIns. (*See* Chapter 5, §2).

The information has to be provided in the language as in the obligation or in a language specified in the agreement concluded with the client. Where insurance services are provided electronically, insurance companies shall be required to provide information to clients on an ongoing basis in an easily accessible format. Before concluding a contract, the insurance company shall obtain a statement from the client, supported by sufficient evidence, to the effect that he/she has received the information. The client shall also state any other information received in connection with the insurance policy in question prior to concluding the contract. It also has to be mentioned that this obligation shall apply to the insurance company vis-à-vis brokers if a broker is involved in the conclusion of the insurance contract.

The contracting party shall be kept informed about all changes in the life of the insurer as well as in the contract, as defined by law.

According to the case law of the courts, the insurer shall be held liable for the conduct of the agent if the agent violated his/her obligation of information and cooperation (JD2004. 109, JD2003. 411), especially if his/her activity is performed within the framework of an employment contract (JD2008. 331, 2344 CDP2011.). The insurer is responsible for the activity of the tied insurance intermediaries.

If the insurer violates his/her obligation to provide information and cooperate, he/he may be held liable for the failure to conclude the contract. (JD2007. 48, JD1997. 481.)

152. The contracting party is also obliged to cooperate, which is of utmost importance in contracting as well as during the term of the contract.[183] The insurer is entitled to request data from the contracting party, the insured, or both of them and is entitled to be informed about the changes of the substantial circumstances in writing (notification of changes). The contracting party (insured party) shall disclose to the insurance company all circumstances of which he/she is or should be aware of and which are important to terms of providing the insurance coverage. In practice, the insurers prepare the questions to which the response is relevant for the undertaking of the insurance in advance. Therefore, the contracting party shall satisfy his/her disclosure obligation by truthfully filling out the questionnaire furnished by the insurer. *Leaving the questions unanswered shall not, in itself, constitute a violation of the disclosure obligation.*

The insured person has to prove that the insurer was aware of the undisclosed circumstance at the time of the conclusion of the contract or that it did not contribute

182. Sections 152–158 of the BIns.
183. Section 6:452 of the CC.

to the occurrence of the insured event; it was within the scope of the plaintiff's obligation of proof. (Curia Pfv. 22.021/2018/4.).

153. The violation of the obligation of disclosure and notification of changes has serious sanctions in the insurance relationship. In the event of any breach of the obligation of disclosure and notification of changes, the obligation of the insurance company shall not take effect unless the contracting party is able to prove that the insurance company was aware of the concealed or undisclosed circumstance when the contract was concluded or that such circumstance had no influence on the occurrence of the insured event.

The insurance contracts usually cover more than one asset or more than one person concurrently. In this case, the breach of the obligation of disclosure and notification of changes pertains to some of them; the insurance company shall not be able to allege the breach of the obligation of disclosure and notification of changes with respect to the remaining assets or persons.

The contracting party (the insured person) is obliged to notify the changes only if it was stipulated in the contract, although the breach of this obligation has the same legal consequences as the breach of the obligation of disclosure.

The contracting party and the insured person are responsible for the conduct of the other party as well. Neither of them shall be entitled to refer to any circumstance that either one had neglected to disclose or report to the insurance company, though he/she must have known about it and should have disclosed or reported it.

II. Attachment to the Offer

154. The CC also takes into account that the insurance competences evaluate the risks according to the received offer and decide whether they wish to enter into a contract with the offeror. During this time of risk evaluation, the offeror shall be bound by the offer. The offeror shall be bound by the offer for a period of fifteen days from the time when it was made and for sixty days if a health risks assessment is required (usually in case of life, accident or health insurance) for the evaluation of the offer.[184]

III. Formal and Material Requirements

155. The CC facilitates the contracting for it allows the contracting party to make his/her offer and to enter into contract by phone or electronically, without the use of electronic signatures.[185] If the contract is not executed in writing, the insurance company shall make out a document so as to verify insurance cover (in practice, this document is called an insurance policy, but it can also be certifying documents, stamps, etc.). This document is able to substitute literacy.

184. Subsection 3 of s. 6:443 of the CC.
185. Subsection 1 of s. 6:443 of the CC.

IV. The Conclusion of the Contract

156. The detailed regulation of the creation of an insurance contract is fairly complicated; furthermore, there are different rules if the contracting party is a consumer. The statements of the contracting person come into effect towards the insurer if they arrive at the insurer. The mass transactions are concluded by insurance brokers who generally do not accept the statements; they just forward them to the insurers.

V. The Conclusion of the Contract (Dispositive Rules)

157. The conclusion of the insurance contract can take place as follows:

(a) One common document (written contract): The insurance contract may be established in a way that—according to the requirements of literacy—a single contract will be signed. In this case, the insurers typically use standard contract terms.

(b) Separate documents with the same content: The contracting party is entitled to submit his/her offer in writing—normally using an offer form introduced by the insurer—which the insurer accepts by issuing an insurance policy. In some cases, the insurer could also make an offer by a document signed in advance (so-called block bonds).

(c) Oral offer or conduct implicitly referring to the offer, respectively, and a document proving the insurance coverage with the same content as the offer (unilateral literacy): The CC regulates this contracting method as a general rule. If the parties don't make written statements (offer or acceptance), the insurer is obliged to make out a document to verify insurance cover. This document (which can be called an insurance policy, certification ticket, etc.) is able to substitute literacy.[186] According to the judicial practice, if either of them makes a written statement (offer or its acceptance), the issuance of the document which verifies insurance cover is not obligatory (JD1995. 110).

(d) Oral offer or conduct implicitly referring to the offer, respectively, and a document proving the insurance coverage with content different from the offer (unilateral literacy): In some cases, the document verifying insurance cover differs from the contracting party's offer. In this case, the contracting party is obliged to contest the difference without delay upon receipt of the document. If the contracting party fails to do this, the contract shall take effect in accordance with the document verifying the insurance cover (the different statement of the insurer). However, the insurer is required to expressly point out such discrepancies to the contracting party in writing at the time the document verifying the insurance cover is delivered (and not later). In the absence of a warning notice, the contract shall be executed in accordance with the contents of the offer.[187]

186. *Ibid.*
187. Subsection 2 of s. 6:443 of the CC.

It has to be considered a derogation from the offer if the contracting party makes an offer which differs from the informative materials transferred to him/her in advance or from the standard contract terms applied by the insurer and the insurer issues a different document verifying insurance cover (JD2013. 151).

VI. Unilaterally Cogent Norms of a Contract Between the Insurer and a Consumer

158. It is important to emphasize that the CC regulates the conclusion of the contract by the implicit conduct of the insurer only in case of a contract with a consumer, although there is no obstacle to using this rule by the parties in cases of contract which cannot be regarded as a consumer contract.

The CC assumes that in case of mass transactions, it is the consumer who makes the offer. Therefore, a consumer insurance contract shall also be executed—retroactively to the date of delivery of the offer to the insurer—if the insurer does not respond to the offer within fifteen days of the time of receipt thereof or sixty days if a health risk assessment is required for the evaluation of the offer.[188]

However, this can only happen if the offer was made:

- upon receipt of the relevant statutory information;
- on the insurance company's own standard offer sheet for the type of policy in question;
- containing the applicable tariffs.

In case of a consumer contract, if an insured event occurs during the risk assessment period, the freedom of contract of the insurance company is restricted because it is entitled to refuse the offer only if:

- the offer sheet contains an express warning to that effect; and
- it is instantly clear from the nature of the insurance cover requested or from other circumstances of risk coverage that the individual risk assessment is necessary for accepting the offer.[189]

In a non-consumer contract, the insurer is not bound to these rules.

159. An insurance contract may be concluded by any person who has a vested interest in the occurrence of or in avoiding the occurrence of an insured event (survival to a stipulated age, birth assurance or marriage assurance) under some form of property or personal relationship; or those who conclude the contract on behalf of an interested person.[190] With his rule, the CC requires the existence of an insurable

188. Subsection 1 of s. 6:444 of the CC.
189. Subsection 3 of s. 6:444 of the CC.
190. Section 6:440 of the CC.

interest in all kinds of insurance. However, the lack of an insurable interest is sanctioned only in case of indemnity insurance and a group fixed-sum policy because these contracts concluded without the existence of an insurable interest shall be null and void.

The insurable interest that is typically related to ownership are linked, for example, in case of vehicles, to the operator as well (JD2000. 59), but in case of contracts for use the insurable interest can be connected not only to the owner but also, for example, a lessee is interested in the preservation of the property (CDP2013. P.3. JD2011. 103) In case of a hire purchase, the buyer does not acquire ownership rights until the full payment of the purchase, but when he possesses the object, he bears the risk of damage and, therefore, he is interested in the preservation of property (JD2005. 319).

VII. Starting Date of Risk Coverage

160. The conclusion of the contract does not necessarily mean the start of the risk coverage because they can be separate from each other.

The coverage of risk can be fixed by the parties in the contract or, failing this, it begins at the time the contract is concluded.[191]

The parties (obviously, such a claim can rise on the side of the insurance company) can bind the starting date of risk coverage to the payment of the fee, which must be expressly provided for in the contract.

If the insurance event occurs, its occurrence becomes impossible, or if the insurable interest ceases before the insurance coverage becomes effective, the contract or the relevant part of it shall be terminated.

If the insured event occurs, its occurrence becomes impossible, or the insurable interest ceases before the insurance coverage becomes effective, the contract or the relevant part of it shall be terminated.[192]

The parties may agree, in writing, that the insurance company is to cover the insurance risk from such point in time preceding the date of conclusion of the contract.[193] This is the so-called preliminary coverage, which shall remain in effect for a maximum of ninety days; nevertheless, it becomes invalid if the contract is concluded or the offer is refused (the contracting party shall pay a fee preliminary defined for this period as well). Preliminary coverage can be stipulated where the parties are unable to conclude a final agreement, but the insurer ensures to provide the services defined by the parties for a fee if the insured event occurs during the defined period.

191. Subsection 1 of s. 6:445 of the CC.
192. *Ibid.*
193. Subsection 2 of s. 6:445 of the CC.

Chapter 4. Obligations of the Insured

Edit Antal Ujvári

§1. Description of Risk

161. The contracting party can be the insured person himself/herself, but in practice, it is common in all types of insurances for the contracting party to be someone other than the insured person or that the contracting party is one of the insured persons, but the contract covers the other persons or their assets.

The contracting party makes the offer or any other declaration and bears the main obligations of the contract, primarily the obligation of the payment of the fee. The contracting party is the "master of the case" because his/her legally relevant acts lead to the formation, the maintenance, and the termination of the legal relationship. Consequently, the contracting party determines the type of risk. Based on the types of risk undertaken in the standard contract terms used by the insurance companies, we can distinguish between "one risk" (e.g., a car racing event), "more risk" (e.g., hailstorms which can occur repeatedly within a given period of time), "one type of risk" (e.g., hailstorms), or "more type of risk," so-called combined insurance. The latter occurs typically in case of consumers (e.g., home insurance) where a contract may include indemnity insurance and fixed-sum policies (accident insurance) as well.

If the contract is not concluded by the insured person, the contracting party and the insured person have separate legal positions. The insured person is a person who bears the insurable interest, who has an interest in the integrity and stability of the value of the insured property or in connection with whose life and health events, which are considered insured events in the contract, can occur. The insured person is the primary subject of rights deriving from the insurance contract, but there are also obligations which are either exclusively borne by him/her (i.e., the obligation of the notification of the event) or which are borne by both the contracting and the insured party.

The insurer has to make his/her declarations to the contracting party, who is required to notify the insured persons of them.[194]

The insured person can unilaterally enter into the contract instead of the contracting party with a written statement addressed to the insurer. Upon entering into the contract, the rights and obligations conferred upon the contracting party shall pass to the insured person, although the insured person shall be liable to cover the contracting party's expenses arising from the contract, including premium payments. If the insured person enters into the contract, the insured person and the contracting party shall be subject to joint and several liabilities for premium payments due for the current insurance period.[195]

194. Section 6:450 of the CC.
195. Section 6:451 of the CC.

A special type of insurance is the so-called group insurance.[196] The specialties of the group insurance are the following:

- there are more insured persons in the contract;
- insured persons are identified according to their affiliation to a natural group, or under the relationship between the insured persons and the contracting party (e.g., employment relationship, association membership), or according to other relationships; and
- the insurance company's risk coverage and the related terms are custom-tailored to the group policyholder.

Group insurance can be linked to financial services. In this case, it is typically, the insurance contract functions as a guarantee of credit or loan contracts

Insurance companies offer group insurance for, e.g.,:

- Bank account contracts in which the bank appears as a contractor and the account holder as the insured person in connection with an insurance event related to his life. The insured person or a beneficiary nominated by him is entitled to the insurance sum.
- Loans granted by the credit institution (e.g., personal loans, insurance in connection with credit cards), group loans or risk life insurance connected to mortgages that provide coverage in certain life situations of the debtor (e.g., incapacity for work, unemployment). The beneficiary is the credit institution. It can also be associated with property insurance or even health insurance. Customers become the insured persons of the insurance contract with the declaration of accession or, in some cases (e.g., in case of certain credit card contracts) automatically, with the conclusion of the credit card contract itself.

In case of group credit insurance related to car leasing products, the contractor is the lessor financial enterprise, the insured person is the lessee national person and the beneficiary is the credit provider. But even Casco and compulsory insurance can be connected to car loans.

The connected or "cross-sold" contracts and terms and conditions are more complicated, which was also pointed out by the Court of Justice of the European Union in case C 96/14. *Jean Claude van Hove v. CNP Assurances SA.*[197] According to the judgment of the European Court of Justice, it is extremely important that the insurance contract drafts the operation of the insurance mechanism in a clear, accurate and understandable way so that the consumer can evaluate its economic consequences. The fact that the insurance contract is linked to loan contracts concluded at the same time may play a role in the examination of compliance with the requirement for the transparency of the contract terms, as the consumer is not considered to be equally careful in assessing the risks covered by the insurance contract.

Group insurance has additional features compared to the general rules, either in connection with the risk-taking of the insurer or the legal situation of the insured

196. Section 6:442 of the CC.
197. https://eur-lex.europa.eu/legal-content/hu/TXT/?uri=CELEX:62014CJ0096.

person. Both the Civil Code and the BIns. provides that the information obligation of the insurer/insurance broker[198] is towards the contracting party, who is obliged to inform the insured person of the statements made to it and the changes in the contract.

From information published by the NBH on the Experience of the procedures of the Board,[199] it can also be concluded that there are many disputes in connection with group insurance (e.g., credit card insurance, travel cancellation group insurance, etc.). The general experience of the legal disputes on group insurance was that the insured person was unaware of the conditions of the given insurance, namely in connection with which type of risks and under what conditions the insurance provides compensation for their damage.[200]

The peculiarity is due to the fact that the contracting person is not considered a consumer for group insurance, and the contract concluded by him is not considered to be a consumer insurance contract by the Civil Code. It means that the rights of the insured person/beneficiary who can be regarded as a consumer are not fully prevail. However, the Board also deals with the disputes of the insured persons/beneficiaries against the insurance companies, i.e., it considers the insured persons/beneficiaries of group insurance as a consumer.

In this case, the insurance contract does not enumerate the insured persons by their name, and the insured assets are also not specified one by one, but the contract refers to them according to their nature (e.g., office buildings, equipment, IT equipment, etc.). A further specialty of the contract is that the family members of any member of such a group may also be covered by the policy. The act also takes into account that there can be a permanent change in the members of the group; therefore, the persons of verified membership in that group at the time of occurrence of the insured event shall be considered insured. With the exit from the group, the insurance relationship also terminates, although the contract may provide that the termination of the relationship between the insured person and the contracting party shall not affect the insurance cover.

A claim for the performance of the contract can typically result from an insurance entitlement. However—especially among the life, accident, and health insurances—it is common that the performance can be claimed not by the insured person but by a person distinct from him/her: the beneficiary. The insurer stands on one side of the contract, while on the other side, the contracting party and the insured person have certain obligations; the insured persons have different rights as

198. *See*: Ujváriné Anal Edit:, *A biztosítási szerződéssel összefüggő, tájékoztatási szabályokkal kapcsolatos kárfelelősség, különös tekintettel a közvetítői helyzetekre* [Liability for Damages Related to Information Rules Related to the Insurance Contract, with Particular Regard to Intermediary Situations]. *Biztosítás és Kockázat,* Vol. 2, 48–59.

Ujváriné Antal Edit: *Fogyasztóvédelem a biztosított szemüvegén át—különös tekintettel a csoportos biztosításra* [Consumer Protection Through the Lens of the Insured—with Particular Regard to Group Insurance]. In *Ünnepi tanulmányok Fazekas Judit tiszteletére* Keserű Barna Arnold, Szoboszlai-Kiss Katalin (szerk.), 747–767. ISBN 978-615-6491-12-1 DOI: 10.59199/salusvocalis.2023 Kiadó: UNIVERSITAS-Győr Nonprofit Kft.

199. https://www.mnb.hu/bekeltetes/tanulsagok-jotanacsok-jogesetek.

200. https://www.mnb.hu/letoltes/pbt-2022-hun-eves-jelentes.pdf.

well, while the beneficiary has the right to the amount of insurance. The rules relating to beneficiaries appear in the CC only among the rules relating to the fixed-sum policies (life, accident and health insurance), although in practice, we meet beneficiaries of property insurance contracts as well.[201]

In liability insurance policies, there is a special person beside the insured person (or the contracting party): the injured party, who is unknown at the time of the conclusion of the contract and who may not certainly become a party. The injured party has direct rights and obligations towards the insurer.

§2. Payment of Premium

162. According to the regulation of the BIns. one of the main specialties of insurance services is that the insurer measures the risks by mathematical and statistical means and establishes and collects a consideration (premium) for the commitment.[202]

Insurance is a business, and the proportion between the services is formed in such a way that the risk in the probability of the potential hazards is balanced within a period: the period of insurance. The insurance period is one year, according to the dispositive rules of the CC.

The insurance premium shall generally not be subject to "bargain" since the rate of insurance premium is adjusted to the pre-assessed risk within the insurance period; therefore, it is usually predetermined by the insurer. As a result of the negotiations of the contract, the insurer may naturally grant a discount (e.g., by property insurance in a longer term of insurance relations, typically in the form of allowance of duration). The payment of premium or its omission concerns, essentially, the liability.

The first insurance premium payment shall be due at a time agreed upon by the parties or, failing this, at the time the contract is concluded, and all subsequent premium payments shall be due on the first day of the period to which they pertain.[203] A single premium shall be paid at the time the contract is concluded.

The insurance premium is obliged to be paid by the contracting party, but if the contracting party and the insured person are different and if the insured person enters into the contract, they shall be subject to joint and several liability for premium payments due for the current insurance period

§3. The Consequences of the Failure or Partial Performance of the Insurance Premium to the Contract

163. Nonpayment of the premium does not result in the termination of the contract by itself. In this case, the insurance company shall dispatch, within thirty days from the due date, a written request for payment to the party in default—indicating

201. Section 6:478 of the CC.
202. Subsection 11 of s. 4 of the BIns.
203. Section 6:447 of the CC.

the potential legal consequences—with an additional thirty-day deadline from the date when the warning was dispatched.[204] In the event of noncompliance within the additional period, the contract shall be terminated with retroactive effect to the original due date. However, the insurer can prevent the termination of the contract if the insurance company forthwith moves to enforce its claim by judicial process.

The contracting party shall not be exempted from paying the premium even if the insurance company does not send him/her a check in case of an agreement of payment of the check (JD2010. 246).

The contracting party can unilaterally trigger the maintenance of the effect of a contract already terminated (right of reactivation). The contracting party may request the insurance company, within 120 days from the time of termination, to reinstate the risk coverage. The insurer is not obliged to restore the contract; the insurance company considers whether to appreciate the application of the contracting party or not. The retroactive payment of the premium does not mean that the insurer undertakes performance obligation retroactively for the period not covered by the risk, but the insurer undertakes the risk for the future due to the follow-up payment of the insurance premium.

It is possible that the insurance premium is not paid as a whole by the contracting party. This fact affects the liability of the insurer differently in case of life or property insurance. The payment obligation can be affected by the termination of the contract with the occurrence of the insured event. In this case, the insurer may claim the insurance premium for the entire period of insurance. If the termination of the contract was caused by other facts, the insurer may claim the insurance premium only up to the date the risk coverage ended (the premium surplus is required to be refunded).

The principle of "indivisibility of the premium" applies, therefore, only to the case where the insurance contract is terminated upon the occurrence of the insured event (CDP2005. 1309)

§4. Obligations in the Case of an Insured Event

164. The performance of the insurance contract is associated with the occurrence of the insured event. The contracts usually stipulate the deadline within which the insured event must be reported. If the contracting party or the insured person fails to report to the insurance company the occurrence of an insured event within the time limit specified in the contract, fails to provide the information necessary, or fails to facilitate verification of the information provided, and, as a consequence, circumstances which are considered material from the point of view of the obligation of the insurance company become undetectable, the insurance company's obligation shall not take effect.

According to sections 123–124 of the BIns., the insurer may demand, as a precondition for payment of settlement, documents (e.g., records from a fire examination, death certification) which are deemed necessary to verify the occurrence of the insured event or for determining the extent of compensation to be provided.

204. Section 6:449 of the CC.

According to judicial practice, the insurance condition which provides an opportunity for the insurer to an unjustified extension of the date of performance is unfair (JD2010. 149) and can be the basis of a public-interest proceeding in the interests of consumers.

The insured person (beneficiary) is generally obliged to necessarily cooperate with the performance of the insurer. The insured person (beneficiary) has to prove that the insured event occurred, and the insured person (beneficiary) is entitled to the insurance sum. According to a rule in consumer protection, it is unfair to require a consumer, who wishes to claim on an insurance policy, to produce documents which could not reasonably be considered relevant as to whether the claim was valid or failing systematically to respond to pertinent correspondence, in order to dissuade a consumer from exercising his contractual rights[205] (*See* General Introduction Chapter 5 Consumer protection).

It is always the task of the insurer to obtain the evidence necessary for the exemption.

The performance of the insurer is usually a financial service and, therefore, the general rules of financial performance apply while the delay of performance will result in the obligation of payment of interest. According to the CC, the insurer is obliged to fulfill the service within the deadline defined according to the period for the preparation of the fulfillment. The residual value generally remains the property of the insured person, but if the insurer reimbursed the total damage, he/she could claim for the residues (e.g., scrap vehicle) as the insurance sum was the entire value of the damage.

According to the practice relating to the statute of limitation of claims arising from insurance contracts, the insurers usually use the possibility of the CC, and they stipulate shorter period of limitation (usually one or two years) compared to the general (five years) limitation period. A shorter limitation period can be stipulated under the general rules of the CC, as the regulation relating to the insurance contract does not stipulate this question.

According to judicial practice, the stipulation of a shorter limitation period differs significantly from the rules generally applicable for insurance relations; therefore, such a standard contract term may only become part of the contract if the insurer separately draws the attention of the insured person and he/she expressly accepts it. (CJD2013. 2875.).

The most recent judicial practice has further tightened in order to protect the consumer and classified such clauses as unfair and invalid with an effect extending to all consumers (Curia Pfv.V.20.152/2020.).

The performance of the insurer terminates the contract only if the insurance contract is related only to a single insured event or to one specific asset which was destructed in connection with the event. In this case, the contract terminates and the insurer shall be entitled to the premium for the whole year (in case of a shorter period of insurance to the premium for this period).

The insured person cannot obtain financial advantage from the performance of the insurer; the property insurance amounts can only restore the financial status before the insured event. If a part of the damage of the injured party is repaid based

205. Point 27 of Annex to PUBC.

on the property insurance contract, he/she cannot claim this part of his damage against the tortfeasor.

Chapter 5. Obligations of the Insurer

§1. Non-life Insurance

Edit Antal Ujvári

I. Obligation of Notification and Cooperation

165. As we mentioned before, the BIns. obliges the insurer to provide the prospective contracting party with easily intelligible, clearly written, and detailed information that is verifiable and documented about the main data of the insurer and about the characteristics of the insurance contract before an insurance contract is concluded. Furthermore, the information shall be sufficient to focus attention on the conditions under which the insurance company is released from liability; on the conditions under which the insurance company is entitled to limit its services; on the exclusions stipulated in the insurance contract; and on all other terms and conditions that differ substantially from common contractual practice, contracting regulations, or any contract clause previously accepted by the parties.

The information has to be provided in the language of the obligation or in a language specified in the agreement concluded with the client. Where insurance services are provided electronically, insurance companies shall be required to provide information to clients on an ongoing basis in an easily accessible format.

The insurance company shall obtain a statement from the client, supported by sufficient evidence, to the effect that he/she has received the information. The client shall also state any other information received in connection with the insurance policy in question prior to concluding the contract.

It also has to be mentioned that this obligation shall apply to the insurance company vis-à-vis brokers if a broker is involved in the conclusion of the insurance contract.

The contracting party shall be kept informed about all changes in the life of the insurer as well as in the contract, as defined by law.

It is possible that there will be a significant time difference between the establishment of the insurance contracts and the (possible) performance of the insurer. Prior to the performance, the obligation of the insurer will be praestare (guarantee) from the beginning of the risk coverage: he/she has to be ready for the performance. The contracting party has an ongoing payment obligation.

Within the insurance contract, the effect of the failure to pay the premium, affecting the termination of the obligation, is partially compensated by the right of the insurer to maintain the legal relationship with its unilateral conduct (forming right). The possibility of enforcement of the failing premium before the court has a similar effect. These issues will be dealt with in connection with the payment of insurance premiums.

In this period, the contracting party can notify the changes relating to the contract, but only those facts which are defined in the contract as notifiable. These conditions must be essential for the undertaking of the insurance. Notification of changes has to be made in writing; its deadline is determined by the conditions of the contract. The failure of notification may lead to the exemption of the insurer as well as the failure of notification during the conclusion of the contract.

II. Transfer of Insurance Portfolio

166. After the nationalization of insurance companies, the first transfer of insurance portfolio took place by law[206] when the state founded the State Insurance Company, Hungarian Insurance and Reinsurance and Export Credit Insurer, by reorganizing the State Insurance as its legal successors on July 1, 1986. The decision shared the insurance portfolio between the newly established organizations and defined which organization has to be recognized as a legal successor for the different kinds of contracts. The legal succession occurred by law without any legal statements from the contracting parties.

The BIns. regulates the possibility of changes in the position of the insurer, which can occur, on the one hand, according to the transfer of the insurance (reinsurance) portfolio by contract between the transferor and the receiving insurers[207] and, on the other, by termination, without a legal successor.[208] The transfer of the insurance portfolio may be carried out, in part or in full, with the permission of the Supervisory Authority.

An insurance portfolio may be transferred to an insurance company established in Hungary, to an insurance company established in another Member State, and to the branch of a third-country reinsurance company established in a Member State.

The transfer of insurance portfolio may occur—besides the agreement based on their own decision—according to a measure of the Supervisory Authority, which can be made in order to protect the interests of the consumers and to ensure that the insurance (reinsurance) activity meets the criteria of the laws and decisions of the Supervisory Authority.

A. *Transfer of Insurance Portfolio by an Agreement*

167. With the transfer of insurance portfolio, the receiving insurance company will become a counterparty to the contracts involved and also the data processor in terms of the personal data and trade secrets of clients, effective as of the date of the

206. According to sub. 1 of s. 34 of Act II on 1979—with MC Decision No. 1016/1986. (IV. 7).

207. For example, on the request of Generali-Providencia Insurance Plc. and Zürich Insurance Plc., the HFSA authorized the Generali-Providencia Insurance Plc. to take over the entire insurance portfolio of Zürich Insurance Plc. The date of the transfer of the portfolio was Mar. 31, 2003.

From the Jul. 1, 2004, Ahico First American-Hungarian Insurance Plc. gave up its home insurance portfolio entitled "Sweet Home" to Uniqa Insurance Plc. The transaction involved 2221 contracts. The TIR Insurance Association sold its compulsory motor vehicle liability insurance portfolio to AIM General Insurance Plc., the transfer was authorized by the HFSA on May 2009.

208. For example, during the transformation, ERGO Life Insurance Plc. merged with VICTORIA-VOLKSBANKEN Life Insurance Private Limited Company on Jan. 1, 2013. The receiving insurance company, VICTORIA-VOLKSBANKEN Life Insurance Private Limited, became the subject of insurance contracts and the obligor of the services.

Authority's authorization. The transferor insurance company may continue to process insurance secrets and trade secrets for the purpose of compliance with the obligation of safeguarding accounting records, for the duration of such obligation, and in the interest of exercising rights and obligations related to insurance activities other than those arising out of the insurance contracts, until the end of the related prescription period.

The CC regulates the legal institution of the transfer of contract,[209] although these rules are only applicable insofar as different legal provisions do not apply, as in the case of the transfer of an insurance portfolio.

The BIns. stipulates—differently from the regulation of the CC—that the consent of the insured persons and the contracting parties is not required for the portfolio transfer. The receiving insurance company shall notify, in writing, all contracting parties concerned of the transfer within thirty days of receiving authorization in the language of the contract. The contracting parties shall have the option to terminate their contracts in a written notice addressed to the receiving insurance company within thirty days of the date of receiving notification.[210]

The insurance portfolio of the Hungarian branch of an insurance company established in another Member State may be transferred, in part or in full, by authorization of the supervisory authority of the other Member State.[211]

B. *Transfer of Insurance Portfolio by the Decision of the Supervisory Authority*

168. Transfer of insurance portfolio can occur during the procedure of the reorganization and liquidation of the insurance company. Furthermore, at the same time as the withdrawal of the operating license, the Authority is obliged to take all measures to protect the interests of the insured persons.[212]

During the reorganization procedure,[213] if the authorization of an insurance company is withdrawn, the Authority may introduce measures for having the insurance company's portfolio affected by the withdrawal of the activity license transferred, in part or in whole, for protecting the insured persons' interest.[214]

At the time of the opening of liquidation proceedings, insurance contracts shall be terminated, with the exception of those in the process of being transferred. Portfolio transfer shall be deemed to be in progress if the application for authorization

209. Section 6:208–6:211 of the CC.
210. Section 118 of the BIns.
211. Section 119 of the BIns.
212. The Commission favors the practice of transfer of portfolio where it is justified and feasible from the point of view of the costs and benefits. WHITE PAPER On Insurance Guarantee Schemes 2010.7.12. COM(2010)370 final.
213. Ujváriné Antal Edit, *A biztosítási tevékenységet végző szervezet reorganizációja, felszámolása* [Reorganization and Liquidation of the Organization Performing Insurance Activities]. In Barta Judit (szerk.), *A fizetésképtelenség aktuális jogi problémái nemzetközi kitekintéssel* [Current Legal Problems of Insolvency with an International Perspective]. Budapest-Miskolc (Patrocinium 2018), 315–330. http://patrocinium.hu/termek/a-fizeteskeptelenseg-aktualis-jogi-problemai-nemzetkozi-kitekintessel/.
214. Subsection 1 of s. 167 of the BIns.

of the portfolio transfer has been submitted to the Authority. During the reorganization procedure, the Authority shall—in order to ensure that the portfolio transfer is carried out successfully—define those insurance portfolios whose insurance contracts will not cease to exist at the time of the opening of liquidation proceedings.

If the transfer of insurance portfolio was unsuccessful and the liquidation procedure was ordered, the insurance contracts terminate according to the conditions defined by law.[215]

As regards mutual associations, the Authority may take measures for the transfer of insurance portfolio with the proviso that taking the measure is not conditional upon the withdrawal of the activity license. The insurance contracts of members affected by the contract portfolio transfer and their membership in the mutual association shall cease to exist on the day of transfer.[216]

During the transfer of insurance portfolio, the rules on competition law also have to be taken into account because the transfer of insurance portfolio is one of the nominated cases for the concentration of companies if a part of a company becomes a part of another company which is independent of the first company. If the concentration reaches a level defined by law, the approval of the HCA must also be obtained beyond the authorization of the Supervisory Authority.[217]

III. Multiple Insurance

169. In connection with indemnity insurance, Hungarian law regulates the prohibition of overinsurance (*see* in indemnity insurance), although multiple insurance is not forbidden (except for the compulsory motor vehicle liability insurance). If the same interest is insured by more than one insurance company, independently (multiple insurance), the contracts are valid, and the insured person shall have the right to submit his/her claim to one or more (or to all) of such insurance companies, and the insurance company shall be liable to make a settlement payment under the terms and conditions fixed in the document verifying the insurance cover and up to the sum insured as specified therein.[218] In this case, the insurer may reserve the right to lodge a claim for compensation relating to the other insurance companies, for the insurance companies shall cover the claims paid jointly in proportion to the amounts of coverage according to which the individual insurance companies would be liable to the insured person.

In connection with the fixed-sum policies, the prohibition of overinsurance does not apply and, therefore, the insured persons are entitled to conclude an insurance contract for the same insurable interest, with the same insurance risk, and with the same content; therefore, they can accumulate the insurance services.

---

215. Sections 187–188 of the BIns.
216. Section 445/B of the BIns.
217. Sections 23–32 of Act LVII of 1996 on the Prohibition of Unfair Trading Practices and Unfair Competition regulate the questions relating to the controlling the Concentration of Companies.
218. Section 6:459 of the CC.

§2. Life Insurance[219]

Judit Barta

170. Life insurance contract is regulated in Chapter LXIV of the CC among the fixed-sum policies, besides the accident insurance.

Life insurance contract is regulated by the general rule of the CC relating to insurance contract, the general rules relating to fixed-sum policies and the rules on life insurance contract, as well as the relevant provisions of the BIns.

The definition of the life insurance contract is determined by the CC as follows:

> Life insurance means a type of policy where the insurance company promises to pay a specific sum of money fixed in the contract, or annuity for life or for a specific period of time, upon the insured natural person's death or attainment of a certain age, or at another predetermined time or occurrence of a specific event.

Life insurance can be, in particular:

(a) term life insurance that provides no benefits upon expiry and that has no cash surrender value; or
(b) ordinary life insurance other than term life insurance, including unit-linked life assurance policies where the investment risk is to be borne according to the contract by the contracting party himself.[220]

I. Special Provision Relating to Life Insurance

A. *Special Relations Relating to the Conclusion of the Contract*

171. According to section 153 of the BIns., before a life insurance contract is concluded—with the exception of net risk life insurance policies that contain no savings elements, which are offered by a financial institution in connection with financial services it provides (*see* Group life insurance Part V, Chapter 5, §2), or where the sum insured is less than HUF 1 million—the insurance company shall assess client demand or shall interview the client in order to ascertain the needs and requirements of the client.

Where the conclusion of the life insurance contract is preceded by the ascertainment of needs, the insurer is also obliged to supply information in the form of a product information guide.[221]

---

219. In connection with life insurance contract *see* further Ujváriné Dr. Antal Edit, *Biztosítási szerződés* [Insurance Contract] In Majoros Tünde (ed.), *Kereskedelmi szerződések alapvető szabályai* [General Rules on Commercial Contracts]. Budapest (Patrocinium Publisher 2015), 219–273.
220. Section 6:477 of the CC.
221. Point B of Annex 4 of the BIns. regulates the minimum contents of the product information. The product information contains brief description of the reasons, as determined by an interview, for

As regards regular, periodical, or single-premium life insurance policies with a savings element, the insurance company shall inform the client about the TCC for the insurance policy and the Internet access thereof.

The contents list of the document to be used by insurance companies for the purpose of client survey and interview (hereinafter referred to as "life insurance questionnaire") shall be decreed by the Governor of the NBH.

The decree of the Governor of the NBH No. 56/2015. (XII.22.) on the material element of the life insurance questionnaire was entered into force on May 1, 2016. This decree was repealed, and the rules of the BIns. have been amended accordingly. According to subsection 1 of section 153 of the BIns., before a life insurance contract is concluded—with the exception of net risk life insurance policies in which no saving element is involved, which are offered by a financial institution in connection with financial services it provides, or where the sum insured is less than HUF 1 million—the insurance company shall assess the client's demands or shall interview the client in order to ascertain the needs and requirements of the client based on the information he has provided.

172. In connection with the general regulation of the CC relating to fixed-sum policies, the written consent of the insured person shall be required to conclude or amend the contract if he/she himself/herself does not conclude it. If an insurance contract is concluded without the approval of the insured person, the section in which the beneficiary is named shall be null and void. In such a case, the insured person or his/her heir shall be construed as the beneficiary; he/she shall, however, reimburse the expenses of the contracting party, including premium payments and the costs of contracting, with the exception of group insurance.[222]

If the insured person is a minor and the contract is not concluded by a parent having legal custody, the *guardian authority's approval shall be required* for the validity of the contract. The consent of the guardian authority is required for the contract if the insured person's legal capacity has been partially limited in respect of making legal statements relating to property or if the insured person is an incompetent adult.

The insured person shall be entitled to revoke his/her consent for the conclusion of a contract at any time, in writing. Group life assurance policies may provide otherwise. If consent is revoked, the contract shall be terminated at the end of the insurance period *unless the insured person enters into the contract.*[223]

---

offering the type of policy for the particular services, term, and amount. It contains the cash surrender value and the discount value in connection with the regulation of the BIns. In the case of unit-linked life insurance policies, the client shall be advised that the value of the underlying units may show a gain or loss. Furthermore, the client must also be notified as to who is to bear the risks from changes in the value of these units determined in accordance with the provisions of the insurance contract pertaining to capital guarantees or capital and yield guarantees.

222. Section 6:475 of the CC.

223. Section 6: 479 of the CC.

B. Notification about the Conclusion of the Contract[224]

173. According to subsection 1 of section 157 of the BIns. following the conclusion of the life insurance contract, the insurance company shall notify—in a clearly verifiable and identifiable manner—the policyholder, within thirty days of the effective date of the contract—in the official language of the Member State of the commitment or in another language, if the policyholder so requests, and if there is an agreement to that effect—that the contract has entered into existence. If the policyholder is a consumer, the insurance company shall be required to draw attention to the possibility of a specific cancellation of the contract (*see* later section 122 of the BIns.). This right of cancellation has to be contained by the provisions of the contract.

C. Obligation of Regular Information by the Insurer

174. According to subsection 1 of section 156 of the BIns. once a life insurance contract has been concluded—other than term life insurance policies with no residual rights attached, supplementary insurance against disability resulting from an accident, or sickness covered under the life insurance branch—the insurance company shall provide written information to the policyholder at least once a year:

- on the benefit value of the life insurance policy;
- its current cash surrender value; and
- the amount of any surplus yield to be refunded (*see*: Part V. Chapter 5, §1).

D. Nomination of a Beneficiary

175. The contracting party is entitled to designate the beneficiary for the performance of the insurer. Once a life insurance contract has been concluded, the contracting party is entitled to designate the beneficiary in a written statement addressed and delivered to the insurance company before the time of occurrence of the insured event. The contracting party may withdraw such a designation in the same way or may supplant the designated beneficiary with another person. If the contracting party is not the insured person, the written consent of the insured person shall be required for all those actions.

224. Dr. Barta Judit, A *biztosító tájékoztatási kötelezettsége a szerződéskötés folyamatában, különös tekintettel az EU vonatkozó irányelveire* [The Notification Obligation of the Insurer During the Conclusion of the Contract with Particular Emphasis on the Relevant EU Directive]. In *Az UNIO-s csatlakozás hatása a letelepedés és a szolgáltatások szabad áramlása körében Tanulmánykötet* (The Effects of the Accession to the EU from the Point of View of the Freedom of Establishment and Services). Miskolc (Novotni Publisher 2005), 28–49.

If the contracting party fails to designate a beneficiary, the CC considers the holder of a bearer policy or, in the absence of such persons or if designation of the beneficiary had not been valid at the time the insured event occurred, the insured person or his/her heir[225] as beneficiary.

In the case of a bearer policy (if the beneficiary is not nominated in the bond), the later designation of the beneficiary will take effect if the bond is destroyed and a new bond is issued.

If the contracting party undertakes, in a written statement addressed to the insured person or the beneficiary, to keep the designation of the beneficiary in effect without any interruption, the designation of the beneficiary may not be withdrawn or altered without the consent of the person to whom the commitment was made (e.g., in case of life insurance contracts connected to a bank credit, where the beneficiary is the bank, *see*: Part V, Chapter 5, §2). The insurance company shall be informed of the contracting party's statement.

Designation of a beneficiary shall become inoperative if the beneficiary dies or dissolves without succession before the occurrence of the insured event.[226]

E. Waiting Period[227]

176. The parties may install a clause in the contract stipulating that the insurance company shall begin to cover the risks of certain perils from a certain point in time following the time of conclusion of the contract or shall be entitled to reduce the amount of coverage if the insured event occurs within the stipulated waiting period. The *waiting period shall not exceed six months*; any length of time in excess of the stipulated waiting period shall be null and void.

F. Consequences of Nonpayment of Premium[228]

177. Contrary to the general rules, in connection with life insurance contracts, the insurance company shall be entitled to bring an action to enforce its claim for premium payments for the entire insurance period in the first year. The insurer shall only be entitled to exercise this right after the first year if the contracting party makes any payment in that year or if they agree on deferred payments. From the

225. According to Hungarian judicial practice, if the heir receives the insurance amount as a beneficiary under the performance of the contract, there is no inheritance condition required to complete the contract. The insurance sum is, therefore, is not part of the estate, and the creditors of the estate cannot claim it (JD1977 553, JD1977, 336, JD1985, 263).

It should be noted that under the Civil Code, an heir can be a legitimate heir or testamentary heir.

Resolution No. 75 of the Civil Law College of the Curia regulates the allocation of the amount of insurance sum between the beneficiaries in the case of several heirs; in the internal relationship of the beneficiaries, the proportion of the insurance sum corresponds to the extent of the amount which the received from the estate.

226. Section 6:478 of the CC.

227. Section 6:480 of the CC.

228. Section 6:481 of the CC.

second year, if the contracting party does not begin to pay the premium, the claim for premium payments cannot be enforced before the courts.

In case of a life insurance contract where the insurer constitutes a repurchase sum, the contract does not terminate in case of nonpayment, but it shall remain in effect with a premium-free reduction (*see* Part V, Chapter 5, §1). The contracting party shall have the option to terminate the contract by notice instead.

G. Breach of the Obligation of Disclosure[229]

178. According to the general rules, the contracting party or the insured person is obliged to notify the insurer of all circumstances necessary for the undertaking of the insurance at the conclusion of the contract. In case of infringement of the disclosure obligation, the insurance company's obligation shall not take effect. However, in case of life insurance contracts, the insurer can be exempt from his/her obligation in case of infringement of the disclosure obligation only *during the first five years of the contract*. Therefore, the insurance company's obligation shall take effect notwithstanding an infringement of the disclosure obligation if the insured event occurs more than five years after the conclusion of the contract.

H. Breach of the Obligation of Notification of Changes[230]

179. The contracting party and the insured person are obliged to notify the insurer about the changes in important circumstances. In case of infringement of this obligation, the insurance company's obligation shall not take effect. However, in case of life insurance contracts, the insurer can be exempt from his/her obligation in case of infringement of the obligation to notify changes only *during the first five years of the contract*. Therefore, the insurance company's obligation shall take effect notwithstanding an infringement of the obligation to notify changes if the insured event occurs more than five years after the conclusion of the contract.

I. Concurrent Insurance[231]

180. The parties may obtain several policies for the same insurable interest and for the same peril and may accumulate insurance services.[232]

229. Subsections 1–2 of s. 6:482 of the CC.
230. Subsection 3 of s. 6:482 of the CC.
231. Section 6:476 of the CC.
232. Sometimes, the possibility of multiple insurance may lead to an insurance fraud. One of the most famous fraud cases in Hungary, from which a book was also written, occurred in 2001. One married couple concluded six different risk life insurance contracts for more than HUF 250 million. They traveled to Greece with a friendly couple and pretended that the husband died in a surf accident. The Greek authorities accepted the tale, the Hungarian court declared the man dead in 2003.

J. Termination by Notice

181. The contracting party shall have the right to terminate the life insurance policy in writing—if the premium for the first year is paid for to take effect at the end of the period of insurance cover by giving thirty days' notice.

The insurance company shall not be allowed to terminate a life assurance policy, with the exception where the insurance risk is increased substantially.[233]

K. Special Cancellation of the Contract

182. According to subsection 1 of section 122 of the BIns. a natural person entering into a life insurance contract, acting for purposes which are outside his trade, business, or profession, shall be entitled to *cancel the life insurance contract in writing—without having to show cause—within thirty days from the date of receipt of the notification.*

Within thirty days following receipt of the policyholder's written cancellation, the insurance company shall account for any and all payments made by the client in connection with the insurance contract in question.

The client's right of cancellation shall not apply:

(a) to credit life insurance;
(b) to life insurance contracts concluded for a term of less than six months.

L. Residual Rights

183. If a life assurance policy is terminated for any reason without payment of the sum insured, the insurance company shall be liable to pay the cash surrender value defined in the policy.[234] (*see* in detail: Part V, Chapter 5, §1).

M. The Exemption of the Insurer from the Payment of the Sum[235]

184. The insurance company shall be exempt from payment of the sum insured if the insured person dies as a consequence of the willful conduct of the beneficiary.[236] In this case, the cash surrender value can be claimed by the heirs, and the beneficiary shall not have a share therefrom.

The insurance companies have been suspicious and started to investigate, and they found the man believed to be dead in the Czech Republic in 2007. Both the two couples were convicted by the Hungarian court for insurance fraud.

http://www.atv.hu/belfold/20150719-ujjlevagas-gyilkossag-karambol-igy-dolgoznak-a-biztositasi-csalok.

http://www.borsonline.hu/aktualis/mindenki-lebukott-az-evszazad-biztositasi-csalasaban/49031.

233. Section 6:483 of the CC.
234. Subsection 1 of s. 6:484 of the CC.
235. Subsections 2–3 of s. 6:484 of the CC.
236. In Hungary, only a half-dozen cases are known of where the beneficiary killed the insured person or contributed in the murder of the insured person in order to obtain a life insurance amount.

The insurance company shall be exempt from the payment of the sum insured if the insured person dies in consequence of or in connection with a serious criminal offense he/she has committed or if the insured person has committed suicide within two years following the time of conclusion of the contract.[237] In this case, the insurance company shall refund the cash surrender value.

237. An interesting case was the murder of Steinherz Rudolf in 1931. The famous wine merchant became indebted and, therefore, concluded several risk life insurance contracts. Later, he charged a man to kill him. He intended to help his family with the life insurances. The murder took place on a train where the assassin beat Rudolf Steinherz to death in a booth with a hammer and disguised the plot as a robbery. During the investigation, it turned out that he had concluded several high-value life insurance contracts before his death. The conductor of the train recognized the man he saw on the train together with the victim from the pictures of the police criminal record. This was confirmed by some passengers as well. The man was captured in Vienna, who said that Steinherz hired him to kill him. Steinherz wanted to disguise the assassination as a robbery in order that his family can obtain the life insurance sum. In the testimony, the judge ordered the exhumation of Rudolf Steinherz and samples were taken from his inner organs. From the internal organs, a drug named Veronal was detected that could be taken by the victim prior to the murder to suppress the pain of the hammer. This also underpinned the confession of the murderer.
https://hu.wikipedia.org/wiki/Steinherz_Rudolf-gyilkoss%C3%A1g.
https://telex.hu/eszkombajn/2021/03/27/steinherz-rudolf-gyilkossag-bergyilkos-vonat-cegled-biztositasi-csalas.
https://napitortenelmiforras.blog.hu/2015/12/09/murder_me_a_steinherz_rudolf_gyilkossag.
https://trove.nla.gov.au/newspaper/article/201425687.
Barta Judit - Kántor Kinga: Az öngyilkosság, mint mentesülésre okot adó esemény az életbiztosítási szerződések körében és annak kivételes büntetőjogi szálai. (Suicide as an exempting event in life insurance contracts and its exceptional criminal law implications).
In: Miskolci Jogtudó, 2019/1., 1–7.
https://jogtudo.uni-miskolc.hu/files/4150/MJ2019iss1art1BartaKantor.pdf.

Chapter 6. Insurance and Third Parties

§1. Entering of the Insured Person the Contract

Judit Barta

185. If a contract was not concluded by an insured person, the insured person shall be entitled to enter into the contract with a written statement addressed to the insurance company. The insurance company's consent is not required to enter into the contract because its position does not change and does not become more burdensome. Upon entering into the contract, the rights and obligations conferred upon the contracting party shall pass to the insured person.

The right of the insurer to the premium is by the rule that if the insured person enters into the contract, the insured person and the contracting party shall be subject to joint and several liabilities for premium payments due for the current insurance period. The insured person entering into the contract shall be liable to cover the contracting party's expenses arising from the contract, including premium payments.[238]

186. The entry of the insured person into the contract seriously affects the position of the contracting party because the insured person occupies his/her position and exercises his/her rights from this point. There are several rights from the contract which the contracting party does not intend to lose, such as the right to designate a beneficiary (either himself or another person dear to him), the right to repurchase, etc. However, the CC does not require the need of consent of the contracting person. The insured person enters into the contract with a written statement addressed to the insurance company without the consent of the contracting party. The CC only allows the insurance contract that contains a clause to limit or exclude the insured person from entering the contract in case of group insurance.[239]

The entrance of the insured person is a right and not an obligation, and therefore, the insured person is not obliged to enter the contract (CDP2013. P3.).

187. In case of life insurance, subsection 2 of section 6:479 of the CC contains a special regulation for the entry of the insured person. If the insured person revokes his/her consent for the conclusion of a contract at any time (except for group life assurance policies) in writing, the contract shall be terminated unless the insured person enters into the contract.

§2. The Beneficiary

Judit Barta

188. The CC contains detailed provisions relating to beneficiaries only within the rules relating to life insurance contract, although it nominates the legal

238. Subsections 1–2 of s. 6:451 of the CC.
239. Subsection 3 of s. 6:442 of CC.

institution within the rules relating to the accident insurance contract where it refers back to the rules of life insurance. A beneficiary is a person who is entitled to the performance of the insurer. Generally, the insured person is entitled to the performance of the insurance contract.

However, it is common that the entire performance or a part of the performance can be claimed not by the insured person but by a third separate person. If the beneficiary is different from the insured person and from the policyholder, he/she is the only bearer of rights. In this case, the insurer stands on one side of the contract while the contracting party, the insured person, and the beneficiary third person stand on the other side. In this case, the insurance contract is a contract in favor of multiple third parties (the insured person and the beneficiary).[240]

The beneficiary of the insurance contract is defined by the contracting party. The beneficiary can be the contracting party, the insured person, or a third person nominated by the contracting party. In connection with life insurance, the CC regulates who can be considered a beneficiary if it was not nominated in the contract. According to the decision of the contracting party, the insured person can also designate a beneficiary. In connection with fixed-sum policies, if an insurance contract is concluded without the approval of the insured person, the section in which the beneficiary is named shall be null and void. In such a case, the insured person or his/her heir shall be construed as the beneficiary.[241]

In case of life insurance, the insured person can be a beneficiary of those services, which are due if he/she is alive. Third parties, which can be the contracting party itself, are usually designated as beneficiaries due to the payment of the insured amount in connection with the death of the insured person. If the insured person dies as a consequence of the willful conduct of the beneficiary, the insurance company shall be exempt from payment of the sum insured.[242]

189. In connection with group risk or savings life insurance concluded by the bank related to bank loans, the banks, as contractors, designate themselves as beneficiaries for the insured events affecting their interests. These contracts include the clause that the insured person cannot enter into the contract for the very reason that he/she shall not be able to change the beneficiary as a contracting party. If the contracting party is not in the bank, it is defined in the loan agreement for which insured events the debtor is required to nominate the bank as beneficiary in the life insurance contract concluded by him/her. These contracts prohibit the possibility of changing the beneficiary.

In case of the employers' group accident insurance, it is common that the contracting employer occupies the position of beneficiary in the event of the occurrence of specified insured events.

In case of indemnity insurance, the CC does not contain rules on the beneficiaries, although this does not prevent the contracting parties from disposing of this legal institution in the insurance contract.

240. Dr. Novotni Zoltán, *A biztosítási szerződések joga* [The Law of Insurance Contracts]. ELTE Jogi Továbbképző Intézet, Budapest (1993), 41.
241. Section 6:475 of the CC.
242. Subsection 2 of s. 6:484 of the CC.

Bank loan contracts connect not only to life insurance contracts but also to property insurance contracts. In this case, the creditor requires the debtor to enter into an insurance contract with coverage of real estate and to designate the bank as a beneficiary in case of the destruction of the real estate or in case of serious damage.

Similar constructions can occur in leasing contracts where the lessor obliges the lessee to conclude a property insurance contract for the leased property and to designate him/her as a beneficiary in case of the defined insured events.

Indemnity insurance contracts are often accompanied by additional accident insurance contracts, which also contain a beneficiary in case of accidental death (CASCO insurance, motor vehicle insurance, home insurance, travel insurance, etc.).

On December 3, 2013, the EIOPA published a material with the title *EIOPA Opinion on Beneficiary Protection Arrangements Regarding Life Insurance Contracts* based on which the MNB started a survey about the Hungarian situation regarding death beneficiary protection. The question was whether the beneficiaries get the death benefits, in general, and what practices are applied by the insurance undertakings to seek the beneficiaries if they don't appear. The result of this analysis is that the visible part of the problem doesn't seem too serious, but there is room to improve the situation within the market itself, considering that the practice of the different undertakings is varying, and also in the quality. Meanwhile, the latent part of the problem is more worrying. These are cases where the insurer doesn't get information about the death of the insured, so it doesn't start to seek the beneficiary. On the analysis of the numbers, this latent part can be much higher, even with one or more orders of magnitude, so it has to be considered significant.[243]

§3. The Legal Position of the Injured Party

Edit Antal Ujvári

190. The injured party is a subject related to a liability insurance contract whose identity is known with the occurrence of the insured event (tort caused by the insured person).

In case of liability insurance contracts, the insurance company shall pay the amount of settlement to the injured party. The insured person shall only be entitled to request the insurance company to pay him/her if he settled the injured party's claim.[244]

If the insured person disputes his/her liability for claims lodged against him/her, or the amount of his payment obligation on grounds which are manifestly unfounded, the insurance company shall pay the amount of settlement to the injured party.[245]

243. Banyár József & NAGY Koppány, *A haláleseti kedvezményezettek védelmének magyarországi helyzetéről* [On the Situation of the Protection of Beneficiaries of Death in Hungary]. Biztosítás és Kockázat, Vol. II/1 (2015), 76–86.

244. Subsection 1 of s. 6:472 of the CC.

245. Subsection 2 of s. 6:472 of the CC.

Unless otherwise provided for by law,[246] the injured party shall not be entitled to lodge his/her claim directly to the insurance company. This rule shall not preclude the injured party's right to bring action against the insurance company, asking the court to determine whether the insured person's liability insurance coverage applied to the injured party at the time of the occurrence of the damage.[247]

Under the former CC, the injured party could not bring legal action against the insurer of the tortfeasor. Therefore, the liability insurance cases took place between the injured party and the tortfeasor. If the judgment rejected the claim of the injured party, it affected the insurer, while a judgment against the tortfeasor only affects the insurer if he/she took part in the procedure, if he/she was represented during the procedure, or if he/she renounces from these.

In this legal context, the judicial practice caused a fundamental breakthrough, which was accepted by the current CC. The injured party still has no possibility to directly demand the performance of the insurer instead of the tortfeasor in the legal procedure. However, according to the established judicial practice,[248] there is no longer a legal obstacle to bringing a so-called declaratory action against the insurer by the injured party. This action seeks to declare that the liability insurance coverage of the insured person existed at the time of the tort, and it covers the damage caused to the injured party.

The judgment of the Court of Justice of the European Union, in its preliminary ruling in the *Prüller-Frey* case, concerns the admissibility of an action for damages directly against the insurer in the event of non-contractual damages according to Regulation 864/2007. According to the Court, Article 18 of the Regulation must be interpreted as meaning that, in a situation such as that of the case before the referring court, a person who has suffered damage is entitled to bring a direct action against the insurer of the person liable to provide compensation where such an action is provided for by the law applicable to the non-contractual obligation, regardless of the provision made by the law that the parties have chosen as the law applicable to the insurance contract. According to this, it is possible that Hungarian law (except compulsory motor vehicle liability insurance) does not recognize the possibility of direct actions against the insurer by the injured party, but the injured party may still sue the insurer directly if the liability insurance contract contains coverage for the activity of the insured person in a county other than the seat of the insurer and the contracting party and if the injured party suffered damage in a Member State whose law permits the direct action against the insurer.

246. For example, Act LXII of 2009 on Insurance Against Civil Liability in Respect of the Use of Motor Vehicles.
247. Subsections 1–2 of s. 6:473 of the CC.
248. JD2000. 335., JD2002. 6.

Part III. Property and Liability Insurance

Chapter 1. The System of the Regulation

Edit Antal Ujvári

191. The CC regulated after the general provisions (Chapter LXII. General Provisions on Insurance Contracts (section 6:439–6:457)) the indemnity insurance (Chapter LXIII. Indemnity Insurance Contracts. (1) General provisions on indemnity insurance contracts (section 6:458–6:469), (2) Liability insurance policies (section 6:470–6:474)).

Chapter 2. General Provisions on Indemnity Insurance Contracts[249]

Edit Antal Ujvári

§1. Insurable Interest: Overinsurance—Underinsurance

192. The CC—contrary to the former regulation where the insurable interest only appeared in the property insurance contract—regulates insurable interest as one condition for the establishment of a legal relationship within the general provisions. Any indemnity insurance contract concluded in contradiction to this provision shall be null and void.

Among indemnity insurance, it is particularly important to determine the insurance value (which is its value in case of property) and the coverage.

A property insurance contract does not result in the enrichment of the insured person; therefore, the determination of the insurance value is very important. The insurance coverage is the amount which represents the upper limit of the obligation of performance of the insurer. Our law determines the prohibition of overinsurance, which means that the coverage shall not exceed the value of the insured property. *The insured person cannot be enriched by the tort, which is strengthened by the unified judicial practice (JD1195. 110).* Any agreement for a coverage higher than the value of the insured interest shall be partially null and void, which means that the insurance coverage shall be replaced by the actual value.

The CC allows some exceptions from this rule of the prohibition of overinsurance; therefore, an insurance policy can include provisions:

- for the estimated future value of a property;
- for the value of restoration; and/or
- for the value of replacement.

193. If the amount of coverage is lower than the value of the insured interest, the insurance company shall be liable to cover the loss in such a manner that the amount of insurance is proportionate to the value of the property.

According to judicial practice, the payment of the acquisition value of the property in a new state cannot be connected to the occurrence of the acquisition in the new state in the insurance contract; this standard contract term is unfair (JD2007. 371.) The court also classified the standard contract term as unfair, according to which the insurer undertook insurance for the new value, while it only undertook an obligation for the refund of the obsoleted value upon reaching an obsolescent of 75% (CDP2010. 2221)

249. *See* further, Ujváriné Dr. Antal Edit, *Biztosítási szerződés* [Insurance Contract] In Majoros Tünde (ed.), *Kereskedelmi szerződések alapvető szabályai* [General Rules on Commercial Contracts]. Budapest (Patrocinium Publisher 2015), 219–273; Dr. Zavodnyik József, *A biztosítási szerződések* [Insurance Contracts]. In Osztovics András (ed.), *A Polgári Törvénykönyvről szóló 2013. évi V. törvény és a kapcsolódó jogszabályok nagykommentárja III. kötet* [General Commentary of the Act V of 2013 on the Civil Code and of the Relating Legal Acts—Vol. 3]. Opten Ltd., Budapest (2014), 1106–1270.

Among indemnity insurance, it is common to stipulate a so-called excess (franchise), which means that the insured person bears a part of the actual damage stipulated in the contract (it can be a defined percentage or a defined amount) while the insurer only reimburses amount above this part. In case of the so-called first risk (*premiere risque*) insurance, the insurance waives the application of the legal consequences of underinsurance, which means the insurer pays the actual damage within the framework of the insurance amount in spite of that it did not insure the whole property of the insured person. This type of insurance contract is typical in case of commercial shops, department stores, or warehouses where the change in stocks is very high.

It can happen that the same interest or asset is insured by more than one insurance company independently (concurrent insurance). In this case, the prohibition of overinsurance relates to the totality of the services of the insurance companies. If the insured event occurs, the insured person is entitled to submit his/her claim to one or more (or to all) of such insurance companies, and the insurance company shall be liable to make a settlement payment under the terms and conditions undertaken by him/her, up to the sum insured as defined in the contract. In this case, the insurer may reserve the right to lodge a claim for compensation relating to the other insurance companies, for the insurance companies shall cover the claims paid jointly in proportion to the amounts of coverage according to which the individual insurance companies would be liable to the insured person.

§2. Other Specialties Relating to the Content of the Legal Relationship

I. Insurance Premium

194. Regarding insurance premium as a characteristic of insurance contracts, the most relevant question is whether insurance contracts can have a gratuitous form or not. The CC answers it unambiguously: the definition of an insurance contract (section 6:439(1)) prescribes that the policyholder shall pay insurance premiums.

In case of indemnity insurance, the insurance premium is adjusted to the value of the insured property because the occurrence of the risk—in addition to the endangerment of property—mainly depends on this. The insurance companies often intend to strengthen the risk community in a way that the contracting parties are tied for a longer period, and they provide them a premium discount, the so-called term discount.[250]

250. The consumer-friendly insurance product is a new product in the insurance market, because the NBH qualifies the contract conditions of the applicant insurance companies according to the tender notice and the relevant regulations and ensures the use of the trademark for applicants who meet the conditions. In 2021, a total of eight institutions obtained Qualified Consumer-Friendly Home Insurance (MFO), which means that a significant part of the home insurance market now offers a consumer-friendly products.
https://www.mnb.hu/letoltes/mfo-vedjegyszabalyzat.pdf.
https://www.mnb.hu/letoltes/kocka-zati-jelente-s-2022-hun-0825.pdf.

Sometimes, the contracting party (the insured person) pays the insurance premium for the defined insurance period but only a part of it (partial payment). In this case, the insurance company shall dispatch, within thirty days from the due date, a written request for payment to the party in default—indicating the potential legal consequences—with an additional thirty-day deadline from the date when the warning was dispatched. If the insurance company's request proves unsuccessful, the contract shall remain in force with the same amount of coverage for a term to which the premium paid corresponds.

II. The Performance of the Insurer

195. The insurance company is required to perform its obligation on the date specified in the contract (usually in the terms and conditions defined in advance). In the determination of this date, the insurance companies have to take into account that they are obliged to remain within the time limit necessary for the performance. The insurer has to calculate the performance between the occurrence of the insurance event and the expiration of the limitation period continuously. During this time, the delayed notification of damage by the insured person does not result, by itself, in the exemption of the insurer unless significant circumstances become impossible to investigate due to the delay. *However, for the duration of the delay of notification, the insured person is not entitled to default interest (CJD2005. 1091).*

CJD2019. 4092. The insurance service (insurance sum) which is to be paid on the basis of the property insurance contract, belongs to the property of the insured person even if a third-party beneficiary has been designated as collateral for another contract. In case of liquidation proceedings against the insured person, the insurance premium is part of the liquidation assets.

196. According to the general rules, the insurance company may demand—in accordance with sections 123–124 BIns., as a precondition for payment of settlement—documents (e.g., records from a fire examination, etc.) which are deemed necessary to verify the occurrence of the insured event, or for determining the extent of compensation to be provided.

197. The insured person (the beneficiary) has the general obligation of cooperation necessary for the performance of the insurer. The insured person (beneficiary) is required to prove that the insured event occurred and that he/she is entitled to the insurance sum insured as an insured person (beneficiary). According to a rule in consumer protection, it is unfair to require a consumer who wishes to claim on an insurance policy to produce documents which could not reasonably be considered relevant as to whether the claim was valid or failing systematically to respond to pertinent correspondence, in order to dissuade a consumer from exercising his contractual rights.[251]

The insurer's payment obligation can occur according to the contract; it depends on whether or not the asset is underinsured, whether the insurance was concluded

251. Point 27 of Annex to PUBC.

for a new value, and on the specified insurance sum since the insurer is obliged to reimburse up to this sum. The insured person is required to prove not only the occurrence of the damage (insured event) and its amount but also *that, for example, he fulfilled the obligation of prevention of damage according to the contract. (JD2002. 98)*

The justified cost of mitigating damages (or in case of under-regulation, a part of it) shall be borne by the insurance company within the limits of the sum insured, even if mitigation of damages has been unsuccessful.

If the insured property is recovered, the insured person shall be entitled to lay claim to it. Of course, this cannot lead to the unjust enrichment of the insured person; therefore, the amount received in settlement shall be repaid. If the insured person does not claim the property, its ownership will belong to the insurance company, but *the transfer of ownership occurs under the general rules of civil law (JD2005. 390.) The fact that the injured person, the owner of the motor vehicle, allowed the loan disbursing bank a right to purchase as collateral for the loan contract does not entitle the insurer to pay the damage not to the injured party (the owner) but directly to the bank. (CJD2003. 776).*

III. Maintaining the Amount of Insurance Cover

198. A specialty of indemnity insurance is that there is a tight connection between the insurance sum and the insurance period. The amount of coverage for a given period of insurance cover shall be reduced by the amount paid for claims of insured events that occurred during that same period unless the contracting party supplements the premium accordingly. The insurance company shall be entitled if the contracting party has been advised thereof in writing, not later than at the time of settlement, and notified of the fee for maintaining the amount of insurance cover.

IV. Exemption from Settlement Obligation

199. Among property insurance, the scope of the exemption of the insurer from the obligation to perform due to the breach of contract of the other party is broader. The insurance company shall be exempt from its payment obligation if it is able to prove that damages have been caused unlawfully, either willfully or by gross negligence, by:

- the insured person or the contracting party or any family member living in their household, any managing partner or any employee, member, or agent working in a position specified in the standard contract terms; or
- a person authorized by the insured legal person as specified in the standard contract terms.

The standard contract terms can only prescribe such legal consequences in connection with the conduct of the executive officer or any member, employee, or agent of such insured legal person authorized to manage the insured property.

200. According to judicial practice, the omission can also be a basis for the verification of gross negligence and, therefore, for the exemption of the insurer (CJD2000. 171.). The insurer is required to prove that the tortfeasor belongs to the persons, resulting in the exemption. (CJD2009. 2008) The person requiring the performance of the insurance contract is required to prove that the conditions for the performance of the insurer are met, as well as the occurrence of the insured event. In contrast, the insurer is required to prove his/her exemption (BDT2009. 2070).

Failure to comply with the official regulations concerning the operation of boilers is a serious conduct of the insured person which leads to the exemption of the insurer (JD1989. 280), but the failure to turn on the alarm system can also be the basis for gross negligence in case of burglary insurance events (JD1995. 642).

201. The contracting party and the insured person shall take reasonable precautions in order to prevent any loss or damage. This rule also prevails if the insurance contract specifies the duties of the contracting party/insured person relating to the prevention of damage (e.g., prescription of tools, procedures, qualification, etc.). The contracting party and the insured person shall mitigate the damage based on the insurance company's specifications, and according to its instructions given at the time when the damage or loss occurred or, failing this, they shall proceed under the principle of reasonable conduct. *According to the judicial practice, for example, it has to be regarded as the omission of the obligation of the prevention of damage and, therefore, can lead to the exemption of the insurer if the insured person leaves the registration certificate of the vehicle and spare key of the vehicle in the motor vehicle (CDP2009. 2046), or if the insured person leaves the ignition key in the vehicle unattended (JD1993. 501). The violation of the obligation of the prevention of damage can only result in the exemption if all the conditions are met (JD2001. 225.).* Safety requirements are relevant conditions for a home insurance contract, which can only become a part of the contract if the client of the insurer receives it during the conclusion of the contract in writing, undersigned by the insurer. *In the absence of this, the insurer shall not be exempted from the obligation to perform in case of any deficiencies in mechanical protection (JD2002. 437).*

The non-performance of the notification about the changes, by the insured person, can only be established for the facts recognized in a timely manner but which failed to be reported (CJD2005. 1256, CJD2004. 940).

The mere violation of the relevant rules and regulations, carelessness, and inattention relating to the activity are not sufficient for the determination of gross negligence (CJD2002. 641).

According to the practice of the courts, gross negligence can also be established if the insured person conveys information about the operation of a motor vehicle with the knowledge that the driver could be under the influence of alcohol (CJD2001. 481).

In order to prevent vehicle theft, insurance companies stipulate in their contracts that it is prohibited to make a copy of the key of the vehicle without their prior consent. According to judicial practice, the breach of this obligation infringes the obligation of the prevention of damage; therefore, the insurer is exempted from the obligation to pay (CJD2000. 319).

However, in the so-called key declaration lawsuits, the judicial practice ruled that the provision of the insurance contract, which provides the insurer with an exemption based on the fact of the breach of the disclosure obligation without any further proof, is contrary to the principle of unilateral cogency. It was a public interest lawsuit initiated by the General Inspectorate for Consumer Protection and the Hungarian Autoklub. The judgment became final and legally binding in the first instance and became a guideline in further court proceedings as well (Decision No. 1.P.91.194/97/6. Central District Court of Pest, JD1999. 505.).

202. After the occurrence of the insured event, the insured person is required to present the damaged property to the insurance company in the same state. The insurance company's settlement obligation shall not take effect if, as a consequence of any change greater than that which is permitted, it becomes impossible to clarify the basic circumstances from the point of view of assessing the payment obligation of the insurance company.

V. Termination by Notice

203. In case of indemnity insurance contracts, both parties are entitled to unilaterally terminate the contract. The parties shall be entitled to terminate a contract of indeterminate duration in writing, to take effect at the end of the period of insurance cover, by giving thirty days' notice. This period can be one year, six months, one month, etc., as regulated in the CC. *The non-compliance with these rules makes the termination invalid (JD1995. 417., JD1995. 209., JD2001. 119.).*

The right to terminate may be excluded for a maximum period of three years, but any other regulation shall be partially null and void.

In case of contracts concluded for a defined period, the right to terminate applies only if the contract covers a period of over three years. In this case, either of the parties shall be entitled to terminate the contract as of the fourth year.

VI. Claim for Compensation of the Insurer (Subrogation)

204. In case of indemnity insurance contracts, the insurance company shall be entitled to lay claim for compensation against the person responsible for the damage up to the amount of settlement it has paid if he/she recompenses the damage in accordance with the insurance contract. In this case, the guarantees for the coverage of the claim of the injured party (insured person) also remain in effect and are transferred to the claim. The insurer is not entitled to compensation if the tortfeasor is a family member of the insured person living in the same household. *According to the judicial practice, the insurer is entitled to claims for compensation against the person responsible for the damage, which cannot be interpreted broadly, that the insurer may act against the subsequent possessors of the insured property as well (JD1999. 507).*

If the insurance company did not provide settlement for the entire claim according to the contract (e.g., because the full value of the asset was not insured), he/she shall inform the insured person and shall also move to enforce the claims of the insured at his/her request, which could be contingent upon an advance on expenses. From the sum recovered, the insured person's claim shall be satisfied first.

§3. LIABILITY INSURANCE POLICIES[252]

I. Specialty of Liability Insurance

205. The significance of liability insurance increases parallelly with the emergence of new risks caused by the development of science and technology and with the tightening of liability (contractual liability, liability for hazardous activity, product liability, etc.).[253] Among the legislations, the number of insurance obligations and the compulsory insurance increases which are especially important for the protection of the contracting parties, the consumers, and potentially injured persons. Special laws apply to insurance obligations of:

- the operator of the motor vehicle;
- the notaries;
- the multiple insurance agents;
- the independent insurance intermediary;
- the health service operators, etc.

---

252. *See* further: Ujváriné Dr. Antal Edit, *Biztosítási szerződés* [Insurance Contract] In Majoros Tünde (ed.), *Kereskedelmi szerződések alapvető szabályai* [General Rules on Commercial Contracts]. Budapest (Patrocinium Publisher 2015), 219–273; Ujváriné Dr. Antal Edit: *Felelősségtan* [Law of Liability]. Budapest (Patrocinium Publisher 2017); Ujváriné Antal Edit, *A kárfelelősségi szabályok sajátosságai a biztosítási jogviszonyban* [The Peculiarities of the Liability Rules in the Insurance Legal Relationship]. In Barta Judit, Barzó Tímea & Csák Csilla (ed.), *Magyarázat a kártérítési jogról.* Budapest (Wolters Kluwer Kiadó 2018), Part I, Ch. 6, 218–223.

Ujváriné Antal Edit, *Felelősség a szerződésen kívül okozott kárért* [Liability for Damage Caused Outside of the Contract]. In Barta Judit, Barzó Tímea & Csák Csilla (ed.), *Magyarázat a kártérítési jogról.* Budapest (Wolters Kluwer Kiadó 2018), Part I, Ch. 3/1, 62–96.

Ujváriné Antal Edit, *Felelősség a szerződésen kívül okozott kárért* [Liability for Damage Caused Outside of the Contract]. In Barzó Tímea & Papp Tekla (ed.), CIVILISZTIKA II. Dologi jog—Felelősségtan Scientia Rerum Politicarum, Dialóg Campus Kiadó, Budapest, 2019, Part II, Ch. II, 261–302.

https://nkerepo.uni-nke.hu/xmlui/bitstream/handle/123456789/12659/web_PDF_ATMA_Civilisztika_II.pdf?sequence=1.

Dr. Fuglinszky Ádám, *Kártérítési jog* [Law on Damage Compensation]. Budapest (Hvgorac Publisher 2015); Dr. Novotni Zoltán, *A felelősségbiztosítási jogviszony alapkérdései a magyar jogban* [Basic Questions on Liability Insurance Relationship in the Hungarian Law] (Candidate thesis, 1981); Dr. Zavodnyik József, *A biztosítási szerződések* [Insurance Contracts]. In Osztovics András (ed.), *A Polgári Törvénykönyvről szóló 2013. évi V. törvény és a kapcsolódó jogszabályok nagykommentárja III. kötet* [General Commentary of the Act V of 2013 on the Civil Code and of the Relating Legal Acts—Vol. 3]. Budapest, Opten Ltd., 2014, 1106–1270; Dr. Kovács Kázmér & Dr. Kovács Szabolcs, *Indemnification and Insurance Contracts.* In István Sándor Dr. (ed.), *Business Law in Hungary.* Magister Books, Budapest (Patrocinium Kiadó 2016), 403–405.

253. Pandurics Anett & Markó Olga, *A felelősségbiztoítások szerepe, jelene és jövője Magyarországon* [The Role, Present and Future of Liability Insurance in Hungary]. Biztosítás és Kockázat 2/3. https://mabisz.hu/wp-content/uploads/2018/08/biztositas-es-kockazat-2-evf-3-szam-5-cikk.pdf.

In some areas, the law determines the content of the liability insurance contract and the minimum insured limit (i.e., in connection with independent insurance agents and financial service intermediaries).

206. The current CC changed the system of tort liability; different rules apply to contractual and tortuous liabilities. The general form of tortuous liability is based on actionable conduct, although there are special, stricter liability rules as well. According to the former rules, a person whose rights relating to personality had been infringed could ask for pecuniary and non-pecuniary damage as well. According to the current CC, any person whose rights relating to personality had been violated shall be entitled to restitution for any non-material violation suffered, which the liability insurance covers—irrespectively that it cannot be qualified as damage.

207. Not only civil liability can be inserted into insurance coverage but also liabilities relating to other areas of law, e.g., labor law liability of the employer, financial responsibility of the employee (public servants) or of a member of a cooperative, etc.

The liability of the insured person can be established based on tortuous or contractual liability, although it has to be highlighted that only liability for damages and the payment of restitution, defined by law, can be insured within the framework of a liability insurance contract. The liability insurance only covers damage for which the insured person is liable under the law. *Therefore, for example, the consent of the injured person in a road accident can eliminate the unlawfulness of the damage and, therefore, exempt the insurer from the liability for damages based on compulsory liability insurance (JD2011. 195). If the non-contractual damage caused by the insured person is considered the insurance event according to the liability insurance contract, he would be liable for the damage caused to third parties on the basis of a liability insurance policy during the performance of the contract (JD2005. 324).*

II. The Legal Position of the Subjects of the Liability Insurance Contract

A. *The Legal Position of the Injured Person*

208. The legal position of the injured person does not change although the tortfeasor has a liability insurance contract; his/her position is determined by the rules of tort (liability issues, burden of proof, etc.), and this is confirmed by judicial practice (JD1993. 570., JD2005. 249.). The injured party is entitled to lodge his/her claim to the insured person (tortfeasor) and is not entitled to lodge his/her claim directly to the insurance company unless otherwise provided for by law or by the contract of the parties (e.g., in case of compulsory motor vehicle liability insurance contracts a special law provides a possibility of direct claim enforcement[254]). This rule shall not prevent the injured party from bringing an action against the insurer

254. *See* more details about motor vehicle liability in Ch. 4.

to have the court decide whether the insured person's liability insurance covered the damage of the injured party at the time when the damage was caused.[255]

B. The Legal Position of the Contracting Party (Insured Person)

209. The insured person occupies the most complex position in the legal relationship.

The liability insurance contract usually regulates the time in which the insured event has to be reported in writing to the insured person (a claim has been filed with respect to his/her activity specified in the contract or if he/she becomes aware of any circumstance that is likely to give rise to such a claim). According to the CC, a time limit of at least thirty days shall be provided for the notification of an insured event. If the notification is not made within the time limit, the general rules apply: if, therefore, material circumstances for the obligation of the insurer become impossible to investigate, the insurer will be exempted.

If the insured person is required to pay damages to the injured person, he/she cannot refuse it, referring to his own liability insurance contract, but he is entitled to invite the insurance company—within the framework of the contract—to perform his/her own obligation. If the insured person compensates the claim of the injured person, he/she may demand the insurer to perform.

C. The Legal Position of the Insurance Company

210. The legal status of the insurance company can be characterized as such: its rights (e.g., claim for premium) are against the insured person, and its obligations are also towards the injured person, but it is required to perform this obligation directly in favor of and to the hand of the injured person. The insurer may only deviate from this rule if the insured person compensates the injured person's claim. It is important to emphasize, however, that the content of the liability insurance contract shall prevail with respect to the extent of the responsibility of the insurer to the injured person instead of the insured person. On the one hand, it does not necessarily comprise the entire responsibility of the injured person (e.g., the insurer takes the risk up to a limited amount), and, on the other hand, the contract usually determines its temporary scope of validity as well.

According to judicial practice, the injured party is required to lodge a creditor's claim during the liquidation procedure against the debtor (insured person) so that the liquidator can take action against the insurer based on the debtor's liability insurance contract (CDP2011. 2420).

The termination of the insured person's liability insurance without a legal successor does not terminate the obligation of the insurer to pay an allowance as compensation; the injured person is entitled to lodge a claim against the insurer for the increase of the amount of the allowance (CDP2008. 1772).

255. Section 6:473 of the CC [Enforcement of the injured party's claim].

If the insurer concluded a liability insurance contract with a company, terminated later without a legal successor in respect of its employees, the legal successor of the insurer shall be liable for claims related to the insurance event (compensation for industrial accident), if its conditions are met (JD1998. 615).

211. The policy covers procedural costs if incurred under the insurance company's guidance or upon its prior consent. The insurance company shall be liable to advance the expenses when so requested by the insured person.

The upper limit of the performance of the insurance company is the insurance sum specified in the insurance contract, although the insurance company shall be liable to cover the legal expenses, including interests, of the insured person if he/she is responsible for the damage, even if they exceed the amount of coverage together with the settlement payment.

The insured person may protest against his/her liability or its extent. If this happens to be clearly unfounded, the insurer is required to perform to the injured person, and the additional costs incurred by the baseless denial shall be borne by the insured person.

212. According to the rules of the former CC, the insurance contract covered the intentional or gross negligent tort of the insured person, but the current regulation leaves the acceptance of these risks to the insurance contract. Therefore, the insurance contracts have differentiated content, which is a particularly important circumstance among professional (medical, legal, etc.) liability insurances. It is important to mention that according to the former CC if the insurance company was held liable for the intentional or grossly negligent damage defined by law (or in the contract), it was entitled to require the amount paid to the injured person from the insured person. Therefore, the law intended to prevent the insured persons from becoming "irresponsible" for their actions which were protected by the insurance coverage, because there was a "threat" that the insurance company could take action against them. This is called the right to recourse (regress) of the insurer. The current CC does not contain this rule, but the dispositivity of the CC does not exclude the possibility that the contracting parties agree to similar rules in the insurance contract. We emphasize that the Compulsory Motor Vehicle Liability Insurance Act explicitly includes the right of the insurer to regress, the reasons for which are listed exhaustively. (*See* for more details Part IV.)

D. *The Insured Person's Acknowledgement, Performance and Settlement of the Injured Party's Claim*

213. The insured person's acknowledgement and settlement of the injured party's claim, and any related composition, shall be considered effective with respect to the insurance company only if the insurance company has granted prior consent or acknowledged it after the fact (that he/she was involved in the making of the statements, in the conclusion of the agreement, he/she represented the insured person during this process or, if this did not occur, he/she either gave his prior consent to the statements or accepted the statement of the insured person, made without his involvement as bounding). However, the law takes into account that the insurer cannot misuse his/her rights. Therefore, these statements have no legal force in respect of the insurance company if the claim is manifestly well founded.

However, if the insurer and the injured person make a settlement, it also has an impact on the tortfeasor because the injured person cannot claim further damages against him/her in respect of the same damage (CDP2004. 1125).

E. The Scope of a Judgment in a Lawsuit Between the Tortfeasor and the Injured Person

214. The judgment in a legal action taken by the injured person against the insured person may be favorable to the insurer if the claim of the injured party proves to be unfounded and is rejected by the court. In such cases, the legal interests of the insurer are not violated even if he/she was not aware of the lawsuit and did not participate in it because there is no payment obligation arising from it. In this case, therefore, if the judgment in a dispute relating to the liability of the insured person is rejected, the scope of the judgment of the court will have an impact on the insurer as well.

If the court has ruled against the insured person, it shall apply, with respect to the insurance company, if it has participated in the lawsuit (e.g., as an intervenor), provided for the insured person's legal representation, or if he/she has waived the above. From this fact, it follows that if the insured person has liability insurance, it is always advisable to call upon the insurer to the lawsuit next to him/her, for they obviously have the same legal interests. The situation is different when the insurer was aware of the lawsuit but resigned from the representation and participation in the litigation. In this case, the insurer obviously does not deserve the protection of the law, and the judgment has an impact on the insurer regardless of its content (either rejecting or condemning).

According to the solution of the Hungarian law, the scope of liability includes services that cover insurance protection, at least to the extent of the scope of liability insurance. This is referred to in the provisions of the law, which concerns the participation in the lawsuit by the insurer.

CJD2018. 3885. If the forwarding agent's liability insurer settles the theft damage caused to the goods transported by public road in the direction of the sender instead of the insured person, a claim for compensation (recourse) arises by the law against the carrier entrusted by the forwarding agent as a direct insured person, whose actionable behavior caused the damage during transportation.

Chapter 3. Fire Insurance

Edit Antal Ujvári

215. In the Hungarian insurance practice, the risks listed in the insurance contracts (either private or corporate) include fire insurance. The concept of the insured event is determined by the conditions of the contract. Usually, a fire can be regarded as an insured event if self-nourishing flames—which do not arise in proper combustion or which do but leave and are able to spread further independently—cause damage to the insured assets. It also can be regarded as an insured event if the fire resulting from overvoltage in electrical appliances damages other assets.

The conditions of the insurance contract contain provisions relating to the exclusion of risks (e.g., if the property is damaged due to a fire which is not able to spread (e.g., scorch on an asset next to cigarette ash, glowing coals, lighting or heating appliance, etc.); if the asset is exposed to the effects of fire, smoke, or heat (e.g., ironing, drying, baking, cooking, etc. during which change in color and shape occurs); if spontaneous ignition occurs; if flammable or explosive material with an amount exceeding the application for domestic use are stored in the secured area, etc.).

Insurers often offer a possibility to conclude a supplementary insurance. The supplementary insurance can be concluded and has to compensate an insured party, for example, if the insured company is forced to pause its normal economic activity due to fire, explosion, or lightning, and if the damage is caused by the suppression, rescue, demolition, or evacuation activities, which became necessary due to these events.

Chapter 4. Loss of Benefits Insurance

Edit Antal Ujvári

216. According to the CC (section 6:439), under an insurance contract, the insurer undertakes to provide coverage for the risk specified in the contract and to provide settlement or benefits for the loss arising upon the occurrence of a specific future event after the starting date of risk coverage, and the insured person undertakes to pay an insurance premium agreed upon. The insurance company's service covers the payment for the insured person's loss in the amount and in the manner defined in the contract and other policy benefits.

Regarding the loss of benefits, we have to distinguish between property insurance and liability insurance.

Among the property insurance contracts concluded by individuals, the service of the insurance company usually connects to the damage in the asset and does not cover loss of benefits, which may potentially occur due to damage in the asset.

Certain insurance contracts may provide companies the opportunity to cover the loss of benefits. One type of it is the so-called *shutdown insurance* which provides coverage for (net) loss of benefits which the insured person loses due to material damage caused by the breakdown of the insured equipment.[256]

217. In case of liability insurance, however, the insured party shall be entitled, under a liability insurance policy, to request the insurance company to exempt him/her, in the manner and up to the limit specified in the policy, from paying for damages or paying restitution, for which he/she is legally liable.

According to the general rules of tort liability,[257] the tortfeasor shall compensate the aggrieved party for all his losses in full, which include the loss of benefits; therefore, the tortuous liability extends to the lost benefit as well. The liability of the insurer is aligned to the liability of the tortfeasor. In the basic insurance contract, the insurers generally do not take the risk of loss of benefits; therefore, they usually exclude the risk of lost profits in the terms and conditions of the contract, or the contract may limit the liability of the insurer by that amount.

256. https://mabisz.hu/wp-content/uploads/2018/09/T%C3%A1j%C3%A9%C3%A1koztat%C3%B3-az-%C3%BCzemsz%C3%BCnet-biztos%C3%ADt%C3%A1sr%C3%B3l-honlapra.pdf.

257. Point a) of sub. 2 of s. 6:522 of the CC.

Chapter 5. Transport Insurance

Judit Barta

§1. Legal Regulations Relating to Domestic Transports

218. The definition of carriage contract is regulated by the CC. Under a carriage contract, a carrier undertakes to transport the consignment to its destination and deliver it to the consignee, and the consignor undertakes to pay the fee agreed upon.[258]

The carrier is responsible for the damage to the consignment between its receipt and its delivery. The carrier shall be held responsible for the loss of the consignment, too. According to the CC, the consignment may be considered lost when it has not been delivered within thirty days after the prescribed period of carriage. If the consignment is recovered following the payment of damages, the carrier shall notify the consignor within the shortest possible time, upon which the consignor shall have the right of disposition over the consignment.[259]

The carrier shall be held liable for the damage caused by the delay in the issuance of transport equipment or by the delay in delivery of the consignment.

The general rules of the CC for domestic carriage of goods are complemented by specific laws relating to certain sectors of transport:

- Government Decree No. 26/1999. (II.12.) on the carriage of goods by air.
- Convention on the Contract for the Carriage of Goods by Inland Waterway (CMNI) (promulgated by Act CXLI of 2005).
- Government Decree No. 32/2009. (II.19.) on the carriage of goods by railway.
- Government Decree No. 120/2016. (VI.7.) on the carriage of goods by road.

International carriage is regulated by transport sectors by multilateral and bilateral agreements and, in case of Member States, by the legal acts of the EU.

§2. Liability Insurance of the Carrier[260]

219. In case of domestic carriage, there is no provision relating to liability insurance except for air transport.

Carriage insurance provides insurance coverage for the damage to goods as well as for the loss of goods between the receipt and the delivery of the consignment.

258. Section 6:257 of the CC.
259. Subsection 4 of s. 6:268 of the CC.
260. There is a website where most of the insurance products distributed in Hungary can be found: http://biztositasifeltetelek.hu/?page=3&biztosito=0&modozat=0&ervkezdetmin=&ervkezdetmax=&nyomtatvanyszam=&kereses=hitel&kereses2=&megnevezes=&mutat=50&rendez=0&szerint=erv_kezdete.

The damage caused by the delay of the carrier is excluded by the insurers. Supplementary insurance contracts can be concluded for the contributor availed by the carrier. The contracts determine limits on the insurance compensation per insured events and per insurance periods. The total compensation paid by the insurance company per insured events in the insurance year shall not exceed the total annual limit.

The contracts contain an excess, which is usually 10%, although it can be reduced in case of the payment of an increased premium.

The determination of fee can be made according to different criteria; it can be based on traffic (e.g., the revenue of carriage fee or the quantity or the risk of goods to be transported), but it also can be determined as a fixed fee per vehicle. In case of a flat fee-based insurance premium, the number or the nature of transport equipment is one of the relevant factors.

Another risk applies to glassware, frozen meat or bulk grain. The nature of transport equipment and transport branch has a significant effect on the insurance premium. Different insurance premium applies to carriage liability insurance contracts relating to transportation by truck, motor vehicle, draft animals, aircraft, boat, etc.

In case of international carriage, the insurance premiums, or even the risk coverage, depend on the route and the countries concerned.

§3. Exclusions

220. The types of exclusions are different in the insurance companies; however, there are common exclusions, e.g.:

- the so-called damage arising from political risks (war, strikes, civil unrest, protest, terrorism, etc.);
- damage in conjunction with radioactive or ionizing radiation;
- damage resulting from the inevitable hazards on the part of a carrier, such as earthquakes, lightning, etc.;
- damage related to the specific characteristics of the different types of goods, e.g., freezing, occlusion, mold, desiccation, etc.;
- damage resulting from the delay;
- damage caused by deficiency in packaging which cannot be noticed from the outside;
- damage caused by improper filling or the non-delivery of transport documents;
- damage caused during loading by the sender or which resulted during the delivery to the recipient;
- risks of transportation goods which has a particular risk or which are qualified as special under the insurance contract, such as entertainment electronics, photography products, precious metals, precious stones, banknotes, securities, museum properties, artworks, tobacco, livestock, oversized and overweight heavy goods, vehicles, self-propelled machinery, corpses, mail (the coverage can be extended with extra charge);

- in case of chilled and frozen goods (transported in a temperature-regulated area), the insurance coverage does not cover the cases when temperature registration equipment did not operate or did not operate sufficiently in the vehicle (thermo-script).

§4. Consignment Insurance

221. Consignment insurance can become necessary if the carrier has no liability insurance contract or the coverage of the liability insurance contract does not cover the consignment to be delivered or the defined damage event.

The consignment insurance provides the owner of the goods with the knowledge that his goods can be fully protected against damage caused during transportation. In case of both domestic and international transport of goods, consignment insurance for all risks, or for identified risks, can be concluded. A consignment insurance contract is concluded between the consignor and the insurer in order to protect the goods against damage during transportation.

There are several types of consignment insurance:

- specific consignment insurance (for one way);
- framework insurance (this insurance provides coverage for all transportation of the insured person within the insurance period, which is one year).

The insurance coverage could be extended to the storage of the goods during the transportation if it does not exceed thirty days, to the damage caused by the breakdown of the cooling device, to damage caused by theft, to damage resulting from the threat of war, etc.

The conditions for domestic consignment insurance are different across insurers and branches of transportation, but for international transportation, insurance companies apply the London conditions of 1963 or 1980, with greater or lesser changes.[261]

261. https://mabisz.hu/wp-content/uploads/2018/08/tajekoztato-a-szallitassal-kapcsolatos-biztositasokrol-20170413.pdf.

Chapter 6. Liability Insurance[262]

Edit Antal Ujvári

222. In Chapter 6 of General Introduction, we explained the rules relating to compulsory insurance, which is the most typical among liability insurance. Some laws relating to compulsory insurance regulate—taking into account the aim of the insurance obligation—the essential elements of the content of the contract to be concluded, but most of the relevant law prescribes only the insurance obligation.[263] It does not specify even to what limit the insurance contract shall provide coverage, what shall be the maximum level of excess, etc. In some cases, the obliged person can satisfy his/her obligations imposed by the law with the provision of other financial guarantees instead of the insurance contract. Among the compulsory insurance contracts, the compulsory motor vehicle liability insurance has to be highlighted because its content is regulated, in detail, by the law.[264] The laws also prescribe the content of the insurance contract, e.g., in the case of independent financial services agents, insurance intermediaries,[265] liability insurance contracts concluded by a person performing the property valuation, and the liability of nuclear damage.[266]

223. If the insurance contracts do not limit the cover, the claim under the liability insurance contract is governed by the rules on compensation. In other words, if cover exists on the basis of the act committed, the damage caused (damage compensation) may be recovered, even if the insurance contract has already been terminated at the time the damage occurred, subject, of course, to the rules on limitation.

If the legislation does not lay down any requirements as to the liability insurance required for the pursuit of the activity, and therefore the temporal validity, in case of the liability insurance contracts offered by insurance companies, it is typical that

262. The market position of liability insurance is analyzed in Pandurics Anett & Markó Olga, *Felelősségbiztosítások szerepe, jelene és jövője Magyarországon.* [Roles, Present and Future of Liability Insurances in Hungary] Biztosítás és Kockázat, Vol. II/3., 78–94.

263. E.g., According of the law (Act CLIV of 1997) an operating licence for a health service can only be issued if the applicant has a liability insurance to compensate for damage caused during the health service. As the lawyer activity Act (Act LXXVIII of 2017), the minimum amount of the liability insurance necessary to ensure the damages calculated per damage event is HUF 15 million.

264. *See* more about it in Part IV.

265. *See* more about it in Part VII.

266. *See* more about it in Ch. 12.

According to the Government Decree No. 155 of 2016. (VI.13.) on the simple notification of the construction of a residential building, in force from Jan. 1, 2017, in case of the construction of a new residential building with a total useful floor area of no more than 300 square meters, it is mandatory to conclude designer's liability insurance for the compensation of damage caused by the architect or other professional designer with a direct contractual relationship with the builder within the scope of undertaken planning and design management activities. The liability insurance contract requires the main contractor too. The insurance contract provides coverage for damages caused under its scope and occurring no later than three years after the termination of the contract.

the insurer covers only the damage caused by activities carried out during the insurance period, and it also turns out during the insurance period, and the insurer is notified about the damage. It is especially problematic in case of professional liability insurances because damage could occur, often, many years after carrying out the activity (if a professional error was committed). Many insurers offer solutions to this situation; therefore, the insurance also covers damage which arises from errors committed before the creation of the insurance. Of course, it is required that the damage becomes known after the conclusion of the insurance contract. This extension is called retroactive coverage or the extension of the temporal scope, and it also has an additional fee.

On this basis, the insurer's risk coverage also covers claims that constitute an insured event, the cause of which arose before the insurance was taken out but of which the insured was not aware, provided that the claim was notified to the insurer during the period of risk coverage. In this case, the insurer may also cover claims for damage and non-pecuniary loss caused within the period specified in the insurance contract (e.g., within one year before the commencement of the risk).

Another way of extending the temporal scope offered by the insurance conditions that—for an extra cost—the risk covers not only reported damage caused during the term of the insurance contract but also the duration of the contract is extended for the future (e.g., for five years from the termination of the contract).[267]

Of course, the insurance contracts may contain exclusions or limits of risk.

The insurance contract usually provides coverage—among others—for the costs of the lawyers or experts incurred, up to the extent determined in the contract.

In the following, we analyze—without detailed description—what the insurance contracts cover on the basis of the general conditions in the insurance market. In some areas, the insurer provides service in the form of an association to its members (e.g., accountants and lawyers). It is also typical that the insurance contracts provide coverage in case of damage to life, physical integrity, and health to the payment of restitution (which is not the element of the damage according to the Hungarian law), to which the insurer is obliged, under Hungarian law, in respect of the violation of the rights relating to the personality.

§1. Liability Insurance of the Employer

224. The insurance companies provide coverage—up to the extent and according to the conditions laid down in the contract—for claims of damages which are supported and opposed against the insured because of a work accident of a person in his/her employment (or in a relationship of public servant, Government service, or voluntary cooperative membership of public interest) and to which the employer is responsible, under Hungarian law.

267. E.g., Architectural designer has a liability insurance contract when designing a family house. After three years he retires, cancels his professional indemnity insurance. After five years, the house collapses (the liability insurance contract has been cancelled for two years), according to the professional opinion, there is a design defect. According to the insurance contract, the cover extends to damage caused by professional errors during the contract period until five years after the contract expires.

§2. Liability Insurance for Service

225. This type of insurance provides coverage—according to the extent and conditions laid down in the contract—for the material damage of the contracting parties of the insured persons caused by the performance of the service provided by the insured or by his/her defective performance (e.g., the painter breaks the window glass with his ladder during the painting), for the payment of restitution directly related to material damage.

The conditions of the contract offered an opportunity—subject to a special agreement—to extend the risks, for example, to:

- damage in the assets in the possession of or rented, leased, borrowed, deposited, or safeguarded by the insured person;
- the liability of damages of the insured person as the lessor of the real estate;
- the liability of damages of the insured person as the lessor of the machinery, equipment, and other objects;
- damage in assets for which the insured person provides his/her service.

§3. Liability Insurance for an Activity[268]

226. This form of insurance contract covers personal injuries and tortuous damage in property caused by the insured person outside his/her service activity as defined in the contract (e.g., during a construction activity, a balcony falls down to a passer due to defective performance).

§4. Product Liability Insurance[269]

227. In Hungary, the Product Liability Directive[270] was implemented in a separate Act[271] at first. During the codification of the CC, it was inserted in the Code which regulates the liability of the manufacturer for damage caused by defective

268. It is not too easy to differentiate between the liability insurance for an activity and for the service.

269. Fazekas Judit, *Hannibal ante portas! Autonóm járművek—Termékfelelősség—Biztosítás* [Hannibal ante portas! Autonomous Vehicles—Product liability—Insurance]. In Barta Judit (ed.), *Biztosítás, több szem-szögéből. Ünnepi kötet Ujváriné dr. Antal Edit c. egyetemi docens 65. születésnapja tiszteletére.* Novotni Alapítvány-Patrocinium Kiadó, Mikolc-Budapest (2019), 139–163.

Ujváriné Antal Edit, *Termékfelelősség* [Product Liability]. In, Barta Judit, Barzó Tímea & Csák Csilla (szerk.), *Magyarázat a kártérítési jogról.* Budapest (Wolters Kluwer Kiadó 2018), Part I, Ch. *3/2.6, 146–163.*

Ujváriné Antal Edit, *A termékfelelősség* [Product Liability]. In Barzó Tímea & Papp Tekla (ed.), Civilisztika II. Dologi jog—Felelősségtan, Scientia Rerum Politicarum, Budapest (Dialóg Campus Kiadó 2019), Part II, Ch. IV/3., 345–357.

https://nkerepo.uni-nke.hu/xmlui/bitstream/handle/123456789/12659/web_PDF_ATMA_Civilisztika_II.pdf?sequence=1.

270. Council Directive 85/374/EEC of Jul. 25, 1985 on the approximation of the laws, regulations and administrative provisions of the Member States concerning liability for defective products.

271. Act X of 1993.

products among the non-contractual liability.[272] On the basis of a product liability insurance contract, the insurance company provides coverage—according to the extent and conditions laid down in the contract—for claims of compensation which are supported and opposed against the insured person for the personal injuries and property damage caused by a defective product manufactured by the manufacturer. Some insurers also provide coverage for the damage caused during the provision of the service.

§5. LIABILITY INSURANCE FOR ENVIRONMENTAL POLLUTION

228. Sudden, unexpected, and unforeseen environmental pollution can be subject to insurance coverage, which could be traced back to an event other than the normal operating activity caused even by an omission, to which the company can be held liable under Hungarian law. In this area, it is a particularly significant problem that although the insurance obligation is prescribed in some areas, the minimum amount which the insurance company has to provide as coverage is usually not defined. In Hungary, the most serious industrial disaster of recent times was the so-called red mud accident of Ajka in 2010. Serious environmental pollution caused the death of ten persons and damaged the health of over 150 persons. The wall of a dam of 400 × 600 square meters which contained the by-product of alumina, the red mud, broke through, and the effluent, more than 1 million cubic meters of red mud, flooded three towns. The highly alkaline, caustic industrial waste spread out about 40 square kilometers, causing inestimable economic and ecological damage in the area and also polluting two rivers, the Raba and the Danube. The company responsible for the damage only had liability insurance with a minimum (HUF 10 million) amount. The home insurance contract did not cover the damage relating to industrial disasters. The restoration of the damage after the red mud catastrophe cost a total of HUF 38 billion to the Hungarian Government of which the restoration of environmental damage cost HUF 21 billion.[273]

§6. PROFESSIONAL LIABILITY

229. The most typical areas of profession liability are the following: tax advisers (accountants), contractors providing security services, health and social activities, pharmacies, pharmacists, independent financial intermediaries, forensic experts, public procurement consultants, common representatives of condominiums, private investigators, architecture, design, engineering, technical inspection activities, educational institutions, health (animal health) and social activities, contractors providing property protection services, lawyers, notaries, bailiffs, etc.

272. Ujváriné Dr. Antal Edit, *Felelősségtan* [Law of Liability]. Budapest (Patrocinium Publisher 2017), 149–159.
Dr. Fuglinszky Ádám, *Kártérítési jog* [Law on Damage Compensation]. Budapest (Hvgorac Publisher 2015), 588–669.

273. https://hu.wikipedia.org/wiki/Ajkai_v%C3%B6r%C3%B6siszap-katasztr%C3%B3fa.

Among the professional liability insurances, insurance obligation appears in several areas; therefore, the insurers offer their services taking into consideration the regulatory requirements. In many cases (e.g., health insurance.), the insurance covers damage caused not only by the insured person but also by other persons who are in an employment relationship or in other relationships of work with the insured person during the performance of the insured activity and in connection with it.

Recently, the liability insurance of the executive officers and the members of the supervisory board came particularly into the fore because of the more and stricter liability rules relating to them. These persons are basically responsible towards the company, but in some cases determined by law, they are also liable to the creditors (e.g., in case of a risk of insolvency if the executive officer does not take into account the interests of the creditors and, therefore, the company's assets are not enough for the satisfaction of the claims). In general, the insurance contracts provide coverage for the damages caused to the company in this kind of activity, but there are also insurance products (mainly the products offered by insurance companies seated in the USA) which provide coverage for damage caused to third parties.

The rising expectations (up-to-date knowledge of the continuously changing legislation, a high level of professionalism) towards the auditors (tax advisors, accountants) mean the strengthening of liability against them. The professional omission of these persons may lead to the imposition of fines which the insurers take over for an additional fee, up to the limit specified in the contract. The auditors set up their own insurance association.

According to the Government Decree No. 155 of 2016. (VI.13.) on the simple notification of the construction of a residential building, in force from January 1, 2017, in case of the construction of a new residential building with a total useful floor area of no more than 300 square meters, it is mandatory to conclude designer's liability insurance for the compensation of damage caused by the architect or other professional designer with a direct contractual relationship with the builder within the scope of undertaken planning and design management activities.[274]

§7. Private Life Liability Insurance

230. The insured event is usually damage—caused exclusively as a private individual listed in the contract—to property and person of another person which has to be compensated by the insured person under Hungarian law and under the performance of which the insured person is exempted by the insurer according to the conditions defined in the contract:

- owner, tenant, user of the insured property (e.g., storer of fuel oil, user of gas cylinders, gas tanks, operator of electric household equipment);

274. *See*: Barta Judit, *Szakmai felelősségbiztosítás—tervezői felelősségbiztosítás* [Professional Liability Insurance—Designer Liability Insurance]. In Dr. Barta Judit (szerk.), *Biztosítás, több szemszögéből. Ünnepi kötet Ujváriné dr. Antal Edit c. egyetemi docens 65. születésnapja tiszteletére*. Novotni Alapítvány-Patrocinium Kiadó, Miskolc-Budapest (2019), 209–223.

- pedestrian causing a road accident;
- user of a bicycle, wheelchair, or manually operated means of transport;
- operator of non-motorized water vehicles (except sailing boats);
- pet owners (except dog owners).

Furthermore, insurance can be concluded for additional risks too (e.g., sports liability; child liability, according to which the insured person as the custodian of the tortfeasor child can be held liable under Hungarian law for personal and material damage caused to third parties; dog owner liability risk).

A private life liability insurance covers not only damage but also restitution in the case of damage to life, physical integrity, and health.

The insurance usually does not cover the loss of benefits and the penalties.

Chapter 7. Motor Vehicle Insurance

Edit Antal Ujvári

231. The motor vehicle insurance concerns two areas of insurance law: on the one hand, the vehicle, as an asset, can be covered by indemnity insurance; on the other hand, the coverage of the damage caused by the operation of the motor vehicle could be provided by liability insurance. The legal regulation and the practice of motor vehicle liability insurance will be analyzed in Part IV; therefore, here, we only present the characteristics of the insurance contracts for the vehicle as an asset.

The insurance companies generally offer the vehicle insurances in a package, i.e., compulsory insurance and property insurance together, offering significant advantages in such cases. The scope of the insurances covers Europe.

The comprehensive insurance—by the choice of the contracting party—includes theft, breakage, natural disaster, damage to the glass, etc. Countless additional insurance can be concluded, e.g., assistance service for technical failure, chauffeur service, legal aid, rental car service, baggage insurance, and accident insurance for passengers injured in a vehicle. Within the framework of supplementary insurance, additional transportation insurance could, in case of full loss, if the vehicle has to be saved, stored, or transported, provide cover, up to the amount specified in the contract.

There are bonus allowances for damage-free years in motor vehicle property insurance as well, but they differ according to the insurance companies. Some insurers give a discount from the basic fee, others reimburse the discount at the end of the insurance period. In case of a loss of interest, the CASCO bonus can be transferred to the CASCO contract of another vehicle, although this benefit can be enforced in a short time (usually one year).

Chapter 8. Legal Expenses Insurance

Edit Antal Ujvári

232. The history of legal expenses insurance is relatively short, although it is now more and more significant. This type of insurance is regulated as a self-insurance activity and as a type of contract, according to EU law.[275] The legal expenses insurance is regulated in section 4 Point 48 of BIns.:

> Legal expenses insurance shall mean a policy offering coverage of costs of litigation along with other services for a premium, such as, in particular:
>
> (a) indemnification of loss suffered by, and restitution awarded to, the insured person by way of out-of-court settlement or in civil or criminal proceedings,
> (b) defense or representation of the insured person in civil, criminal, administrative or other proceedings or if a claim is filed against the insured person for compensation for damages or for any claim for restitution.[276]

233. According to the regulation in the pursuit of legal expenses insurance:

(a) the insurance company employees engaged in the settlement of legal expenses claims and the employees providing legal advice are not performing the same or similar services in any of the insurance company's other divisions or for any other insurance company in connection with any class of insurance defined in law and that any senior executive of the insurance company installed as a superior officer for these employees shall not be installed in a similar position in connection with the settlement of claims in other branches of insurance;
(b) the insurance company entrusts another organization, whose name and address are indicated in the legal expenses insurance contract, for the management of legal expenses claims and for providing legal advice in respect thereof; or
(c) the insurance contract states that the insured party is entitled to appoint a legal representative of his/her choice to represent his/her interests upon the occurrence of an insurance event. The insurance company may propose a legal representative, upon the express written request of the policyholder, if the policyholder does not wish to exercise his right of choosing a legal representative. The insurance company shall offer at least three legal representatives for the policyholder to choose from.

Under special authority:

(a) the insurance company's employees assigned to handle legal expenses claims and provide legal advice in respect thereof;

275. Solvency II Directive.
276. The detailed rules are regulated by ss. 160–166 of the BIns.

(b) the authorized representatives of a company delegated by the insurance company for handling legal expenses claims and for providing legal advice in respect thereof;

are entitled to provide representation for the insured person in any administrative or court proceedings unless otherwise provided for by law.

234. The settlement of claims shall be entrusted only to a limited company, a private limited-liability company, or the branch of a foreign-registered company specializing in the management of legal expenses claims, provided it does not have any financial, commercial or administrative links with the insurance company and it is not in any direct or indirect relationship that may have any effect on impartiality in the settlement of claims and whose other activities shall not obstruct its objectivity in terms of the management of claims.

Information between the legal expenses insurance company and the company entrusted with the management of claims shall take place under adequate facilities to prevent the legal expenses insurance company from using such data in connection with the settlement of claims arising from other classes of insurance contracts.

235. In case of legal expenses insurance, the terms and conditions of a contract for legal expenses insurance shall expressly provide:

(a) The free choice, of the insured person, of a lawyer in any court or administrative proceedings, or before the opening of such proceedings, or in any proceeding aimed at reaching a settlement without such proceedings, where this is deemed necessary to represent or serve his/her interests.[277]
(b) The designation of an unbiased arbitration procedure in which the parties are required to participate in case of any disagreement between the insurance company and the insured person in connection with the insurance company's services. If the outcome of the arbitration procedure is in favor of the insured person, the costs of the procedure shall be borne by the insurance company; otherwise, the policyholder and the insurance company shall cover their own expenses. Unless otherwise stipulated in the insurance contract, the insured person shall have the right to retain a lawyer of his/her choice in the event of any disagreement. If the lawyer adopts the position of the insured person, the insurance company shall be required to proceed accordingly. If there is a dispute between the insurance company and the insured person in connection with the insurance company's services, the insurance company shall be required to inform the insured party in writing about his/her possibilities.

277. The European Court of Justice in its *Eschig* case (C-199/08) argued that the right to free choice of lawyer does not depend on the conflict of interest; the insured person is entitled to it in all procedure. The judicial practice is analyzed in Dr. Zavodnyik József, *Jogértelmezés a biztosítási piacon. Az uniós jogszabályok értelmezése az előzetes döntéshozatali eljárások során.* [Legal Interpretation In The Insurance Market. Interpretation of Union Laws During Preliminary Rulings] Biztosítás és Kockázat, Vol. II/4, 35.

(c) The right of the insured person to the free choice of a legal representative to represent or serve his/her interests arising out of, or in connection with, the insurance contract if the procedure fails.
(d) The advice for the insured person, in writing or in some other verifiable manner, of his/her rights in case of any conflict with the insurance company.
(e) The rules of the procedure to be followed by the parties if two or more adverse parties have legal expenses or liability insurance coverage with the same insurance company in connection with an event that serves as the basis of the insurance company's obligation to provide services.

236. If legal expenses insurance is provided as part of an insurance contract covering other risks as well, the legal expenses section of the insurance contract shall be clearly separated so that it may be easily identified by the clients.

The insurance company shall be required to draw attention to the existence of legal expenses coverage on all of the documents that are supplied to the client; furthermore, the premium payable for legal expenses insurance shall be shown separately from all other premiums in the currency in which the policyholder is required to pay the insurance premium.

In Hungarian insurance practice, legal expenses insurance does not generally form part of the basic insurances, but it can be concluded as an additional (add-on) insurance or as a stand-alone form of insurance. Legal expenses insurance can be concluded as a private person and as an employee or as a collective group legal expenses insurance.

237. The main types of legal expenses insurance are, in particular:

(a) Transport legal protection: the protection against damage caused by a motor vehicle operated by the insured person or by a foreign motor vehicle driven by the insured person.
(b) Legal protection for practitioners of a profession.
(c) Family protection.
(d) Legal protection in connection with an ownership or rental of a real estate, even for residential communities.

238. Legal expenses insurance contracts typically provide coverage for the following:

(a) The support of the insured person with professionals specialized for the settlement of damage claims, jurists employed by the insurance company, or a lawyer selected by the insurer.
(b) The risks of the total cost, up to the insurance limit, according to the following:
   - the usual fees of a lawyer chosen by the insured person;
   - the procedural duty of litigation;
   - the court and court bailiff fees;
   - the costs of witnesses summoned by the court and experts appointed by the court;

– the costs of the court opponent, which the insured person is obliged to pay on the basis of the court decision.

Chapter 9. Aviation and Space Insurance

Judit Barta

239. Section 69 of *Act XCVII of 1995 on air transport* lists the activities for which the conclusion of liability insurance is compulsory.

The operation of a public airport, a registered civil aircraft or an aircraft not obliged to be registered, as well as the civilian air traffic control activity can only be carried out under the coverage of liability insurance.

A license for the operation of a public airport, for civilian air traffic control activity, and for the carrying out of an aviation activity can only be issued in case of a coverage of liability insurance.

The prerequisite for the authorization of aviation activity for economic purposes is the existence of liability insurance under Article 11 of Regulation (EC) No. 1008/2008, Regulation (EC) No. 785/2004 of the European Parliament and of the Council of April 21, 2004, on insurance requirements for air carriers and aircraft operators, and Regulation (EU) No. 285/2010 of April 6, 2010, modifying this.

The compulsory liability insurance concluded by the operator has to include compensation for damage caused to third parties by the conduct of the aircraft or by the persons serving on the board of the aircraft.

The detailed rules of compulsory liability insurance are determined, in a decree, by the Government.

According to Government Decree No. 39/2001. (III.5.) on compulsory aviation liability insurance, the insurance should cover, at least, death, restitution in connection with death, bodily injury, and actual damage to property.

The decree defines the minimum amount of liability insurance in respect of the following:

- non-contractual damage caused by aircraft operators not covered by the Regulation 785/2004/EC;
- damage in connection with the operation of a public airport operator;
- damage in connection with the civilian air traffic control activity;
- contractual damage in connection with aviation activity (passenger's death, physical injury or damage in their luggage, or, in case of freight and mail transportation, the damage in the freight and the consignment).

240. The maximum insurance sum of damage that occurred in connection with the activity, without financial compensation, of an aircraft with a maximum take-off weight of 2,700 kg is XDR 100,000 (special drawing right) per passenger.

In case of any insurance coverage, the excess shall not exceed 5% of the insurance sum.

The insurance obligations defined in the regulation should include cover for any damage caused by potential violent activities (war risks).

The existence of insurance coverage is certified by a certificate issued by the insurer.

The operator of the aircraft is required to keep the certificate of insurance onboard the aircraft and present it to the officials entitled to the control on request. In the absence of a valid certificate, the aircraft cannot operate for air travel.

The operator of the aircraft can conclude an air accident insurance for the conductors of the aircraft and its staff for accidents in connection with the use of the aircraft. The usage of the aircraft includes when the aircraft is rolling on the ground or when the insured persons aboard have left the machine.

Insurance can be concluded for the aircraft themselves, for the damage in them. This covers damages in the aircraft in flight, while taxiing, when standing, and on landing.

Chapter 10. Theft and Embezzlement Insurance

Edit Antal Ujvári

241. Insurance for events of burglary and robbery can be covered by insurance concluded in private life or by corporate property insurance. It is usually a part of basic insurance, but sometimes these kind of risks are only covered in case of a conclusion of an additional insurance.

The concept of both insurance events is defined in the insurance contract, which is not necessarily the same as the criminal law definition.

Burglary is usually an insurance event when the perpetrator enters a closed room using violence and steals the insured asset. Robbery is an insured event when a perpetrator takes away a thing to which he/she is not entitled, by force or threat, against life or bodily integrity. Insurers generally undertake the damage to property caused in connection with these insured events (for a limited amount).

The contracts prescribe additional conditions if the burglary or the robbery is committed for assets stored in containers (safes, wall safes, etc.).

It is essential to point out in this context that the BIns. explicitly stipulates that the insurer shall determine, in the terms and conditions of the insurance contract, what kind of services he/she will provide and against the presentation of what kind of documents in case of the occurrence of the insurance event. Insurance companies may demand, as a precondition for payment of settlement, documents which are deemed necessary to verify the occurrence of the insured event, or for determining the extent of compensation to be provided, and may not render the payment of settlement subject to the final and binding conclusion of any criminal or misdemeanor proceedings that may have been opened in connection with the insured event notified. Therefore, the law breaks this insurance practice, which lasted several decades, according to which the payment of settlement was always the subject to the final and binding conclusion of proceedings against the perpetrator, because of which the payments usually dragged on.

Embezzlement insurance is less typical in the Hungarian market. However, U.S.-based insurance companies usually offer coverage where an employee has committed robbery, fraud, embezzlement, or any other criminal act, alone or in groups, with premeditation, which resulted in damage by the loss of money or any property to the employer.

A special insurance method is the so-called supplementary insurance, linked to the fleet CASCO insurance, which provides coverage for the embezzlement of the insured motor vehicle. The additional insurance may only be concluded with the theft insurance contract.

Chapter 11. Agricultural Insurance, Hail Insurance, Livestock Insurance

Judit Barta

242. The main groups of agricultural insurance are the following:

- plant insurance;
- animal insurance; and
- forest insurance.

The stock of plant insurance is the largest, the stock of animal insurance remained below 4% in 2019, and the stock of forest insurance is minimal.[278]

§1. Plant Insurance

243. Similar to other countries, extreme weather, which makes the agricultural industry extremely vulnerable, causes more and more problems in Hungary as well. Therefore, the Hungarian Government started supporting, since 2012, agricultural insurance premiums, developed and approved, in advance, by the relevant ministry within the limits set by law. *Act CLXVIII of 2011 on the management of weather and other natural risks affecting agricultural production* allows state support within the framework of tenders for agricultural insurance fees, concluded for the coverage of certain weather risks, set out by law (section 16). This system created a risk community for the mitigation of the risk impact caused by the weather, with the participation of farmers concerned, and provided the possibility for the strengthening of the farmers based on their self-reliance.

In addition to the fee-subsidized agricultural insurance, traditional plan insurances can also be concluded. In the case of non-fee-subsidized plant insurance, most people conclude insurance for ice, fire and storm damage.[279]

§2. Forest Insurance

244. Of more than 2 million hectares of forest in Hungary, less than 100,000 hectares (about 5%) are insured. Three insurance companies deal with forest insurances. Their total annual income is only a few multiples of HUF 10 million. The basic insurance always involves damage caused by fire, hail, or storm. The additional insurance may also cover damage which occurs only in forests, such as snow, ice, and freezing rain damage. The payment of the insurer is not linked to the damage but to its prevention. For example, the insurer undertakes the costs of the prevention of damages caused by twenty-one species of insects, including the gypsy

278. http://repo.aki.gov.hu/3557/1/Mezőgazdasági%20biztosítások%202019.%20év.pdf.
279. *Ibid.*

moth, which has caused great damage in recent years. The insurance premium will depend on whether the forest consists of evergreen pines or hard-or soft-leaved trees. The basis of the fee is the cost of specific installations—per hectare—in case of a fresh forest, while it is the exploitable amount of the wood in case of an older forest. The annual insurance premium begins from 0.8% of them and can rise to 2.7% of them in case of total protection.[280]

§3. Insurance of Breeding Animals, Livestock, and Horses

245. Within the framework of the insurance for breeding animals, livestock, and horses, an insurer covers the losses in horses, breeding cattle, pigs, sheep, and goats due to illness and accident. The insurance provides compensation in case of death or the emergency slaughtering of the insured animals.

As a supplementary insurance, a so-called additional cost insurance can be concluded, which covers expenses which arise in case of infectious diseases (e.g., mouth and nail disease, swine fever, etc.), resulting in a notification obligation and regulatory extermination of livestock (cattle, pig, sheep, goat), set out in the Animal Health Act. The compensation will help in the reestablishment of the insured livestock farms.

There are insurances for poultry, which provide sickness and accident insurance for a variety of species of farmed poultry (chickens, ducks, geese, turkeys). The insurances provide compensation in case of the death or the emergency slaughtering of the insured animals.

There also are insurances for natural disasters, which covers damage caused by fire, lightning, storm, hail, flood, earthquake, landslide, unknown cavern collapse, and the failure of water and steam lines to the farm animals (cattle, pig, sheep, goats and poultry). The insurances provide guaranteed compensation in case of the death of the insured animals.

Within the framework of livestock and breeding animals' insurance, only the animals registered in the official records, provided with chips, tattoos, or other official marks, can be insured.

The animals can be insured up to a defined age. In case of animal disease as the insured event, insurance companies stipulate a waiting time, which is usually sixty to ninety days. The condition for the conclusion of an insurance contract is the disclosure of data about the stock concerned (about their state, illnesses, deaths, etc.) back to three years.

The insurance contracts contain a number of exclusions, e.g., depreciation of the animal due to its age and flaw, the cut of the animal based on these reasons (culling), the cut of the animal due to chronic disease, the cut of the animal because its keeping is not efficient further (technological culling).

The total number of animals of the same age group kept on the same premises has to be provided. If the actual number is greater than the number of insured animals, proportional payment has to be carried out.

280. https://erdo-mezo.hu/index.php/hirek/olvas/erdeszeti-biztositas-egy-kiaknazatlan-terulet.

§4. Other Types of Insurance Contracts

246. For enterprises operating in the agriculture sector, the insurance companies offer agricultural property insurance, which provides coverage for general and specific assets of the rural sites and factories, as well as occupational accident insurance and liability insurance.

Chapter 12. Catastrophe Insurance

§1. Nuclear Risks

Edit Antal Ujvári

247. Insurers do not cover the risk of a nuclear explosion or nuclear radiation events. Based on the authorization of section 67 Point (g) of the Act CXVI of 1996 on nuclear energy, the Hungarian Government—taking into consideration Decree No. 24/1990 (II.7.) on the ratification of the International Convention on Civil Liability for Nuclear Damage undersigned in Vienna, May 21, 1963—adopted the Government Decree No. 227/1997. (XII.10.) on the nature, conditions, and amount of insurance, or other financial cover, for nuclear liability. According to this, the licensee of the nuclear installation is obliged to have a contract providing insurance (liability insurance) or other financial coverage for the reimbursement of nuclear damage arising from his/her nuclear liability towards a third party.

The licensee is entitled to conclude liability insurance contracts with more insurance companies and conclude contracts for the purpose of undertaking financial coverage with more credit institutions. The presence of liability insurance or other financial collateral and the existence of the statutory requirements relating to them may be verified by the authority with the licensee. The organization with the liability insurance or other financial collateral shall not terminate or suspend the contract unless the termination or suspension has been notified, in writing, to the licensee, and to the body defined in the law, at least two months in advance.

The liability of the licensee is strict; there is no room for exculpation unless the licensee proves that the nuclear damage occurred due to an unavoidable nuclear accident that falls beyond the realm of nuclear activity (armed conflict, war, civil war, armed uprising, and extraordinary natural disaster).

The licensee is, wholly or partially, exempt from liability if he/she proves that the nuclear damage was, wholly or partly, the result of the gross negligence or the deliberate and unavoidable act or omission of the person claiming compensation for nuclear damage suffered by him/her.

Except for statutory exceptions, the limitation or exclusion of liability for nuclear damage shall be null and void.

In case of nuclear power plants, nuclear heating plants, and installations producing and processing nuclear fuel, the amount of the absolute liability of the licensee shall not exceed XDR 100 million per nuclear accident that occurred in the installation; in case of other nuclear installations and during the transport or storage of nuclear fuel it shall not exceed XDR 5 million. The Hungarian state reimburses the nuclear damage which exceeds these sums, but the total amount of the compensation for nuclear damage cannot exceed XDR 300 million.

§2. Natural Catastrophes

Judit Barta

248. In Hungary, the following natural risks are included in the property insurance coverage: earthquake, landslide, flood, inland water, storms, rainstorms, hailstones, snowstorms, clouds, and lightning strikes.

As water damage, the insurer reimburses the physical damages of the insured assets caused by flood, drift, breakage, destruction, and contamination resulting from large amounts of water from flood, inland water, or rainstorm.

As earth movement damages, the insurer reimburses damage in the insured property caused by landslide, rockslide, or collapse of unknown structures or cavities.

As storm damage, the insurers cover:

- physical damage in the insured assets caused by the pression and suction effect (e.g., breaking of roofs);
- damage caused by the objects drifted by the storm;
- damage caused by the object falling due to the storm (e.g., fallen poles and trees);
- damage caused by rain, snow, or ice during storms (e.g., crash of glass windows, leak of roofs).

Storms are generally considered to be air movements in which the strongest winds reach or exceed the speed of 75 kilometers per hour.

Insurers do not compensate damage caused, by storm, to the temporary collateral (film, tarpaulin, etc.) for protection from weather, in the glazing of greenhouses, in the overlaid structures, buildings, exterior plastering, envelopes, paintings, landslides, landslides, and in freely stored property.

Hailstorm is a precipitation in the form of ice crystals, of varying sizes, causing damage to the roof, facades or exterior structures of buildings, structures, and car bodies (in the form of bumps).

The insurer reimburses the damages caused to the insured buildings, structures, and the movable property therein by the snow load exceeding the normal amount.

In Hungary, most of the problems are typically caused by floods (53.6%), extreme temperatures (17.9%), and storms (17.9%). According to the data of the AHIC, most of the storms with sudden rainfall and high precipitation within a relatively short period and with strong gusts occur from the beginning of May to the end of August. According to the experience over the recent years, 100,000–130,000 damage events were reported in this period.[281]

In Hungary, earthquakes occur rarely. January 2014 was the last such event, which resulted in 2,500 insurance claims.

Despite the frequent damage caused by extreme weather, the number of home insurances has decreased by 93,000 since 2010. According to the data of the AHIC, the insurance companies managed 2.98 million individual home insurance contracts at the end of 2013.

281. https://mabisz.hu/tag/vihar/.

In light of growing earthquake, storm, or flood damages, it is a particularly bad tendency that the number of individual home insurance contracts has decreased by some 93,000 since 2010, and the decreasing number of individual insurance contracts could only be partially compensated by condominium housing insurance contracts.

In 2016, the housing insurance stock started to grow, which is also due to the boom in the real estate market and real estate lending.

The level of home insurance premiums is low in a European context, and the protection against natural damage belongs to the basic coverage in the Hungarian market. In Hungary, insurers do not undertake insurance against damage in adobe houses, greenhouses, and foil tassels.

Protection against natural damage can also be found beyond home insurance in corporate property insurance and motor vehicle property insurance.

Chapter 13. Credit and Caution Insurance

Judit Barta

249. In Hungary, a separate Act, Act XLII of 1994 on the Establishment and Activities of the Hungarian Export Credit Insurance Limited Company, founded Mehib Plc., after the change of regime, in 1994. Its owner is 100% the Hungarian state; the shareholders' rights are exercised by one of the ministers acting on behalf of the state. Mehib is a private limited company. For its insurance activity, the regulation of BIns. shall be applied with the derogations contained in the Act governing Mehib Plc.

The activities of Mehib Plc. cover *marketable and non-marketable* insurance, reinsurance, and related information services in the following insurance sectors:

(a) loans;
(b) guarantees;
(c) various financial losses.

Mehib Plc. has the right to perform export-related foreign trade transactions, international aid operations, supplier transactions, export-oriented investments, foreign investments and domestic sales by Hungarian investors, and travel organization services performed by Hungarian companies or by Hungarian branch or representative of foreign companies. Mehib Plc. can also provide foreign exchange risk arising from the abovementioned activities separately.

The Government ensures the long-term and stable functioning of Mehib Plc.

The state undertakes a first-loss guarantee for the fulfillment of the payment obligations arising from insurance and reinsurance commitments of Mehib Plc. under the terms of the law and Government decrees.

The provisions of the BIns. shall not apply to the activity of Mehib Plc. performed under the first-loss guarantee of the state.

The mission of Mehib Plc. is:

- to encourage and assist external relations;
- to promote export;
- to share financial risks which cannot be guaranteed by traditional market instruments;
- to facilitate funding;
- to increase the competitiveness of enterprises;
- to reduce the risks of export-related lending and guarantee with state-based insurance products.

The parties of the insurance are, on the one hand, Mehib Plc., as an insurer or reinsurer, and on the other hand:

(a) a Hungarian company undertaking foreign trade activity;

(b) a Hungarian company directly or indirectly investing in a foreign enterprise if the risk coverage of Mehib Plc. covers the transaction;
(c) financial institutions (banks, credit institutions);
(d) a domestic enterprise providing travel services for short-term transactions as an insured person; or
(e) a foreign-based credit insurer or a domestic credit insurer, as a reinsured person.

The clients of Mehib Plc. are:

- financing banks;
- large companies;
- small- and medium-sized enterprises (SMEs);
- travel companies (travel agencies).

In all cases, Mehib Plc. assists exporters through their individual and general-purpose insurance products provided directly to companies or indirectly to financing banks. Most of the potential exporters come from SMEs.

Among short-term transactions,[282] the pharmaceuticals, processing, machine, food, and chemical industries are the largest insured companies.

In case of medium- or long-term transactions,[283] the unique, high-value export of goods of consumers is ensured.

In connection with foreign investments, the export of Hungarian machinery and equipment or the provision of services by a Hungarian company and of complex projects implemented abroad by Hungarian exporters are insured.

Mehib Plc. has insurance products covering all the cycles of export businesses, which cover the various risks, from the conclusion of the business to the delivery to the payment.

Mehib Plc. provides factoring transactions and loans to banks.

Characteristics of short-term export credit insurance contracts are:

- low excess (5%-10%), which can be 1% in case of banks;
- services with listed price, under the same conditions for everyone;
- framework insurance contracts for an undetermined period with annual insurance periods; new purchasers may be involved in the insurance at any time during the year.

There is a type which typically provides insurance coverage for larger companies exporting to customers in non-marketable countries. Supplementary insurance can be concluded for manufacturing risks.

For factoring companies, the insurance covers the purchased claims receivables after delivery.

---

282. *Short-term transaction:* transaction in which the insured total risk period including the manufacturing period and the duration of the loan is less than two years.
283. *Medium- or long-term transactions:* transaction in which the insured total risk period including the manufacturing period and the duration of the loan is at least two years.

The type developed for medium and small businesses provides coverage for payment risks related to exports, including EU and OECD countries. Supplementary insurance can be concluded for manufacturing risks.

Carrier credit insurance provides insurance coverage to the Hungarian exporter when the exporter provides credit to the importer by postponing payment for the consideration of the goods or services delivered.

Purchaser credit insurance provides insurance coverage for payment risks of credit provided by banks for foreign purchasers or foreign banks with the aim to purchase goods and services of Hungarian origin.

Manufacturing risk insurance provides insurance coverage for the risks during the production period, before the performance of the exporter, for the costs of the production of the product or service under a foreign trade contract.

Investment insurance provides coverage for capital and yield invested in a foreign enterprise. It provides protection for the foreign investments of domestic investors in a foreign country, for risk events primarily related to the country, of the investment for up to fifteen years.

Guarantee insurance provides insurance for a tender guarantee, a deposit repayment guarantee, and a warranty guarantee based on the guarantee scheme relating to the whole life cycle of the contract concluded by the insured person.

250. The insurance activities of Mehib Plc. typically covers transactions with the following countries:

- Central and Eastern Europe, especially the countries of the Carpathian Basin.
- CIS countries, in particular Russia and Ukraine.
- Non-EU Member States of the Balkans.
- China, India, certain states of Southeast Asia, North Africa, and the Middle East (to carry out individual transactions of higher value, having a national economic significance).

In relation to insurance modes:

- short-term: Russia, Ukraine, Serbia, Kazakhstan, neighboring EU states, and the Balkan countries;
- medium or long term: Russia, Ukraine and other CIS countries, Romania, and the Western Balkans.

251. The *conditions of non-marketable risk insurance,* which can be undertaken by Mehib Plc. under the first-loss guarantee of the Hungarian state from the central budget, are regulated by *Government Decree No. 312/2001. (XII.28.)*

The Government Decree defines:

- the subject of eligible insurance, *see* the abovementioned modalities;
- the insurance events, such as the insolvency of the contracting party or the insured person, nonpayment, late payment, unlawful termination of the export

contract, unlawful refusal of receipt of export goods, unauthorized bank guarantee calling, unexpected state measures (imposition of an import ban), other political events having a negative impact on the contract, outbreak of war, nuclear disasters, etc.;

- the duration and amount of risk-bearing, the amount of excess which is at least 5% of the total amount of insurance premium for export credit insurance linked to medium- and long-term transactions and at least 20% of the total amount of insurance for all other insurance;
- the main rules for risk evaluation;
- the main aspects of the establishment of insurance premium rates;
- the main aspects of the provisions relating to the reserves obtained from unearned premiums;
- the possibility of reimbursement: according to the Government decree, in case of damage exemption or low damage claims, the reimbursement of the premium may be granted to the insured person;
- the determination of the length of the patience period (30–180 days) in case of payment of damages, which is used to ensure that the insurer can determine whether the damage occurred or whether activities relating to the mitigation of damage have taken place or not;
- the main rules for the notification of claims;

  exception rules other than the exemption rules of the Civil Code relating to indemnity insurance; for example, if the insured person provided false or misleading information to the insurer, if the insured person breached, intentionally or with gross negligence, his obligations arising out of the insurance contract and damage occurs or the amount of risk increases in connection with this, or if the insured person commits a criminal offense in connection with the insured transaction, etc.;
- the rules relating to the obligation to prevent and mitigate damage which exceeds the rules of the CC, whose costs shall be borne by Mehib Plc. and the insured person in proportion to the amount of the liability provided that they are approved by Mehib Plc. These costs include legal costs of proceedings and other legal costs incurred in connection with the minimization or prevention of damage but do not include costs for determining the validity of the damage claim;
- the supplementary terms and conditions of the insurance contract;
- the obligations of the insured (e.g., notification obligation, obligation to mitigate damage) which exceed the rules of the CC, such as an assignment obligation,[284] a transfer obligation,[285] or an inspection obligation.[286]

284. Simultaneously to the payment of damage, the insured person is obliged to assign the claim up to the damages paid and the amount of excess to Mehib Plc. as the representative of the state, together with the right to enforce the claim.

285. The insured is obliged to transfer immediately after the payment of damages any sums received in connection with the insured transaction to Mehib Plc.

286. The insured person must allow Mehib Plc. or his authorized representative to completely look into his books and business correspondence with his debtors in the context of the given insurance relationship.

Chapter 14. Credit Protection Insurances

Judit Barta

252. About the topic of credit protection insurance, *see* Part II, Chapter 6 and Part V, Chapter 5, §2.

Chapter 15. Technical Insurance

Judit Barta

§1. Machinery Fracture Insurance

253. The most widespread product is the so-called machinery fracture insurance. It is unavoidable during the activity of a business that an unexpected fracture or breakage (due to internal or external force) may prevent the proper functioning of a machine or a whole production line and, therefore, make the production or service partially or completely impossible.

The insurance service covers the costs of the repair of the equipment or its replacement with a similar one. Nowadays, practically every type of machine and equipment can be insured, from metalworking machines to helicopter motors to ski elevators.

One especially important machine or several selected machine groups can also be insured.

Most of the products are total risk management insurance, which means they compensate for all damage which is not included in the excluded risks. Exclusions are, e.g., molding or material defects, defective design, improper installation, damage due to the lack of know-how or handling error, damage in water boilers due to water shortage, physical explosion, short circuit, windstorm damage, etc. The insurance can be extended to cover risks of fire and natural damage, burglary, robbery, as well as theft and delivery risks.

§2. Supplementary Fire and Shutdown Insurance[287]

254. The shutdown insurance provides coverage for financial losses due to the occurrence of damage to property. It is a supplementary insurance which means it can only be concluded if the undertaking has a property insurance contract with the insurer concerned. If the basic property insurance contract terminates, the supplementary insurance will also terminate.

The insured event can be fire damage, explosion and collision damage, lightning strike damage, water damage resulting from plumbing, storm damage, water damage resulting from inland water or rainstorm, hail or snow damage, damage resulting from the breakdown of a technological pipeline, damage resulting from a shutdown due to damage caused by aircraft, provided that the underlying valid property insurance covers the damage concerned and the insurer is required to perform the service as a result of the property damage insurance event. Shutdown damage is

287. There is a website where most of the insurance products distributed in Hungary can be found: http://biztositasifeltetelek.hu/?page=3&biztosito=0&modozat=0&ervkezdetmin=&ervkezdetmax=&nyomtatvanyszam=&kereses=hitel&kereses2=&megnevezes=&mutat=50&rendez=0&szerint=erv_kezdete.

the gross loss in profit caused by the insurance events affecting the insured assets, which includes the permanent costs incurred by the insured person during the shutdown period.

§3. Cyber Insurance

255. The demand for cybersecurity and the insurance of good repute also increased in the Hungarian corporate market. Data loss or data theft can be insured in Hungary, but the incidence of cyber-insurance products is far below 10% of the potential market.

At the moment, only a few insurers are dealing in Hungary with cyber-insurance, which aims to mitigate the loss of data loss or data theft. According to this insurance, the insurer not only compensates for the damage but also provides specialists who can help in such crises (data security specialists, IT specialists, lawyers specialized in data protection and PR specialists).

The insurers offering cyber products also provide additional risk management services. Most of the customers do not have internal resources to adequately assess their risk exposure and to effectively reduce it.

The professionals employed by the insurer cover, collectively, almost all the major areas of information security, so they can provide a comprehensive picture of the cybersecurity situation of the contracting person, and they suggest potential solutions to how to change it in order to effectively increase the security. Since total security can never be reached, it is still worthwhile for a company to conclude an insurance contract, and the insurance premium is adjusted to the potential damage and the probability of its occurrence after the proposals have been made. In Hungary, AIG insurance offered a cyber-insurance product for the first time in September 2013.[288] The number of insurers offering the product is constantly expanding.

§4. Business Continuity Service in the Insurance Market[289]

256. Allianz Hungária Insurance Company, in cooperation with one of the major Hungarian electricity companies and an electronics company, has developed an insurance system. Within the framework of this, they jointly provide expert assistance in the event of the occurrence of an unforeseen catastrophe.

Based on the Allianz Global Corporate & Specialty Risk Report from 2016, a survey was also conducted in Hungary. In Hungary, most enterprises are mostly aware of fire and explosion (42%), natural disasters (42%), shutdowns and breakdowns in the supply chain (31%).

Disaster situations can occur for a number of reasons in a company's life, e.g., due to flood, fire, power blackout, bomb alarm or even pipe breaking. All of these events can bring the company to a disadvantage because it has to suspend its business.

288. https://kkvmagazin.com/v/biztositas-kiberbiztonsag-casco-kotelezo-bizalmi-index/.
289. https://mabisz.hu/wp-content/uploads/2019/10/biztositas-es-kockazat-6-evf-3-szam-4-cikk.pdf.

In 2015, the NBH prepared a recommendation for the companies under its jurisdiction (banks, insurance companies, funds, etc.) for the first time, which stipulates what plan, measures and IT protection are required in order to prevent disasters. This was replaced by Recommendation No. 7/2017 (VII.5.) of the NBH on IT system protection.

Therefore, Allianz Hungária Plc. undertakes, as an insurance service, the preparation of a disaster relief plan for the seamless operation as a unique solution in the insurance market and in addition, if there is trouble, Allianz Hungária Plc. provides an auxiliary office for the insured persons within forty-eight hours, where continuous IT and office aid is also provided for the aggrieved company.

In line with the expectations, the insurance service can affect not only the companies within the scope of the NBH but also multinational corporations and SSC service centers, as well as service providers, irrespective of the industry, who are of the utmost importance to ensure continuous business.

In case of a disaster, sixty workstations on 450 square meters can be claimed together with the related infrastructure within the framework of the insurance. With the current technology solutions, a restart within four hours after the occurrence of the disaster event can be achieved.

§5. Construction and Installation Insurance

257. The insurance covers all building constructions and civil engineering equipment, auxiliary equipment and construction machinery in the area of the construction as well as other costs related to damage: costs of cleaning of ruins, expert costs, printing costs of plans and other documents, costs of repairing existing or adjacent buildings can be insured.

Construction and installation insurance is generally an all-risk type of insurance. The insurance covers, e.g.:

- damage in property arising from construction work during the construction, the occurrence of which is sudden, accidental, unforeseeable;
- damage resulting from the theft of construction materials and other secured assets;
- personal and property damage caused to a third party (supplementary liability insurance).

The complete installation work of the insured person, including all necessary structural elements and mounting material, is insured. Furthermore, construction site installations, auxiliary structures, construction machinery, additional costs resulting from the damage (costs of cleaning of ruins, expert costs, printing costs of plans and other documents), and existing works can also be insured.

It is also possible to conclude insurance that covers only installation work, which is usually also an all-risk type of insurance. Insurance coverage includes, e.g.:

- damage in property arising from installation work during the installation, the occurrence of which is sudden, accidental, unforeseeable;

- damage resulting from the theft of construction materials and other secured assets;
- personal and property damage caused to a third party (supplementary liability insurance).

Part IV. Motor Vehicle Insurance

Edit Antal Ujvári

Chapter 1. The Legal Regulations

258. Motor vehicle insurance affects two areas of insurance law:

– insurance of the motor vehicle as an asset, which belongs to the area of indemnity insurance;
– the other area is the liability insurance, which is the coverage of the damage caused by the operation of the motor vehicle.

259. At international level, the need to provide compensation for road users who suffered damage has led to bilateral and multilateral agreements in which participating Member States have undertaken to introduce compulsory insurance in their countries since the middle of the last century. Participants of the Conventions guaranteed that compulsory insurance also provides protection against damages which are caused by the motor vehicle outside the borders of their own country but in the territory of a country, which is the Member of the Convention (Green Card Convention and Licence plate number Convention).[290]

In Hungary, the compulsory motor vehicle liability insurance was governed first by the Government Decree No. 30/1959. (V.10.). Regulation concerning insurance obligation was justified by the fact that Hungary has been part of the Convention since 1961. The insurance network was fully established by the year 1970.[291]

A remarkable stage of the history of motor vehicle liability insurance was, also at international level, when the premiums of compulsory liability insurance were incorporated into gasoline fuel prices, so the insurance relationship was created by law (ex lege), and it eliminated the process of concluding a contract, the registration, the traditional payment of fee, and consequently the lack of insurance coverage too.

290. Since Jul. 1, 2020, AHIC, as the Hungarian National Office, has enabled its members to issue green cards in black and white format, therefore the mandatory green color will no longer be used. https://mabisz.hu/fekete-feher-alapszinnel-bocsatjak-ki-a-jovoben-a-zoldkartyat/.

291. Kiss Eszter, *A kötelező gépjármű-felelősségbiztosítás rövid története és alapvető jellemzői* [Short History and Basic Features of Compulsory Motor Vehicle Liability Insurance]. Debreceni Jogi Műhely, 2013/3, 17–36.

This solution, which has operated since 1982, was replaced by the contractual structure of compulsory liability insurances for motor vehicles from July 1, 1991, which was established in line with the second motor vehicle liability Directive of the Community.

The special rules of compulsory motor vehicle liability insurance can be found in the MVI from January 1, 2010, but the BIns. also contains special provisions in relation to the compulsory liability insurance relationship and to the insurance companies which provide such services.[292] The Act is specialized compared to the rules relating to insurance contract of the CC because the provisions of the CC can be applied to motor vehicle liability insurance contracts if the MVI does not contain different provisions.[293]

---

292. Act LXII of 2009 serves to comply with the following EU legal acts:
   (a) Council Directive 72/166/EEC of Apr. 24, 1972 on the approximation of the laws of Member States relating to insurance against civil liability in respect of the use of motor vehicles, and to the enforcement of the obligation to insure against such liability (Official Journal L 103, 02/05/1972).
   (b) Council Directive 72/430/EEC of Dec. 19, 1972 amending Council Directive 72/166/EEC of Apr. 24, 1972 on the approximation of the laws of the Member States relating to insurance against civil liability in respect of the use of motor vehicles and to the enforcement of the obligation to insure against such liability (Official Journal L 291, 28/12/1972).
   (c) Second Council Directive 84/5/EEC of Dec. 30, 1983 on the approximation of the laws of the Member States relating to insurance against civil liability in respect of the use of motor vehicles (Official Journal L 008, 11/01/1984).
   (d) Third Council Directive 90/232/EEC of May 14, 1990 on the approximation of the laws of the Member States relating to insurance against civil liability in respect of the use of motor vehicles (Official Journal L 129, 19/05/1990).
   (e) Council Directive 90/618/EEC of Nov. 8, 1990 amending, particularly as regards motor vehicle liability insurance, Directive 73/239/EEC and Directive 88/357/EEC which concern the coordination of laws, regulations and administrative provisions relating to direct insurance other than life assurance (Official Journal L 330, 29/11/1990).(f)Directive 2000/26/EC of the European Parliament and of the Council of May 16, 2000 on the approximation of the laws of the Member States relating to insurance against civil liability in respect of the use of motor vehicles and amending Council Directives 73/239/EEC and 88/357/EEC (Fourth motor insurance Directive) (Official Journal L 181, 20/07/2000).
   (g) Directive 2005/14/EC of the European Parliament and of the Council of May 2005 amending Council Directives 72/166/EEC, 84/5/EEC, 88/357/EEC and 90/232/EEC and Directive 2000/26/EC of the European Parliament and of the Council relating to insurance against civil liability in respect of the use of motor vehicles (Official Journal of the European Union L 149/14, 11.6.2005).
   (h) Directive 2009/103/EC of the European Parliament and of the Council of Sep. 16, 2009 relating to insurance against civil liability in respect of the use of motor vehicles, and the enforcement of the obligation to insure against such liability (Official Journal of the European Union L 263/11, 7.10.2009).

   There is a new Directive: Directive (EU) 2021/2118 of the European Parliament and of the Council of Nov. 24, 2021 amending Directive 2009/103/EC relating to insurance against civil liability in respect of the use of motor vehicles, and the enforcement of the obligation to insure against such liability (Official Journal of the European Union, L 430/1, 2.12.2021.).

   By Dec. 23, 2023 Member States shall adopt and publish the measures necessary to comply with this Directive. They shall immediately inform the Commission thereof.
293. Further laws, which contain relevant detailed rules: the Decree No. 21/2011. (VI.10) NGM of the Minister for National Economy on the bonus-malus system and being rated in it, and on the rules for issuing loss history certificates, the Decree No. 20/2009. (X.9.) of the Minister of Finance on

The MVI Act contains the general rules of motor vehicle liability insurance and defines the tasks of the organizations and the main tasks in relation to control and registration.[294]

In connection with insurance contracts for motor vehicle fleets, the parties may derogate from the provisions of this Act in terms of the conclusion and termination of the contract, the period of insurance cover and terms of payment of premiums.

Motor vehicle fleet shall mean a group of motor vehicles for which a policyholder—whether a legal person, private entrepreneur or sole proprietorship—has obtained insurance from a given insurance company, provided that the fleet contains at least five motor vehicles on the first day of the period of insurance cover.

---

the categories of motor vehicles applied in the compulsory motor vehicle liability insurance, the Decree No. 34/2009. (XII.22.) of the Minister of Finance on the rules on certification of compulsory motor liability insurance for motor vehicles in Hungarian place of business and Hungarian place of destination.

294. The appearance of e-scooters in traffic caused a serious debate. The rules of road traffic do not specifically classify it in the category of vehicles, but according to the practice of the authority, the regulations regarding mopeds are requested from those driving them. It means that anything that starts on the accelerator cannot be a bicycle and cannot be driven without a helmet. A liability insurance and a driver's license is also required, and it is forbidden to drive them on the pavement, and people can only drive them with a maximum of 45 km/h on public roads, like all motorcycle riders. https://www.parlament.hu/irom41/07930/07930-0001.pdf The relevant ministry is preparing a proposal to amend the rules of road traffic in relation to the e-scooters.

JD 2022.12.319: Decision No. Bfv.II.442/2022/5. of the Curia stated in a criminal case that the electric scooter is a mechanically propelled vehicle. Therefore, driving it under the influence of alcohol or other psychoactive substances on a public road or on a private road not closed to public traffic constitutes a criminal offense.

Chapter 2. Rules of Damage Liability[295]

260. The liability rules of the CC shall be mentioned as well because the rules of the compulsory motor vehicle liability insurance are based on the Codex.[296] Civil liability insurance covers such tortuous activities, which shall be under liability in accordance with the law.

Therefore, the consent of the injured party of the road accident eliminates the unlawfulness of the tort, and it exempts the insurance company from the liability based on the compulsory liability insurance. (JD2011. 195.) The CC prescribes stricter rules for the liability for hazardous operations, which means that these stricter rules shall be applied to liability relating to operation of motor vehicles (section 6:535 of the CC).

Anyone who engages in activities involving increased risk must compensate for the resulting damage. The operator of the activity involving increased risk is considered to be the one for whose benefit the dangerous plant operates. If the hazardous activity has more than one operator, they must be considered a joint tortfeasor.

The definition of the Civil Code also allows that in case of damage caused by a hazardous activity, it is not the actual user but the person for whose benefit the hazardous activity operated who is responsible according to the liability rules for hazardous activity.[297]

---

295. Ujváriné Dr. Antal Edit, *Biztosítási szerződés* [Insurance Contract] In Majoros Tünde (ed.), *Kereskedelmi szerződések alapvető szabályai* [Basic Rules of Commercial Contracts] Budapest (Patrocinium Publisher 2015), 258–268.

296. The appearance of artificial intelligence in motor vehicle traffic requires a rethinking of new dangers and liability and related insurance issues worldwide.

A significant topic of the 2020–2021 period was the regulation of unmanned aerial vehicles, which opened up a new mandatory liability insurance market for insurers. Act CLXXIX of 2020 on the amendment of certain laws related to the operation of unmanned aircraft (so-called Drone Act) came into force on Jan. 1, 2021. With this Act Hungary fulfilled its legal harmonization obligation. The Drone Act modified Act XCVII of 1995 on Aviation. In addition, Government Decree No. 39/2001 (III.5.) on compulsory aviation liability insurance was also supplemented with regulations on the mandatory liability insurance of drones. However, the regulation of drones did not stop here, the development of additional legal frameworks necessary for harmonized operation is ongoing, as well as the implementation of the technical background.

Fazekas Judit, *Az autonóm mobilitás stratégiai és szabályozási keretei az Európai Unióban* [Strategic and Regulatory Frameworks of Autonomous Mobility in the European Union]. In Lévayné, Fazekas Judit & Kecskés Gábor (szerk.). *Az autonóm járművek és intelligens rendszerek jogi vonatkozásai Győr*, Magyarország, Universitas-Győr Nonprofit Kft. (2020), 348, 221–254.

Pusztahelyi Réka, Mesterséges intelligencia által okozott károk: A no-fault kártalanítási rendszer bevezetésének előnyei és hátrányai [Damage Caused by Artificial Intelligence: Pros and Cons of Introducing a No-Fault Compensation System]. Infokommunikáció és jog 2020/2, (e-különszám). https://infojog.hu/pusztahelyi-reka-mesterseges-intelligencia-altal-okozott-karok-a-no-fault-kartalanitasi-rendszer-bevezetesenek-elonyei-es-hatranyai-2020-2-75-e-kulonszam/.

Pusztahelyi Réka, Toward a European AI Liability System. *Multidiszciplináris Tudományok: A Miskolci Egyetem közleménye* 2021/5, 319–321. https://ojs.uni-miskolc.hu/index.php/multi/article/view/894/648.

297. Pusztahelyi Réka, *A veszélyes üzemi felelősség egyes kérdései az új Ptk. rendszerében* [Certain Issues of Liability for Hazardous Activity in the New Civil Code]. Publicationes Universitatis Miskolcinensis Sectio Juridica et Politica, Tomus XXXIII (2015), 306–325. http://midra.uni-miskolc.hu/document/22054/16382.pdf.

For example, in the case of spouses, the maintenance and operation of the motor vehicle is for the benefit of both spouses—typically the entire family—the spouses are joint operators, regardless of which of them is the owner of the motor vehicle, and also of which of them regularly carries out the activity involving increased risk (PK. 40.).

On this basis, allowing the use of a car free of charge on one occasion does not establish the operator's responsibility in relation to the user (JD1992. 242), while in judicial practice, it is also the rule that the person who maintains and operates the hazardous activity on a long-term basis, or the person who checks, supervises and manages the source of danger is also considered to be the operator.

The operator can be relieved from liability if he is able to prove that the damage occurred due to an unavoidable cause that falls beyond the realm of highly dangerous activities. For example, the operator is not liable if the damage was caused by a detonated bomb which is placed by a third party on a bus; t*he assassination must be qualified as an unavoidable cause that falls beyond the realm of highly dangerous activities (JD2000. 200.). After the vehicle has been stopped and the engine is stopped the opening of the door of the motor vehicle belongs to the operation of the vehicle, so the damage caused in relation to this situation, shall be compensated by the liability insurance company (CJD2007. 1692.). If the vehicle was stopped for a short time, the dangerous feature does not disappear if the stopping happened with the intention of going forward (JD2005. 54. JD1999. 552.). The driver shall inform the passenger that the seat belt shall be switched on, if the passenger is injured because the seat belt was not switched on, the driver is responsible for the damage (JD2008. 61.).*

When examining an external cause outside the scope of operation of the hazardous activity, the traffic situation leading to the accident must also be evaluated (Decision No. Pfv.III.20.215/2020/9. of the Curia). The concept of hazardous activity cannot be restricted to the means of the activity involving increased risk; it covers not only the motor vehicle on the public road but also the operating conditions (Decision No. Pfv.III.20.539/2020/3. and Decision No. Pfv. 20.587/2021/6. of the Curia).[298]

Pusztahelyi Réka, *A veszélyes üzemi felelősség szabályozási környezete* [The Regulatory Environment of Liability for Hazardous Activity]. Nemzeti Közszolgálati Egyetem, Budapest (2018). https://nkerepo.uni-nke.hu/xmlui/bitstream/handle/123456789/12954/Pusztahelyi_A%20veszelyes_uzemi_felelosseg_szabalyozasi_kornyezete_2018.pdf?sequence=1.

Pataky Tibor, *A kötelező gépjármű-felelősségbiztosítás szabályozása és továbbfejlesztésének lehetőségei* [The Regulation of Compulsory Motor Vehicle Liability Insurance and the Possibilities for Its Further Development], Budapest (HVG–ORAC 2019), 236.

298. From the point of view of the mandatory motor vehicle liability insurance, in terms of classification as damage caused during the operation of the motor vehicle, the judgment in Case C-100/18 Línea Directa of the Court of Justice of the European Union (Luxembourg, Jun. 20, 2019, ECLI-:EU:C:2019:517) has great importance. According to the judgment, a situation in which a vehicle parked in a private garage of a building for more than 24 hours has caught fire, causing a fire originating in the vehicle's electrical system and causing damage to the building falls within the concept of "use of vehicles" within the meaning of the directive on insurance against civil liability in respect of the use of motor vehicles.

Especially in the context of traffic accidents, it is difficult to judge whether the behavior of the injured party involved in the occurrence of the damage was unavoidable or preventable. In case of unavoidable behavior of the victim, the dangerous activity as a whole is exempted from liability, however, in the case of preventable public influence, there is room for sharing of damages (JD2009.359., JD2014.146.). Such contributory influence leading to the sharing of damages can be considered if the passenger of the vehicle fails to use the safety devices installed in the vehicle (the seat belt) or does not comply with other safety regulations (JD2016.115. and JD2014.146.).

In judicial practice, the protection of the injured party prevails, especially if the responsible person has liability insurance.

261. If two or more hazardous operations cause the damage (if the injured person is not the operator of the hazardous activity when two motor vehicles crash, but, for instance, a pedestrian or cyclist), in the outer relationship, so in relation to the injured person, they shall be liable jointly in line with the rules of hazardous activity. In such cases, in the inner relationship of hazardous operations and in events when the motor vehicles cause damage to each other, the first thing which shall be examined is which party performed the attributable activity which caused the damage. If damage is caused by one hazardous operation to another, the operators shall be liable to provide compensation as commensurate according to attributability. Attributability can be, e.g., drunk driving, significant overspeed, improper technical condition of the vehicle, serious driving technical error (JD2007. 409., cDP2007. 1690.).

If the damage is not attributable to either party in accordance with the general rules, the compensation shall be provided by the party whose highly dangerous activity is responsible for the malfunction that contributed to causing the damage (e.g., unexpected failure of the braking system, malfunction, driver's illness), but *the traffic situation at the time of the malfunction has also relevance (JD2002. 359.).* If the cause of mutual damage is a malfunction that occurred in the scope of both parties' highly dangerous activity, or if such malfunction cannot be attributed to one of the parties, each party shall, where individual responsibility cannot be established, bear liability for his own loss (e.g., more vehicles crash because of an animal, which jumps in front of the vehicle within the braking distance*)*. According to the judicial practice, the situation shall be regarded as a malfunction, which cannot be attributed to one of the parties, if the "priority is mandatory" sign is removed by an unknown person. *(JD2001. 275.). The insurance company shall be liable in accordance with the rules of compulsory motor vehicle liability insurance if the damage is caused by a machinery because of a breach of traffic rules. (JD2006. 152.)*

262. Due to the compulsory liability insurance, the insurance company is obliged to perform a situation as though the damage event has not happened. Therefore, in the case of a hire purchase of a motor vehicle, the amount of the contractual interest, which was determined as the consideration for the credit contract, cannot be passed to the insurance company. *(JD2001. 120.).*

Any exclusion or limitation of liability for highly dangerous activity shall be null and void; this prohibition shall not apply to damage caused to a tangible thing.

The CC stipulates a three-year period of limitation for the enforcement of claims, which is shorter than the general (five years) period of limitation. The damage liability is based on the compensation of the whole damage, which means that the whole pecuniary damage (any depreciation in value of the property of the aggrieved party, any pecuniary advantage lost, and the costs necessary for the mitigation or elimination of the financial losses sustained by the aggrieved party) shall be compensated. With the adaption of the new regulations of the CC, the legal institution of the non-pecuniary damage was abolished and the restitution[299] became the pecuniary sanction for personal damage. We need to mention that the liability insurance—and consequently the compulsory liability insurance too—covers the restitution as well, which is not damages.

299. Section 2:52 of the CC.

Chapter 3. Subjects of the Legal Relationship[300]

263. The subject of the compulsory liability insurance can be such an insurance company which is authorized in the home Member State to conduct the activity.[301]

The organizations need to be mentioned, which are established by the insurers, and their aim is to coordinate and settle the claims of injured parties in relation to international vehicle traffic (in accordance with the international treaties and the Directives of the European Union). The National Insurer's Bureau, as the organization of insurers, performs the tasks arising from international treaties; the Information Center is obliged to communicate the data in connection with the enforcement of damage claims.

The National Office is only obliged to pay compensation for damage caused in Hungary by the operation of a motor vehicle located in a third country if there is an international motor insurance agreement with the country of origin of the motor vehicle causing the damage or if the operator (driver) of the motor vehicle has concluded border insurance and maintained it continuously during his stay in Hungary (JD2019. 79.)

Insurers operate the Claims Organization in their home Member State, which provides due compensation for claims of a domestic injured party in respect of any loss or injury caused by motor vehicles based in other Member States in any state that is party to the Green Card System, if the insurance company of the responsible party, or the claims representative of such insurance company failed to evaluate the claim for compensation and to provide settlement.

The AHIC operates the tasks of the National Insurer's Bureau and of the Claims Organization as well.[302]

264. During the formation of the single internal market, cross-border services became more and more important, but in such cases, the insurance company is

300. Ujváriné Dr. Antal Edit, *Biztosítási szerződés* [Insurance Contract] In Majoros Tünde (ed.), *Kereskedelmi szerződések alapvető szabályai* [Basic Rules of Commercial Contracts]. Budapest (Patrocinium Publisher 2015), 258–268.

301. The yearbook of the AHIC contains the distribution of compulsory motor vehicle liability insurance by insurance companies in terms of premium income and number of contracts for the year 2020.
https://mabisz.hu/wp-content/uploads/evkonyv/mabisz-evkonyv-2021-V6j4-HU.pdf.
For the business data of insurers *see*: MNB, *Biztosítási, pénztári, tőkepiaci kockázati és fogyasztóvédelmi jelentés*, (2022), 33–35.p. https://www.mnb.hu/letoltes/kocka-zati-jelente-s-2022-eng-1207.pdf, https://www.mnb.hu/en/publications/reports/report-on-insurance-funds-capital-market-risk-and-consumer-protection/report-on-insurance-funds-capital-market-risks-and-consumer-protection-2022.

302. In 2020, the National Office received 5,352 new claims, as a result of which it paid HUF 1.611 billion in compensation to foreign national offices and insurance companies. In 2020, approximately 10% of the cases handled by the National Office were claims settled as Compensation Organizations (135 damage claims).
In 2021, the National Office received 2,225 new claims, which is less than the outstanding number of the previous year, but still significantly higher than the average of previous years. In 2021, 6,355 motor vehicle, property, personal injury or annuity claims were charged to the Compensation Account, which represents a 7.3% increase compared to the previous year.
https://mabisz.hu/wp-content/uploads/evkonyv/mabisz-evkonyv-2022-hu.pdf.

obliged to appoint a claims adjustment representative for the settlement of claims (who provides the representation of insurers in judicial or nonjudicial processes), and claims representative shall be appointed by an insurance company to conduct the business of motor vehicle insurance against civil liability to operate in a Member State other than the home Member State, for handling and settling claims for compensation arising from an accident involving a vehicle covered by the insurance contract in the injured party's Member State of residence, and for representing the insurance company against the injured party.

265. Compensation Fund (Guarantee Fund, which is operated by the AHIC) is of great importance, which is established by the insurance companies. The tasks of the Compensation Fund will be detailed later. Claims Guarantee Fund is also established and financed by the insurance companies, which provides compensation to victims of accidents caused by motor vehicles with sufficient insurance cover at an insurance company undergoing liquidation.[303]

266. Insurance obligation stipulated by the law burdens all of the operators of all motor vehicles registered in the territory of Hungary. The insurance obligation burdens the operator with the conditions declared by the Act, which means he has to conclude and maintain the insurance contract in accordance with the legal conditions. Operator shall mean the person shown in the document (traffic license) issued by the competent authority of the country where the motor vehicle is based as having custody of the vehicle or failing this, the owner of the vehicle. As regards the obligation to obtain insurance, the operator shall mean any person named by the owner of the motor vehicle to have custody of the vehicle as verified by contract or some other credible form of evidence. *According to the judicial practice, in case of compulsory motor vehicle liability insurance, the insurance interest connects to the*

303. In Case C 409/11, The request has been made in proceedings brought by Messrs Csonka, Isztli, Juhász, Kiss, and Szontágh against the Magyar Állam (Hungarian state) concerning the liability which, according to the applicants, the Hungarian state incurs as a result of the incorrect transposition of that directive into Hungarian law. The Insurance Directives against civil liability in respect of the use of motor vehicles must be interpreted as not including, among the obligations which that provision imposes on Member States, that of establishing a body to ensure that compensation is provided to victims of road accidents in situations where, although the persons responsible for the damage had taken out insurance covering their civil liability in respect of the use of motor vehicles, the insurer has become insolvent.

Insurers carrying out compulsory motor vehicle liability insurance activities are obliged to pay a maximum of 0.25% of their business premium income—1% of their annual premium income—into the Compensation Fund every quarter, as long as the Fund's available assets do not exceed 6% of the total compulsory motor vehicle liability premium income of the market in the previous year. Until now, three insurers under liquidation, ASTRA (the liquidation of ASTRA legally began in 2016), MÁV and AIM, have accepted claims for the burden of the previous compulsory motor vehicle liability insurances and assessed them at the expense of the Fund. At the end of 2020, the amount of assets managed by the Compensation Fund, as well as current account and deposit amounts, was around HUF 7.7 billion. https://mabisz.hu/wp-content/uploads/evkonyv/mabisz-evkonyv-2021-V6j4-HU.pdf.

At the end of 2021, the amount of assets managed by the Compensation Fund, as well as current account and deposit amounts (after the liquidation of MÁV ÁBE in 2008 and AIM in 2014 and asset withdrawal due to Astra payments) was approximately HUF 8.9 billion.

https://mabisz.hu/wp-content/uploads/evkonyv/mabisz-evkonyv-2022-hu.pdf.

property right or to the operator of the motor vehicle. Therefore, the owner of the motor vehicle or the operator, who is registered into the traffic license, is entitled to conclude the contract. (JD2000. 59.)

267. Where insurance is obtained due to the transfer of title, the new operator is required to conclude the insurance contract in accordance with this Act without delay after the transfer is completed.

In case of the operator's death, if the person subject to the obligation in respect of compulsory insurance of vehicles cannot be identified, the policy shall remain valid for a period of thirty days upon the operative date of the resolution adopted in conclusion of the probate proceedings, if the person having custody of the motor vehicle notified the insurance company of the death, and paid the applicable premium to keep the policy in force (Decision No. Pfv. 20.563/2016/5. of the Curia).

268. The owner of a motor vehicle that is registered in the territory of another Member State—if the motor vehicle's Member State of destination is Hungary—shall obtain insurance coverage under this Act for a period of thirty days from the time when the vehicle is delivered after the transfer of title.

269. In order to properly distribute the burdens of the community of the risk of those obliged to enter into contracts, in order to determine the premiums of the contracts in proportion to the risk, the insurers create a claim history register (hereinafter: claim register) for the purpose of using the claims history data, performing the tasks related to claim settlement, issuing the claim history certificates, as well as verifying the existence of the insurance cover. This task is performed by the claims registration body, which is the AHIC with its special organizational unit set aside for this purpose.[304]

270. The operator is the party who concludes the contract with the insurance company, but the insurance protection does not only cover the damage caused by the operator. The insured party shall mean the operator of the motor vehicle who owns an insurance policy, and the driver of the motor vehicle. This party does not mean the operator in all of the cases.

According to the legal regulations which are aimed at the protection of the injured party, we can determine that due to the relationship of compulsory motor vehicle liability insurance, the insurance event is the damage which is caused in connection

304. The activities of AHIC are divided into two main areas: the professional advocacy activities of the association and the tasks related to third-party insurance.

https://mabisz.hu/wp-content/uploads/2018/09/mabisz-alapszabalya-20171204.pdf.

The AHIC's Separated Organization Unit (ESZE) has a statutory mandate for dealing with tasks concerning third-party insurances. Among other things, it handles the Compensation Account which provides compensation to victims who were harmed by vehicles lacking third-party insurance, or in other cases, when the one causing damage is unknown. Also AHIC ESZE manages the Compensation Fund which role is to compensate people, who had their third-party insurance at insurers becoming insolvent. AHIC ESZE also operates the Information Center for international claims settlement and the Hungarian Green Card Office. An also known activity is the operation of Central Damage History Registry for registering damages and Bonus-Malus degrees.

with the operation and driving of the insured party's motor vehicle, for which the insured party shall be liable. *The judicial practice emphasizes that liability insurance covers the damage, for which the insured party is liable as an employer, if the business accident was caused by the operation of the vehicle (JD2001. 372.).*

271. The insurance not only covers the compensation of pecuniary damage because loss or injury and compensation shall also be construed, respectively, as a violation of personality rights underlying any claim for restitution. (Decisions No. P. 22.919/2016/69., P. 23.012/2017/19. and Pf. 20.709/2020/6. of the Tribunal of the Capital).

When determining the amount of non-pecuniary compensation, the legal practice developed in the injured party's place of residence abroad is not applicable; all claims arising from the given damage must be assessed uniformly on the basis of Hungarian law and related legal practice (CJD2020. 4252.).

All operators of motor vehicles registered in the territory of Hungary—other than the motor vehicles exempted under specific other legislation—are required to enter into a contract with an insurance company to obtain coverage for any injury arising from the use of motor vehicles under the terms and conditions defined by the law and to pay the premium charged in order to keep the policy in effect (obligation in respect of the compulsory insurance of vehicles).

According to the general rules of the liability insurance, the service obligation of the insurer exists for the injured party at the time of the occurrence of the insurance event, whose legal situation has specialties, compared to the general rules.

Chapter 4. Features of the Contract

§1. Insurance Obligation: Obligation of Concluding the Contract

272. We mentioned above the insurance obligation, which means the operator (in the case of property transfer, the new operator) shall conclude and maintain the contract in accordance with the legal provisions.

Pursuant to Directive 2009/103/EC on the insurance against civil liability in respect of the use of motor vehicles and the enforcement of the obligation to insure against such liability, the minimum insurance coverage amounts must be revised every five years in accordance with the European consumer price index. Pursuant to this, the Act XX of 2022 modified the maximum amounts of the insurance coverage defined in the law as follows:

In connection with any claim, regardless of the number of victims, in the case of damage to property, the insurance company shall cover up to the forint equivalent of EUR 1,300,000 per claim, and in the case of personal injury up to the forint equivalent of EUR 6,450,000 per claim, including any and all related claims arising out of or in connection with the accident, the costs of enforcement of the claim (including legal expenses), and interest for the period until the settlement payment is in fact made.

(These amounts incorporate the costs of claim enforcement and interests, too. The Act contains detailed regulations in relation to the procedure of the insurance company if the claims of more injured parties exceed the maximum damage coverage.) The Act lists the damage claims which are not covered by liability insurance. For instance, the property damage and the loss of profit arising from the claims of the insured persons of the vehicle which caused the damage.

Requiring the injured party to have the vehicle damaged in the accident repaired at a branded service center that procures the parts from the dealers designated by the liability insurer may involve additional obligations and burdens that the injured party cannot be expected to bear, and cannot be assessed as a violation of the obligation to mitigate damages, which is results in a burden that exceeds the expected level for the injured party (JD2021. 260.).

When entering into contracts with insurance associations, clients must be aware that by becoming a member of the insurance association, in addition to paying the insurance premium, they may also be required to pay membership fees in accordance with the articles of association of the insurance association. Furthermore, when the articles of association allow this, the supreme body of the insurance associations (general assembly, meeting of the delegates) is entitled to impose an additional payment obligation if other sources are not sufficient to fulfill the association's obligations for the current year.

273. If the policyholder caused the accident in the territory of another Member State or in the territories of any states which are parties to the Green Card System and where there is a valid agreement between the national bureaus of such states and the Hungarian National Bureau, the amount of minimum cover of the insurance companies shall be determined based on the regulations of the motor vehicle liability insurance in the country where the accident took place. If the minimum amount of cover fixed in the contract for insurance companies is higher than the amount prescribed in the country where the accident took place, the guarantee obligation of the insurance companies shall apply up to the amount limits fixed in the relevant insurance contract.

274. The insurer is under a contractual obligation in accordance with the conditions of the MVI Act, and the refusal right of the insurer is limited in the Act.

One of the special restrictions of the contract freedom is the rule that if the insurance contract terminates during the period of insurance due to the nonpayment of the premium:

- the operator is required to conclude a contract with the insurance company where his previous policy was terminated due to nonpayment of premium;
- the renewed contract is based on the premium tariff rates in effect on the first day of the period of risk coverage;
- only this insurer is entitled and obliged to accept the offer (except if the activity license of the insurer was canceled because in this case the contract can be concluded with other insurers as well).

275. For the sake of fair competition between the insurance companies, the insurance company may not accept the request made sixty days before the beginning of the period of insurance cover and may not conclude a contract before that time; any contract concluded as such shall be null and void.

276. Another feature of the contract is that the content of the insurance relationship is regulated by the law; the contract comes into existence in line with that, and the insurance company shall make available the contracting terms (fee tariffs) in accordance with the law.

The insurance contract is valid in written form—as a general rule—but the contract can be concluded by way of the contracting operator delivering his request—made out in compliance with premium tariff rates and policy conditions—to the insurance company or the insurance company's agent upon receipt of information as to policy conditions, using the application form prescribed by the insurance company. The contract comes into existence, too, if the operator's request fails to comply with the fee tariffs and with the insurance conditions, but the insurance company does not respond to the request within fifteen days. The contract shall be deemed executed at the time the request is delivered under the conditions contained in the request. In the event of liability insurance contracts, the "additional" insurance is prohibited, so any additional insurance contract concluded for the same period of insurance cover or for a part of such period of insurance cover shall be null and void.

The contracting party shall disclose all material information that may be of consequence concerning the policy from the insurance company's point of view (for instance, data of the insurance contracts in the former insurance cycle, claims records system identification number, information necessary for determining the amount of noninsurance fee, etc.).

The insurance companies shall establish claims records, which contain the information defined by the law relating to the insurance contracts (such as the event which caused the damage and the date of the damage). The claim record system promotes better apportioning the collective burden of those required to participate in the compulsory motor vehicle liability insurance regime and for determining the premium charged for such policies reflecting the risk involved.

§2. Exemption of State Motor Vehicles

277. The operators of motor vehicles that were exempted by the minister directing the ministry that exercises operator's rights, or by the minister exercising control or supervisory rights over the body that exercises operators, shall be exempted from the obligation of concluding an insurance contract under this Act. The minister in charge of asset management may grant exemption to operators of the motor vehicles if measures are adopted before the effective date of exemption concerning the settlement of damages that may occur in the future involving the exempted motor vehicles, including the financial resources required for such settlements, (e.g., a list shall be compiled and regularly updated on the exempted motor vehicles, or measures shall be taken relating to the register of exempted motor vehicles, including access made available to this register for the National Bureau in discharging the functions conferred upon the Information Center, a body responsible for providing compensation for damages caused by exempted motor vehicles, and the body responsible for settlement shall be appointed in Hungary and other Member States).

Now from the members of the Government the Minister of Defence makes use of the possibility, and the liability insurance obligation does not cover the vehicles of the Ministry of Defence and the Hungarian Defence Forces (for military vehicles) from January 1, 2012.[305]

§3. The Territorial Scope and Term of Validity of the Contract

278. The territorial scope of the contract extends beyond the borders of the country because it shall cover the territories of Member States and the territories of countries which are parties to the Green Card System where there is a valid agreement between the national bureaus of such states and the Hungarian National Bureau according to the Internal Regulations.

The liability insurance covers the territory of the EEA and of Switzerland, furthermore, the territory of the countries, in which the damage was caused and which are Member States of the international agreement.

The term of insurance contracts for motor vehicles which is required to bear permanent registration plates shall continue indefinitely, and the insurance period is one year. The coverage of risk by the insurance company (insurance cover) shall commence at the time fixed by the parties in the contract, or failing this, at the time the contract is executed. The law makes it possible that the parties can agree differently

305. Decree No. 17/2011. (XII.23.) of the Ministry of Defence.

than the legal regulations, but any contract (insurance) term introduced by the insurance company unilaterally, without the knowledge of the other party, stipulating that the insurance company's coverage of risk shall commence following payment of the premium (the first installment of the premium) shall be null and void. According to the Act, there is the possibility of the discontinuance of the contract for a maximum six-month period.

§4. The Insurance Fee[306]

279. The insurance fee, which has to be paid due to the insurance contract, is determined by the insurance companies in line with the legal regulations.

The operator shall be entitled to a discount consistent with any accident-free period (bonus) or must pay a surcharge (malus) based on the number of claims for which the insurance company was liable to provide settlement on his behalf (malus).

Insurance companies are required to use accident and claims records in accordance with another decree, to operate a bonus-malus system relying on such accident and claims records, and to issue accident and claims certificates.

For example, the insured can obtain a discount on the no-damage premium (bonus) or pay an additional fee (malus) according to the number of damage events, or it is possible to apply individual fees established according to the announced tariff. The advantages and disadvantages associated with the bonus-malus system are attributed to the contracting operator, regardless of who drove the vehicle of the insured person. When the vehicle is sold, the bonus-malus grade acquired by the operator is not transferred to the new owner; he has his own bonus-malus rating, according to which a new contract must be concluded. The transfer of a more favorable bonus classification is only possible in case of termination of the previous contract due to loss of interest (e.g., sale or withdrawal of the previous vehicle) for two years.

The NBH creates and operates a contract and claims database related to the determination of the fee tariff in connection with the compulsory motor vehicle liability insurances (hereafter: "KKTA").[307]

For the operation of the KKTA, the Supervision uses data received in the context of data provision in accordance with subsection 13 of section 269 of the BIns., provided that the KKTA does not contain personal data.[308]

306. https://www.mnb.hu/letoltes/kgfb-index-infografika-2022q1.pdf.

307. Based on a complaint submitted by Hungarian Autoclub, the report of the Commissioner of Fundamental Rights in case AJB-39/2020. suggested the modification of Decree No. 21/2011 (VI.10.) of the Minister of National Economy, which regulates the bonus-malus system. As a result of this, the regulation clearly regulates the rules for the use of loss history data by insurers, the way the data is used, and its detailed rules.
https://www.ajbh.hu/documents/10180/3190211/Jelent%C3%A9s+a+k%C3%B6telez%C5%91+g%C3%A9pj%C3%A1rm%C5%B1-felel%C5%91ss%C3%A9gbiztos%C3%ADt%C3%A1st+%C3%A9rint%C5%91+szab%C3%A1lyoz%C3%A1ssal+%C3%B6sszef%C3%BCgg%C3%A9sben+39_2020/e7343ce3-fb47-1f56-380d-5515fd599e35?version=1.0.

308. https://www.mnb.hu/felugyelet/adatszolgaltatas/biztositok/2018-evre-vonatkozo-adatszolgaltatasok/a-kozponti-kgfb-teteles-adatbazis-kkta-technikai-segedletei.

The KKTA, to which insurers operating compulsory motor vehicle liability insurance business provide contract and claims data dating back to 2011, provides all market players with sufficient statistical background to establish well-founded premium rates.[309]

The Price Navigator, which is the information tool of the AHIC created for the purpose of consumer protection, not only reliably serves customers who want to be fully informed about the current mandatory motor vehicle liability insurance premiums but also provides a way to offer an authentic comparison and control point for all players in the market, including consumers and the intermediary side as well.[310]

Insurance companies shall calculate the premium based on the premium tariff rate published for each individual insurance policy, in effect on the first day of the period or term.[311] It has occurred many times that insurers failed to comply with the statutory obligation relating to the publication obligation, and it resulted in a supervisory procedure and the imposition of a serious fine. The insurer shall not make any changes during the period of insurance cover to which it pertains, with the exception if the premium shown in the contract differs from the one to be calculated based on the premium tariff rate due to the policyholder operator's breach of the obligation of disclosure or cooperation at the time of conclusion of the contract. Consequently, in the case of indefinite duration contracts, the insurance premium can be modified (due to the premium tariff rate applicable on the first day of the period of insurance cover), but it cannot be modified during the time of the concrete insurance. Insurance companies shall send out information pamphlets more than fifty days before the last day of the period of insurance cover to inform the policyholders concerning the annual insurance cycle and the estimated premium for the next period of insurance cover calculated based on the premium tariff rate and on information available at that time. According to this, the contracting party can decide in time whether or not to maintain the legal relationship. The insurance company is entitled to the premium for the period of risk coverage. The premium (part of the premium) shall be paid previously. The consequence of the insurance obligation and the payment obligation of the parties of the risk community is that if the operator fails to comply with the insurance obligation, he shall pay the missed fee and the so-called noninsurance fee too, which shall be calculated and collected by the insurance company that provides a contract for the operator after the duration of

309. Decree No. 42/2019 (XII.3.) MNB on Detailed Rules for Requesting Data from the Contracts, Claims and Settlements Database Covering Compulsory Motor Vehicle Liability Insurance Policies. In effect from Dec. 4, 2019.

310. https://mabisz.hu/dijnavigator/.
https://alk.mnb.hu/fogyasztoknak/tematikus_oldalak/kgfb/dijtarifa.

311. As a result of the investigations of the NBH, it has been determined that fee discounts must be determined in such a way that each customer can accurately determine the fee to be paid in the following year. It is also important that the tariff cannot include a discount that is only for new contract holders, i.e., it can only contain a distinction in favor of the existing contract. *See*, for example: Decision No. H-JÉ-II-B-58/2020. of the NBH on the completion of a comprehensive investigation for GROUPAMA Insurance Plc.
https://alk.mnb.hu/data/cms2485099/keksz_25810567.pdf.

noninsurance. The manager of the Compensation Fund is entitled to the noninsurance fee.[312] (The noninsurance fee shall be calculated in accordance with the Act.)

§5. Termination of the Contract

280.

(a) Lapse of interest (e.g., the operator's changing or withdrawal of the vehicle from the traffic if reinstatement of the vehicle does not take place within one year, and in the case of the transfer of the ownership, if the operator, who is obliged to conclude the contract is changed).
(b) Nonpayment of the fee. In the event of nonpayment of the premium, the insurance company affected shall—in a verifiable manner—dispatch within thirty days from the due date a request for payment to the party in default—indicating the potential legal consequences—with an additional sixty-day deadline from the original due date permitted. In the event of noncompliance with this grace period, the contract shall be terminated on the sixtieth day following the due date if not already terminated for other reasons. (Within this time, the insurance company shall bear the risk).
(c) Resignation. Both the insurance company and the contracting party are entitled to terminate the contract by a unilateral statement for future purposes. Resignation shall be in writing and shall be effective on the last day of the period of insurance cover, which shall be communicated to take effect at least thirty days before. The resignation shall not be justified.
(d) Mutual agreement.
(e) Revocation of the activity license. The contract is terminated in the event too, if the activity license concerning motor vehicle liability insurance of the insurance company will be withdrawn.

281. The insurance company shall notify the operator in writing, if the insurance contract is terminated, within thirty days (in the case of nonpayment of the fee within fifteen days) of the time of termination or the time of gaining knowledge of such termination. (At the same time, the insurance company shall inform about the bonus-malus classification.) The insurance company is the subject of an increased cooperation obligation in this case too, because the company is obliged to send a notification to the operator about the termination within fifteen days. The Parliamentary Commissioner for Citizens' Rights completed an inquiry, and then a judicial decision was born, which resulted in the determination that the notice of termination of the contract must be sent to clients in a verifiable manner.[313]

---

312. https://www.mnb.hu/letoltes/fedezetlensegi-dijtablazat-2022.pdf.
https://mabisz.hu/fedezetlensegi-dijak-2023/.

313. Decision No. 3293/2019. (XI.18.) of the Constitutional Court stated that it is a constitutional requirement that the sending of the notification must be done in a way that can be verified after the fact for each recipient, without any doubt.
https://public.mkab.hu/dev/dontesek.nsf/0/165126b4063f0406c1258403004de6d4/$FILE/3293_2019%20AB%20hat%C3%A1rozat.pdf.

§6. LEGAL SITUATION OF THE INJURED PARTY

282. The injured party shall report the loss to the insurance company within thirty days of the time when the accident occurred (or to other institutions who are obliged to the compensation) because in the event of noncompliance with this time limit, the sanctions for any delay in the payment of compensation shall not apply to the insurance company (with the exception of the self-faulted delay).

I. Claim Enforcement Against the Insurance Company[314]

283. The injured party is in a more favorable legal position, compared to the general rules of civil liability insurance, because he is entitled to enforce his claim directly against the insurer (which means he can file not just a declaratory action but a condemnation action in the court), but only within the framework of the limited insurance contract.

284. The persons involved in an accident shall, at the scene of the accident, exchange the necessary information for identifying their persons and motor vehicles and for verifying liability insurance coverage, as well as information describing the accident. The data and information supplied in this fashion shall be processed according to the relevant provisions of the BIns. pertaining to insurance secrets.

285. The online IT solution operated by AHIC for the reporting of compulsory motor vehicle liability insurance claims facilitates the reporting of claims.

286. The e-claim form shall mean an IT solution made available by AHIC for filing a claim falling within the scope of compulsory motor vehicle liability insurance online.

According to judicial practice, the injured party can sue the tortfeasor directly for the indemnification of the damage (JD2013. 43.).

If there is more than one injured party due to a damage event, who want to enforce the damage claim, the Act contains detailed provision about the insurance company's procedure because of the limited amount liability insurance. The termination of the corporate existence of the insured party of liability insurance does not

See further: Report of the Commissioner of Fundamental Rights in case AJB-39/2020 in connection with regulations concerning compulsory motor vehicle liability insurance.

https://www.ajbh.hu/documents/10180/3190211/Jelent%C3%A9s+a+k%C3%B6telez%C5%91+g%C3%A9pj%C3%A1rm%C5%B1-felel%C5%91ss%C3%A9gbiztos%C3%ADt%C3%A1st+%C3%A9rint%C5%91+szab%C3%A1lyoz%C3%A1ssal+%C3%B6sszef%C3%BCgg%C3%A9sben+39_2020/e7343ce3-fb47-1f56-380d-5515fd599e35?version=1.0.

314. The applications submitted to the FAB in connection with the compulsory motor vehicle liability insurance were related to the lack of coverage fee, the tortfeasor's surcharge, the bonus-malus classification, the change in the fee schedule, and the compensation claims submitted by the injured parties in the year 2021. https://www.mnb.hu/en/hungarian-financial-arbitration-board/introduction/report-on-the-activities-of-the-hungarian-financial-arbitration-board, https://www.mnb.hu/bekeltetes/bemutatkozas/eves-jelenteseink/jelentes-a-penzugyi-bekelteto-testulet-eves-tevekenysegerol-2022.

terminate the insurer's obligation to pay the compensation annuity. In line with the general rules of civil law, the injured party is entitled to bring an action against the insurance company to *raise the amount of the annuity (JD2009. 12.). In line with the judicial practice, the operator and the insurer of the motor vehicle are obliged to compensate the damage under joint and several liabilities, so they both can stand trial (CJD2011. 2514., CJD2021. 4320.).*

In accordance with the rules and the practice, the compulsory motor vehicle liability insurance dispute between the injured party and the insurer cannot constitute a consumer dispute (there is no contractual relationship between them), so there is no legal possibility to turn to an alternative dispute settlement forum.

II. Claim Enforcement Against the Compensation Fund[315]

287. Because the Hungarian rules put great emphasis on the "protection of the injured party," the enforcement of damage claim is provided for victims of accidents caused:

- by uninsured motor vehicles in violation of the obligation in respect of the compulsory insurance of vehicles; or
- by the motor vehicles of unidentified operators or unidentified vehicles under the limits set out in the Act; and
- by the motor vehicles of unidentified operators, furthermore;
- compensation of such damage caused during the time of discontinuance (maximum six months); and
- if the damage was caused by a motor vehicle that was not placed into service or that was deregistered.

In these cases, the injured party can turn to the Compensation Fund (In the case of an unknown tortfeasor, some damage (e.g., losses occurred in the motor vehicle) cannot be compensated except if the accident results in death or serious personal injuries).

If the Compensation Fund reimburses the injured party's damage, it will be entitled to claim for reimbursement and can claim the reimbursement of all the costs which occurred in relation to compensation by the party determined by the law (for instance, from the operator who failed to obtain insurance cover and from any driver who used the motor vehicle without the operator's permission or in full knowledge

315. In 2020, a total of 4,892 claims related to motor vehicle, property, personal injury and annuity were charged to the Compensation Account, on the basis of which the Separate Organizational Unit managing the Compensation Account paid HUF 2.037 billion in compensation for the substantiated claims, together with the annuity disbursements.
https://mabisz.hu/wp-content/uploads/evkonyv/mabisz-evkonyv-2021-V6j4-HU.pdf.
In 2021, the Separate Organizational Unit managing the Compensation Account paid out HUF 3.716 billion in compensation for substantiated claims, together with the annuity payments. In 2021, the total result of the recourse activity reached HUF 1.190 million, which is a significant increase compared to the previous year.
https://mabisz.hu/wp-content/uploads/evkonyv/mabisz-evkonyv-2022-hu.pdf.

that the vehicle was not covered by compulsory insurance. We have mentioned before that in such cases, the tortfeasor is obliged to pay a noninsurance fee.)

The compensation for the damage of the victim of an accident is provided by the rule if there is any disagreement between the manager of the Compensation Fund and the insurance company as to liability for providing compensation to the victim of an accident; the manager of the Compensation Fund shall pay the amount of compensation in advance and settle with the insurance carrier of the responsible party at a later date. The same is required if the manager of the Compensation Fund shall advance the amount of compensation where there is any dispute between the insurance companies involved as to liability for providing compensation to the victim of an accident.

The operator of the Compensation Account may assert a compensation claim against the persons specified by law in the event that he fulfilled the claim of the injured party in the absence of mandatory motor vehicle liability insurance (JD2017. 229.)

Instead of the owner who caused an accident abroad and does not have motor vehicle liability insurance, the operator of the Hungarian compensation account compensates the injured party—through the foreign insurance company—for the damage caused. After this, he can claim reimbursement from the operator for the costs incurred. During this, it is sufficient to prove that he examined the merits of the injured party's claim, while the tortfeasor, on the other hand, must prove that some item of the compensation paid was unnecessary or the amount was exaggerated (CJD2022. 4484.)

III. Claim Enforcement Against the Claims Guarantee Fund

288. As we mentioned before, if the insurer with which the insured party concluded the motor vehicle liability insurance contract was under liquidation, the claim of the injured party against the insurer will be covered by the Compensation Fund.

IV. Claim Enforcement in Case of Damage Caused by a Motor Vehicle from Another Member State

289. If the damage is caused by a motor vehicle which has the establishment in the territory of another Member State or in the territory of a Member State of the Green Card System, the injured party living in the territory of the country can file the claim:

- to the claims representative, who is appointed within the territory of the country by the insurance company of the tortfeasor's vehicle, who is obliged to make the procedure in Hungarian; or
- to tortfeasor; or
- to the insurance company of the tortfeasor directly.

JD 2019.10.270 I. If the motor vehicle of the Hungarian business organization suffers an accident in Germany caused by a third party, the existence and scope of the obligation to compensate shall be governed by Rome II. Regulation. As a result of this, German law must be applied regardless of whether the injured party sues the tortfeasor or the insurer directly.

V. Claim Enforcement Against the Claims Organization

290. If the insurance company or its claims representative of the vehicle which caused the accident has not provided a reasoned reply to the points made in the claim within three months of the date when the injured party presented his claim for compensation, the injured party can enforce the claim against the Claims Organization (which was established by the insurance companies). The injured party can turn to the Claims Organization if the insurance company has failed to appoint a claims representative (except if the injured party presented a claim for compensation directly to the insurance company and if he received a reasoned reply within three months of presenting the claim). It can happen that the tortfeasor motor vehicle, which seat is another Member State or the insurance company of the tortfeasor motor vehicle cannot be identified after two months of the accident (even with the database of the Information Center). In this case, the Claims Organization can help the injured party.

§7. The Legal Situation of the Insurance Company

291. According to the law, the insurance company shall include the examination of liability and the settlement of justified claims for any loss or injury as a result of accidents caused by the insured persons using the motor vehicle shown in the insurance contract. Insurance companies shall determine the justification of claims for compensation relying on the policyholder's statement as to responsibility and on the facts and information available relative to the policyholder's liability in damages. The insurer is obliged to give a justified answer within fifteen days from the receipt of the necessary documents and within three months if the company does not get the documents, and if the company takes suggestions for damages, and if the company does not recognize on the basis of the amount. (The insurance company shall be required to pay the sum awarded to the injured party within fifteen days following the acceptance of the offer of compensation or of the date of delivery of the final judgment for the award of damages.)

§8. The Legal Situation of the Insured Party

292. The insured party shall notify his insurance carrier in writing within five working days, and he must report within five working days if any judicial or non-judicial charges are filed against him in connection with the accident. The insurance company is entitled to provide representation for the insured party in such proceedings. (The operator who has no insurance also shall notify the Compensation Fund.)

In accordance with the Act, the scope of any legally binding judgment dismissing the injured party's compensation claim shall also include the policyholder, if the court so rules in a lawsuit between the injured party and the insurance company, the claims adjustment representative, the National Bureau, or the manager of the Compensation Fund. Consequently, the scope of a condemnation will affect the insured party if he participates in the lawsuit.

The agreement between the insurer and the injured party affects the damage causer to the extent that, due to the same damage, the injured party can no longer be subject to another indemnification (JD2005. 249.).

§9. The Assignment and Recourse Right

293. If the compensation has been provided by the insurance company (the National Bureau or the manager of the Compensation Fund), it shall be subrogated to the insured party or the operator or driver in their rights (assignment) against the person who caused the accident—up to the amount of compensation. The Act lists the events when the insurer (the National Bureau or the manager of the Compensation Fund) is entitled to demand repayment of the amount of the paid compensation. The most important events from these cases are the following. The Compensation Fund can demand repayment:

- from the insured party/parties if they have wilfully and unlawfully caused the loss or injury collectively (in the case of several insured parties, jointly and severally);
- from the driver, if he drove the motor vehicle while under the influence of alcohol or any substance that has the capacity to impair one's ability to drive;
- from the driver if he did not have a driver's license;
- from the driver, if the loss or injury was caused by the failure to provide help, or if driving recklessly in the case of professional drivers.

The recourse right of the insurance company is limited by amounts, which amount depends on the feature of the sanctioned activity.

§10. Control

294. Operations such as placing a motor vehicle into service, making any entry into the registration certificate relating to the operator, issuing or renewing a temporary use certificate, replacing the motor vehicle's distinguishing sign (registration plate), and carrying out the periodic inspection of a motor vehicle may be carried out only if the obligation in respect of compulsory insurance of vehicles is satisfied. According to the Act, in the process of registration of any data of the operator in the certificate of registration and during the motor vehicle's periodic inspection, and also upon the inspection of the motor vehicle operated on public roads, the competent authority shall check insurance cover by way of electronic means, directly from the bureau of insurance policy records through a computer communication link. If the bureau of insurance policy records determines—upon cross-referencing the motor vehicle registry with the insurance policy records carried out quarterly—that a vehicle has no valid insurance cover, or if the authority vested with powers to check insurance cover discovers that a motor vehicle has no valid insurance cover, the competent authority shall deregister the motor vehicle.

Part V. Insurance of the Person

Judit Barta

Chapter 1. Legal Regulation of Accident and Sickness Insurance

§1. Legal Regulation of Accident and Sickness Insurance in the BIns.

295. Annex 1 of the BIns. lists the accident and sickness insurance in the non-life insurance branch.

According to the BIns., accident insurance also covers occupational accident and disease as well as injury to passengers.

According to the BIns., the insurers may provide, according to the accident insurance, fixed pecuniary benefits (e.g., HUF X thousand in case of bone fracture, HUF X per day in case of hospital care), benefits in the nature of indemnity (e.g., reimbursement of costs of medical treatment, reimbursement of costs of medicines), or the combinations of these two (fixed pecuniary benefits and benefits in the nature of indemnity).

The BIns. also lists the sickness insurance in the non-life insurance branch. According to sickness insurance the insurer may provide:

(a) fixed pecuniary benefits;
(b) benefits in the nature of indemnity;
(c) combination of the two (fixed pecuniary benefits and benefits in the nature of indemnity).

If the insurer has the authorizations which simultaneously cover both branches, the BIns. uses the name "Accident and Health Insurance" or "Health Insurance."

296. Point 1 c) of Annex 2 of the BIns. classifies the supplementary insurance underwritten in addition to life insurance in the life insurance branch according to the following: "insurance against personal injury including incapacity for employment, insurance against death resulting from an accident and insurance against disability resulting from an accident or sickness."

The CC regulates a system and terminology other than the BIns. The accident insurance contract can be found within the fixed-sum policies, though, according to the BIns. the insurer may provide not only a fixed amount but also compensation. Therefore, this contract has a mixed nature, which is also emphasized in the CC, although the sickness insurance which has a similar nature is regulated as health insurance and in a separate chapter. The accident insurance contract is regulated in addition to the life insurance contract in Chapter LXIV "Fixed-sum policies," while health insurance is regulated in a separate title in Chapter LXV. In our view, it would have been closer to the thinking of the BIns. if accident and sickness insurance had been regulated in a separate chapter of the CC as a mixed type of insurance from the point of view of the service.

§2. Regulation of Accident Insurance Contract in the CC

297. General rules relating to accident insurance contract is defined by the CC. The accident insurance contract is regulated in addition to the life insurance contracts within the framework of the fixed-sum policies.

Accident insurance means a type of insurance where the insurance company promises to pay a specific sum of money or annuity fixed in the contract or other benefits as contracted upon the insured person's accidental death, health impairment, or disability resulting from an accident.[316]

The parties shall not be entitled to agree on limiting the right of termination.

The written consent of the insured person shall be required to conclude or amend the contract if he himself does not conclude it. If an insurance contract is concluded without the approval of the insured person, the section in which the beneficiary is named shall be null and void. In such a case, the insured person or his heir shall be construed as the beneficiary; he shall, however, reimburse the expenses of the contracting party, including premium payments and the costs of contracting, with the exception of group insurance.[317]

For accident insurance, the CC contains a mixed regulation because the regulation of indemnity insurance and life insurance has to be applied according to the law.

Usually, the rules on indemnity insurance have to be applied with the derogations defined by the law.

The regulation of life insurance has to be applied only within the limit defined by the CC.

Under subsection 1 of section 6:486 of the CC, the regulations governing life insurance shall apply to accident insurance policies with respect to:

(a) the revocation of the insured person's statement of consent;
(b) the designation of beneficiary and his rights;
(c) the exemption of the insurance company if the death of the insured person has been caused by the beneficiary of the insurance money.

Under subsection 3 of section 6:486 of the CC, provisions on indemnity insurance shall apply to accident insurance policies subject to the following exceptions:

316. Section 6:485 of the CC.
317. Section 6:475 of the CC.

(a) the insurance company shall not have the right to enforce any claim for compensation against the person who caused the accident;
(b) the insured person shall not have the obligation to preserve the scene upon the occurrence of the insurance event.

The CC allows the parties to obtain several policies for the same insurable interest and for the same peril. Each contract will be valid, and the prohibition of over-insurance shall not be applied. The parties therefore may accumulate insurance services.[318]

According to section 6:456 of the CC, if the contracting party is a consumer, the contract shall be allowed to derogate from the exclusion of derogation only to the benefit of the contracting party, the insured person, and the beneficiary with respect to fixed-sum and health insurance policies.

318. Section 6:476 of the CC.

Chapter 2. Workmen's Compensation and Occupational Disease

§1. Group Accident and Health Insurance Contracts Concluded by the Employers

298. In Hungary, Act LXXXIII of 1997 on the Services of the Compulsory Health Insurance System (CHIS) lists the accidents at work and occupational disease in the social security services.

Under section 51 of CHIS, accident benefits shall be due and payable in the cases of accidents at work or occupational diseases. Accident benefits are provided in the form of emergency medical services, benefits for accident-related injuries,[319] and accident allowance.[320] In case of accidental death, the relatives may receive an accident benefit.

Under subsection 1 of section 52 of CHIS, accident at work means any accident sustained by the insured person at his/her workplace while performing work or in connection with his/her occupation. Accident at work shall also include if suffered while commuting to and from work and to and from the insured person's home (residence) (hereinafter referred to as "accident in commute") commuting to and from work and to and from his/her home (residence). Accident at work shall also cover those sustained by the insured person while performing work in the public interest or while claiming certain social security benefits.

Under subsection 3 of section 52 of CHIS, occupational disease means any acute and chronic disease contracted at work or while engaged in an occupation or any chronic disease diagnosed following the performance of work:

(a) that is closely related to work or occupation and that may be attributed to physical, chemical, and biological factors, psychological stress or ergonomic considerations arising at work or during the work process; and/or
(b) that is attributed to the degree of engagement of the worker if greater or lesser than normal.

299. With regard to social security benefits, employers have the option to conclude accidental insurance and health insurance in a complementary and voluntary way as a main rule.

319. Under sub. 3 of s. 55 of the CHIS, benefits for accident-related injuries shall be due and payable—irrespective of any prior insurance period or whether or not drawing sick pay—for a period of one year, which may be extended maximum by one additional year.
320. According to sub. 1 of s. 57 of the CHIS, accident allowance shall be due and payable to any person who sustained an accident at work and consequently a degree of health impairment of over 13%, but is not eligible to the benefits provided to workers with disabilities. If the degree of health impairment is below twenty percent, the accident allowance shall be paid for maximum of two years, if it is over twenty percent it shall be paid for the entire duration of health impairment. The rate of accident allowance varies according to the degree of health impairment resulting from the accident at work.

An accident at work (e.g., at an office or university) may occur at any employer, not only in case of hazardous occupations. The most frequent announcement in connection with corporate accident insurance is related to bone fracture, and incapacity due to accident is also common. Accident insurance is mostly combined with sickness insurance.

Employers conclude accident and health insurance contracts voluntarily for two reasons:

- expressing their appreciation of their employees, increasing their commitment to the employer;
- in cases of health and accident cases, risk is higher than the average. Insurers determine what they consider to be a dangerous occupation in this contest.[321]

There are several constructions:

> The insurance sum can only be paid to the insured person, but the amount can be divided between the employer and the employee. In the latter case, the insurance also supports the employer, e.g., it covers the costs of replacing the lost labor, such as the cost of the replacement of temporary workforce or staffing, and covers the contractual penalty for the possible infringement of a deadline, and the portion of sick pay which has to be paid by the employer.

The services can also be formulated according to certain group of employers (groups of specific occupation, job position, and status), which means that several different employers' groups can be insured with an insurance.

Insurances may cover all employees of the employer or only just a specific group of employees.

In general, group insurances can be concluded from at least ten people.

A twenty-four-hour accident protection can also be stipulated which can be insurance for non-work-related accidents outside the workplace, for workplace accidents, or for both workplace accidents and workplace commute accidents.

---

321. Most of the contracts are regarding the following occupations dangerous:

(1) Non-civil aviation workers: Workshop pilot, advertising flying, aerial photography, helicopter rescue, helicopter police, helicopter construction, helicopter transportation, helicopter pest fight.
(2) Flight crew members of the Armed Forces, parachute jumper.
(3) Mining workers: operators of mining machinery, deep drilling, collier, carter, quarry worker, oil miner, solid mineral extractor.
(4) Metallurgical machine operator, foundry worker, boiler operator, iron and nonferrous metallurgical fusion, roller.
(5) Blaster, pyrotechnician, industrial alpinist, industrial diver.
(6) Electric power industry workers.
(7) Armed profession: bodyguard, commando, legionnaire, intelligence agent, armed man, security guard, pyrotechnist, diver.
(8) Peacekeeper.
(9) Stuntman.

Insurers offer a separate accident and health insurance for senior employees within the framework of which they provide premium services, e.g., manager screening, higher sums, and higher amount of compensation.

300. Occupational safety and security are also of paramount importance for the state, therefore, the collective health and accident insurance contracts concluded by the employers can be considered eligible costs if the employees or their family members are the beneficiaries. Occupational accident insurance is benefit-free from taxes and other contributions under the current laws if the monthly insurance premium per capita is lower than 30% of the minimum wage.

Insurance services are free from taxes and other contributions, except for the daily allowance with a specified amount defined in the tax laws. (*See also* Part IX.)

The employers with a high risk of occupational accident may—in addition to accident benefits provided by social security—also voluntarily conclude collective accident insurance contracts in order to cover damage caused by employment accidents, although with a higher fee than the average. Within the framework of a public procurement procedure, the Ministry of the Interior concluded a group life and accident insurance contract for two years for the employees belonging to the accelerated staff (police, anti-terrorists, specialists of the national defense service, employees of prisons, employees of disaster management, etc.) in 2015. At the same time, they will no longer conclude an accident insurance contract for the active members of the armed forces according to the decision of the competent minister. Damage caused by military accidents and not covered by the social security system is covered by the Ministry's own resources.

301. At the same time, a part of the employers exposed to particular or high risk is obliged to conclude an accident insurance contract by law. Act CXXXIII of 2005 on Security Services and the Activities of Private Investigators, employers of security guards and private investigators are obliged to conclude an accident insurance contract, even if the private investigator or the security guard is a subcontractor.

302. In accordance with the Act XXXI of 1996 on firefighting, technical rescue and fire brigades (section 41), and Government Decree No. 259/2011. (XII.7.) on its implementation, the operator of the fire department is obliged to conclude life and accident insurance contracts for firemen and for persons providing technical rescue.

The concluded insurance contract must cover at least accident and death caused by fire suppression, technical rescue and the preparation of these, and during standby duty.

Chapter 3. Accident Insurance

§1. Accident Insurance Concluded by the State for Persons Between the Age of 3 and 18

303. In Hungary, health insurance belonging to the social security system provides adequate health-care services to insured persons in the event of an accident. In case of incapacity for work due to an accident, employees receive a certain amount of financial benefits. In the case of an accident of minors, public health care provides health services, but legal representatives (parents) also have costs during the nursing, treatment, etc. of the minors. *Therefore, according to Government Decree No. 119/2003. (VIII.14.), the Hungarian state concludes a special accident insurance contract with all minors who have a residence in the territory of Hungary and who are Hungarian citizens from the age of 3 until the age of 18.*[322]

The accident insurance contract is for a calendar year, and the Ministry determined by the state concludes the contract within the framework of a public procurement procedure with the insurance company that provides the winning offer. The insurance premium is paid by the state.

The accident insurance relationship comes into existence by law on the date on which the insured person reaches the age of 3 and ends on the day on which he reaches the age of 18.

In the case of an accident of the insured person, the insurer is obliged to provide the services specified in the law, e.g.,:

- an insurance sum of HUF 200,000 in the event of accidental death;
- an insurance sum of HUF 3,000 (about EUR 10) in the case of bone fractures;
- an insurance sum of between HUF 3,000 and HUF 300,000 in case of disability, depending on its extent.

The accident is obliged to be reported to the insurer by the legal representative of the minor within thirty days after its occurrence.

According to the law, the definition of the accident is the following:

> a sudden external impact independent of the will of the insured person, in consequence of which the insured person dies within one year of the occurrence of the accident or suffers permanent health damage or fleeting injuries (bone fracture) defined by the law within two years of the occurrence of the accident.[323]

304. The law identifies certain diseases as well as deaths resulting from accidents, like:

---

322. According to the data of the HCSO from 2016, approximately one-and-a-half million children between 3 and 18 years of age are affected by the state-financed accident insurance.

323. According to the statistics of the insurance companies (2014–2015), the most common personal injuries occur due to bone fracture among the 3- to 18-year-old children. More than 80% of damage claims are reported as injuries.

(a) polio;
(b) brain cavity and/or cerebral inflammation due to tick bite;
(c) rabies and tetanus infections.

The beneficiary of the contract is the minor himself or, in the case of his death, the heir of the insured person.

The insurer can be exempted from the obligation to provide services if he proves that the insurance event was caused unlawfully, intentionally, or grossly negligent by the insured person. The law classifies as gross negligence if the insured person:

(a) was under the influence of alcohol during the occurrence of the accident (the blood alcohol concentration exceeding 1.5% in general and 0.8% during driving);
(b) was under the influence of drugs, narcotic substances, or medicines unless they were prescribed by a doctor and they were used in accordance with the prescription;
(c) drove a motor vehicle without a valid registration certificate or a valid driving license required to drive the vehicle.

The insurer can be exempted from the obligation to provide services in case of breach of the obligation to prevent and mitigate damage. The insured person is obliged to act during the mitigation of damage like it can be expected of or by a person in a particular situation.

The insurer can be exempted from the obligation to provide services if the notification obligation is violated and, therefore, essential circumstances become undetectable.

The insurer can be exempted from the payment of the insurance sum if the insured person has lost his life as a result of the deliberate conduct of the beneficiary.

The legislation includes exclusions as well, e.g.: the insurer does not perform if the insured person has been involved in a competition or a preparation for a competition that involves the use of a motorized land vehicle, watercraft, or aircraft. The insurance does not cover accidents which are caused directly or indirectly, in whole or in part, by ionizing radiation, nuclear energy, war or crime against the state.

305. There are insurance companies which provide group student accident insurance for schools and kindergartens in addition to state-funded accident insurance. The contract is concluded by the educational institution, but the insurance premium is paid by the parents and the legal representatives instead of the insured persons who are students or kindergarteners.

§2. PUBLIC ACCIDENT INSURANCE

I. Basic Accident Insurance

306. In Hungary, much less accident insurance is concluded than in the Western countries.[324]

Most people conclude insurance for accident-related death or disability.

Accident insurance contracts usually provide a specific amount for the following events:

- payment of a specific amount to the beneficiary in the case of accident-related death;
- payment of daily allowance in the case of nursing in a hospital due to an accident, sometimes from the first day, sometimes only from the fourth day;
- payment of a specific amount for an operation due to an accident, even in the case of more surgeries;
- payment of a specific amount in case of accidental disability or permanent damage to health (there are insurers who already pay form 10% of disability in case of accident disability, but the basic level is usually 25% of disability and the amount of insurance sum increases depending on the severity of the disability);
- payment of a specific amount for bone fracture;
- payment of a specific amount for a coma due to an accident;
- payment of daily allowance in case of incapacity for work resulting from an accident for a specified number of days;
- payment of a specific amount in the case of a burn injury, the financing of plastic surgery;
- payment of a specific amount in case of death or injuries due to a traffic accident;
- payment of accidental expenses (rescue, transportation, and dental expenses in the territory of Hungary certified by invoices, therapeutic appliances up to a fixed amount).

Insurers, applying the rules on indemnity insurance, usually stipulate their right to normal termination of the contract by the end of the insurance period, with a thirty-day notice period.

The insured person is obliged to report the changes in his activity (occupation, work, sport) within the stipulated time limit. If the risk increases in connection with this, the insurer is entitled to propose the modification of the contract (e.g., payment of surcharges) or, if the insurer cannot undertake the risk (e.g., this is excluded or the offer could have been rejected), he can terminate the contract.

324. According to the data of the AHIC, in Hungary, approximately 633,000 individual accident insurance contracts were registered in 2015. In addition to housing, motor vehicle and life insurances, an additional 1 million accidents and sickness insurance contracts increase the level of public safety. According to the estimated data, 11% of the population is protected by accident insurance. Source: https://mabisz.hu/szemle/?p=5728.

The accident insurance can also contain a value tracking clause when the amount of insurance sum and on the basis of this, the insurance premium is raised by the insurer once a year by the same proportion.

Accident insurance can also be concluded as an additional insurance next to life, home or other insurance. The cost and value proportion of additional insurance is less good than those of individual accident insurance.

Exclusions and exemptions are largely based on rules relating to the student accident insurance concluded by the state.

II. Extreme Sports Accident Insurance

307. From January 1, 2007, social security does not provide free services for accidental injuries resulting from extreme sports activities determined by separate laws in Hungary, except for life-saving emergency care. (*See also* Part VI.) In case of an accident, such sportsmen are expected to face serious additional costs. For this reason, the number of such accident insurance contracts has increased. Extreme sports accident insurance, as a basic service, covers medical expenses (costs of outpatient care, inpatient care, medical rehabilitation, oral surgery) and the cost of patient transport if it is certified by invoice. As supplementary insurance, it supports the cost of the necessary medicines and therapeutic appliances and provides a specified amount in case of accident-related death, disability, bone fracture, and daily allowance in case of accident hospital care.

Chapter 4. Private Health Insurance

§1. The Regulation of the Health Insurance Contract in the CC and in the BIns.

308. The law seeks to meet the social needs which have emerged in the last decade by introducing health insurance—temporally only with some rules. CC regulates the health insurance contract in a separate chapter (Chapter LXV.).

The definition of health insurance is the following:

> Health insurance is a type of insurance where the insurance company promises to pay benefits as provided for in the contract in the event of the insured person's sickness. The insurance benefits may also cover the costs of health-care services specified in the contract provided to a person in good health.[325]

According to the notion, the insurer provides services mainly in case of sickness, but according to the needs of the age, it is also possible that the insurer pays the costs of health-care services used by a healthy person (the health-care screenings, programs, and the purchase of sports equipment are more and more common).

This type of contract has a mixed character because partly the regulation of indemnity insurance and partly the regulation of life insurance has to be applied.

The regulations governing life insurance shall apply to health insurance policies:[326]

(a) with respect to group insurance;
(b) with respect to the consent of the insured person if he is not the contracting party;
(c) with respect to the revocation of the insured person's statement of consent; and
(d) when the insurance company's obligations take effect upon the infringement of the disclosure obligation.

If health insurance was obtained as an indemnity insurance, the provisions on indemnity insurance shall apply with the following exceptions:

(a) in the obligation to mitigate damages, the insured person's refusal—in exercising the right of disposition to which he is entitled by virtue of law—to a medical procedure shall not constitute a reason for the insurance company's exemption; and
(b) the insured person shall not have the obligation to preserve the scene upon the occurrence of the insurance event.[327]

325. Section 6:487 of the CC.
326. Subsection 1 of s. 6:488 of the CC.
327. Subsection 2 of s. 6:488 of the CC.

It follows from the essence of health insurance that the general rules on the significant increase of the insurance risk cannot in all respects be applied.

According to the general rules, in case of a considerable increase in the insurance risk, the insurer is entitled to make a proposal to amend the contract or terminate the contract.[328] Subsection 1 of section 6:490 of the CC states that the insured person's health deteriorates with age due to natural causes which shall not constitute a considerable increase in insurance risk.

The CC expressly excludes the possibility that the insurance company can terminate a health insurance policy by notice in an ordinary way.[329]

In case of health insurance contracts, the CC contains a provision on waiting period,[330] according to which the parties may install a clause in the contract stipulating that the insurance company shall begin to cover the risks of certain perils from a certain point in time following the time of conclusion of the contract, or shall be entitled to reduce the amount of coverage if the insured event occurs within the stipulated waiting period.

In case of health insurance contract, waiting period can be stipulated in two cases:

- where the policy pertains to nursing care services;
- if the insurable person suffers from a permanent illness and it was known to both parties at the time the contract was concluded.

The maximum waiting period is three years, according to the CC.[331]

Under section 6:456 of the CC, if the contracting party is a consumer, the contract shall be allowed to derogate from the exclusion of derogation only to the benefit of the contracting party, the insured person, and the beneficiary with respect to fixed-sum and health insurance policies.

309. Some provisions of the BIns. also directly affect the health insurance contract.

According to subsection 1 of section 134 of the BIns. the following actions of insurance companies shall not be construed as a violation of the principle of gender equality defined in Act CXXV of 2003 on Equal Treatment and the Promotion of Equal Opportunity (hereinafter referred to as "ETOA") based on sex if the insurance company processes, stores, and uses data related to sex solely for the purpose of risk assessment in connection with life, accident, and health insurance policies.

Under subsection 4 of section 156 of BIns. if a medical examination of the prospective policyholder is required for the conclusion of an insurance contract—life insurance and non-life insurance alike—the insurance company must inform the client of his right to have access to the results of such tests and examination at the health-care service provider pursuant to the Healthcare Act.

328. Section 6:446 of the CC.
329. Subsection 2 of s. 6:490 of the CC.
330. Section 6:480 of the CC.
331. Section 6:489 of the CC.

§2. The Health Insurance Market and the Health Insurance Products

310. Between 2012 and 2019, the fee for health insurance concluded by the employer was free from taxes and other contributions.

311. From January 1, 2019, the tax exemption has ended; the insurance premium paid by the employer is taxed in the same way as the salary and is considered income on the employee's side. The employer is also charged with the employer's contribution after the paid insurance premium, in the same way as after the wage.

312. Insurance services of the insurers are also tax-free. (*see* Part IX). Corporate group health insurance can be offered by insurance companies for a minimum of ten people.

The constructions of health insurance products are varied; there are fixed-sum policies, indemnity insurances, and insurances providing medical services. In the case of indemnity insurance, the service of the insurer is the reimbursement of the pecuniary damage suffered by the insured person (e.g., the cost of a health-care service or the cost of a medicine). In the case of fixed-sum policies, the insurer pays a predetermined amount, regardless of the effect of the insurance event on the financial situation of the insured person (e.g., daily allowance for the days spent in the hospital, payment of a specific amount for a particular illness).

Health services provided by health insurances may be complementary to social security services (benefits which are not funded by social security system, such as dental interventions, specific screening tests can be claimed from the private service provider contracted with the insurer or higher-quality care covered by the insurer can be claimed in the state hospital, e.g., single room in the hospital). They can be of a substitute or alternative nature when the private health-care institution contracted with the insurer provides the same health-care service as the state but with better infrastructure (hotel-type catering, a la carte meal, more modern diagnostic equipment, etc.).[332]

Insurance contracts offered by insurers have only been fixed-sum policies and indemnity insurances for years, primarily because there were no private health-care service providers. The fixed-sum policy constructions are not considered "real" health insurance in the literature, as opposed to "real" health insurance (service providing health insurance) covering part or all of the health-care costs.

Nowadays, the first private service providers appeared in the Hungarian health-care sector, and the number of their patients is increasing. Nevertheless, the health insurance market does not grow in line with expectations.[333] In recent years, the growth of the private health-care sector has been more dynamic than that of the relevant insurance products.

---

332. About the rulings of health insurances *see*: Dr. Tőkey Balázs, *Kitekintés a magán-egészségbiztosítások legelterjedtebb szabályozási megoldásaira* [Outlook for the most Common Regulation Models of Private Health Insurances] Biztosítás és kockázat, 2015/4. 12, 48–61.

333. In 2014, 32,700 health insurance contracts are concluded, which increased for 33,600 in 2015. In 2021, 39,171 health and sickness insurance contracts were active. Compared to the slow portfolio growth, premium income shows a significant increase, however, the proportion of insurance claims to premiums has increased significantly between 60%–80%.

This is primarily due to the fact that the health insurance contract can be concluded mainly by healthy clients who undertake to pay the insurance premium for a longer period of time, possibly without any insurance event. This presupposes a serious personal foresight to which the Hungarian population is less susceptible. The other reason is that most private health-care service providers provide outpatient care or one-day surgery, the cost of which is still payable by a part of the population or is covered through health insurance. The costs of inpatient care are much higher; therefore, it is worthwhile to conclude insurance contracts which cover these costs. Today, the most popular service is the obstetric and dental private practice.

Most health insurance companies provide the following services:

- the payment of a specified amount per day for the days of illness as a replacement for lost income;
- the payment of daily allowance in case of hospital treatment, depending on the number of days spent in the hospital;
- the payment of a specified amount in case of the so-called dreadful illnesses defined in the contract (there are insurers who provide services for forty illnesses, while the majority only covers four to five illnesses);
- the coverage of the costs of illness during a stay abroad;
- outpatient care in the following fields: internal and child medicine, otolaryngology, ophthalmology, gynecology, urology, dermatology;
- support of costs of anti-influenza vaccination annually;
- laboratory tests (standard): basic blood, urine and stool tests, hormone tests, prostate cancer screening (PSA);
- diagnostic tests (standard): gynecological cytology, ECG (ultrasound, under load), ultrasound (UH), X-ray, mammography, Doppler and arteriography examination, filter audiological examination, bone density test (ODX, DEXA);
- allergic tests;
- (Call Center) twenty-four-hour telephone health line (e.g., availability of medical, hospitality services, pharmacy services, counseling in the field of prevention, health care and healthy lifestyle);
- booking of date, organization of health services;
- providing ambulatory surgeries;
- physiotherapy and therapeutic massage annually on defined occasions;
- dental inspection once a year;
- the financing of vaccinations not reimbursed by social security;
- the partial or full reimbursement costs of centrally sponsored stem cell withdrawal;
- the reimbursement of home care and financing of therapeutic appliances;
- the payment of a specified amount for malignant cancer;
- the payment of a fixed amount for permanent damage to health.

It is important to point out that insurers stipulate in the contract that the insurer is not responsible for the professional quality of the health-care services provided

https://www.portfolio.hu/gazdasag/20230105/husz-ev-alatt-nyolcszorosara-nott-az-egeszsegbiztositasi-piac-588196.

for the insured person and for the damage and restitution caused to the insured person during the performance of the health-care service, for which the health-care provider is responsible.

Health insurance contracts also stipulate that the contract terminates when the insured person reaches his 70th (sometimes 80th) birthday. Nowadays, insurers do not offer insurance contracts for the nursing of elderly people (*see* Part VI.).

Most of the contracts are health insurance combined with life insurance; therefore, they belong to the life insurance branch, according to the BIns. Most insurance contracts stipulate a waiting period, which is usually six months after the beginning of the contract. Health insurance contracts contain a number of exclusions, only a few of them are:

- pregnancy and childbirth, if the conception occurred before the beginning of the risk;
- induced abortion;
- sterilization;
- change of gender;
- treatment by a nonmedical practitioner and their consequences;
- suicide;
- regular alcohol consumption, events related to regular drug consumption;
- psychiatric illnesses;
- cosmetic interventions and disadvantages caused by them;
- claims related to specific infectious diseases;
- events related to specific sports activities.

Chapter 5. Life Insurance

§1. Individual Life Insurance

313. Unlike the European trends, most of the life insurance products are combined with savings element in Hungary. There are several reasons for this, e.g., low bank interest rates; it is not worth keeping money in bank deposits, investment-linked life insurance, or pension insurance supported by tax benefits. The purely risk products are typically concluded to reduce the risk of bank loan repayment for the provisions of the banks. The classical risk-bearing nature of life insurance products is, therefore, less effective in Hungary.

In practice, life insurance products can be in many cases combined with supplementary insurance such as sickness and accident insurance.

The Hungarian insurance market offers countless life insurance products in various combinations. In the following, we tried to categorize the most important characters and we tried to present their most important variants.

I. General Types of Life Insurance Contracts

A. *Life Insurance with Savings Element and the So-Called Attainment Insurance*

314. According to Point 75 of subsection 1 of section 4 of BIns., life insurance with a savings element shall mean life insurance policies, other than death risk policies, that generate a savings element and that provide benefits upon expiry or that feature the option of surrendering the policy for its cash surrender value, or both in some cases

B. *Risk Life Insurance*

315. In the case of risk life insurance, if the insured person dies within the duration of the insurance, the insurer undertakes to pay a certain amount for a third person, the beneficiary. If the insurance period terminates and the insured person is alive, the insurance contract is terminated without payment.

"Whole life" insurance is a special type of risk insurance. Here, the contract lasts during the life of the insured person; therefore, it always terminates with a payment. It is typical in case of whole life insurance that insurers limit the payment period, e.g., until the age of 80 of the insured person, and then the insurance remains valid without payment.

Risk life insurance can also be used as a *collateral life insurance*. In this case, in the event of the death of the insured person (debtor), the creditor bank will receive the insurance sum which will be included in the amount of the loan.

C. *Mixed Insurance*

316. One of the most common life insurance products is the mixed insurance, which is a combination of risk and attainment insurance. In this case, the insurance event is the survival of the insured person at the end of the insurance or the death of the insured person during the insurance period. The main derogation from the purely life insurance policy is that if the insured person is still alive when the fixed term expires, the insurer still pays the specified amount of insurance. The insurer is also required to perform his service in case of the death of the insured person.

II. Insured Event

317. Insured events are:

- survival to a stipulated term;
- death of the insured person;
- persistent deterioration of health of the insured person defined in percentage;
- marriage, birth, pension entitlement.

III. Criteria in Connection with the Insured Person

318. These are:

- determination of the maximum age of the insured person, usually 60–65 years; if the insured person reaches this age, no life insurance contract will be concluded;
- in the case of life insurance with savings element, the determination of the maximum age of the insured person is generally around 70 years; although in the case of piety life insurance[334] and whole life insurance, the contract will last until the end of life of the insured person;
- health insurance statement or even medical examination.

According to subsection 4 of section 156 of BIns. if a medical examination of the prospective policyholder is required for the conclusion of an insurance contract, the insurance company must inform the client of his right to have access to the results of such tests and examination at the health-care service provider pursuant to the Healthcare Act.

In the case of life assurance concluded without a medical examination, insurers usually stipulate a waiting period (*see* Part II, Chapter 5, §2).

334. In the event of piety life insurances, the costs of the funeral are covered by the amount of insurance, if the insured party dies.

IV. The Payment of Insurance Premium

319. The insurance premium can be a single premium, which means that there is one premium payment, which is payable upfront at the beginning of the insured period.

The payment of the insurance premium can be regular or periodical.

Flexible payout: There are life insurance contracts which allow the contracting party, after the conclusion of the contract to pay an extra fee higher than the stipulated fee (extraordinary charge) depending on his contractual income options. The minimum of this fee is usually determined (approximately EUR 150). If, for example, the contracting party does not pay a continuous fee but has paid an extra fee, the insurer will reimburse the extra fee to cover the continuous fee.

Another option is the possibility of *dynamic rate adjustment* when the contracting party can increase the insurance premium per contracting period.

V. Investments in Insurance Technical Reserves (Decision of Investment and Investment Risk, Capital Guarantee, Yield Guarantee)

320. In the case of conventional savings insurance, the insurer decides on the investment of the technical reserves and the insurer bears the risk of the investment. It does not promise a yield but pays the amount determined on the termination.

Under Point 6 of subsection 1 of section 4 of BIns., *unit-linked life insurance* shall mean a type of life insurance product where the insurance company places the amount of the technical provisions relating to the insurance contract into individual, separately managed stocks of assets (asset funds) created by the insurance company comprising theoretical settlement components of identical value (investment units) having its own investment policy, or into other investment funds operated by a company authorized to manage investment funds, whichever is selected by the insured party, for the purpose of investment, according to the terms and conditions laid down in the contract.

If the investment decision is made by the contracting party, he bears the risk of the investment.

According to subsection 3 of section 156 of BIns., as regards unit-linked life insurance policies, the insurance company must provide the policyholder with access to information on the placement of investments, to wit, the cross rate of the various investment forms used to cover the policyholder's investment, the types of each form of investment, and the current value of his investments.

A. Capital Guarantee and Minimum Guaranteed Yield

321. During the capital guarantee, the insurer promises that the amount of the technical reserves constituted from the insurance premium will not be reduced even in the case of unfavorable investments, or the insurer will reimburse it in the event of a loss. Insurers do not always promise to keep 100% of the capital, and there are insurers who promise the retention of only 50%–70% of the invested amount.

When calculating the life insurance premium, the insurers assume a yield which will inevitably be achieved and determine the extent of the service, taking into account this.

The amount of this yield is the technical interest rate.

Under Point 96 of subsection 1 of section 4 of BIns., *technical interest rate* shall mean the rate of interest used by the insurance company when calculating the premiums and premium reserve for life and sickness insurance policies and benefit payment reserve for accident and liability insurance policies, where the ceiling rate is specified in the relevant legislation.

In the case of a yield guarantee, the insurer must perform the undertaken service even if the investment income is below the technical interest rate. Some insurers promised and guaranteed yields which could not be performed, therefore they jeopardized the other reserves of the insurer. For this reason, the NBH determines the maximum amount of yield which can be promised by 2016. The NBH decree determines the maximum amount of the minimum guaranteed yield which is 2.3% in HUF contracts from July 1, 2016, according to the *NBH Decree No. 54/2015 (XII.21.)*. From December 2022, technical interest rates (guaranteed yield) applicable for services payable in HUF are:

(a) 4% per year for products with a regular fee;
(b) 7% for single-fee products with a duration of five years or less;
(c) 4% in the case of single-fee contracts lasting longer than five years.

According to subsection 2 of section 125 of BIns., the performance guarantee incorporates a guarantee to preserve the capital invested, lacking any specific reference thereto.

B. Bonus

322. According to Point 100 of subsection 1 of section 4 of BIns., *bonus* shall mean the difference between the return on investment of mathematical provisions comprising a part of technical provisions of accountancy and the yield calculated by the technical interest rate.

Before January 1, 2016, the BIns. obligatory provided the return of 80% of the bonus to the contracting party. From January 1, 2016, it is not compulsory, and the insurers are free to decide whether they return from the extra investment bonus to the contracting party or not.

Several provisions of the BIns. require the insurer to inform the contracting party about the return of the bonus (and its amount) in the terms of the contract and the customer's prospectus. The insurer also must inform the contracting party if he does not return the bonus at all. According to the subsection 6 of section 6 of NBH Decree No. 55/2015. (XII.22.), if the insurer does not stipulate the minimum proportion of the profit sharing in its contractual terms, the percentage of profit sharing is considered to be 0%, i.e., the whole profit remains with the insurer.

Several insurers undertake the rebate, usually between 80% and 90%, but there are those who promise 100%.

Several insurers undertake the return of the bonus, usually between 80% and 90%, but there are insurers who promise 100% of reimbursement.

VI. Service

323. Type of services are:

- single payment service;
- annuity benefits which mean payments made to the beneficiary periodically under contract.

Types of annuities:

- in the case of an immediate starting annuity, the annuity payment starts in the year when the contract is concluded (annuity purchased by pension funds);
- in the case of delayed annuity payments, the annuity payment starts only after the expiration of a term specified in the contract (usually 5–10 years);
- the annuity may be up to the end of the life of the insured person (simple annuity) or for a defined period of time or duration, but at most up to the date of death of the insured person if it happens before the aforementioned date (fixed-term annuity);
- the purpose of the so-called front guarantee benefit is that the insurer guarantees the annuity for the period specified in the contract even if the insured person dies in the meantime; in this case, the beneficiary (or the heir) receives the annuity;
- in case of the so-called back guarantee life annuity, the insurer will pay the annuity for a few years after the death of the insured person for the beneficiary;
- in case of a double annuity, there are two insured persons, usually a married couple, where the two insured persons jointly accumulate the jointly purchased annuity. The amount of the annuity may be reduced if one party dies, but the annuity service is terminated only if both parties die.

VII. Other Services

324. Point *63 of subsection 1 of section 4 of BIns.* offers the insurer to provide a so-called *policy loan* which means a loan—not treated as a financial service—that may be provided by the insurance company to the holder of a life insurance policy up to its cash surrender value and which is settled by the insurance company and the policyholder upon or before the occurrence of the insurance event or when the contract terminates.

VIII. Residual Rights

325. Under Point 72 of subsection 1 of section 4 of BIns., *residual rights* shall mean the rights defined in the terms and conditions of a life insurance contract that remain in the case of nonpayment of premium and/or the termination of the contract without payment of the sum insured.

A. Cash Surrender Value

326. Subsection 1 of section 6:484 of the CC regulates the cash surrender value: if a life assurance policy is terminated for any reason without payment of the sum insured, the insurance company shall be liable to pay the cash surrender value defined in the policy.

The payment of the cash surrender value can be led back to the dual purpose of the life insurance premium: the life insurance premium partially is the consideration of the risk of the insurer and partially is a reserve-raising tool, which serves as the coverage of the insurance company's service (the coverage of the service of the insurer consists of the premiums paid and from the yield resulting from the investment). For this reason, it would be an unjustified advantage for insurers if they keep the premium reserve while they are not obliged to pay the insurance sum.[335]

The amount of minimum cash surrender value is determined by section 124/A of the BIns. based on the percentage of the insurance premiums paid. Insurers can determine a higher minimum cash surrender value than the value determined by law, which is not uncommon in the insurance market.

Insurers stipulate that the supplementary insurance terminates at the time of the repurchase.

B. Partial Repurchase

327. Some contracts also allow the contracting party to repurchase only the extra fees paid or part of the insurance premium. In such cases, the contract remains in force but with a reduced insurance amount left in the insurer.

C. Premium-Free Reduction

328. According to subsection 2 of section 6:481 of the CC, in the event of nonpayment of premium, an ordinary life insurance policy other than term life insurance shall remain in effect with the premium reduced accordingly (hereinafter referred to as "premium-free reduction"). The contracting party shall have the option to terminate the contract by notice instead. The contract may not be rendered premium-free if the surrender value has not been calculated at the time of premium-free reduction. In this case, the contract shall be terminated in the absence of a settlement value.

---

335. Dr. Zavodnyik József, *A biztosítási szerződési jog alapjai* [Basis of Insurance Contract Law-].Budapest, BOI (2004), 101.

In the case of premium-free reduction, the contracting party cannot pay the continuous insurance premium for a certain reason but does not use the option to repurchase because he does not want to terminate the contract for this reason. In this case, the insurer will provide an insurance service with a lower amount from the reserves made up of the insurance premiums paid up to that date and from its investment.

There are contracts which provide the opportunity to recommence the payment, and then the contracting has the opportunity to reraise the previously reduced insurance amount and resume payment.

The possibility of premium-free reduction is linked to a defined amount of insurance premium paid or to the number of years covered by the insurance premium.

The determination of the premium-free amount is based on the premium-free table forming part of the contract.

IX. Inflation Escalation

329. Under Point 27 of subsection 1 of section 4 of BIns., *inflation escalation* shall mean the annual adjustment of the insurance premium and the amount of coverage, irrespective of the number of claims, consistent with the level of inflation.

Insurance contracts almost always use inflation escalation. Basically, their annual fees are increased according to the inflation rate published by the HCSO prior to the given year. The indexing raises both the amount of insurance and the insurance premium. Insurers usually change these two at the same level, but this is not decisive.

Under subsection 2 of section 156 of BIns., in connection with an inflation escalation clause in an insurance contract, the client is to be clearly informed concerning the components to which the inflation escalation clause applies and to which it does not apply. The insurance company shall be required to emphasize the existence of inflation escalation clauses, including the rights of the client relative to such clauses.

X. Compulsory Elements of Life Insurance Contracts According to the BIns.

330. According to subsection 1 of section 121 of BIns., the terms and conditions of the insurance contract shall cover:

- the detailed rules for inflation escalation, where applicable;
- a description of the rights of the insured person, the contracting party, and the beneficiary and the obligations of the insurance company that apply when the contract is terminated, including information on the provisions concerning the termination of the contract;
- the detailed rules for the provision of residual rights and/or a life insurance policy loan, if available in the case of life insurance policies;
- optional daily access to information concerning the placement and value of unit-linked life insurance policies;
- the procedure for crediting the bonus;

- the detailed rules concerning the suspension and separation of asset funds in the case of unit-linked life insurance policies (*see* Chapter 6);
- in the case of life insurance, the option to change the technical rate of interest during the term of the insurance contract, under the condition that it may be changed only if the highest technical rate of interest fixed in the decree on the highest technical rate of interest is amended.

§2. Group Life Insurance

I. Employer Group Life Insurance

331. The conclusion of employer group life insurances occurs mainly in three cases in Hungary:

(1) In Hungary, employers can give employees nonwage benefits in a statutory value. These can be meal tickets, wellness weekends, clothing exchange, travel allowances, etc. The nonwage benefit cannot be considered taxable income, therefore the employee does not have to pay taxes and contributions afterward. It is also referred to as a cafeteria system because the employee can choose from the opportunities offered by the employer. Life insurances can also be awarded within the framework of nonwage benefits as an eligible option, but employees prefer to choose other nonwage benefits, which can be transformed into cash or can be used immediately.
(2) Some employers, in addition to the cafeteria system, conclude group life insurance for their employees, combined with accident and sickness insurance. The employer expresses his care and appreciation for his employee.[336]
(3) It is also popular that the employee pays the insurance, but the employer organizes the conclusion of the insurance because the insurer provides a discount because of the number of insured persons.

According to the surveys, if the employer concludes separate life insurance for his employees or for a part of them in addition to the cafeteria system, he has a better position in the labor market.

Risk life insurance is more common in large companies than in SMEs.

Larger companies tend to conclude them as an additional benefit and care for everyone, typically creating different insurance groups with different service content.

According to surveys, insurance rates are low compared to the European average. Hungarian companies spend less money on insurance; one of the reasons for this is that employees do not always prefer this. At the same time, the conclusion of

336. For some budget-funded employers, the list of life insurances is also listed at the level of allowances outside the cafeteria system, such as in the Act on courts. In addition to "cafeteria" benefits, judges may be given other benefits, such as in particular: life insurance policy with savings element in recognition of the length of service.

group life insurance contracts can help to increase the insurance proportion of a fairly underinsured Hungarian society compared to Western Europe.[337]

II. Group Life Insurance Concluded by Credit Institutions (Banks)

332. Among life insurances and the supplementary accident and sickness group insurances, insurances concluded by bank occupy a special position. These contracts are concluded by banks mostly for two reasons in Hungary.

333. The purely risk life insurance is concluded by a credit institution for individuals who take long-term loans from him. The contracting party is the credit institution; the insured person is the debtor, i.e., the borrower. The premium is paid separately by the debtor or it is calculated into the costs of the given loan, into the incurred expenses of the credit institution. In case of occurrence of the insured events, the beneficiary is the credit institution. Insurance events are the debtor's death or incapacity for work (illness, accident). Life insurance is therefore an additional guarantee of the loan contract besides the mortgage loan because in the event of the death of the debtor, the insured amount is paid to the credit institution, and the sum is included in the amount of loan which has not been paid back. In the event of a temporary incapacity for work of the debtor, the insurer pays the repayment sums instead of the debtor for a specified period of time (usually ten months), or in the event of a long-term incapacity for work of the debtor (disability), the insurer pays a specified amount, which is also received by the credit institution and is imputed into the unpaid loan.

The disadvantage of these contracts is mostly that the insurer does not require a health declaration or a medical examination, but the contract states that the insurer does not provide the service if the insured event occurs within X years (usually two–five years) from the conclusion of the contract in connection with a disease which already existed during the conclusion of the contract. The insured persons or their relatives later realize that the insurers fail to pay when the insured event occurs because the insured was under medical treatment prior to the conclusion of the contract, and the subsequent insurance event is related to this. Insurers therefore conduct a "health investigation" during the administration following the occurrence of the insurance event. Insurers request a medical expert and collect the necessary health information in order to determine whether the death or illness may be traced back to the period prior to the conclusion of the contract. During the conclusion of individual life insurance contracts, the common process is reversed: first, the insurance comes into existence, then the insurance event occurs, and finally, the health condition is examined.

334. Conclusion of life insurance with a savings element. The bank concludes the contract, the debtor is the insured person, and the bank is the beneficiary. The debtor pays the fees associated with the loan and the insurance as well. The essence of the loan construction is that it allows a deferred capital repayment. The debtor

337. Biztosítási Szemle [Insurance Review] https://mabisz.hu/szemle/?p=6085.

only pays the interest and handling costs to the bank and accumulates the capital repayment in the life insurance, and when the life insurance expires (which is equal to the termination of the loan), the amount of the insurance is used for the repayment of the capital of the housing loan. The insurance has coverage and a savings function. If the amount of the insurance is greater than the amount of the loan, the difference is paid to the insured person or to another beneficiary designated by him.

335. It is not so widespread, but a few banks offer a premium account life insurance contract with a payment account. In some cases, the bank organizes the conclusion of the contract, and the premium paid by the client will be more favorable because of the group. In other cases, the bank offers the life insurance together with the account contract; the bank is the contracting party and the client is the insured person, but the beneficiary can be determined by the client, and the insurance premium is included in the account management fee. With respect to the market price of life insurance, it is possible to conclude an insurance contract with a much more favorable price, even for half of the market price.

In case of these life insurances, there is no medical examination prior to the conclusion of the contract and no health questionnaire has to be completed.

336. The insurer also does not pay if the insured event occurs within X years (usually two–five years) from the conclusion of the contract in connection with a disease which already existed during the conclusion of the contract. There are contracts where other exemptions are stipulated. In this case the insurer does not pay if the insured event is caused partly or wholly by a disease which has been diagnosed or treated within three years prior to the conclusion of the contract.

The contracts are concluded for an undetermined period, usually up to 65 years old and they terminate when the contracting party is 70 years old.

Chapter 6. Pension Funds

337. In Hungary, no classical pension funds have been created within the framework of the supplementary pension system. The institutions of the supplementary system, the voluntary mutual insurance funds,[338] the private pension funds,[339] and the occupational retirement provider collect the retirement savings and invest them as their own assets. The forefront savers have an individual account to credit the payments and their investment yields, from which an amount determined by law can be deduced in order to finance the operation of these institutions.

The premium income from pension insurances concluded by insurers is also an isolated part of the assets of the insurer determined by law which is managed by the insurer.

The pension institutions manage the collected savings under the applicable laws themselves or delegate them to external experts.

The Act LXXXII of 1997 on Private Pensions and Private Pension Funds (PPF) allows the assets of the private pension fund to be managed by a private limited-liability company,[340] while the external organization entrusted with the management of the fund's assets may only be an investment firm, a financial institution, an insurance company, or an investment fund management organization.[341]

338. The main reason that the law allows an insurance private limited company to manage the assets of a private pension fund is that an insurer can also establish a private pension fund as an employer under the law. However, after the establishment of the fund, the insurer cannot operate the fund longer because it became the property of the members, and the members can make any decisions regarding the private fund.[342]

---

338. According to sub. 9 of s. 2 of VMIF Act, the organization, financing, and provision of services to supplement, substitute, or replace social security services and social services, as well as services for health protection under the conditions laid down in this Act, funded from membership payments kept on the members' individual accounts shall be treated as voluntary mutual insurance fund activities.
339. According to sub. 4 of s. 4 of PPF Act, private pension fund activity shall include the admission of fund members, the collection of membership payments on the members behalf, the investment of these funds, and keeping individual accounts from which to provide pension plan benefits and lump-sum payments.
340. According to sub. 9 of s. 66 of PPF Act, *asset management for pension funds* shall mean performance of obligations and exercising, in a specified scope, the ownership rights pertaining to a fund's assets, within the framework of contracts concluded with the fund.
341. Subsection 9 of s. 66 of PPF Act.
342. According to sub. 1 of s. 7 of PPF Act, funds may be established by employers separately or jointly, chambers of trade (hereinafter referred to as "chambers") separately or jointly, professional associations separately or jointly, or together with a chamber (or chambers), as well as employees' and/or employers' interest representation organizations, separately or jointly, or together with the aforementioned entities.

    Under sub. 1 of s. 11 of PPF Act, the organizations may undertake to partly or entirely assume the founding and operational costs of the fund.

    According to sub. 1 of s. 5 of the PPF Act, after the establishment of the fund, the rights of the founders terminates, and in accordance with the principle of self-administration, fundamental decisions related to the fund shall be made exclusively by fund members.

Insurers could earn revenue from the management of the assets of private funds and from the revenue they received from it, which compensates for the huge amount invested in the establishment of the fund.

Because of this, Annex 2 of BIns. contains a separate point for the management of pension assets when defining the sectors of the life assurance sector.

339. Insurers participating in the foundation of private funds, however, do not fundamentally deal with the management of the funds. The law allows the provision of other services and that private pension funds purchase allowance from insurers. In this field, there is a rather intensive link between private funds and insurers.

According to the Act XCVI of 1993 on Voluntary Mutual Insurance Funds (VMIF), voluntary pension funds have developed in other constructions, therefore the law does not stipulate expressly that their assets can be managed by insurance private limited companies. With the exception of this, the voluntary fund can manage its assets with the same institutions as the private pension fund. The same applies to occupational retirement providers and insurance companies: they either manage their retirement assets themselves or entrust them to an abovementioned external expert defined by law statutory, already listed.

In most cases, insurers delegate the investment of the collected premiums of retirement insurances to external trust companies, and they do not invest themselves. There are groups of companies in which there are insurance companies and investment fund management organizations, and in this case the assignment is given within a group of companies.

§1. MANAGEMENT OF ASSETS OF INSURERS

340. Pension insurances may also be unit-linked insurances.

Under Point 29 of subsection 1 of section 4 of the BIns., asset fund shall mean assets set aside from the premiums of unit-linked life insurance policies—less the deductions provided for in the insurance contract—for investment purposes.

In addition to the general investment rules for the technical insurance reserves of the insurers (*see* Part I, Chapter 4), special provisions apply to unit-linked asset funds.

341. With respect to assets held as cover for technical provisions in respect of life insurance contracts where the investment risk is borne by the policyholders and where the benefits provided under the contract are directly linked to the value of assets contained in an internal fund held by the insurance companies (asset funds), comprising theoretical settlement components of identical value (investment units), the technical provisions in respect of those benefits must be invested in units represented as closely as possible by those assets.[343]

In connection with the investment and management of the assets held as cover for the reserves of unit-linked life insurance policies, the following provisions shall be observed:

343. Subsection 1 of s. 105 of BIns.

(a) The investment policy of the asset funds shall, *inter alia,* contain the data and information provided for in Annex 12 of the BIns.
(b) The policyholders must be informed on a regular basis concerning the market value of the liquid assets and financial instruments comprised in the portfolio of their choice.
(c) The performance of the portfolio shall be demonstrated according to the criteria specified in Annex 10 of the BIns.
(d) Insurance companies may not purchase for any portfolio they manage:
   - securities of their own issue;
   - securities issued by their related companies,[344] with the exception of securities admitted to trading on a regulated market or that are subject to quote-driven trading.

(e) An insurance company may not transact any deals involving financial instruments—with the exception of Government securities with a maturity of less than six months and open-ended public investment units—that are not listed on a regulated market on behalf of any portfolio it manages with a company in which it has a qualifying interest or with a company that has a qualifying interest in the insurance company.

The investment shall be made for the clients, in accordance with the investment policy, professionally, under the general principles of fairness, transparency, and with due care, with particular regard to the price and expenditures—including any refund received and other deductions in asset management—and the return expected.

Insurance companies shall specify any price, fee or commission they charged and any deduction they applied in proportion to provisions so as to ensure that such specification and the related description clearly demonstrate their purpose and underlying content.

Insurance companies shall adopt regulations to fix the evaluation principles for the securities and concerning the means and frequency of disclosure of information to policyholders.

Insurance companies shall be allowed to make changes in the investment policy of asset funds in compliance with the contract terms and conditions, and only in a way that ensures such change shall not affect the level of risk of the given asset fund. Changes in the investment policy can be made only if the original investment policy cannot be implemented due to changes in the investment climate or to changes in the accessibility or availability of assets.

Insurance companies shall communicate to the clients concerned any changes made in the investment policy at least sixty days in advance. Insurance companies shall post an information bulletin on their websites on any changes made in their investment policy. The clients concerned shall be demonstrably notified of any

344. According to the BIns., for this purposes related company shall mean the company's parent company and subsidiary, a subsidiary of the company's parent company, a shareholder with a qualifying interest in the company or any other company in which the company or the owner, supervisory board member, managing director of the company, or one of their close relatives has a qualifying interest.

changes in the investment policy as provided for in the contract or in the relevant agreement either orally, in writing, or by way of electronic means. Following the date of notification, clients shall be given the opportunity to switch to another asset fund free of charge within a period of sixty days.[345]

342. The insurance companies offering unit-linked life insurance policies shall notify the Authority of the asset funds it offers with such life insurance policies within fifteen working days from the day they were introduced. The notification shall indicate the name of the asset fund and the underlying investment policy.[346]

I. Capital and Performance Guarantee[347]

343. The name, investment policy and commercial communication of the managed fund, or the policy terms and conditions may contain any reference for guarantee to protect the capital invested and may undertake to guarantee the earnings (hereinafter referred to as "capital guarantee, performance guarantee"), where the guarantee is accompanied by appropriate guarantee arrangements.

The performance guarantee incorporates a guarantee to preserve the capital invested, lacking any specific reference thereto. (*See* further: Chapter 5, §1).

II. Capital and Yield Protection

344. The name, investment policy and commercial communication of the managed fund, or the policy terms and conditions may contain any reference to a pledge to protect the capital invested (capital protection) and may undertake to guarantee the earnings (yield protection), where yield and capital protection are supported by an adequate investment policy pertaining to financial instruments.

The promise to pay dividends incorporates a pledge to preserve the capital invested, lacking any specific reference thereto.

III. Asset Fund Suspension

345. Insurance companies shall suspend the buying and selling of units of the managed fund connected to unit-linked life insurance policies (hereinafter referred to as "asset fund suspension") in the interest of the clients if the net asset value of the managed fund, and, consequently, the price of the investment units cannot be determined due to the fact that the assets of the managed fund have become illiquid in part or in whole.

Insurance companies shall implement the asset fund suspension immediately upon gaining knowledge of the underlying circumstances with retroactive effect to

345. Section 107 of BIns.
346. Subsection 1 of s. 270 of BIns.
347. Section 125 of BIns.

the valuation date (hereinafter referred to as "opening date of asset fund suspension") before which the net asset value of the asset fund could have been determined for the last time.

The BIns. contains detailed regulation relating to the notification of the clients, to the client instructions, and to the transactions affecting the suspended asset.

The maximum duration of asset fund suspension is one year, which the insurance company may extend in justified cases by another year.

§2. Supplementary Pension Annuities of Insurers[348]

346. The institutions of the supplementary system, the voluntary mutual insurance funds, the private pension funds, and the occupational retirement provider may perform the obligatory pension service by purchasing yield from the insurer under the law applicable to them.

According to subsection 6a of section 47 of the VMIF Act, if the fund member wishes to receive pension payments in whole or in part in the form of annuity, the fund shall have the option to satisfy the obligation to provide annuity benefits either by providing annuity from its own resources or by purchasing a life annuity contract from an insurance company. Under subsection 6d, a life annuity purchased from an insurance company is a contract where premium is paid upon the annuitant reaching retirement age in return for a stream of payments for the rest of the annuitant's life. In the insurance contract, the fund functions as contracting party.

Under section 27 of the PPF Act, the fund shall provide the fund member with pension plan benefits in the form of a fund benefit of the type chosen by the fund member or in the form of an annuity purchased from an insurance company or an institution for occupational retirement provision.

According to section 33 of the PPF Act, the fund may also fulfill its pension benefit obligations through the purchase of pension benefits from insurance companies. The benefit shall be purchased from the fund's relevant benefit reserves. The insurance company providing the pension benefit may be selected either by the fund or by the fund member using such benefits. The fund member may choose to have a pension benefit from another insurance company even if the fund provides the same pension benefit. The contract for the provision of pension benefits shall be concluded between the insurance company and the fund, which shall also act on behalf of the fund member(s).

The person eligible for pension benefits shall receive at least a life annuity. Life annuities purchased from insurance companies may not be terminated by fund members.

According to subsection 7 of section 34 of the applicable law, the occupational retirement provider may perform the obligatory pension service by purchasing yield from the insurer falling within the scope of the BIns.

---

348. According to Point 45 of sub. 1 of s. 4 of BIns., *annuity benefits* shall mean payments made to the beneficiary periodically under contract.

§3. Specialties of the Pension Insurance in the Life Insurance Branch

347. From January 2014, the state supports pension insurances, supplementing the social security pensions with tax benefits. The tax allowance only entails pension insurance which meets the criteria laid down in the tax code (*see* Part IX.). The tax benefit gave an impulse to the pension insurance market. On the one hand, several pension insurance products were created by insurers, and on the other, the number of contracting persons of pension insurance contracts increased dramatically.

For these reasons, the *NBH issued a recommendation No. 1/2017. (I.12.)* on pension insurance products and their intermediation.

348. It is recommended that the contracts have to be simple, transparent—especially in terms of construction and costs—and worthy of value, therefore they can serve as a voluntary pre-care. During the intermediation of contracts, a high priority is the professional and objective but easily understandable information. The structure of the product has to be constructed in such a way that the expected outcome of investments tailored to the purpose of the product has to be at least equal to the costs and the inflation, and the tax incentive applies as an actual customer advantage. It is expected that the tax advantage linked to the products will increase the retirement savings of the contracting party and not the insurance companies.

The central bank also makes a recommendation on the level of the TCC.[349] In the case of guaranteed yield or capital higher than the average or in case of special insurance risk, higher TCC is allowed.

Since pension is a regular, lifelong income after retirement, it is necessary that these products also include annuity services.[350]

In respect of life unit-linked pension insurance contracts where the investment risk is borne by the policyholders, the insurer is expected to offer investment opportunities which take into account the age of the customer. The client must clearly identify the size and type of investment risk they face.

It is an important expectation that pension insurances are sold by intermediaries with appropriate expertise who are able to offer the right product after a proper assessment of the needs of the customer. The NBH recommends that in the case of pension insurance, insurers drop the commission to the intermediaries in order for them to be interested in the long-term maintenance of contracts.

---

349. According to Point 97 of sub. 1 of s. 4 of BIns., *TCC* shall mean an indicator showing all costs charged to life insurance policies with savings element in a percentage figure.

350. It can be a good practice, beside the traditional annuity, if the insurance company shares the service time, for example, a fixed-term annuity before the insured person turns 80–85 years of age, or for a simple scheduled withdrawal, which parameters can be changed by the client and for a deferred annuity which starts after this. This solution can provide an adequate level of supplementary pension. If the amount of the savings does not allow the granting of an annuity or the client does not request it reasonably, a fixed-term annuity can also be granted. The fixed-term annuity should not be shorter than ten years.

Provision of an exclusively lump-sum service can be justified in the case too in the event of the clear demand of the client (e.g., to cover the lump-sum costs of placement in the home of elderly people, or to buy annuity from another insurance company), or if the amount of the saving is so short, that it cannot provide the sufficient amount of the annuity service.

It is recommended that insurers create new pension insurance products, therefore the NBH expects that insurers do not promote or encourage practices in the process of the sale of funds according to which they transfer assets from other previous savings and savings forms to the pension insurance. This essentially complies with the OECD Policy Options for the Payout Phase.

349. In the past years, pension insurance has become an appealing product of the life insurance branch, whose primary reason is the annual tax allowance applicable since January 1, 2014. In 2015, a pension insurance contract could be concluded with seventeen insurers. By the end of 2015, the pension insurance portfolio consisted of nearly 200,000 pension insurance contracts, 75% of which were unit-linked contracts and approximately 5% of which were single-premium insurance.[351]

350. The number of regular premium pension insurance contracts in 2021 was nearly 420,000, of which 75% were unit-linked contracts. The expansion of the regular premium, traditional pension insurance stock is lagging behind that of unit-linked insurances. Its growth has slowed down since 2019; the increase was +2.5% from 2020 to 2021.

351. In 2022, twelve institutions became active in the pension insurance market. Among them, two insurers only offer traditional products and two insurers only offer unit-linked products.[352]

351. https://www.mnb.hu/letoltes/publikalando-jelentes-v4-digitalis.pdf.
352. Report of the NBH 2022., p. 28.
https://www.mnb.hu/letoltes/kocka-zati-jelente-s-2022-hun-0825.pdf.

Chapter 7. Ethical Life Insurance Concept of the NBH[353]

352. In the last twenty-five years, the savings life insurance market has grown dynamically. Among the life insurance with a savings element,[354] first, the traditional types of life insurance policies (life insurance policies with savings element other than unit-linked policies with a cash surrender value[355]) appeared in the 1990s, where the client only knew the premium and the amount of service guaranteed by the insurer but did not see the link between these two and the content of the insurance premium. Unit-linked products appeared in 1997.[356] Customers have already been informed of certain costs by the insurer, but not all of the costs. It was not clear and transparent how much the insurer deducted from the fee to the costs of the insurance and how much is the amount of money the insurer invested for the benefit of the client. Sales of unit-linked products raised many problems:

- Intermediaries received a high commission, which, on the one hand, increased the cost of the products, and on the other, intermediaries placed their own interests before the interests of their clients, and therefore, the number of the so-called apart divestments (divestment of a product not in compliance with the needs of the client) increased.
- Besides the too-high cost, the yield of the products was low; therefore, the contracting parties soon became disappointed. The period of retention of the products (the duration of contracts) shortened; the contracts existed for an average of 6.4 years.

353. József Banyár – Petra Turi The Evolution of the Insurance Consumer Protection Approach in Hungary, Public Finance Quarterly v 2019/2, 200. p.
https://unipub.lib.uni-corvinus.hu/4223/1/PSz_Banyar_Turi_2019.pdf.
Mátyás Miklós Dániel et al., *Etikus életbiztosítás: evolúció vagy revolúció—Az etikus életbiztosítási szabályozás előzményei, elemei, hatása, nemzetközi párhuzamok* [Ethical Life Insurance: Evolution or Revolution—Preludes, Elements, Effect and International Parallel of Ethical Life Insurance] In Biztosítás és kockázat, 2016/4. 12., 12–38.
http://real.mtak.hu/44961/1/biztositas_es_kockazat_3_evf_4_szam_2_cikk_u.pdf.

354. According to Point 75 of sub. 1 of s. 4 of BIns., *life insurance with savings element* shall mean life insurance policies, other than death risk policies, that generates a savings element and that provides benefits upon expiry or that features the option of surrendering the policy for its cash surrender value, or both in some cases.

355. According to sub. 1 of s. 6:484 of the CC, if a life assurance policy is terminated for any reason without payment of the sum insured, the insurance company shall be liable to pay the cash surrender value defined in the policy.

356. According to Point 6 of sub. 1 of s. 4 of BIns., *unit-linked life insurance* shall mean a type of life insurance product where the insurance company places the amount of the technical provisions relating to the insurance contract into individual, separately managed stocks of assets (asset funds) created by the insurance company comprising theoretical settlement components of identical value (investment units) having its own investment policy, or into other investment funds operated by a company authorized to manage investment funds, whichever is selected by the insured party, for the purpose of investment, according to the terms and conditions laid down in the contract.

As a solution unique in Europe, AHIC developed the self-regulatory definition and publication of TCC in 2010.[357] This was a step forward, but it did not moderate the too-high costs.

The next step for the enlargement of transparency was the recommendation of the NBH on pension insurance in 2014 and 2017 (*see* Part V, Chapter 6).

In order to remedy the remaining problems in the life insurance market, the so-called *ethical life insurance concept* of the NBH was born which can result in one of the most comprehensive changes of the past decades in the life insurance market.

This concept was developed in 2015–2016 as a result of the tripartite cooperation in which the NBH as the supervising body, the Ministry of National Economy as the legislator, and a member of the AHIC Life Insurance Department as the representative of the market took part of.

One of the elements of this system based on customer confidence and long-term sustainability is applicable from 2016, but it mostly takes effect from January 1, 2017.

Taking into account the ambitions of the EU (single, brief information KID, TCC-like indicator RIY—Reduction in Yield, Commission Transparency Requirements, which appear in IDD or commission limits), the NBH has also developed its own recommendation.

353. The evolving regulatory system—improved along the lines of the fair concept—may bring the most comprehensive change of the past decades in the assurance market. The goal of the system is to ensure long-term sustainability by increasing the trust of the customer. In order to reach the goal, the NBH, the Ministry for National Economy, and the AHIC created the fair assurance regulatory system along the lines of the fair treatment principle. The result is a wave of comprehensive development of products that may lead to a new generation of investment-based assurance products. This article presents, with the assistance of the experts of the organizations involved, the antecedents, the elements, the expectable impacts of the fair assurance regulatory system, and some international examples. The MNB, along the lines of the fair treatment principle and as part of their strategy, created the fair bank framework in 2014, which was followed by the fair assurance concept in 2015. The elements of the complex regulatory system, that takes into account both prudential aspects and consumer protection, were built with the cooperation of the market participants and regulators. The system is aimed at strengthening transparency, creating more stringent investment rules, reducing misspellings, and evolving products that can create real value for customers in low-interest environment as well. As the goals to reach are in line with the international trends, we present some known and probably less known examples in order to show the similarities and differences of the fair assurance regulatory system. The system, based on customer trust and long-term sustainability, is partially applicable as of 2016; however. The system will be applied from 2017. The MNB continues to work

357. Under Point 97 of sub. 1 of s. 4 of BIns., *TCC* shall mean an indicator showing all costs charged to life insurance policies with savings element in a percentage figure.

on improving the system, which is ongoing.[358] It will most probably have a significant impact on the assurance market and the whole range of products. We strive to give an estimation of the scale and the direction of the impact with the help of a few examples. We expect that—after a transitional period—customers can benefit from the longer life cycles of the contracts, which provide stable portfolios and sustainable profitability for insurance companies as well.

354. In case of life insurance with savings element, international regulatory practice focuses primarily on transparency in costs and commissions. The ethical life insurance concept goes beyond this and its aims are:

- the transparency of the costs and services charged by the insurers (transparency), therefore the visualization of the hidden costs, the ban of marginalization, the description of the costs, the demonstration of the assets actually invested;
- a fair value for money (providing adequate and secure service for the costs incurred, higher yields than the total costs for the customers), minimum investment yield, minimum repurchase value, definition of TCC limit;
- the imposition of stricter investment rules, obligatory custodians with daily valuation of assets, professional regulations for the trustee, etc.;
- a higher level of information for customers (evaluation of needs with adequate content, welcome calls).

§1. The Elements of the Regulation

355. In order to achieve these objectives, various regulatory instruments have been developed:

- the BIns. changed at several points;
- the NBH issued the Decree No. 55/2015 (XII.22.) on the calculation and publication of the TCC (TCC Decree);
- the NBH issued Decree No. 56/2015 (XII.22) on material element of the life insurance questionnaire (*see* Part II, Chapter 5, §2 Life insurance) (it was repealed on February 23, 2018);
- the NBH issued the Recommendation No. 8/2016. (VI.30) on the application of prudential and consumer protection principles in relation to (unit-linked) life insurances (UL Recommendation).

The NBH issued the Recommendation No. 7/2021. (VI.21) on the prudential and consumer protection requirements of automatic portfolio management services applicable to unit-linked life insurance.

358. Marina Magnava, *Hungary: The MNB is Working on a New Concept to Improve Life Insurance*. 5. 12. 2023. (online).
https://www.xprimm.com/HUNGARY-The-MNB-is-working-on-a-new-concept-to-improve-life-insurance-articol-19-21167.htm.

356. In the UL Recommendation, NBH laid down basic expectations for the calculation and presentation of costs, which the insurance companies have to comply with from January 1, 2017:

- the insurance company shall separate the fees charged for risk cover, for the cost of the collection of fee, and for the savings;
- the insurer should not unduly charge multiple types of costs for the same purpose;
- the number of types of costs deducted from the fee intended for savings should remain within reasonable limits and do not preferably include more than three types of costs ((1) costs incurred in the first years of the contract and directly arising out of the conclusion of the contract, (2) asset management costs, (3) administrative costs);
- the extent of the costs has to be reasonable in each case, and it has to be determined in proportion to the costs involved with the costs of the insurers.

The MNB expects that in the case of unit-linked life insurances which may be settled by the insurer for a regular payment of at least ten years, the value of the TCC calculated on the basis of the TCC Decree shall not exceed:

(a) maximum 4.25% in case of the ten-year maturity;
(b) maximum 3.95% in case of the fifteen-year maturity;
(c) maximum 3.5% in case of the twenty-year maturity.

In addition to the abovementioned major expectations, it prohibits the ascertainment of hidden costs, prohibits the marginalization, and sets out standards for the proper presentation of costs.

The *TCC Decree* regulates the calculation and publication of TCC for life insurance with savings element products from January 1, 2016. The Regulation (based on the TCC Code developed by AHIC) has been extended with a step-by-step entry into force to all types of contracts with savings element and requires regular reporting and disclosure obligation. It is a novelty that in case of unit-linked products, insurers publish not only the minimum and maximum TCC value but also calculate and publish the indicator for all asset funds offered in connection with the product. With this, prudent customers can get information on the price of investment in each asset fund, and they will have the opportunity to take this into account when deciding which asset fund they intend to invest in. The TCC Decree expects further methodological changes from January 1, 2017.

Under subsection 6 of section 153 of BIns., insurance companies shall publish the TCC on their websites.

From January 1, 2018, based on the Packaged Retail Investment and Insurance-Based Products (PRIIPs) EU regulation, the Hungarian insurance companies also have to publish the so-called KID which includes:

- the most important objectives (the investment vehicles);
- the level of risk (from a scale of 1 to 7);

- the costs and their impact on yield (Reduction in Yield (RIY) is similar to TCC, which has been known in Hungary since 2010) of unit-linked and mixed savings insurance.[359]

It also sets example calculations for the customer which shows which amount of sum he can pick up after one, ten, and twenty years in the case of four different market scenarios if he pays HUF 3 million investment in lump sums or HUF 300,000 for regular insurances.

The KID also includes:

- the exact name and address of the service provider;
- the type of target investor;
- the insurance service and its costs;
- where the customer can file a complaint;
- what happens if the insurer cannot pay; and
- in what case the contract will terminate.

§2. Modification of the Regulation of the BIns.

I. Strengthening Payment and Investment Rules

357. From January 1, 2016, all insurers are obliged to apply a custodian, and the custodian must perform a daily asset valuation.[360] Insurance and reinsurance companies shall conduct all financial transactions in connection with operations through payment account opened at a credit institution.

Insurance and reinsurance companies shall keep funds, other than the funds required for operating expenses, which are invested in financial instruments in investment accounts maintained by a depositary used for such task.

The manager of such investments shall inform the depositary fully of daily transactions.

The manager of investments and the depositary shall calculate the net asset value if the unit price of the asset fund differs from the price of the underlying fund.

The asset values calculated shall be confirmed for each valuation date.

359. The calculation methodology of the RIY indicator is similar to the Hungarian TCC, but there are some important differences between the two systems:

- RIY assumes the future of the yields of the past while TCC calculates with a fixed rate of yield fixed by the NBH.
- TCC calculates with maturity interests, while the RIY calculates with repurchase with the exception of the recommended period (in this case twenty years). The indicated times are also different: TCC calculates with ten, fifteen, and twenty years, while RIY with one, ten, and twenty years.

360. Section 104/B of BIns.

II. In the Case of Self-management, the Professional Criterion System Is Recorded by BIns.[361]

358. Where the assets of an insurance or reinsurance company are managed—in part or in whole—by the company itself, that activity shall be entrusted to a person—under contract of employment—who:

(a) has no prior criminal record;
(b) has a university-level or master's degree in the relevant field, such as in the field of actuarial studies, natural sciences, economics, law, or engineering, or has a diploma in auditing or a diploma in higher education or postgraduate qualification in the banking profession;
(c) complies with fit and proper requirements; and
(d) has at least three years of experience in investments and asset management at a financial organization.

III. Maximizing[362] the Technical Interest Rate[363]

359. The Governor of NBH shall decree the highest permissible technical interest rate that can be used to calculate the premiums on life insurance, accident, and sickness insurance (health insurance) policies, as well as reserves and benefit payments.

The insurer must also perform the service undertaken if the investment result is below the technical interest rate. The excessive yield promise is restricted by *NBH Decree No. 54/2015 (XII.21.).*

IV. Separate Records of Asset Funds.[364] Correct Registration of the Investments of the Contracting Party

360. Insurance companies shall keep separate records of each managed fund attached to unit-linked life insurance policies, apart from the funds covering other technical provisions of accountancy and from the assets used for the insurance company's own investments.

In the case of unit-linked life insurance policies, the insurance company may show on the policyholder's account only such investment units that have actually been placed into an asset fund or investment fund, showing the values at which the assets in question were placed.

---

361. Section 104/A of BIns.
362. Subsection 1 of s. 133 of BIns.
363. Under Point 96 of sub. 1 of s. 1 of BIns., *technical interest rate* shall mean the rate of interest used by the insurance company when calculating the premiums and premium reserve for life and sickness insurance policies, and benefit payment reserve for accident and liability insurance policies, where the ceiling rate is specified in the relevant legislation.
364. Section 110 of BIns.

The insurance company's records and the statements of account given to the customer must correspond.

This rule seeks to curtail bad insurance practice, according to which many insurers do not invest the initial payments but only reveal their perceived value, but actually deduct it as a cost.

V. Determination of Minimum Investment and Repurchase Value[365]

361. In the case of unit-linked life insurance policies with savings element, the insurance company shall invest:

(a) at least 20% of the premiums due and paid for the first year, minus risk premium;
(b) at least 50% of the premiums due and paid for the second year, minus risk premium;
(c) at least 80% of the premiums due and paid for the third and subsequent years, minus risk premium.

With the proviso that the proportionate deduction from the related provision need not be taken into consideration from the beginning of the fourth year for the purpose of compliance.

If the policyholder exercises his residual rights,[366] settlement shall be based at least on the invoiced value of the minimum investment ratios. In the settlement, the costs incurred in connection with the client's instructions—other than those pertaining to the residual rights—may be enforced.

In the case of life insurance policies with savings element other than unit-linked policies, if the policyholder exercises his residual rights, the cash surrender value shall be calculated based on the period of insurance cover from the beginning of the contract until the time of claiming residual rights, representing:

(a) at least 20% of the premiums due and paid for the first year, minus risk premium;
(b) at least 50% of the premiums due and paid for the second year, minus risk premium;
(c) at least 80% of the premiums due and paid for the third and subsequent years, minus risk premium.

365. Section 124/A of BIns.
366. Under Point 72 of sub. 1 of s. 4 of BIns., *residual rights* shall mean the rights defined in the terms and conditions of a life insurance contract that remain in the case of non-payment of premium and/or the termination of the contract without payment of the sum insured.

VI. The Determination of Commission Limit by Law[367]

362. The amount of commission paid in connection with a life insurance policy with savings element may not exceed the amount of the premium the insurance company has received by the time of payment of the commission.

As regards stipulated premium life insurance policies with savings element, commission may be paid on the first year calculated from the date of the contract—at the earliest after the first premium payment is received by the insurance company as stipulated— a maximum of fourteen monthly premiums (2017), thirteen monthly premiums (2018) and, from 2019, only twelve monthly premiums can be paid to the insurance broker.

The amount of commission paid in total for the full term of the contract may not exceed the amount of the premium the insurance company has received for the full term of the contract.

VII. Transparent Presentation of Costs[368]

363. In connection with the investment and management of the assets held as cover for the reserves of unit-linked life insurance policies, the following provisions shall be observed: the investment shall be made for the clients, in accordance with the investment policy, professionally, under the general principles of fairness, transparency and with due care, with particular regard to the price, expenditures—including any refund received and other deductions in asset management—and the return expected.

Insurance companies shall specify any price, fee, or commission they charged and any deduction they applied in proportion to provisions so as to ensure that such specification and the related description clearly demonstrate their purpose and content.

364. The regulation is required to achieve a complex market impact:

- transparent costs;
- decreasing commissions;
- ethical operation;
- extension of the persistence period for contracts (eight–ten years);
- the spread of pension insurance.

367. Section 377 of BIns.
368. Point f) of sub. 1 of s. 107 and sub. 1a of s. 107 of BIns.

Part VI. Private Insurance—Social Security

Judit Barta

Chapter 1. Connections Between Social Security Benefits and Private in General

365. In the EU, social security and social security systems are not the subject matter of harmonization issues. So, each Member State is entitled to freely decide which services will be provided in relation to the taxes and contributions.

In the field of social security, only the coordination rules can be applied, which facilitates the citizens to avoid a disadvantageous situation by crossing borders. Although EU legislation cannot be found in the field of social security benefits, there are a lot of policy areas (internal market, social cases, market supervision, business and economic policy) which allow the Union to take effect in the area of social security benefits too, as we are going to see it in relation to funded private pension funds. Besides, the soft law legal instruments (such as the Open Method of Coordination) and community JD also have an impact on social security systems.[369]

366. In Hungary, the comprehensive social security system, which concerns everybody, was established in 1975 by the adoption of Act II of 1975 on Social Security Benefits. New rules were needed because of the changes in the social and economic environment, which resulted in the transition to the market economy. In 1997, three Acts were adopted, which incorporated the new rules of social security. There is a comprehensive Act, which regulates the general provisions, and there are separate acts in relation to the social security pension benefits and the services of the Compulsory Health Insurance System:

- Act LXXX of 1997 on the Eligibility for Social Security Benefits and Private Pensions and the Funding for These Services.
- Act LXXXI of 1997 on Social Security Pension Benefits.
- Act LXXXIII of 1997 on the Services of the Compulsory Health Insurance System.

369. Vallyon Andrea PhD dissertation, *A kiegészítő biztosítások szerepe az egészségügyben az Európai Unióban és Magyarországon*. [The Role of Supplementary Insurances in the Fields of Health-Care System in the European Union and in Hungary.] Szent István University Gödöllő, Faculty of Economic Sciences, Doctoral School of Economics and Organizational Sciences, 2011, 52–60.

367. According to the Act LXXX of 1997 on the Eligibility for Social Security Benefits and Private Pensions and the Funding for These Services, social security means a societal pooling system covering—in accordance with the rules laid down in this Act—the citizens of Hungary and other natural persons working in Hungary subject to the special provisions set out in this Act. Participation in the social security system is mandatory in accordance with the law. Insured parties shall pay a contribution to the system of social security. For this, they can obtain the right for themselves and for their relatives, described by law, to social security benefits.

The insurance relationship is created on the strength of the law simultaneously with the underlying relationship. In order to ensure sufficient financial cover for benefits provided under the social security system, employers are required by law to pay contributions and other provisions of the like.

Everybody is an employer who employs insured parties or himself. *Health insurance and pension insurance services are provided* in the system of social security.

Health insurance can be:

- in-kind health services; or
- cash benefits (infant care benefits, child care benefits, sick pay);
- accident benefits (emergency medical services, benefits for accident-related injuries, accident compensation); and
- benefits provided to workers with disabilities (invalidity allowance, rehabilitation allowance).

Pension insurance benefits are the social security pension benefits on one's own right (old-age benefits), dependents' benefits (widow's pension, orphans' pension, parent's benefits, accident-related dependent's benefits), and rehabilitation benefits.

368. According to the legal literature, private insurances can have three roles besides state insurance (social security):

- substituting, when in certain areas, private insurance recognized by the state can be chosen instead of social security benefits;
- supplementary, when private insurance is based on the basic state insurance services, and it meets higher demands or special needs. The two together can provide a higher level or better quality of services. The supplementary feature is known as a parallel service, and this is reflected in the field of health insurance mostly when the private system provides the same service as the state insurance but at a better level. In this case, the insured party shall pay the social security contribution and the private insurance premium, too; eventually, it means a double payment;
- complementary, in the areas where social security benefits do not provide services or for those who are not insured in social security benefits.

Nowadays, in Hungary, private insurance roles are mainly the supplementary function both in the field of the pension system and in the area of health care.

Chapter 2. Connection Between Social Security and Private Security in the field of Health Insurance

369. The health insurance branch of social security benefits provides services in the event of illness, accident, occupational disease, and occupational accident also. The BIns. regulates the accident and sickness insurance as a sector of the non-life insurance branch, and it rules health insurance in the case of joint operation of them.

In Hungary, private health insurance, which completes the compulsory health insurance, can be divided into two major services:

- the so-called auxiliary health insurance services provided by the voluntary mutual health insurance funds; and
- services provided by the health insurance contracts (accident and sickness) which are provided by business insurance companies.

Services can be classified into three groups:

(1) reimbursement of in-kind benefits (for health) services;
(2) price support for medicine and medical aids;
(3) to provide a specified amount of compensation.

§1. Health Funds

370. The introduction of health insurance funds in Hungary is a part of the reform of social security benefits after the change of regime. In 1993, when the VMIF Act was born, health insurance funds played an important role. The legal definition of recognized fund[370] also refers to this important role because its objective is to provide the substitute function. The Governmental ideas at that time could not be realized, nor the health reforms, which targeted the strengthening of health services. Thanks to that, the role of supplementary health funds is marginal besides the social security benefits, but their accumulated assets should not be underestimated. The self-care which occurs in the field of health care is smaller because of the accustomed patronizing role of the state at the time of socialist state arrangements, so the state tried to make the fund membership desirable by tax benefits.

According to the VMIF Act fund, organizations can be established on the basis of the decision of private individuals or by employees at the employer's initiative.

A voluntary mutual insurance fund cannot be only a health fund, but it can be a pension fund and mutual aid fund too.[371]

---

370. VMIF Act. s. 2., sub. 2 Point (c) recognized fund shall mean any voluntary mutual insurance fund that arranges social security benefits in a particular social insurance and social sector and/or provides services to replace or supplement such benefits in accordance with the legal regulations contained in sub. (1), and based on the authorization granted in specific other legislation.

371. In 2015, in the cashier sector *forty-four voluntary pension funds, twenty-six health funds, and ten self-administered funds* operated.

Pension funds shall be authorized to provide pension benefits only, and mutual aid funds shall be allowed to provide mutual aid services exclusively. A health fund may engage in subsidizing medicinal products and medical aids, supplementing part or all of the income of a fund member lost due to incapacity for work on account of sickness, as well as providing support to the survivors of a deceased fund member (collectively as mutual health-care aid).

According to the law, the voluntary mutual insurance fund means an association created by natural persons (fund members) under the principle of independence, mutuality, solidarity, and voluntary participation for funding services to *supplement, supersede,* or *replace* social security benefits and benefits for health protection (services). The fund shall record the membership payments it receives from members in individual accounts and shall organize, finance, and provide its services accordingly. Regulations concerning financial management and liability and entitlements related to fund activities are governed by the Act.

The *membership contribution* shall mean a regular cash contribution paid under commitment by fund members that is used to finance the fund's services and the operation of the fund; employers may, subject to the provisions laid down in the Act, undertake to partly or entirely assume these contributions under the title of employer's contribution. The minimum amount of membership contributions that is payable by all members (compulsory membership fee) is stipulated in the basic rules of the fund.

371. A health fund may organize its service by itself or may hire a service organization institution to do so. A health fund may provide in-kind benefits only through a health fund service provider.

The costs of the various services shall be covered, as instructed in the basic rules of the fund, from the individual health fund account of the fund member to whom the services are provided or shall be charged equally to the individual accounts of several fund members, and shall be financed from the mutual cover fund.

Fund members shall have the option, in accordance with the instructions laid down in the basic rules of the fund, to tie up a specific part of the balance available on their individual accounts for a period of two years. Tying up funds in accordance with the above shall constitute the fund member's agreement to refrain from using the tied-up funds during the two-year period for financing fund services.

The health fund shall refund at least 90% of the payments, which means it can use a maximum of 10% for its costs.

Health funds may engage in providing auxiliary health insurance services and life-improvement health fund services to fund members or to their close relatives where instructed by the fund members. Health funds shall be authorized to provide the following auxiliary health insurance services from the services which are not subsidized by the health insurance administration agency or subsidized partially only:

(a) health services, which mean services provided in addition to or in place of the health-care services available within the framework of social security benefits under contract with a health service provider;
(b) home care for a fund member or his/her close relative;

(c) support for curative gymnastics, curative massage, and physiotherapy;
(d) support provided in connection with special aids designed to assist the visually impaired, for example, financial support for the purchase of Braille books and magazines and in connection with the costs of guide dogs;
(e) life-improvement services, which mean financial support provided for the purchase of special aids designed to assist handicapped people and the mentally impaired and to finance improvement works to rearrange their living environment to accommodate their special needs (such as support bars, handles, doors, exits, wide corridors, hoists, and similar lifting devices);
(f) support for treatment for quitting pathological addictions;
(g) financial support for the purchase of medicines and medical aids;
(h) lump-sum auxiliary health insurance services which are the financial supports provided to persons with no income to cover the whole or part of the income lost due to being incapacitated;
(i) support to survivors in the case of the death of a fund member;
(j) support provided for the purchase of gluten-free special foods;
(k) payment of the fees charged by health insurance (sickness insurance) funds financing the services.

372. Health funds are allowed to provide life-improvement health fund services too, for example, holistic medical services, financial support for the purchase of sports goods, purchase of protective equipment (wristbands, elbow and knee supports, helmets), financial support for the purchases of herb teas and dental hygiene products.

Health funds can support preventive services too, such as:

> cervical cancer screening, breast cancer screening, colon cancer screening, prostate cancer screening, screening for locomotor disorders, AIDS test, test for the early detection of mental disorders, and dental examination.

§2. Health Insurance Contracts Offered by Insurance Companies

373. Since the function of health insurance contracts offered by insurance companies is to provide supplementary services in Hungary, their services, therefore, act upon the social security benefits. Products primarily target the services which are not or partially financed by social security, or the social security provides them with additional expenses or provides no services at all, or where the state health insurance service is reasonably unsuitable for some reason or is too long.[372]

372. One of its reason can be the hospital waiting list and the patient admission list.
Their definition can be found in the s. 5/B of CHIS:

> k) "*hospital waiting list*" shall mean a register showing the sequence in which patients receive treatment in the inpatient medical institution that is carried out in the interests of providing medical treatment—with the exception of health-care services provided under the central waiting list—in a specific order and/or to prevent shortage of capacity (Paragraphs j and k) hereinafter referred to collectively as "waiting list";

374. Subsection 6 of section 18 of the CHIS. lists the cases which cannot be financed by the Health Fund. The list expanded significantly from January 1, 2007, for example:

- occupational hygiene examinations and controls described in specific other legislation;
- employment health-care core services described in specific other legislation;
- medical treatment provided to professional athletes;
- non-curative health-care services, such as those provided solely for aesthetic or recreational purposes;
- sterilization if carried out for non-health-related reasons;
- procedures, medicinal products, and medical aids that have been approved in Hungary but not for financing under the health-care system;
- immunization of the insured person by non-compulsory vaccination.[373]

375. According to section 23 of the CHIS., the costs of some health-care services are supported in partial by social security benefits. These are, for example:

(a) dental plates for persons under 18 years of age;
(b) prosthodontics of the type specified by ministerial decree to restore mastication;
(c) procedures for changing one's sexual characteristics, with the exception of reconstructive surgery required to correct a genetically determined developmental anomaly.

According to the section 23/A, the insured persons shall be entitled to the following subject to additional compensation:

(a) premium services requested of his/her own motion within the framework of medical treatment; and
(b) room and care at a contracted health-care service provider if the insured person's condition so requires, including the necessary medication and meals.

376. It is necessary to clarify certain issues in order to develop insurance products that provide health-care services. Such a question is the professional quality of public and private health care (medical, nursing), which is not measured or controlled. There is no quality assurance in this field. Quality is more apparent in terms of infrastructure (waiting rooms, examiners, wards, community rooms, hygiene

---

m) *"patient admission list"* shall mean a register maintained in an outpatient medical facility containing the sequence in which patients are admitted for treatment by appointment according to the medically requested services, unless the insured person requires immediate attention due to his/her health condition.

373. About the health-care services available at a fee *see* in details: Dr. Barzó Tímea, *Praxisjog. Aktuális kérdések az egészségügyi alapellátásban* [Praxis Law. Actual Issues on Basic Health-Care Service]. (Medicina Publisher 2007), 146–147.

rooms, equipment, medical instrumentation and its standard) and of subsidiary services (bedding, meals, etc.), but there are no actual quality measurements and control. Noticeable disadvantages are the already mentioned waiting list and patient admission list. Insurance services try to offer more in these areas, where the quality of public health care is inappropriate. This requires private service providers also. Until 2012, health insurances were largely amount and indemnity insurances because of the tight private service market. Nowadays, in the field of outpatient care and one-day surgery, there are many private providers, while private inpatient care develops much slower.

This is due to the strict legal regulation and the substantial capital requirement, which restrict entry into the market.

Health insurers are mainly able to contract with private service providers under the current social security conditions. Private providers can provide more comfortable services without waiting lists and patient lists, primarily in the field of patient or one-day surgical procedures, diagnostics, and laboratory testing. If the insurers wish to meet the needs of a wider range, they should provide inpatient care within the insurance services. Most of this is provided by public infrastructure; there are private hospitals, mostly in the fields of obstetrics, gynecology, internal medicine, and surgery. There are insurers too, who have concluded with a private hospital.

It should be mentioned that in the inpatient care sector, adequate statistics are lacking for insurers (case number, demographic characteristics, interventions, outputs and costs), and organizing services is hard without the necessary information.

In professional circles, there is an agreement that because of the demographic changes and the aging of the population, nursing insurance will become an emerging area for private services,[374] but social security is not prepared for it.

According to the legal literature, health insurance products of insurance companies can supplement social security services in the following areas:

- Within the framework of public hospital care or in private hospitals and further comfort services.
- Nursing of elderly and sick people.

374. This is strengthened by the modification of the CC in Jun. 1, 2016.

According to the sub. 2 of s. 4:196 of the CC, maintenance obligation shall primarily prevail in the relation of the parent and his/her child and in the relation of the adult child and his/her parent in need support.

According to the s. 4:205 of the CC, the parent can turn to the court if the adult child is unwilling to the maintenance. The court shall determine the amount of maintenance upon due consideration of the entitled person's justified needs and on the financial ability of the person owing maintenance. Justified needs shall cover the justified expenses and the costs of living of the person entitled to maintenance. The obligation of maintenance of a relative in need of care due to his/her old age, health, disability, or other reason shall cover the costs of nursing and care, as well as other related services which are deemed necessary. The maximum amount the person owing maintenance is required to provide shall not exceed half of his/her income.

According to the sub. 1a of s. 4:208 of the CC, where a person provides maintenance without any contractual or legal obligation to a parent in need of support instead of the parent's child legally obligated to do so, such person may demand compensation for the expenses arising in connection with providing such justified care from the child owing maintenance within a preclusive period of one year from the date when maintenance was actually provided.

- The world's leading insurance companies strive to provide insurances for the most commonly accidental or death-related illnesses (dreaded diseases). There is an insurance company in Hungary that provides insurance for the forty most disastrous illnesses, but the majority only provides insurance for some illnesses.
- Remuneration of the prices of medicines which are not supported by social security.
- Providing dentistry services which are not supported by social security.
- Means for the preservation of health services which are not directly belonging to health care (sport, recreation).
- Waiting list, patient care without patient admission list, one-day surgery, laboratory tests, diagnostic tests.

§3. Accident Insurance Offered by the Insurance Companies and the Insurance Relating to Work Accidents

377. Subsection 6 of section 18 of the CHIS Act lists the services which cannot be financed by the health insurance fund from January 1, 2007. These are, for instance, the highly dangerous extreme sports defined by law,[375] services because of accidents that happened during leisure-time activities, except emergency care.[376] To cover the costs of non-subsidized services, private insurance companies may provide extreme sports insurance.

However, those who are incapacitated or disabled due to extreme sports accident receive sickness benefits and invalidity benefits.

We have already mentioned in line with the occupational accidents (*see* Part V) that an employee is entitled to social security benefits according to the CHIS Act. Employee can enforce more damage against the employer if their liability can be determined in line with the legal regulations.

According to section 67 of the CHIS., the employer shall reimburse the costs of social security benefits in special cases. The employer shall be liable to reimburse any health insurance benefits paid in connection with an accident at work or an occupational disease if the accident or the disease occurred due to the employer's

375. Government Decree No. 217/1997 (XII.1.) on the Implementation of Act LXXXIII of 1997 on the Services of the Compulsory Health Insurance System:

    Section 5/B *

    (1) *In the application of Paragraph *e)* of Subsection (6) of Section 18 of the CHIS, the following shall be considered as particularly dangerous (extreme) sports or self-amusement activities: *
    a) water skiing; *b)* jet-skiing; *c)* white-water rafting; *d)* mountain and rock climbing of degree V and above;
    e) high-mountain expeditions; *g)* base jumping and bungee jumping; *h)* wall climbing; *i)* junk car (autocrash) sport, rally; *j)* hot-air ballooning; *k)* single-handed and open-sea sailing; *l)* kiting, parachuting, paragliding, aerobatics.

376. A separate law defines the area of emergency treatment.

or its representative's infringement of the mandatory occupational safety regulations. The employer shall be liable for the actual determined and granted health-care services and for the health-care services provided and subsidized under the health insurance system.

The liability of the culpable employer has two directions. On the one hand, the employer shall be liable to the worker who suffered the damage (to the relative who is entitled to maintenance), and on the other, the employer shall be liable to the social security institution.[377]

The abovementioned provision of the CHIS urges the employers to conclude liability insurances for such cases.

377. Dr. Mádi Sarolta, *A társadalombiztosítási szerv megtérítési igénye, mint az üzemi balesetek és foglalkozási megbetegedések prevenciójának egyik eszköze* [Compensation Claim of Social Security Institution, as an Instrument of Prevention of Occupational Accidents and Sickness]. Miskolci Jogi Szemle, 2013/1, 68–73.

Chapter 3. The Connection Between Social Security Benefits and Private Insurance in the Field of Pension Fund[378]

378. In Hungary, the private sector also has an additional role in the field of pension insurance.

Its task is to provide a higher level of livelihood to the retired, together with the state pension.[379] The private sector, which also covers the pension insurances offered by insurers too, started to evolve after the change of regime. In Hungary, the first law introducing institutional voluntary retirement savings was born in 1993, allowing the foundation of so-called voluntary mutual pension funds (VMIF Act). It was followed by *a mandatory private pension fund system based on the principle of full funding,*[380] which was dominating the additional pillar for more than a decade.

379. In the mid-1990s, the situation was ripe for the Government in power at the time to set out to restructure the pension system. The huge debt accumulated toward the World Bank had a substantial impact on the process of transformation by promoting and encouraging the reduction of pension-related expenses with the introduction of a more moderate version of the *so-called Chilean model.* Hungary was the first among the Central-Eastern European countries to introduce a mandatory pay-as-you-earn private pension system as an additional pillar, with the others following suit, except Slovenia and the Czech Republic. In 1997, the Hungarian Parliament adopted the three laws that implemented the transformation.[381] As a result of the changes, the pension system became a three-pillar system, with the inclusion of a mandatory two-pillar pension system consisting of a pay-as-you-go state pension system and a pay-as-you-earn private pension system.[382] The third pillar included several voluntary pension saving forms, such as the voluntary mutual pension funds mentioned above and occupational pension scheme providers. As a result

378. Dr. Barta Judit & Dr. Dezse Tivadar, *The Hungarian Pension System: The Present and a Possible Future.* In *European Integration Studies*, Number 1 (Miskolc University Press 2017).
379. Pensions of 65- to 74-year-old retirees compared to the income of 50–59 years of age, it can be stated that the amount of the pension is 61% compared to the income, which is the fifth highest in the Union. The problem is that the purchasing power of old-age pension in Hungary was in the last third on the rank of the Union in 2012. The situation has not changed since then.
380. The essence of the pay-as-you-earn principle is that the monthly payments of private pension fund members are reserved and invested by the fund during the so-called accumulation or waiting period (its minimum duration is fifteen years as determined by law), creating the financial basis for future pension services. Biometric, investment risks, and the risk of untimely death or becoming disabled are all taken by pension fund members.
381. Dr. Barta Judit, *The Role And Function of the PAY-AS-YOU-EARN Pension System in the Hungarian Pension System.* In *European Integration Studies*, Vol. 9, Number 1 (Miskolc University Press 2011), 5–15.
   Dr. VARGA Zoltán, *Analysis of the Changes in the Hungarian Pension System in 2011.* XXVI. microCAD International Scientific Conference, March 29–March 30.
   Conference Book, University of Miskolc Innovation and Technology Transfer Centre.
382. *See* more about the topic: Dr. Barta Judit, *Visszatérés az egypilléres kötelező nyugdíjrendszerhez (a 2010. december 13-án elfogadott törvénycsomag értékelése)* [Return to the One-Pillar Compulsory Pension System (The Evaluation of the Package of Laws Adopted on Dec. 13, 2010)] In Gazdaság és Jog, 2011/3., 9–15.

of the compulsory implementation of the Directive of the European Parliament and the Council of Europe *2003/41/EC*, *Act CXVII of 2007 on Occupational Retirement Provisions and the Institutions* was adopted in Hungary which has facilitated the foundation of occupational pension scheme providers since 2008.[383]

380. In September 1997, the first mandatory private pension funds were established in Hungary. The private pension fund members *paid a membership fee mandatorily deducted by their employer from their taxable income* as the base of pension contribution as well as *a pension contribution to the pension insurance fund*. Members of the state pension fund system paid a pension contribution of 8%, while private pension fund members paid only 2% to the central pension insurance fund and another 6% as a membership fee, so the greater part of their pension contributions was received by the private pension funds. As a consequence, the income of the state pension insurance fund decreased in proportion to the number of entrants to the private pension funds. The lack of missing pension contributions due to membership fees was compensated from the revenues of the state budget. No one expected, however, that instead of the projected two hundred thousand people, more than 3 million would enter the private pension fund system, thus causing an enormous shortage in the pension insurance fund, which constantly had to be compensated from the state budget.

In return for the payment of shared pension contributions, private pension fund members were entitled to receive only three-fourths of the entire social security pension, and they would have received the remaining one-fourth, or even more in an ideal case, from the private pension funds. The members of the so-called mixed pension system would have received three-quarters of their pensions from the state and a quarter from the private pension funds.

After the accession and with the expiry of the given grace period, the EU began to resent the serious budget deficit indirectly generated due to the introduction of the mandatory private pension fund system. Consequently, in the summer of 2010, not only Hungary but also all the other EU Member States that had previously introduced an additional pay-as-you-earn pension system turned to the European Commission with the request of changing the rules of calculating state deficit and national debt. Their goal was to achieve that the EU would not take the budget deficit generated by the introduction of the private pension fund system into consideration in the accounts, and they also wanted to achieve that the mandatory membership fees paid to the private pension funds could be recorded as budget revenue. In the event of the acceptance of this request, the budget deficit in Hungary would have been only 2.4% on paper instead of the existing 3.8% which, in turn, would have met the required maximum of 3%. The EU rejected the request, so the Hungarian Government resolved the situation with administrative means, intervening in the private pension fund system by quick and successive law amendments. The greatest change was brought about by the law adopted on December 13, 2010. The members of mandatory private pension funds had to decide whether they

383. Only one institution of the kind was established in Hungary in 2010. It was acquired by the Allianz Group in 2015, turning the name of the company into Allianz Foglalkoztatói Nyugdíjszolgáltató Zrt. It consisted of only three employers in 2014.

wanted to remain in the private pension funds or return to the state pension system until January 31, 2011. Those who did not return to the social security pension scheme, with effect from December 1, 2011 onward, could not gain any additional period of service in the social security pension system and lost their entitlement to receiving any state pensions. The accumulated capital on the individual accounts of those who decided to return to the state pension system was transferred to a fund specially created for this reason.

They were allowed to make a decision on what to do with their return on investment above the inflation rate. According to the data released at the beginning of February 2011, 98% of private pension fund members decided to return to the state pension system. The law was attacked by several people at the Constitutional Court; presumably, it was also the reason why the Hungarian Parliament adopted another law in 2011, amending the previous one. *This law terminated the mandatory payment of membership fees* to private pension funds, and the members were allowed to pay voluntarily a so-called contribution deducted from their taxed income, *the amount of which was not determined by the law any longer but by the private pension funds themselves. Thus, the mandatory retirement provision schemes ceased to exist in Hungary.*

It was made possible for private pension fund members to return to the state pension system again; the membership of those who decided to return to it terminated on May 1, 2012. The strict provision was also repealed, according to which those who had previously chosen membership in any of the private pension funds lost their entitlement to receiving state pension in the future. The termination of mandatory membership and the mandatory payment of membership fees to the private pension funds, as well as providing the opportunity to return to the purely state pension system in two stages, were not left without serious consequences: the number of private pension fund members was drastically reduced, forcing several private pension funds to close down.[384]

On a systemic approach, the Hungarian pension system has turned back to its former two-pillar structure again: the first pillar is a mandatory pay-as-you-go state pension system, and the second pillar is a voluntary, additional one, including all institutional forms of pension savings such as pay-as-you-earn private pension funds, voluntary mutual pension funds, occupational pension schemes, the so-called tax-assisted pension savings account (NYESZ account) and life insurance policies designed for pension savings.[385]

384. The number of the members of the private pension funds exceeding 3 million decreased to 99,299 persons by the end of 2011 and dropped to 74,400 persons by the end of March, 2012. By 2014, only four pay-as-you-earn private pension funds were standing with approximately 61,000 members.

385. Dr. Barta Judit, *Visszatérés az egypilléres kötelező nyugdíjrendszerhez (a 2010. december 13-án elfogadott törvénycsomag értékelése)* [Return to the One-Pillar Compulsory Pension System (The Evaluation of the Package of Laws Adopted on Dec. 13, 2010)] In Gazdaság és Jog, 2011/3., 9–15.

Chapter 4. Voluntary Mutual Pension Funds and Private Pension Funds

381. The actual Hungarian Government came under pressure at the time of the introduction and the repression of the regime of compulsory funded private pension. Meanwhile, the regime of compulsory funded private pension "failed" in the other Central-Eastern European Member States (with the exception of Slovenia and the Czech Republic) and in most of the South American and Latin American countries, too. Indeed, there are exceptions, but they are less common. World Bank experts have also figured out the problems of the system, primarily the problems of the budget deficit caused by the introduction, and they are no longer recommending this model so enthusiastically.

The organizational structure of the private pension fund system developed in a special way in Hungary, which also contributed to the failure of the system because of its contradictions.

With the elimination of the element of compulsory self-care and the abolition of statutory guarantees, the funded pension system became nowhere more or better than the voluntary mutual pension fund system nowadays.[386]

Voluntary mutual pension funds and private pension funds operate on a pay-as-you-earn principle. Two periods are distinguished in these systems: the *so-called accumulation period* and the *so-called service or annuity period.*

During the accumulation period, savers collect the cover of their future pension; the minimum duration of accumulation is stipulated by the relevant laws (it is ten years in the case of voluntary mutual pension funds and ten years in the case of private pension funds). During this period, the members perform so-called payments to *their individual accounts*, which amounts are invested in by the pension funds in accordance with their investment policy in the framework of a portfolio investment scheme chosen by the members, and the yields achieved are credited to their accounts. After the expiration of the accumulation period and receiving the entitlement to state pension, members are also entitled to the additional pension service which is calculated based on the amounts accumulated in their individual accounts, mostly in the form of annuity. The pension or annuity is provided by the pension fund itself, or it enters into a contract with an insurance company and purchases an insurance annuity.

Savers pay their contribution deducted from their pretax income to both forms of institutions.

During the accumulation period, the amount accumulated in the individual account is in the ownership of the members, but their freedom to act is restricted only to the designation of beneficiaries. In preparation for the possible event of their

386. Dr. Barta Judit, *A kiegészítő nyugdíjpillér ezen belül a magánnyugdíjpénztári rendszer aktuális helyzete és értékelése* [The Current State Of The Supplementary Private Pension Fund System From The Aspect Of Contributors]. The Publications of the MultiScience—XXIX. microCAD International Multidisciplinary Scientific Conference University of Miskolc, (Apr. 9–10, 2015). ISBN 978-963-358-061-5 http://www.uni-miskolc.hu/~microcad/publikaciok/2015/E2_Barta_Judit.pdf.

death during the accumulation period, *pension fund members are allowed to designate a beneficiary* with regard to their individual accounts for whom the amount accumulated in the individual account should be paid. If a beneficiary is already designated, the amount in the deceased pension fund member's account cannot be inherited, but it is paid to the beneficiary as part of the service the pension fund provides. It depends on the choice of a fund member to designate a beneficiary who can be not only an heir but also anyone else. More than one beneficiary can be designated up to different levels of entitlement; the designation of beneficiaries can be either withdrawn or changed.

During the service or annuity period, a beneficiary could not be designated to receive the amount not yet paid, which resulted in some criticism because the amount accumulated over the decades (up to tens of millions of Hungarian forints) remained at the private pension fund in the case of the untimely death of the member during the annuity period. In 2015, the laws on voluntary mutual pension funds and private pension funds were amended which facilitated the payment of the remaining amount on the service or annuity account to the designated beneficiary even in the case of a member's death during the annuity period. If the deceased pension fund member does not designate any beneficiaries, the rules of inheritance must be applied. The possibility of a beneficiary designation or heritability needs to be provided even if it is not the pension fund that provides the annuity service but it "buys" that from a private insurance company; that is, it enters into a contract with a private insurance company for providing annuity service.[387]

Voluntary mutual pension funds and private pension funds provide annuity services only for their members, and their relatives or beneficiaries are not entitled to them. This possibility was earlier provided by the mandatory private pension funds. For relatives, the possibility of a beneficiary designation or heritability can provide the "care."

---

387. Dr. Barta Judit, *Örökölhetőség, és hozzátartozói ellátás kérdése a magyar kiegészítő nyugdíjpillér egyes intézményeiben* [Issues on Inheritance and Relatives' Care in Certain Institutions of the Hungarian Supplementary Pension Pillar] In Mélypataki Gábor (ed.), *A szociális jog aktuális kérdései Magyarországon és az Európai Unióban* [Actual Issues on Social Law in Hungary and in The European Union]. Conference volume, 2016.2.11., 22–29.
University of Miskolc, Faculty of law, (ISBN:978-963-358-123-0).
https://oszkdk.oszk.hu/storage/00/02/02/22/dd/1/A_szoci__lis_jog_aktu__lis_k__rd__sei_Magyarorsz__gon___s_az_Eur__pai_Uni__ban.pdf, vagy Friedrich Ebert Stiftung.
http://fesbp.hu/common/pdf/A_szocialis_jog_aktualis_kerdesei_2017.pdf.

Chapter 5. Occupational Pension Scheme Providers

382. The unique feature of this form of saving for retirement is that it is focused on the employer's engagement and not that of the saver's. The employer makes a decision about the introduction of an occupational pension scheme; if there is no such scheme offered by the employer, the employees can only collectively put pressure on the employer. One can become a member if they have an employment contract with the founder of the scheme, and their contract includes the employer's commitment to paying contributions. The terms of pension services are determined by the employer within the framework of the related rules and regulations.

The occupational pension scheme basically operates according to two models:

- it can be financed *by the principle of predefined levels of retirement service (fully funded pension scheme)* where the financial and biometric risks are borne by the employer; or
- it can be defined *by payment (partially funded pension scheme)* where the retirement service is not determined, and it depends on the magnitude of the contributions and the yields of their investment. The employer is obliged to pay a certain amount of contributions, and the risks of investment fall on the employee.

Employers in Hungary mostly prefer fully funded pension schemes, that is, retirement services determined by paid contributions.

Retirement service is provided by accumulation during *the waiting period* which is primarily paid by the employer in the form of regular payments and investments of pension contributions. The waiting period starts from the beginning of membership; although the employer determines its duration, it is maximized in ten years by legal provisions. Pensions can be provided after the waiting period. The employee may decide to pay *supplements to the contribution* paid by the employer. The employer has the right to stipulate that the employee has to pay a supplement as well.

The amount credited to members' accounts[388] and its yields are the property of the member. In the case of both pension schemes—in order to bond employees—a period of conditional acquisition of rights can be determined which is the shortest period of time spent in employment, after which the employer gets the ownership of the employer contributions and the yields credited to their account. The period of conditional acquisition of rights can range from zero to three years.

In the event of death, members may designate a beneficiary in a public document (death beneficiary). More beneficiaries can be designated; a member may also appoint a new beneficiary at any time. It is also possible to withdraw a beneficiary designation. If the member does not designate a beneficiary or the designation is repealed, the member's natural heir or heirs should be considered a beneficiary in the share of their inheritance. The beneficiary becomes the exclusive owner of the account at the time of the member's death.

388. Contributions paid by the employer. Membership payments and investment yields are credited to a member account. After reaching retirement age, the pension service is calculated based on the amount held in the member account.

The pension scheme might contain a provision that in the event of a member's death, no beneficiaries can be appointed. In this case, the amount in the account is transferred to the member's occupational pension provider at the time of death of the member, and it is further transferred to member accounts of the pension scheme, calculated in proportion to the credit balances. If the employer payment of members' contributions is subjected to the payment of supplements by the employee, the pension scheme cannot contain any provision on the exclusion of beneficiary designation.

In the case of fully funded pension schemes, the law allows for designating a beneficiary for providing reversionary pension.

Chapter 6. Individual Retirement Account

383. Individual retirement account (NYESZ account) can be opened by any individual who is not entitled to a pension yet and puts at least HUF 5,000 in the account. The required period of savings qualifying as a pension service is a minimum of three years but getting full tax benefit becomes possible only after ten years of savings. There can be two types of pension savings accounts: (1) money accounts or (2) securities accounts. The account manager is not obliged to pay interest for the retirement savings placed in the money account because the goal is to invest the money primarily into securities. The discounts are therefore mainly related to the securities account when the saver invests the retirement savings in securities. The state supports the opening of NYESZ accounts in a way that an amount specified in the personal income tax (PIT) is returned to the NYESZ account of the individual in the form of benefit (savings support). The National Tax and Customs Administration (NTCA) transfers a maximum of HUF 100,000 or 20% of the amount in the pension savings account after paying taxes in a given tax year.

384. An additional benefit is that the profits and yields (interest, capital gains, etc.) of the transactions of investment assets in the securities account are exempt from taxation—except for stock dividends—and pension services paid from the account are also tax-free. Income tax is to be paid for the interest on financial assets held in the account. The amount of money paid by the saver is accumulated in the money account together with its potential interests and the part of income tax returned by the NTCA; in the securities account, however, the yields of investment assets and the part of income tax returned by the NTCA are collected. The account manager may charge a fee for managing the account and providing investment services.

Payment from an NYESZ account is considered *a tax-free pension service* if, in the case of the termination of the account, the account holder is entitled to receive pension, or, in exceptional cases, after ten years following the opening of account, if the account holder is declared permanently disabled and becomes entitled to receive invalidity pension.

Payment from an NYESZ account is considered *a taxable pension service* if the account holder becomes entitled to receive pension, saves for at least three years, but the termination of the account happens no more than ten years after opening the account. In this case, the account holder can keep the savings support, but the overall yield achieved on the entire portfolio until the date of terminating the account—money and securities—qualifies as other income for which income tax and health contributions are to be paid.

In the case of payment not qualifying as a pension service, the payment support has to be paid back to the NTCA increased by 20% as a self-employed taxpayer, and income tax has also to be paid if any income is generated by the investment.

The assets held in the securities account—according to the rules of the inheritance of ordinary securities accounts—are a part of the inheritance. The inheritors can choose between the options of asking to sell the existing securities and receiving their yield or, if they have a securities account, of deferring the securities in the

NYESZ account. The inheritors are exempt from taxation in terms of the yields or returns in the NYESZ account regardless of the number of passed tax years and the entitlement to receive pension.

In respect to the amount held in the money account, the situation is similar, the only difference is that a beneficiary can be designated in the event of death by applying the specific statutory rules to this type of payment account.

Chapter 7. Pension Insurance Contracts Concluded with Insurers

385. Pension insurance belongs to the life insurance branch, it is one of its branches, and it is provided by life insurance companies only. According to the main rule, the insurance event is the reaching of the retirement age, but it can be combined with risk elements too, such as disability or death before the reaching of the retirement age. Only pension insurance shall enjoy tax benefits, which comply with the regulations of the Act on Personal Income Tax (*see* Part IX.).

The annuity insurance, which has insurance elements, serves to cover care for retired years. This provides for the insured party the annuity, which shall be paid monthly until the death of the insured party. According to the Tax Act, it can be only a non-degressive annuity, which shall be provided until the end of the tenth year from the first payment or until the insured person's death.

In the event of pension insurance, if the insured party dies, the amount, which was not paid as annuity, cannot be inherited, and there is no possibility of nominating a beneficiary. The reason for this is that the insured parties create a risk community and the savings of the dead insured shall be transferred to those who live up to the age calculated by the insurance company.

The number of life insurance for retirement provided by insurance companies has increased, and the state urges the conclusion of these contracts with tax benefits from 2014. (*see* Part IX).[389]

Twenty percent of the fee paid in the year will be credited by the state from the paid tax up to a maximum of HUF 130,000 per year for the benefit of the insurance contract.[390] Insurers offer more and more types of pension insurance products, and currently, there are about eighty different pension insurance schemes in the market; all insurance companies which deal with life insurance have at least two to three kinds of pension products.

389. In light of the insurers' data from 2016, the pension insurance is the most dynamically development area among the pension targeted self-care services thanks to the tax allowance.
Source: https://mabisz.hu/szemle/?p=5617.

390. For the HUF 130,000 tax credit, an average of HUF 54,000 per month shall be paid, which means HUF 650,000 per year. For this, only a small percentage of the contractors are able to pay. They pay an average of HUF 200,000 annually to their pension insurance account, which will entitle them to a tax credit of HUF 400,00 in the next year.
Source: https://mabisz.hu/szemle/?p=6166.

Part VII. Insurance Intermediaries

Chapter 1. Law of Establishment and Supervision

Judit Barta

§1. Basic Conditions of the Activity of Insurance Intermediaries

386. The condition of the insurance intermediary and ancillary insurance intermediary activity is that the NBH registers the intermediary and issues a registry number for the intermediary. Insurance mediation activities can be carried out if the insurance intermediaries are in active status in the register maintained by the NBH.[391] Ancillary insurance intermediaries may engage in the pursuit of insurance distribution activities on behalf of insurance companies, brokers, multiple agents, and ancillary insurance intermediaries only if, depending on the person, they are included in the registers of the NBH.[392,393] The register of the NBH shall comprise the register of natural persons engaged in the activities of insurance intermediaries, the register of economic operators engaged in insurance mediation, the register of economic operators engaged in ancillary insurance mediation, and the register of deregistered insurance intermediaries.[394] In the course of the registration procedure, the Authority shall assign a registration number to each natural person and economic operator insurance intermediaries, and economic operators engaged in ancillary insurance mediation.[395] Insurance intermediaries and economic operators engaged in ancillary insurance mediation shall be registered upon notification—by way of the means decreed by the Governor of NBH—by the insurance company, multiple agents, or broker on whose behalf they perform insurance mediation activities.[396]

391. Subsection 2 of s. 369 of the BIns.
392. According to sub. 1 of s. 407 of the BIns., the Authority shall maintain a register on insurance intermediaries and the managers of such insurance intermediaries responsible for distribution operations, and on economic operators engaged in ancillary insurance mediation and the managers of such economic operators responsible for distribution operations notified or authorized under this Act in order to carry out authorization and supervisory functions relative to them.
393. Subsection 2a of s. 369 of the BIns.
394. Subsection 3 of s. 407 of the BIns.
395. Subsection 1 of s. 410 of the BIns.
396. Subsection 1 of s. 411 of the BIns.

Insurance mediation activities may be taken up and/or pursued by a natural person who:

(a) has a professional qualification as defined by law, e.g., a university-level degree or secondary education in the field of economics, insurance intermediary professional qualification;
(b) complies with the requirement of continuing professional training;
(c) is of sufficiently good repute.[397]

Insurance companies, multiple agents, and brokers are required to maintain an internal records system:

- on the natural persons they employ or engage with to mediate insurance;
- if they engage an economic operator to mediate insurance, on that economic operator, and the natural persons who pursue the mediation of insurance at such economic operator;
- on the economic operators engaged in ancillary insurance mediation they commission, and on the natural persons engaged in ancillary insurance mediation at that economic operator;
- the persons provided for in subsection (1) of section 368 employed[398] for the purpose of facilitating the registration and supervision of insurance intermediaries of

397. Section 69/A:

The following shall not be deemed of sufficiently good repute:

a) a person who does not have a clean criminal record; or
b) a person who is or has been an executive officer of an insurance company, reinsurance company or a financial organization, or who is or has been a senior executive of a business association that was able to avoid insolvency solely as a result of intervention by the competent supervisory authority, or that was liquidated or is undergoing liquidation, or that was removed from the register of companies by way of involuntary de-registration procedure or is undergoing involuntary de-registration, and whose personal responsibility for this situation was established by court ruling or regulatory decision not more than five years previously.

398. Subsection 1 of s. 368 of the BIns.: Unless otherwise provided for in this Act, the provisions of this Book shall not apply to any person who carries on the activity of ancillary insurance mediation pertaining solely to insurance contracts if all the following conditions are met:

a) the insurance contract is complementary to the product or service supplied by any provider and it covers the following:
   aa) the risk of breakdown, loss of or damage to goods supplied by that provider, or the risk of nonuse of the service supplied by that provider, or
   ab) damage to or loss of baggage and other risks linked to the travel booked with that provider; and
b) the amount:
   ba) of the premium paid for the insurance product does not exceed six hundred euro calculated on a pro rata annual basis, or
   bb) of the premium paid per person does not exceed two hundred euro, and the duration of the service provided for in Paragraph *a)* is equal to, or less than, three months.

the NBH.[399] Registration by the Authority is not required for taking up the pursuit of insurance mediation activities where the mediation of insurance is performed by a natural person employed by a credit institution specified in the CIFE or by a universal postal service provider provided for in the Act on Postal Services or any contributor delegated by the universal postal service provider, in accordance with the employer's instructions, in the customer area of the employer's premises, or by the way of a mobile postal service establishment.[400]

Natural persons shown in the register of insurance intermediaries shall be in possession of a picture identification document issued by the insurance company or by the insurance intermediary.[401]

The natural persons engaged in the pursuit of insurance mediation activities shall be required to attend continuing professional training programs prescribed by the BIns. for the purpose of maintaining the active status. This facilitates up-to-date knowledge concerning the insurance products they mediate.

The continuing professional training may be provided by the insurance company that employs the natural person insurance intermediary under contract of employment or otherwise or by the independent insurance intermediary or a specialized vocational institution which is defined by the BIns.

The insurance company or independent insurance intermediary shall keep records of attendance in the continuing professional training and shall verify the participation of the NBH in supervisory control proceedings.[402]

§2. Authorization for the Employment or Delegation of a Principal Agent

387. The employment or delegation of a principal agent shall be authorized by the NBH. The principal agent may be in a personal service contract or employment relationship with the insurer.[403]

§3. Conditions Concerning the Activities of Multiple Agents[404]

388. Multiple agents can carry out their activities with the authorization of the NBH and in certain forms. The BIns. defines the forms, which are the followings:

(a) limited company;
(b) private limited-liability company with at least HUF 5 million in equity capital;

399. Subsection 1 of s. 412 of the BIns.
400. Subsection 1 of s. 370 of the BIns.
401. Subsection 1 of s. 374 of the BIns.
402. Section 376 of the BIns.
403. Sections 395–397 of the BIns.
404. Sections 388–393 of the BIns.

(c) Hungarian branch of a third-country insurance intermediary company with at least HUF 5 million in capital.

After granting the authorization, the NBH shall register the multiple agents in active status.

Multiple agents, in line with the insurance mediation activities intended to be pursued:

(a) shall have ownership title or the right to use or lease premises suitable for receiving clients;
(b) shall have continuous systems of files and records permitting individual identification of the activities performed;
(c) shall have in place the means required for compliance with the obligation of disclosure to the NBH;
(d) shall meet the personnel conditions prescribed for insurance mediation activities.

Multiple agents shall employ a natural person delegated for the management of insurance mediation activities under contract of employment. The natural person responsible for the management of insurance mediation activities shall be a person who has no prior criminal records and meets the professional conditions defined by the BIns.[405]

Multiple agents shall maintain a records system with sufficient facilities to permit individual identification of concluded insurance transactions. Rules for the reports to be filed by multiple agents shall be decreed by the Governor of the NBH.

Multiple agents shall—at all times—carry professional indemnity insurance covering liability in connection with their activities:

(a) representing at least EUR 1,300,380 applying to each insured loss and in aggregate EUR 1,924,560 per year for all claims covering the entire territory of the EU; or
(b) shall have EUR 1,924,560 of secured financial reserves.[406]

Multiple agents may not engage in independent insurance mediation activities.[407]

405. Conditions:

(a) has a university-level degree and at least three years of experience as an insurance executive at an insurance company, or have a total of at least five years of experience in the field of insurance in the employment of an insurance company; or
(b) graduated from a secondary education institution and have at least seven years of experience as an insurance executive at an insurance company or an economic operator engaged in insurance mediation activities;
(c) is engaged in mediating exclusively at the given insurance intermediary;
(d) is not employed by any insurance company under contract of employment or any other work-related contractual relationship;
(e) complies with fit and proper requirements.

406. Subsection 6 of s. 391 of the BIns.

407. Subsection 2 of s. 387 of the BIns.

§4. Conditions of the Activities Carried Out by Insurance Brokers[408]

389. The activities of insurance brokers can be carried out with the authorization of the NBH and in given forms. The forms are defined by the BIns., which are:

(a) limited company;
(b) private limited-liability company with at least HUF 5 million in equity capital;
(c) Hungarian branch of a third-country insurance intermediary company with at least HUF 5 million in capital.

After granting the authorization, the Authority shall register the broker in active status. As appropriate for the insurance mediation activities intended to be pursued, brokers:

(a) shall have ownership title or the right to use or lease premises suitable for receiving clients;
(b) shall have continuous systems of files and records permitting individual identification of the activities performed;
(c) shall have in place the means required for compliance with the obligation of disclosure to the NBH;
(d) shall meet the personnel conditions prescribed for insurance mediation activities.

Brokers shall employ a natural person delegated for the management of insurance mediation activities under contract of employment, who shall have no prior criminal record and shall meet the professional requirements defined by the BIns.[409]

Brokers shall maintain a records system with sufficient facilities to permit individual identification of concluded insurance transactions. Rules for the reports to be filed by brokers shall be decreed by the Governor of the NBH.

Brokers shall—at all times—carry professional indemnity insurance covering liability in connection with their activities:

(a) representing at least EUR 1,300,380 applying to each insured loss and in aggregate EUR 1,924,560 per year for all claims covering the entire territory of the EU; or

408. Sections 399–406 of the BIns.
409. Conditions:
  (a) has a university-level degree and at least three years of experience as an insurance executive at an insurance company, or have a total of at least five years of experience in the field of insurance in the employment of an insurance company; or
  (b) graduated from a secondary education institution and have at least seven years of experience as an insurance executive at an insurance company or an economic operator engaged in insurance mediation activities;
  (c) is engaged in mediating exclusively at the given insurance intermediary;
  (d) is not employed by any insurance company under contract of employment or any other work-related contractual relationship;
  (e) complies with fit and proper requirements.

(b) shall have EUR 1,924,560 of secured financial reserves.[410]

§5. Registration of Insurance Intermediaries by the Authority

390. The NBH shall maintain a register on insurance intermediaries and the managers of such insurance intermediaries responsible for distribution operations, and on economic operators engaged in ancillary insurance mediation and the managers of such economic operators responsible for distribution operations notified or authorized under this Act in order to carry out authorization and supervisory functions relative to them.[411] The register shall comprise the register of natural persons engaged in the activities of insurance intermediaries, the register of economic operators engaged in insurance mediation, the register of economic operators engaged in ancillary insurance mediation, and the register of deregistered insurance intermediaries.[412] In the course of the registration procedure, the NBH shall assign a registration number to each natural person and economic operator insurance intermediaries, and economic operators engaged in ancillary insurance mediation.[413]

The NBH shall make available on its website the public data of persons engaged in the activities of insurance intermediaries (name and registered address of companies) and other data prescribed by the BIns.[414]

§6. Authorization by the NBH[415]

391. The NBH's authorization shall be required:

(a) for the pursuit of the activities of multiple agents and brokers;
(b) for the employment of a natural person for the management of activities of multiple agents and brokers;
(c) for starting up the activities of a branch to be established by an insurance intermediary established in a third country;
(d) for the employment of the general representative of a branch set up by an insurance intermediary established in a third country;
(e) for termination[416] and suspension[417] of the activities of multiple agents and brokers upon request;

410. Subsection 1 of s. 403 of the BIns.
411. Subsection 1 of s. 407 of the BIns.
412. Subsection 3 of s. 407 of the BIns.
413. Subsection 1 of s. 410 of the BIns.
414. Section 410 of the BIns.
415. Section 413 of the BIns.
416. According to s. 420 of the BIns., where a multiple agent or a broker proposes to terminate his activities, the NBH shall authorize the termination of activities if the multiple agent or broker has satisfied all its commitments and liabilities stemming from those activities. If the Authority has authorized the closure of operations, it shall at the same time withdraw the multiple agent's and broker's authorization and shall change their status in the relevant register to inactive.

(f) for the employment or delegation of a principal agent.[418]

§7. Notification Requirement of Multiple Agents and Brokers[419]

392. Multiple agents and brokers shall notify the NBH within the deadline defined by the BIns.:

(a) any changes in the person managing the insurance mediation activities;
(b) any change in the address of their registered office;
(c) if the own funds drop below the limit of the minimum capital requirement specified by the BIns.;
(d) any increase or reduction of the equity (share) capital;
(e) the termination of their liability insurance policy, including the date of termination; and
(f) if a new liability insurance policy is obtained, including the date when it concluded, as well as documentary proof thereof.

Multiple agents and brokers shall send a duplicate of their annual account, which is deposited with the court of registry, to the Authority by the last day of the fifth month following the balance sheet date.

§8. Actions of the NBH Related to Insurance Intermediaries and Ancillary Insurance Intermediaries[420]

393. The NBH can issue the following measures:

(a) issue a warning for the implementation of the provisions specified by the law, in other regulations relating to insurance mediation activities and in supervisory decision, and in justified cases, issue a mandatory order to that effect, with the deadline prescribed;
(b) impose a supervision fine;
(c) prohibit the pursuit of any unauthorized multiple agencies and brokering activity, as well as the activities of unregistered insurance intermediaries;
(d) order to change the status of the insurance intermediary in the relevant register to inactive;
(e) order the multiple agents or broker to increase their subscribed capital to the required minimum prescribed by the BIns.;

417. According to s. 421 of the BIns., the NBH shall authorize the suspension of multiple agency or brokering activities upon request, for a maximum term of six months. At the time of issuing the resolution of authorization of suspension, the NBH shall change the status of the multiple agent or broker in the relevant register to inactive.
418. Point n) of sub. 1 of s. 237 of the BIns.
419. Section 424 of the BIns.
420. Sections 431–435 of the BIns.

(f) order the hearing of the general representative of a branch set up by an insurance intermediary established in a third country or the person managing the insurance mediation activities;
(g) move to recommend the dismissal of the person managing the insurance mediation activities or the general representative of a branch set up by an insurance intermediary established in a third country;
(h) suspend the authorization of multiple agents or broker;
(i) withdraw the authorization of multiple agents or broker;
(j) prohibit the transfer of the broker's contracts for insurance mediation services;[421]
(k) order the cessation of the infringement or prohibit any further infringement;
(l) in the event of infringement of conduct of business rules relating to the distribution of insurance-based investment products by the managing director of an insurance intermediary company, ban such managing director for a specific period of time from discharging his functions;
(m) order the suspension or prohibition of marketing of certain insurance products or all insurance products through intermediaries;
(n) order the broker or multiple agents to remove its ancillary insurance intermediary from its internal records;
(o) refuse the registration if the close link indicated in the registers exists with a natural person or economic operator established in a third country where there are legal impediments liable to prevent the NBH from the effective exercise of its supervisory functions.

In order to enforce the obligations of ancillary insurance intermediaries and to safeguard the interests of clients, and in order to enforce compliance with the provisions of this Act and other relevant regulations on insurance mediation activities, and with the NBH's resolutions, the NBH shall have the power to take the measures provided for in paragraphs a), b), c), d), k), m), n), and o) with respect to the ancillary insurance intermediary.

In order to meet the requirements prescribed by the BIns., in other regulations on the activities of insurance intermediaries, and in the NBH's resolutions, the NBH shall have powers to instruct insurance intermediaries to draw up an action plan for a specific time frame and to execute the action plan if approved.

§9. Supervision Fee Paid by Multiple Agents and Brokers[422]

394. Multiple agents and brokers—including the Hungarian branches of third-country insurance intermediaries engaged in the pursuit of multiple agency and brokering activities—shall be required to pay a supervision fee to the NBH.

421. According to s. 406/A of the BIns., the transferring broker may transfer its portfolio of contracts for insurance mediation services—including the rights and obligations arising out of such contracts, with the terms and conditions of the insurance contracts connected to the said service contract unaltered—in part or in whole to another broker, or to the branch of a broker established in another Member State (hereinafter referred to collectively as "receiving broker").
422. Section 436 of the BIns.

395. The supervision fee shall comprise the minimum charge plus the variable-rate fee.

396. The minimum charge shall be HUF 75,000, to be increased by HUF 75,000 for each fifty natural persons engaged in the activities of insurance intermediaries, employed or commissioned by the multiple agent or broker or by the economic operator hired by the multiple agents or broker.

397. The annual variable-rate fee shall be 0.25% of the annual commission income.

§10. Insurance Intermediary Activity in Another Member State

398. Where an insurance intermediary or ancillary insurance intermediary proposes to establish a branch or permanent presence in another Member State or to take up the pursuit of insurance mediation activities or ancillary insurance mediation activities in the form of cross-border services for the first time through the branch or in the form of permanent presence, it shall notify the Authority in advance. Any permanent presence of an insurance intermediary or ancillary insurance intermediary in the territory of another Member State that is equivalent to a branch shall be treated in the same way as a branch unless the insurance intermediary or ancillary insurance intermediary lawfully sets up such permanent presence in another legal form. Such could be the case where the insurance intermediary's or ancillary insurance intermediary's permanent presence consists merely of an office managed by the staff of the insurance intermediary or ancillary insurance intermediary or by a person who is independent but has permanent authority to act for the insurance intermediary or ancillary insurance intermediary as a branch would.[423]

Within one month of receiving the notification, the NBH shall communicate the information defined in the BIns. to the supervisory authority of the other Member State.

The NBH shall without delay provide EIOPA with the information of insurance intermediaries and ancillary insurance intermediaries—including a website address where such information is available and any changes in such information—which have notified the Authority of their intention to carry out activities in the form of cross-border services or to establish a branch in another Member State.

If the NBH considers that the organizational structure or the financial situation of the insurance intermediary or ancillary insurance intermediary is inadequate, meaning, in particular, that they are unable to comply with the relevant legal requirements or the personnel and infrastructure they have available appears insufficient, it shall adopt a resolution within one month of receiving the notification referred to in subsection (4) so as to refuse to transfer data to the competent authority of the host Member State and shall inform the notifier that it may not commence operations in the form of a branch.

423. Subsections 1–2 of s. 422 of the BIns.

In the case of cross-border services, the NBH shall inform the insurance intermediary or ancillary insurance intermediary in writing that the information the NBH has forwarded has been received by the competent authority of the other Member State and that it has acknowledged its receipt, that it may commence its business in the other Member State, where applicable, about the means to access the legal provisions of the other Member State on insurance distribution activities at the competent authority of that other Member State, or on the website of EIOPA, and that the notifier must comply with those legal provisions.

In the case of branches, the NBH shall inform the insurance intermediary or ancillary insurance intermediary in writing that the information the NBH has forwarded has been received by the competent authority of the other Member State and that it has acknowledged its receipt. If the competent authority of the other Member State communicates to the NBH within one month of receipt of the notification forwarded by the NBH the legal provisions on insurance distribution activities which are applicable in its territory, the NBH shall communicate to the insurance intermediary or ancillary insurance intermediary in writing the existing legal provisions communicated by the competent authority of the other Member State on insurance distribution activities, and that it may commence its business in the other Member State provided that it complies with the legal provisions.

Where no communication is received from the competent authority of the other Member State within one month of receipt of the notification forwarded by the NBH, the NBH shall inform in writing the insurance intermediary or ancillary insurance intermediary that it may establish the branch and commence its business.[424]

§11. Rules Relating to Insurance Intermediaries Established in Other Member States Taking Up Activities in Hungary

399. Insurance intermediaries residing or established in another Member State shall be allowed to pursue activities on the territory of Hungary in the form of cross-border services or through a Hungarian branch if they are duly registered in their home Member State.[425]

The authorization of NBH is not required for the branch of a multiple agent established in another Member State if pursuing activities through a branch or in the form of cross-border services. The authorization of the Authority is not required for the branch of a broker established in another Member State if pursuing activities through a branch or in the form of cross-border services.

Upon receipt of notice from the competent supervisory authority of another Member State in regard to an insurance intermediary registered under its jurisdiction that is planning to set up a branch or pursue activities in the form of cross-border services for the first time on the territory of Hungary for the pursuit insurance

424. Subsections 5–9 of s. 422 of the BIns.
425. Subsection 1 of s. 371 of the BIns.

mediation activities, the Authority shall communicate the Hungarian regulations pertaining to such activities to the insurance intermediary in question within one month of receipt of said notice.[426]

The NBH may periodically request information from the Hungarian branches of insurance intermediaries and ancillary insurance intermediaries established in other Member States or from insurance intermediaries and ancillary insurance intermediaries established in other Member States in connection with their insurance mediation and/or ancillary insurance mediation activities performed in the form of cross-border services and the related documents in order to verify their compliance with the legislation.[427]

If an insurance intermediary or ancillary insurance intermediary established in another Member State that is engaged in operations in the territory of Hungary through a branch or in the form of cross-border services breaches the regulations in effect in Hungary on branches and cross-border services, or if the NBH detects any discrepancies in their operations, the NBH shall inform the supervisory authority of the home Member State and may move for taking the measures it considers appropriate.[428]

Where, despite the measures taken by the supervisory authority of the home Member State or because those measures prove to be inadequate or are lacking, the infringement persists, or if the infringement is clearly detrimental to the interests of consumers on a large scale, or to the orderly functioning of insurance and reinsurance markets, the NBH may, after informing the supervisory authority of the home Member State, take the measures provided for in the BIns., or may refer the matter to EIOPA and request its assistance in accordance with Article 19 of Regulation 1094/2010/EU. Where immediate action is necessary in order to protect the rights of consumers, the NBH shall have the power to take these measures, with the proviso that in the case of branches on condition that the equivalent measures of the home Member State are inadequate or lacking. If the NBH takes measures, it shall inform the supervisory authority of the other Member State, EIOPA, and the Commission concerning its resolution.[429]

If the supervisory authority of the home Member State of an insurance intermediary or ancillary insurance intermediary has withdrawn the authorization of the insurance intermediary or ancillary insurance intermediary and has notified the Authority accordingly, the NBH shall take all measures it deems appropriate to prevent the insurance intermediary or ancillary insurance intermediary affected to continue the pursuit of further activities.[430]

Upon prior notification of the NBH, the supervisory authority of another Member State where an insurance intermediary or ancillary insurance intermediary that is engaged in operations in Hungary through a branch or in the form of cross-border services is established shall be entitled to inspect the operations of such branch or

426. Section 423 of the BIns.
427. Section 425 of the BIns.
428. Subsection 1 of s. 426 of the BIns.
429. Subsections 2–4 of s. 426 of the BIns.
430. Subsection 5 of s. 426 of the BIns.

the cross-border service in Hungary; the inspection may be carried out by the supervisory authority itself or by a person it has authorized. The NBH may take part in the inspection. When requested by the competent supervisory authority, the NBH shall have the right to inspect the operations on site of an insurance intermediary or ancillary insurance intermediary established in another Member State that are performed in Hungary through its branch or in the form of cross-border services and to request information. If the head office of the insurance intermediary or ancillary insurance intermediary established in another Member State is situated in Hungary, the NBH may reach an agreement with the competent authority of the home Member State that the NBH shall function as the competent authority with regard to organizational requirements relating to the insurance distribution, information requirements, and business rules—including additional requirements in relation to insurance-based investment products—and to sanctions and other measures to be applied in relation to insurance distribution activities.[431]

Where the activity of the Hungarian branch of an insurance intermediary or ancillary insurance intermediary established in another Member State, or its activity carried out in the form of cross-border services:

(a) is entirely or principally directed towards the territory of Hungary;
(b) the sole purpose of setting up a registered office in another Member State is to avoid the legal provisions applicable in Hungary; and
(c) seriously endangers the interests of consumers.

The NBH shall have the power to take the measures referred to in the BIns. following notification of the competent authority of the other Member State, or may refer the matter to EIOPA and may request its assistance in accordance with Article 19 of Regulation 1094/2010/EU.[432]

§12. Insurance Intermediary Activity in Another Member State

400. Where the supervisory authority of another Member State notifies the NBH of any infringement by an insurance intermediary or ancillary insurance intermediary in connection with their activities performed through a branch or in the form of cross-border services of the provisions governing such activities, the NBH may apply the measures provided for in the BIns. vis-à-vis the insurance intermediary or ancillary insurance intermediary in order to eliminate the infringement.

The NBH shall inform the competent supervisory authority of the other Member State concerning the measures it has taken at the time of taking those measures.

If the supervisory authority of the other Member State takes action directly or takes additional measures, the Authority may refer the matter to EIOPA and may request its assistance in accordance with Article 19 of Regulation 1094/2010/EU.[433]

431. Section 427 of the BIns.
432. Subsection 2 of s. 427/A of the BIns.
433. Section 427/B of the BIns.

If the head office of the insurance intermediary or ancillary insurance intermediary established in Hungary is situated in another Member State, the NBH may reach an agreement with the competent authority of the home Member State that the competent authority of that other Member State shall function as the competent authority with regard to organizational requirements relating to insurance distribution, information requirements, and business rules—including additional requirements in relation to insurance-based investment products—and to sanctions and other measures to be applied in relation to insurance distribution activities. The NBH shall without delay inform the insurance intermediary or ancillary insurance intermediary, as well as EIOPA, concerning this agreement. In the other Member State, the competent authority of that other Member State shall have supervisory power over the branches of insurance intermediaries and ancillary insurance intermediaries established in Hungary in order to uphold the provisions relating to insurance distribution, information requirements, and business rules—including additional requirements in relation to insurance-based investment products—and to apply sanctions and other measures in the event of any infringement of these provisions.[434]

§13. Provisions Relating to the Supervision and Activity of the Hungarian Branches of Insurance Intermediaries Established in Third Countries

401. Insurance intermediary companies established in a third country shall be allowed to pursue activities on the territory of Hungary only through a Hungarian branch.[435]

Third-country insurance intermediaries that have a branch in Hungary shall send the official Hungarian translation of their balance sheet and profit and loss account prepared according to the laws of their home countries and approved by an auditor to the Authority within thirty days of approval.[436]

The NBH may take measures if the supervisory authority with jurisdiction over the registered office of a third-country insurance intermediary has taken measures against the given insurance intermediary or one of its branches operating in any country for a reason that affects the safe operation of the Hungarian branch. When requested by the competent supervisory authority, the NBH shall have the right to inspect the operations on site of the Hungarian branch of a third-country insurance intermediary and request information from it. The NBH, if there is reciprocity or under a valid supervisory agreement, may give its consent for the inspection of the Hungarian branch of a third-country insurance intermediary to be carried out by the supervisory authority of the country where it is established or by an auditor or other expert on its behalf.[437]

434. Section 427/C of the BIns.
435. Subsection 1 of s. 372 of the BIns.
436. Section 428 of the BIns.
437. Section 429 of the BIns.

Chapter 2. Insurance Intermediaries and the Insurance Contract

Edit Antal Ujvári

§1. General Rules Relating to Insurance Intermediaries[438]

402. Separate laws have been adopted concerning insurance intermediaries in the unified European insurance market.[439] In light of compliance with Directive 2002/92/EC of the European Parliament and of the Council of December 9, 2002, and with Directive (EU) 2016/97 of the European Parliament and of the Council of January 20, 2016, on insurance distribution,[440] the sections 368–436 of the BIns. stipulate the legal situation of insurance intermediaries, but its further regulations deal with intermediaries. The minimum content requirements of liability insurance contracts relating to multi-agents and brokers are regulated by separate legislation.[441] Furthermore, the rules of the CC can be applied to the relationship between the intermediary and the principal.

403. The BIns. regulates the situation of insurance intermediaries in line with the rules of the norms of the EU, so insurance mediation activities may be carried out by tied insurance intermediaries and independent insurance intermediaries. The conditions of carrying out the activity are defined by the BIns. The BIns. contains common rules relating to insurance intermediaries and ancillary insurance intermediaries (sections 368–382 of the BIns.)

438. Ujváriné Dr. Antal Edit, *A közvetítői szerződés* [Agency Contract]. In Osztovics András (ed.), *A Polgári Törvénykönyvről szóló 2013. évi V. törvény és a kapcsolódó jogszabályok nagykommentárja. III. kötet* [General Commentary of the Act V of 2013 on the Civil Code and of the Relating Legal Acts—Vol. 3]. Opten Ltd., Budapest, 2014, 729–768 and Ujváriné Dr. Antal Edit, *Közvetítői szerződés* [Agency Contract]. In Majoros Tünde (ed.), *Kereskedelmi szerződések alapvető szabályai* [General Rules on Commercial Contracts]. Budapest (Patrocinium Publisher 2015), 91–106.

Harsányi Gyöngyi, A közvetítők szabályozásának speciális vonásai a befektetési ügyletek körében. A biztostásközvetítés és a befektetésközvetítés szabályozásának kapcsolódási pontjai [Special Features of the Regulation of Intermediaries in Investment Transactions. Connection Points of Regulation of Insurance Brokerage and Investment Brokerage]. In Barta Judit (szerk.), Biztosíltás, több szem-szögéből. Ünnepi kötet Ujváriné dr. Antal Edit c. egyetemi docens 65. születésnapja tiszteletére, Novotni Alapítvány-Patrocinium Kiadó, Miskolc-Budapest, 2019, 19–30.

439. Council Directive 77/92/EEC of Dec. 13, 1976 on measures to facilitate the effective exercise of freedom of establishment and freedom to provide services in respect of the activities of insurance agents and brokers (ex ISIC Group 630) and, in particular, transitional measures in respect of those activities.

Commission Recommendation 92/48/EEC of Dec. 18, 1991 on insurance intermediaries.

Directive 2002/92/EC of the European Parliament and of the Council of Dec. 9, 2002 on insurance mediation.

440. The implementation of the latter directive took place with Act CXLV of 2017 which modified the BIns. It took into effect with s. 440 of the BIns., the transitional provisions that can be found in Arts. 441–452/L of the BIns.

441. Government Decree No. 44/2015. (III.12.).

The definition of insurance mediation activity can be found in Point 14 of subsection 1 of section 4 of the BIns.[442]

Insurance mediation activity shall mean the business of insurance distribution carried out by insurance intermediaries and the arrangement thereof, including consultancy by independent insurance intermediaries, with the proviso that the activities shall not qualify as insurance mediation activities (Points 123 of section 4 of the BIns.):

(a) the provision of information on an incidental basis in the context of another professional activity, where the provider does not take any additional steps to assist in concluding or performing an insurance contract;
(b) the management of claims of an insurance company on a professional basis, and loss adjusting and expert appraisal of claims;
(c) the mere provision of data and information on potential policyholders to insurance intermediaries or insurance companies where the provider does not take any additional steps to assist in the conclusion of an insurance contract;
(d) the mere provision of information about insurance products, an insurance intermediary, or an insurance company to potential policyholders where the provider does not take any additional steps to assist in the conclusion of an insurance contract.

Insurance distribution shall mean the business of insurance distribution activities of advising on, proposing, or carrying out other work preparatory to the conclusion of contracts of insurance, or—in particular contracts of insurance concluded by credit institutions specified in the CIFE—of concluding such contracts, or of assisting in the administration and performance of such contracts—or the joining of new policyholders to group insurance contracts in particular by credit institutions specified in the CIFE—in particular in the event of a claim, including the cases when the client is able to make an offer directly or indirectly for the conclusion of an insurance contract using a website or other media, and to conclude an insurance contract on that basis, and the provision of information concerning insurance contracts in accordance with criteria selected by clients and the compilation of an insurance product ranking list, including price and product comparison, or a discount on the price of an insurance contract, where the following shall not be considered to constitute insurance distribution:

(a) the provision of information on an incidental basis in the context of another professional activity, where the provider does not take any additional steps to assist in concluding or performing an insurance contract;
(b) the management of claims of an insurance company on a professional basis, and loss adjusting and expert appraisal of claims.[443]

442. These provisions took into effect on the Feb. 23, 2018.
443. Section 43 of Act XX of 2022 modified the BIns. It is effective from Aug. 6, 2022.

The regulations relating to the obligation to provide information to the insurance intermediaries are in compliance with the European norms, the Solvency II Directive, the PRIIPs Regulation, and the IDD Directive.

Ancillary insurance intermediary shall mean any natural or legal person other than a credit institution or an investment firm as defined in Points (1) and (2) of Article 4(1) of Regulation 575/2013/EU of the European Parliament and of the Council, who, for remuneration pursues the activity of insurance distribution in addition to its principle activity on an ancillary basis, on behalf of an insurance company, multiple agents or broker, under their responsibility, provided that all the following conditions are met:

(a) the principal professional activity of the person is other than insurance distribution;
(b) the insurance product is complementary to the product or service supplied by any provider;
(c) the insurance products concerned do not cover life insurance or liability risks, unless the cover of such life insurance or liability risks complements the good or service which the intermediary provides as its principal professional activity;
(d) any sum of money is not collected from the insurance company on the client's behalf in advance Point 125 of section 4 of the BIns.).

Insurance distributor shall mean any insurance intermediary, ancillary insurance intermediary, or insurance company (Point 126 of section 4 of the BIns.).

Remuneration shall mean any commission, fee, charge or other payment, including an economic benefit of any kind or any other financial or non-financial advantage or incentive offered or given in respect of insurance distribution activities (Points 127 of section 4 of the BIns.).[444]

In connection with the obligation to provide information, it is important to take into account whether the obligation is subject to an insurer or an insurance intermediary (dependent or independent insurance intermediary); whether there is a life (including those with investment elements or not) or non-life insurance contract; whether it is associated with counseling or not; whether there is a cross-selling (i.e., the insurance product is offered with an additional product or service, or conversely, the insurance is the ancillary product) or not.

404. It is important to emphasize the information obligation,[445] which is the obligation of the intermediary (in the official language of the undertaking's country of affiliation or in a different language in the case of an agreement with the client). It obliges the intermediary before the conclusion of the insurance contract (in the event of changes in the data, which can be found in the contract, it obliges him at

444. Points 123–127 of Sub. 1 of s. 4 of the BIns.
445. Section 378, 378/A of the BIns.
Ujváriné Antal Edit, A biztosítási szerződéssel összefüggő, tájékoztatási szabályokkal kapcsolatos kárfelelősség, különös tekintettel a közvetítői helyzetekre [Liability for Damages Related to Information Rules Related to the Insurance Contract, with Particular Regard to Intermediary Situations]. Biztosítás és Kockázat, V. évf. 2. szám, 48–59.
https://mabisz.hu/wp-content/uploads/2018/08/biztositas-es-kockazat-5-evf-2-szam-4-cikk.pdf.

the time of the modification and renewal of the contract) in line with the law. Similar to the regulation relating to the insurers, the information has to be easily intelligible, clearly written, accurate, not misleading, fair, detailed, free of charge, verifiable, and documented:

(a) He shall inform the client about the intermediary (branch, headquarters, supervisory authority, branch office, address, registration number, etc.), whether it is a dependent or independent insurance broker and which insurance company's products are distributed. It is important to draw the attention of the contractor to the fact who shall be liable in the case of damage (restitution), the possibility of complaining, and the competent authority.
(b) The insurance intermediary is an intermediate link between the insurer and the contractor, so the information obligation about the right of representation has great importance. It means he shall inform the client whether he can conclude the contract on behalf of the insurer, and he is entitled to receive the insurance premium from the client.
(c) It is also necessary to inform the party wishing to conclude a contract about the main data of the insurer and the characteristics of the insurance contract. This obligation obliges the insurer, too (if a broker contributes during the conclusion of the contract, then the insurer is obliged against the broker, too). For example, he/she shall be informed about the rules of the exemption of the insurer, the conditions for limiting the service, the provisions which differ from the usual contractual practice, the application of a different law from Hungary, or the exclusive jurisdiction of a court other than a Hungarian.
(d) Information obligation concerning life insurance, *see* in Part V, Chapter 5.

405. The insurance company shall provide the prospective policyholder with easily intelligible, clearly written, and detailed information. The insurance company shall obtain a statement from the client, supported by sufficient evidence, to the effect that he has received the information. (In the event of e-service, contractual party shall be informed by electronic means.)

That these rules can be found in public law norms; the breach of the information obligation connotes the public law legal consequences defined by the BIns. The rules of the CC are relevant in the issue of how the breach of the obligation can affect the insurance contract.

406. Insurance intermediaries and all the insurance shall be subject to the obligation of professional secrecy[446] with regard to all of the data, which concerns the clients' personal circumstances, financial position, and contractual relationship with the insurance company. Exceptions are listed in the act exhaustively. The insurance intermediaries shall be subject to the obligation of professional secrecy without any time limitation. The BIns. contains separate regulations in relation to the retention of data. It is a general rule that all insurance intermediaries shall comply with the professional rules of insurance.

446. Sections 379–381 of the BIns.

§2. TIED INSURANCE INTERMEDIARIES[447]

I. The Agent

407. The "tied insurance intermediary" is the "insurance agent" and the "multiple agent."

The Agent shall mean any person who carries on the activity of insurance mediation:

(a) for and on behalf of one insurance company or for and on behalf of one or more insurance companies in the case of insurance products which are not in competition;
(b) any person who carries on the activity of insurance mediation—including for and on behalf of more than one insurance company in the case of insurance products which are in competition—if the insurance is complementary to the goods or services supplied in the framework of this principal professional activity and he does not collect premiums or amounts intended for the client.[448]

408. The agent is an intermediate who prepares the conclusion of the insurance contract, and he is entitled to participate in the conclusion of the contract and carry out other mediator tasks only with the authorization of the insurance company.

The relationship between the agent and the insurer can be an employment relationship or a civil law relationship. If an insurer and an agent establish a civil law legal relationship, usually a permanent mediation relationship is established, which means that the agent is entrusted to mediate insurance contracts continuously. The BIns. regulates differently from the rules of the CC and stipulates that an agent pursuing insurance mediation activities on behalf of an insurance company shall be entitled to indemnification provided for in section 6:298 of the Civil Code only under an agreement concluded with the insurance company for such activity in writing, and under the conditions set out therein.[449]

If the agent (or the person who has used in the performance of the contract) causes damage while engaged in mediating insurance, the insurance company shall be liable for the damage on whose behalf the mediation took place.

II. Multiple Agents

409. Activity of multiple agents shall be authorized, and the BIns. stipulates strict requirements in connection with the authorization. Multiple agents offer the competing products of several insurance companies, and unlike the brokers, on the

447. Ujváriné Dr. *Antal Edit: Biztosítási szerződés* [Insurance Contract] In Majoros Tünde (ed.), *Kereskedelmi szerződések alapvető szabályai* [General Rules on Commercial Contracts]. Budapest (Patrocinium Publisher 2015), 221–228.
448. Section 43 of Act XX of 2022 supplemented the BIns. with a new Subs. 1a and 1b of s. 383. It is effective from Aug. 6, 2022. It formulates special provisions if the intermediary activity is carried out as an agent by the credit institution defined in the Act on Credit Institutions.
449. Section 386 of the BIns.

basis of their relationship with the insurance company. Consequently, they cannot carry out independent insurance intermediary activity.[450]

Typically, a permanent brokerage contract can be concluded between the insurance company and the multiple insurance agents because the multiple insurance agents are usually mandated to mediate insurance contracts. In such cases, similarly to the situation of the agent, the BIns. prescribes that a multiple agent shall be entitled to indemnification provided for in section 6:298 of the Civil Code only under an agreement concluded with the insurance company for that purpose in writing, and under the conditions set out therein.[451]

The task of the multiple agents is the preparation of the conclusion of the contract, and other intermediate tasks can be carried out by the separate authorization of the insurance company.

Although the multiple agent carries out the activity in the representation of the insurer, but as a person familiar with the insurance profession, he is required to draw up the contracting party's attention to their needs regarding the conclusion of the contract and to the choice of the product. According to the professional rules, it is the obligation of the intermediary to provide detailed, product-matching information, which allows the contracting party to choose the most appropriate product from the "competing" products, which facilitates the appropriate and satisfying choice.

In the case of non-advised sales, in carrying out work preparatory to the conclusion of insurance contracts, the multiple agent shall—in addition to and in accordance with the requirements set out in this Act on non-advised sales—perform an analysis for the purpose of comparison in the product group giving appropriate consideration to the needs of the client, so as to allow the client to find the best products to meet his needs.

In the case of advised sales, in carrying out work preparatory to the conclusion of insurance contracts, the multiple agent shall—in addition to and in accordance with the requirements set out in this Act on non-advised sales—perform an analysis for the purpose of comparison in the product group giving appropriate consideration to the needs of the client, and shall provide the client with a personalized recommendation relating to a particular insurance product or products on the basis of and depending on certain analytical requirements consistent with the client's demands and needs ascertained relying on information given by the client, explaining why that product would best meet the client's demands and needs.

The information shall indicate whether the analysis covers the full spectrum of competing products distributed by the multiple agent or a sufficient number of such products, and the analysis is to be given to the client by means which can be proved.[452]

410. The multiple agents shall keep a record of the mediated contracts. Liability for damages caused by the multiple agent while engaged in mediating insurance and

---

450. It is effective from Feb. 23, 2018. Before the amended of the BIns. with Act CXLV of 2017, the multiple agent was considered an independent intermediary.

451. Section 394 of the BIns.

452. Subsections 3–5 of s. 387 of the BIns.

for the payment of restitution incurred shall fall upon the insurance company on whose behalf the multiple agent was acting when the damage occurred on account of his act or negligence. The situation of the injured party is enhanced by the rule, which prescribes that if in doubt as to the insurance company whose product the multiple agent was mediating when the action that resulted in the damage or the claim for restitution took place, or if such insurance company cannot be identified, the multiple agent shall cover the losses.

Multiple agents shall—at all times—carry professional indemnity insurance covering liability in connection with their activities:

(a) representing at least EUR 1,300,380 applying to each insured loss and in aggregate EUR 1,924,560 per year for all claims covering the entire territory of the EU; or
(b) shall have EUR 1,924,560 of secured financial reserves.[453]

The minimum content requirements for the liability insurance policies shall be decreed by the Government.[454]

III. Mutual Regulation in Both Intermediaries

411. In insurance relationships, it can be of great importance when the contractor has fulfilled his obligation to pay the fee. This can be especially important if, in accordance with their agreement, the insurer's risk-taking connects to the payment of the fee. This is the reason for the regulation of the BIns., which prescribes that if the contracting party has made a premium payment to the insurer's agent authorized to collect premium payments, the premium shall be considered to be received by the insurance company—on account or in cash—on or before the fourth day following the date of payment; however, the contracting party shall be entitled to prove that the premium had been received earlier.[455] The judicial practice supports it, too *(BH2008. 147.).*

IV. The Principal Agent[456]

412. The BIns. maintains the legal institution of the principal agent, which has old traditions in the Hungarian insurance law. The principal agent is entitled to work

453. Subsection 6 of s. 391 of the BIns.

Subsection 2 of s. 453/A of the BIns., effective from Dec. 26, 2020, regulates provisions required for the implementation of Commission Delegated Regulation (EU) 2019/1935 of May 13, 2019, amending Directive (EU) 2016/97 of the European Parliament and of the Council with regard to regulatory technical standards adapting the base euro amounts for professional indemnity insurance and for financial capacity of insurance and reinsurance intermediaries.

454. Government Decree No. 44/2015. (III.12.) Korm. rendelet on the minimum content requirements of multiple agent and broker liability insurance.

455. Sections 384 and 187/A of the BIns.

456. Ujváriné Dr. Antal Edit, *Biztosítási szerződés* [Insurance Contract] In Majoros Tünde (ed.), *Kereskedelmi szerződések alapvető szabályai* [General Rules on Commercial Contracts]. Budapest (Patrocinium Publisher 2015), 221–228.

for only one insurance company. Rights of principal agent are much wider than those of agents in general. A principal agent is an agent of the insurance company who is fully authorized to perform functions within the insurance company's system of business management (he is entitled to conclude the contract in the name of the insurance company, to write out the insurance policy, and to receive the fee without special authorization).

Principal agent can be natural person and firms which engage in the pursuit of principal agency activities, but in the latter case, the firm shall employ a natural person for the management of principal agency activities. This natural person shall meet strict and high professional requirements defined by the BIns.

§3. The Independent Insurance Intermediary[457]

413. The broker who acts on the contractor's behalf is considered to be an independent insurance broker. The broker shall not act as an agent or as a multiple agent (so it is excluded that he connects to the insurers in this way).

The Act defines strict requirements for the registration procedure against independent insurance intermediaries, such as in the case of multiple agents. The independent insurance intermediary shall employ the natural person who is responsible for the management of insurance mediation activities within the organization.

During the performance of the activity, the independent insurance intermediary shall meet the professional requirements of insurance, for which he shall be liable.

Within the framework of the liability, some "professional malpractice" can occur. These can be, for example, false advice, irregular handling of premiums, or false or delayed transmission of statements, for which the intermediary also shall be responsible. The independent insurance intermediary is entitled to employ other persons for the performance of the activity. They are acting on his behalf, but he is also responsible for the conduct of these persons toward his principal. It can happen that the false information or the false statement happened because of an error in the form or document, which is used by the insurance company. This circumstance can lead to the broker's exemption from liability if he can prove this circumstance.

Brokers shall—at all times—carry professional indemnity insurance covering liability in connection with their activities:

(a) representing at least EUR 1,300,380 applying to each insured loss and in aggregate EUR 1,924,560 per year for all claims covering the entire territory of the EU; or
(b) shall have EUR 1,924,560 of secured financial reserves.

The professional indemnity insurance and financial security of brokers shall cover damages caused during their such activities as well as claims for restitution, also if

457. *Ibid.*

the damages are realized or reported and the claim for restitution is notified within five years after the expiry of the contract for professional indemnity insurance or for the financial security.[458]

The minimum content requirements for the liability insurance policies shall be decreed by the Government.[459]

414. An independent insurance intermediary, like a multiple agent, shall keep a record of the insurance transactions he carries out. If he fails this obligation, it does not affect the validity of the contracts, but administrative sanctions can be imposed.

Activity of an independent insurance intermediary can also cover the "mediation" of the payments of the client (insurance premium) and the payments to the client from the insurer (insurance amount, damage amount). The insurance intermediary cannot manage these funds as his own, and he shall keep these funds in a separate account (customer account). Consequently, the payments are protected from the bankruptcy of the insurance broker. The funds, which are on the client accounts, are not part of the assets of liquidation in the case of liquidation of the broker.

Transfer of Portfolio

415. The transferring broker may transfer its portfolio of contracts for insurance mediation services—including the rights and obligations arising out of such contracts, with the terms and conditions of the insurance contracts connected to the said service contract unaltered—in part or in whole to another broker to the branch of a broker established in another Member State. (hereinafter referred to collectively as "receiving broker").

From the time specified in the portfolio transfer agreement, i.e., the date of transfer, all rights and obligations of the transferring broker arising out of or in connection with the contracts for mediation services shall accrue upon the receiving broker, moreover, the receiving broker shall become entitled to process the personal and other data of affected clients, insurance companies and insurance contracts.

The requirement of confidentiality concerning insurance secrets shall not apply to the transferring broker vis-à-vis the receiving broker from the date of transfer with respect to the insurance secrets related to the transfer provided for in subsection (2).

The consent of clients of the contracts for mediation services (customer) affected by the transfer is not required for the transfer of the portfolio.

The receiving broker shall notify the customers in writing in the language of the contract, within thirty days from the date of transfer, concerning the transfer and the rights of customers arising in connection with the transfer.

458. Section 403 of the BIns.

459. Government Decree No. 44/2015. (III.12.) Korm. rendelet on the minimum content requirements of multiple agent and broker liability insurance.

Customers shall have the right to terminate the transferred contract for mediation services with a thirty-day notice—also if the contract contains any clause to the contrary or if it is for a fixed term—within thirty days from the date of receipt of the notice referred to the right to terminate by way of a written statement addressed to the receiving broker.

The right to terminate shall not apply to the customer whose contract for mediation services contains a clause according to which the customer gave prior, unrestricted consent for its transfer or if the customer did not reserve the right to withdraw his statement of consent.

The receiving broker shall publish an announcement on its website at the latest on the date of transfer, or if the receiving broker does not have a website, shall post it in the customer area of its premises and shall keep it continually accessible for ninety days from the date of transfer. The announcement shall also contain the right of the customers provided for in subsection (6), arising in consequence of the transfer, and the related deadlines.

Transferring brokers shall report to the Authority their intention to transfer their portfolio at least sixty days before the date of transfer.

The Authority shall have the right to prohibit the portfolio transfer within forty-five days calculated from the date of submission of notification, if the conditions set out are not satisfied and if it learns of any fact, data or circumstance by way of site inspection or otherwise, giving rise to reasonable suspicion that the receiving broker is unable to handle the transferred portfolio in accordance with the requirements laid down by the relevant legislation, in particular, e.g., it appears that the transfer is likely to harm the interests of customers affected by the transfer.

The provisions of section 6:208–6:211 of the Civil Code on the transfer of contracts shall not apply to the transfer of the broker's portfolio.[460]

I. Main Features of the Broker's Transaction[461]

416. In the legal relationship established due to the brokerage contract, the broker mediates on behalf of the client who is in the position of the insured party or the contracting party if the insurance contract is concluded. The main obligation of the broker is to prepare the conclusion of the insurance contract on the basis of the client's mandate. This obligation covers the conclusion of the contract or to the enforcement of the client's claims only in the case of a special mandate from the principal.

The principal client requires the broker, in accordance with the contract, to mediate the most favorable insurance contract. The broker is obliged to offer the best product on the insurance market to the contracting party, taking into account the insurance premium, the insurance period, and the terms. In the case of non-advised sales, in carrying out work preparatory to the conclusion of insurance contracts, the broker shall—in addition to and in accordance with the requirements set out in this

460. Section 406/A of the BIns.
461. *Ibid.*

Act on non-advised sales—perform an objective analysis of a sufficient number of insurance products competing on the market, and shall provide that analysis to the client by means which can be proved.

In the case of advised sales, the multiple agent shall—in addition to and in accordance with the requirements set out in this Act on non-advised sales—give advice to the client on the basis of a fair and personal analysis and, to that end, perform an objective analysis of a sufficient number of insurance products competing on the market in carrying out work preparatory to the conclusion of insurance contracts, and shall provide the client with a personalized recommendation relating to a particular insurance product or products on the basis of and depending on certain analytical requirements consistent with the client's demands and needs ascertained relying on information given by the client, explaining why that product would best meet the client's demands and needs.

The broker shall provide the analysis referred to in subsection (6) to the client by means which can be proved.[462]

The service of the broker—of course, depending on the contract—can extend to the continuous management of the concluded contract (collection of fees and parts of the fees, announcement of changes in the insurance, cooperation in the modification, assistance in dealing with damages, etc.) and to the renewal of the insurance. The legal relationship between the broker and his client can be regarded as a permanent mediation contract, even if the task of the broker is the mediation of only one contract, but they agreed that he is also obliged to maintain or renew the legal relationship.

417. Typically, the premium of the broker, which is calculated into the insurance premium paid by the client, is paid by the insurer who undertakes the insurance or reinsurance risk in the contract.

In the case of independent insurance intermediaries, the commission shall be construed as remuneration comprising a specific percentage of the insurance premium payable by the insurance company.

418. The principal can enforce the claims arising from the breach of the brokerage contract against the broker (e.g., the broker breaches his information obligation), but the broker is not responsible for fulfilling the obligations of the insurer arising from the insurance contract (but he is not liable to the insurer either for the client's conduct).

II. Relationship Between the Broker and the Insurance Company

419. The broker, who is independent from the insurance company, can connect to the insurer in a specific way. In the event of the consent of the insurance company, but on the assignment of the client, the broker can be entitled to receive the premium, and he can contribute to the assessment of risks and to the performance

462. Section 398 of the BIns.

of rights and obligations arising from the contract, in case of the consent of the insurance company or upon the mandate of the client.

III. Rules in Connection with the Commission of Insurance Intermediaries

420. In recent years, the Authority has revealed several factors in the insurance intermediary market, which have made it possible to abuse the commission, change the proper functioning of the market, injure the client's interests, and result in the incensement of the insurance premium.

421. This is the reason for the regulations relating to the commission of the insurance intermediaries. The definition of commission can be found in subsection 1 of section 4 of the BIns.

The *commission* shall mean any form of remuneration, comprising a specific percentage of the insurance premium, provided to the insurance intermediary in exchange for his services for brokering an insurance contract or in connection with the performance of the insurance contract he has brokered or maintained, also if the contract is retained for a designated period of time, directly by the insurance company underwriting the risk.

The *entitlement to the commission* shall mean the tied insurance intermediary's entitlement to commission accrued for the insured period in connection with an insurance contract he has brokered or maintained within the framework of an intermediary relationship, in certain specific cases and to a predetermined extent also covering a period following the termination of the intermediary's relationship if the insurance contract existed continually.

The *commission repayment* shall mean the tied insurance intermediary's obligation imposed on the basis of the intermediary relationship to repay the commission under certain conditions in part or in whole, as commensurate with changes in the circumstances underlying the payment of commission, if the insurance contract the insurance intermediary has brokered is prematurely terminated (independent of any insured event) or the premium changes to an extent where it no longer covers the amount of the commission paid.

422. The BIns. regulates the rules relating to life insurance with savings element.[463] The objective of the regulations is to make insurances and costs customer-friendly and transparent, especially in the field of life insurances.

The amount of commission paid in connection with a life insurance policy with savings element may not exceed the amount of the premium the insurance company has received by the time of payment of the commission. As regards stipulated premium life insurance policies with savings element, commission may be paid on the first year calculated from the date of the contract—at the earliest after the first premium payment is received by the insurance company as stipulated—in an amount not exceeding the premium due for fourteen months.

463. Section 377 of the BIns.

The amount of commission paid in total for the full term of the contract may not exceed the amount of the premium the insurance company has received for the full term of the contract.

Commissions may not be paid to insurance intermediaries in advance.

Apart from the commission for brokering insurance contracts, insurance intermediaries shall not be entitled to any other form of payment from the insurance company. In addition to the commission, insurance companies shall be allowed to reward insurance intermediaries for services provided outside the scope of insurance intermediary services, properly documented in a manner that is transparent and verifiable, with the underlying reason clearly indicated.

The law prescribes the compulsory elements of the intermediary contract.

IV. Insurance Meditation in Electronic Way

423. Insurance contracts are increasingly concluded by electronic means. The relevant rules have consumer protection features and a special law; the Act XXV of 2005 on financial service contracts concluded in the framework of teleshopping has to be applied. Hungary implemented the Directive 2002/65/EC[464] with the abovementioned law. The personal scope of the law covers, *inter alia*, insurance companies and insurance intermediaries too. The law lays down further rules in connection with the information obligation and regulates the consumer's right to withdrawal from the contract of teleshopping in accordance with the maximum harmonization requirements of the Directive.

During the examination of the domestic contractual practice, it can be stated that the electronic interface is mainly used in the conclusion of compulsory motor vehicle liability insurance contracts, in addition to the field of motor vehicle property insurance and in the conclusion of travel insurance contracts.

424. Electronic broadcasting has many advantages: the activity of comparable websites is really useful because they can increase the competition between insurers and can promote transparency; they can improve the framework of information by the comparison of the products, so they can help the customer to choose the right product. However, it has disadvantages too, e.g., if the information is not complete or not up-to-date, it can cause many problems. It distorts the result of the comparison if the intermediary does not have the full market offer. In such a situation, the consumer is deceived because he thinks he received information about all the domestic products. The Directive 2016/97 on insurance sales (IDD), which came into force on February 22, 2016, intends to settle this situation.

425. The NBH issued Recommendation No. 5/2015. (V.55) on the electronic platform used for the presentation, comparison, and insurance intermediation of insurance products. It sets out the requirements relating to the minimum content,

464. Directive 2002/65/EC of the European Parliament and of the Council of Sep. 23, 2002, concerning the distance marketing of consumer financial services and amending Council Directive 90/619/EEC and Directives 97/7/EC and 98/27/EC.

function, and customer information of the electronic platform, the guidelines for assessing the insurance needs of the e-client, and the promotion of transparency of the interface.

V. Complaints Handling by Insurance Intermediaries

426. Multiple agents and brokers shall provide facilities for their clients to submit any complaint they may have relating to the multiple agent's or broker's conduct, activity, or any alleged infringement orally (in person, by telephone) or in writing (delivered in person or by others, by post, fax transmission, or by electronic mail). The expectations can be found in the BIns.[465]

VI. Contractual Relationship Between the Insurance Intermediary and the Principal

427. Commercial agents played an important role in the process of the European Single Market. It is typical that the Community examined and regulated the commercial broker agreements primarily from the viewpoint of competition law, which is based on section 1 of Article 85 of the Treaty of Rome. The Commission issued a recommendation[466] in 1962, and nearly twenty-five years of preparatory work and consultation preceded the Council's Directive.[467] The process of the unification of the European Contract Law also affects the legal status of commercial intermediaries. As a result of the activities of the working groups (European Network of Excellence Common Principles of European Contract Law (CoPECL)), which are developing the so-called Common Frame of Reference (CFR), the Draft Common Frame of Reference (DCFR) was published and discusses the rules relating to commercial agents, franchise, and distributorship agreements within the regulations of commercial agents.[468]

428. For Hungary, the obligation imposed by the European Agreement, which was signed on December 16, 1991, and promulgated by Act I of 1994 and by the White Paper of Cannes, was to make the Hungarian rules on intermediaries compatible with the community law. The most important harmonization areas were the following: the remuneration of commercial agents, the definition of the minimum content requirements of the contract, and the standardization of certain competition laws and business confidentiality rules. We fulfilled our harmonization obligation with a separate law, the Act CXVII of 2000, on the Commercial Representation

465. Section 382 of the BIns.
466. Notice on exclusive dealing contracts with commercial agents (OJ 1962/2921).
467. Council Directive 86/653/EEC of Dec. 18, 1986 on the coordination of the laws of the Member States relating to self-employed commercial agents (OJ 1986 L 382, 31.12.1986).
468. Book IV., Part E. Commercial Agency, Franchise and Distributorship, 347–364.
Christian von Bar, Eric Clive & Hans Schulte-Nölke, *Principles, Definitions and Model Rules of European Private Law. Draft Common Frame of Reference (DCFR) Outline Edition*, Sellier, Munich (European Law Publishers 2009).

Contracts of Self-employed Commercial Agents. At the time of the adoption of the CC, the main aim was to bring the rules on intermediaries into the Code. Consequently, the CC regulates the general[469] and special rules[470] of the agency contracts in a separate Chapter (Chapter XLI) within Title XVI (Engagement-type Contracts). They can be found after the rules of Personal Service Contracts (Chapter XXXIX.) and of the Consignment Contracts (Chapter XL.).

429. It is a characteristic feature of the Hungarian legal system that the various types of intermediary (agency) activities and the conditions of performing the activity can be found in public law norms, which public law standards have been analyzed in relation to insurance brokers. However, in the legal relationship between the principal and the intermediary, the rules on intermediary contracts of the CC shall be applied. We have referred to the fact that the dependent insurance intermediary is entitled to claim compensation (rules of which can be found in section 6:298 of the CC) only in the case of an agreement between the insurer and the intermediary.

469. Section 6:288–6:292 of the CC.
470. Section 6:293–6:301 of the CC.

Part VIII. Reinsurance, Coinsurance, Pooling

Edit Antal Ujvári

Chapter 1. Reinsurance

§1. Reinsurance as Insurance Activity

430. Reinsurance cannot be regarded as a class of insurance, but it means the share of risks between insurance companies.[471]

The BIns. concerns all of the insurance activities and it regulates reinsurance activities too in line with Solvency II.[472]

According to the authorization of the BIns., the Government Decree No. 43/2015. (III.12.) regulates the solvency and technical provisions of reinsurance companies.

In the case of a reinsurance contract, the insurer that enters into a contract with the client is called a direct insurer (ceding company or direct signatory). This company transfers the risks, or typically only a part of them, assumed by the client to another insurance company, i.e., the reinsurer, for a fee. In this process, the first company performs passive reinsurance activities, and the second one performs active reinsurance activities. It is also possible that the reinsurer passes on part of the assumed risks; this is called retroceding.

An insurance joint-stock company (according to Hungarian law) can carry out both active and passive reinsurance activities.

According to the BIns., "reinsurance" shall mean the activity consisting of accepting risks ceded by an insurance company or reinsurance company, or a third-country insurance company or reinsurance companies, in whole or in part, in return for a fee under contract.

471. The "Principles of Reinsurance Contract Law (PRICL) 2019" were produced by the Project Group on Principles of Reinsurance Contract Law (PRICL) in cooperation with the International Institute for the Unification of Private Law (UNIDROIT). The PRICL provide reinsurance specific rules on contract law in areas where reinsurance practitioners felt that there was a need to improve legal certainty. At the same time, the PRICL incorporate uniform rules on general contract law by virtue of a reference to the UNIDROIT Principles of International Commercial Contracts (PICC 2016). https://www.ius.uzh.ch/en/research/pricl.html.

472. Ujváriné Antal Edit, *Az érvénytelenség különös szabályai a biztosítási jogviszonyban* [Special Rules of Invalidity in the Insurance Relationship]. In Dr. Stefán Ibolya PhD hallgató (szerk.) & Dr. Pusztahelyi Réka PhD docens (lektor), *Miskolci konferenciák 2018–2019 in Memoriam Novotni Zoltán. Emlékkönyv Novotni Zoltán professzor halálának 25. évfordulója alkalmából.* Tanulmánykötet, Novotni Alapítvány, Miskolc, 2021, 199–219.

431. Its objective is the financial enhancement of the stability of insurance company and the share of risks between insurance companies. In the case of reinsurance, the direct insurer will pass on the part of risks assumed from the client. Legal relationships are only between the two insurers. Only the first (direct) insurance company is in a contractual relationship with the client, and reinsurance is a "background" activity from the viewpoint of the insured party. Reinsurance contracts can be called sum and damage reinsurances.

The BIns. contains supplementary rules for reinsurance and special-purpose vehicles.[473] Insurance and reinsurance companies which conclude finite reinsurance contracts or pursue finite reinsurance activities must be able to properly identify, measure, monitor, manage, control, and report the risks arising from those contracts or activities. These provisions shall be applied in conjunction with the provisions adopted by the Commission within the meaning of subsection 2 of Article 21 of the Solvency II Directive. In the territory of Hungary, a special-purpose vehicle—with entitlement to assume risks from insurance and reinsurance companies—may be established upon the Authority's consent if it meets the requirements set out in the Commission regulation adopted within the meaning of Article 211(2)a)–g) of the Solvency II Directive. The Authority has exclusive jurisdiction to initiate the opening of liquidation proceedings in court against special-purpose vehicles.

§2. Reinsurance, as a Private Law Contract

432. The rules of the CC leave room for the freedom of contract, and the CC contains unilaterally mandatory, consumer-protecting rules only in relation to consumer contracts, and the provisions are nonmandatory (dispositive) in relation to other subjects. Because the subjects of reinsurance contracts are not consumers, they are allowed to determine the content of the contract freely.

The CC makes no distinction in line with the form of the insurers, and, in fact, it extends the scope of the regulations relating to insurance contracts[474] because its provisions shall also be applied to insurance relationships on the basis of association membership.[475]

473. Section 198–199 of the BIns.
474. Section 6:439–6:490 of the CC.
475. Section 6:457 of the CC.

Chapter 2. Coinsurance

§1. Coinsurance as Insurance Activity

433. Public law regulations of coinsurance can be found in the BIns. which stipulates that coinsurance shall mean a service provided by several insurance companies for a global premium by means of a single contract for covering loss arising upon the occurrence of a specific future event in connection with risks specified in a contract or providing benefits under contractual conditions in the proportions laid down in writing in advance as well as the creation and management of reserves by each insurance company as consistent with their respective share of the commitment.

434. Sections 201–203 shall apply to coinsurance operations which shall be those coinsurance operations which relate to one or more risks classified under classes 3–16 of Part A) of Annex 1 and which fulfill the following conditions:

(a) the risk is a large risk;
(b) the risk is situated within the territory of the EU;
(c) the contract defines the leading insurance company;
(d) at least one of the coinsurers participates in the coinsurance contract through:
  (da)a head office; or
  (db)a branch established in a Member State other than that of the leading insurance company.

435. The rules laid down in the BIns. shall be applied to the leading insurance company named in the coinsurance contract. Where coinsurance is connected to compulsory motor vehicle liability insurance, the responsibility for the appointment of a claims representative shall lie with the leading insurance company in relation to the coinsurance contract. In the case of coinsurance, technical provisions shall be provided by insurance companies participating in the coinsurance contract as commensurate with their respective share of underwriting obligations. The technical provisions provided by insurance companies participating in the coinsurance contract shall be at least equal to those determined by the leading insurance company according to the rules of its home Member State. Insurance companies participating in the coinsurance contract shall keep records showing the extent of coinsurance operations in which they participate and the Member States concerned.

§2. Competition Law Aspects of Coinsurance

436. Coinsurance is also subject to competition law, but there is no overlap between the two legal areas since both areas are intended to achieve their specific goals and use different tools.[476]

Competition law protects the competition itself and its intensity when it tries to determine the boundaries of legal and illegal cooperation in relation to the long-term cooperation of insurers.

According to section 11 of the Act LVII of 1996 on the Prohibition of Unfair Trading Practices and Unfair Competition (PUTP) agreements and concerted practices between companies, as well as the decisions of the organizations of companies established based on the right of association, their public bodies, associations and other similar (hereinafter referred to collectively as "association of companies") (hereinafter referred to collectively as "agreements"), which are aimed at the prevention, restriction, or distortion of economic competition, or which may display or in fact displays such an effect, are prohibited. An agreement concluded between companies that are not unrelated shall not be construed as such.

437. According to section 16 of the PUTP, certain groups of such agreements may be exempted by the Government in a decree from the prohibition. The Government is entitled to regulate the exemption of specific groups of agreements with regard to the criteria set out in the Act.

The insurance group exemption decree was repealed in the meantime.[477]

An agreement is exempted from the prohibition of cartel provided that:

(a) it contributes to a more reasonable organization of production or distribution, the promotion of technical or economic progress, or the improvement of competitiveness or the protection of the environment;
(b) it allows trading parties not participating in the agreement a fair share of the resulting benefit;
(c) the concomitant restriction or exclusion of competition does not exceed the extent necessary to attain economically justified common goals; and

---

476. Dr. Miskolczi Bodnár Péter, *A versenyjog és az új Ptk* [Competition Law and the New CC] Versenytükör, 2014/1, 73–90; Miskolczi Bodnár Péter, *Biztosítók közötti információcsere kartelljogi megítélése* [Cartel Law Assessment of Information Exchange Between Insurers]. In Dr. Barta Judit (szerk.), *Biztosítás, több szem-szögéből.* Ünnepi kötet; Ujváriné Dr. Antal Edit, *c. egyetemi docens 65. születésnapja tiszteletére*. Novotni Alapítvány-Patrocinium Kiadó, Miskolc-Budapest, 2019, 43–55.

477. Government Decree No. 203/2011. (X.7.) on the exemption of certain groups of insurance agreements from the prohibition of competition restrictions was repealed by s. 346 of Government Decree No. (XII.28.), repealed with effect from January 1, 2018. This is due to the fact that Regulation 267/2010/EU, known as the Insurance Group Exemption Regulation, lost its effect on Mar. 31, 2017. On May 11, the European Commission adopted the new vertical group exemption regulation and the new vertical guidelines (after a thorough evaluation and revision of the 2010 rules), which entered into force on Jun. 1, 2022. *See*: Commission Regulation (EU) 2022/720 of May 10, 2022, on the application of Art. 101(3) of the Treaty on the Functioning of the European Union to categories of vertical agreements and concerted practices.

(d) it does not enable the exclusion of competition with respect to a substantial proportion of the goods concerned.

The burden of proving that an agreement is exempted from the prohibition shall rest on the person claiming the benefit of the exemption.

In order to regulate the behavior of insurance companies, the AHIC developed the "Code of Ethics and Competition" for its member insurers, which insurance companies are aware of during their activities.[478]

§3. COINSURANCE AS A PRIVATE LAW CONTRACT

438. Article 6:441 of the CC regulates the legal situation when more than one subject appears on the side of the insurance company. This is the so-called coinsurance. In the event of the coinsurance, the contracting party shall have a legal relationship with all of the insurance companies. The insurance risk is covered—in a predetermined percentage—jointly by more than one insurance company, and the insurance services are performed collectively, and the service obligations of insurance companies shall be limited by their commitment to the sharing of risks. A coinsurance contract that fails to specify the share of participating insurance companies in risk coverage shall be null and void. The creation and management of reserves by each insurance company shall be consistent with their respective share of the commitment. The insurance companies shall be represented in respect of the contracting party by the leading insurer, and if the leading insurer has not been named in the contract, the contracting party shall have the option to lawfully perform and to make legal statements—at his discretion—to either of the insurance companies.

478. https://mabisz.hu/wp-content/uploads/2018/09/etikai-es-versenykodex.pdf.

Chapter 3. Pool Insurance

439. Third form of risk pulverization is pooling. The essence of pool insurance is to combine many insurers' similar contracts into a large stock because the stocks are severally too small. This means that the insurers add the premium incomes to one place, and the damage will be paid by all of them, too. They can share the profit in line with the proportion of premium income.

The essence of pool-based insurance is that the insurers provide the risks in groups, and they "pulverize" the payment obligation of damages between each other. The "international pooling" combines threat/risk communities in different countries.

For example, the Hungarian Atompool Insurers have won the public procurement tender, which was written for Radioactive Waste Management Nonprofit Ltd. and covered the property insurance services relating to nuclear risks, too.[479] The HCA[480] exempted the cooperation agreement of the Hungarian Atom Pool which was established by eleven insurance companies, from cartel prohibition, with the agreement that they could only deal with property damage in relation to nuclear installation and to damage arising from the operation of a nuclear installation.

479. http://kozbeszerzes.hu/ertesito/megtekint/portal_322_2016.
The consortium made up of Allianz Hungária Plc., Generali Insurer Plc., Groupama Insurer Plc., the Hungarian Branch of HDI Versicherung AG, and Union Vienna Insurance Group Plc. undertook nuclear liability insurance for the Paks Nuclear Power Plant for 2022, for a net EUR 1 million 290 thousand (about HUF 464 million). The estimated consideration was EUR 465 million (about HUF 1.7 billion).

480. Number of Decision: Vj-100/1997/24.

Part IX. Taxation of Insurance

Judit Barta

Chapter 1. Personal Income Tax Preference

440. The Hungarian states provide state subsidy for pension savings determined by law. Currently, three retirement savings enjoy such state aid:

(1) savings in voluntary mutual pension funds;
(2) the pension pre-savings account (NYESZ);
(3) pension insurance contract concluded with insurers with the content defined by law.

The state subsidy is actually a tax benefit. This means that 20% of the personal income tax paid by the pre-saver person, but not more than the amount determined by law,[481] will be transferred by the State Tax Office to the institution providing the service.

441. Pension insurances which form part of the life insurance policies which can be concluded with insurance companies are complementary to old-age pension benefits provided by the state pension scheme. However, the state subsidy introduced in 2014 does not cover all pension insurances but only the insurances with the characteristics specified by Act CXVII of 1995 on Personal Income Tax (PIT).[482] Under Point 93 of section 3 of the PIT Act, pension insurance shall mean a type of *life insurance*[483] where the insured person is the sole beneficiary of the benefits—other than death benefits—for the entire term of the pension insurance contract and where the payment of benefits is triggered:

481. It is HUF 150,000 in case of savings in voluntary mutual pension funds, 100,000 forint in case of NYESZ, and HUF 130,000 in case of pension insurance. Section 44/A of PIT.
482. According to the data published by the AHIC, the tax benefit has greatly increased the number of pension insurances. By the end of September 2015, the number of pension insurance contracts reached 111,000 and the insurance premium income paid for these contracts exceeded HUF 18.2 billion. In December 2022, the number of tax-advantaged pension insurances reached 460,000. https://ado.hu/ado/ev-vegere-meghaladhatja-a-460-ezret-az-adokedvezmenyes-nyugdijbiztositasok-szama/.
483. Under Point 92 s. 3 of the PIT Act, *life insurance* shall mean a type of personal insurance where the insurance company promises to pay a specific sum of money fixed in the contract, or annuity

(a) by the insured person's death;
(b) upon the insured person acquiring eligibility for pension benefits in his own right according to the legislation on social security pension benefits (meaning the state of being retired);
(c) upon health impairment of a degree of at least 40%, provided that the degree of health impairment of the insured person did not reach 40% at the time of conclusion of the pension insurance contract (irrespective of whether the insured person is entitled to invalidity or rehabilitation allowance); or
(d) upon the insured person reaching the retirement age in effect at the time of conclusion of the contract,[484] provided that at least ten-year lapses from the date of conclusion of the pension insurance contract *(from the date of signature by the client of the offer or contract amendment)* until benefits are in fact paid in connection with a specific insured event (excluding the insured person's death, health impairment of a degree of at least 40%, and if pension payments provided by the insurance company are *non-degressive*[485] and such payments are provided until at least the end of the *tenth year* from the date of conclusion of the contract, or until the insured person's death).

According to the provisions of the PIT Act, the pension insurance scheme has four insurance events from which actual retirement or the reaching of the retirement age can actually be considered a pension insurance aim (risk of death and health damage is an integral part of retirement provision but can only be considered indirectly as part of old-age care). According to the law, it is no longer possible to use the tax benefit after the retirement age.

No new life insurance category was born by defining the tax-related aspects of pension insurance; the legislator had only stated that he does not want to benefit all pension-related life insurances.

The Act only points out that insurers do not necessarily have to create a new product and contract with it in order to match the criteria of the PIT Act, but the existing products can also be converted: "from the date of signature of the offer or the modification of contract by the customer." Insurers decided, at their own discretion, to modify the existing products or to create new ones and to modify existing life insurance policies together with the contracting parties (endorsement), according to which they meet the statutory requirements in order to make the tax benefit available.[486]

---

for life or for a specific period of time, upon the natural person's death or attainment of a certain age, or at another predetermined time or occurrence of a specific event.

484. For persons born after Jan. 1, 1957, the retirement age is 65.

485. According to Point 97 of s. 3 of the PIT Act, *non-degressive annuity benefits* shall mean benefits provided by the insurance company, where the amount of the last payment from among the regular payments—expressed in money or any other monetary unit—exceeds or is equal to the amount of benefits the insurance company has paid immediately before the last payment, including the case when any change in the amount of benefits is attributed solely to variations in the frequency of payments and/or in the payment attributes.

486. In 2016, BIns. was also amended in order to maintain the tax allowance, giving a limited scope for amending the insurance contract:

A further condition of the subsidy is that the contracting party has to pay personal income tax. The tax advantage relates to the personal income tax paid. In fact, it means a right of disposal of a part of the tax paid, and the statutory amount of the tax is transferred by the tax office to the insurer who credits it in the pension insurance balance of the contracting party at the end of each year. The tax shall be payable after the so-called consolidated tax base (which includes the income, the revenues, and other income determined by law), but the tax benefits determined by law may be deducted from it.

The party to a pension insurance contract may convey an instruction in a pension insurance statement enclosed with his tax return or provide to the employer in the case of tax assessment by the employer regarding the transfer of a sum from the part of the tax payable on the consolidated tax base that remains following the deductions of tax allowances as per the following (hereinafter referred to as "*pension insurance statement*"): *20% of the sum* said party has paid under one or more pension insurance contract concluded with an insurance company established in Hungary, and which have been credited to a pension insurance contract in the given tax year, or in another EEA Member State during the tax year, *not exceeding HUF 130,000* in the tax year.

A pension insurance statement may not be made in connection with any sum paid for optional *complementary insurance*[487] cover obtained for pension insurance, as the original policy.

If the risk premium payable for the original policy is higher than 10% of the premium payable for the original policy, a pension insurance statement may not be made based on the risk premium of the original policy.

There is therefore no tax benefit after non-pension savings. According to the PIT Act, the threshold of the risk premium payable for the original policy below which

---

Section 122/A:

(1) In the event of any changes in the legal provisions on tax relief or tax credit available in connection with insurance contracts, after the conclusion of such contracts, the insurance company shall have the right to present a proposal within sixty days after the effective date of the legislative changes for the amendment of the insurance contract or the related standard contract terms so as to reflect changes in the legislative environment and to update the contract to bring the relevant terms in line with the conditions for claiming said tax relief or tax credit.

(2) In the absence of the policyholder's refusal to accept the amendment proposal within thirty days from the time of receipt of notice thereof, the contract shall be amended subject to the terms and conditions set out in the amendment proposal effective as of the time when the relevant legislative changes enter into force.

(4) The policyholder's refusal to accept the amendment proposal shall not serve as grounds for termination of the contract by the insurance company.

487. Point 99 of s. 3 of the PIT Act contains the definition of *complementary insurance*: it shall mean, in the application of pension insurance regulations, a type of insurance cover that—regardless of the type of risks covered—has its own unique terms and conditions and its premium is shown according to accounting regulations separately from pension insurance premiums (including if the premium is fixed under the terms and conditions of the contract and collected subsequently by way of withholding).

the tax benefit can be enforced for the full premium is 10%. The aim of the legislator was to ensure that no tax benefit could be applied for the supplementary insurance premium, irrespective of the risks involved.

The holder of the pension insurance policy may exercise said right of disposition based on the amount of premium paid until the first pension payment, or partial pension payment, made by the insurance company—excluding if partial payment is made due to health impairment—or at the latest until reaching the retirement age for old-age pension.

The tax authority shall effect the transfer of the sum the private individual has indicated in the pension insurance statement to the insurance company's payment account. The tax authority shall effect transfer of the sum specified by the private individual in proportion to the sums paid under pension insurance contracts underlying the private individual's right of disposition if said right of disposition is based on payments made to more than one pension insurance contracts.

The private individual shall repay the full amount of the state subsidy (tax benefit) plus 20% if withdrawal of valuable consideration takes place by means other than the payment of pension benefit under the pension insurance contract.

Any withdrawal of valuable consideration has the consequence of the repayment of state benefit, which is not a pension service. The PIT Act contains a non-exhaustive list of the cases which can be considered withdrawal, e.g., cases whether it is actually withdrawn or not, when the retirement savings (the coverage of the amount of the future "pension," i.e., the accumulation) decrease, even through cost deduction. The law does not only penalize the termination of the contract (full repurchase) or the partial repurchase but also, for example, the reduction of the coverage due to the nonpayment of the fee, specifying the amount which does not require the obligation to repay the benefit.

Cases nominated in the PIT Act:

- the surrender of the contract in part or in full;
- the accounting of installment payments of an insurance policy loan against any savings for retirement;
- if more than six months' worth of risk premium (not including the minimum mandatory risk premium of the original policy) is accounted against any savings for retirement in a period not covered by premium payment in part or in full, including, furthermore;
- any unlawful annuity benefits, irrespective of whether or not the contract ceases in consequence or if the contract is amended where in consequence it no longer meets the criteria of a pension insurance contract under this Act.

The private individual shall not be liable to repayment obligation in the event of full compliance with the conditions of payment of tax-exempt pension benefits. Moreover, no repayment obligation applies if the contract is terminated due to the liquidation of the insurance company.

The insurance company shall establish the private individual's repayment obligation, and shall deduct it from the sum payable to the private individual, if any, and shall pay it to the tax authority under the title of personal income tax by the twelfth day of the month following the date when the event invoking the repayment obligation took place.

If the aforementioned obligation cannot be deducted in part or in whole for any reason, the insurance company shall indicate in the certificate the amount which could not have been deducted in part or in whole and shall inform the private individual of his obligation to pay the sum that was not deducted. The private individual affected shall declare the amount of the repayment obligation that was not deducted by the insurance company in the tax return prepared without the assistance of the tax authority based on the certificate made out by the insurance company and shall pay it by the deadline prescribed for filing the tax return.[488]

If a private individual has provided for the transfer of a specific portion of his tax in a voluntary mutual fund statement, an individual retirement account statement and a pension insurance statement alike, the sum transferred by the tax authority may not exceed (on the aggregate) HUF 280,000.[489]

488. Subsections 1–8 of s. 44/C of the PIT Act.
489. Subsection 1 of s. 44/D of the PIT Act.

Chapter 2. Taxation of Income from Insurance Activity

442. The PIT Act generally determines the taxpayer's taxable income and revenue, after which he has to pay personal income tax. The tax payable on the income covered by this Act is 15% of the tax base.[490] In relation to insurance contracts, the law refers to two types of revenues which may result in a tax payment obligation:

- the insurance premium paid by the other party (contracting party), the so-called taxable insurance premium, since the insurer increases with this amount because it does not pay the insurance premium from its own income, which is tax-exempt income only in cases determined by law; and
- the *service of the insurer,*[491] which is a tax-exempt income except from the statutory exceptions;

  The *insurance premium is considered to be the taxable income of the insured person* if the insurance contract was concluded for the insured person by another person (in particular in case of life insurance or liability insurance) and the premium is paid by the third party. In the following cases, the insurance premium paid by another person cannot be considered taxable income:
- a premium paid for the purchase of an annuity from the insurer by a private pension fund (*see* Part V, Chapter 6).

Under subsection 2a of section 4 of the PIT Act, no revenue shall be considered acquired upon payment of the premium for liability insurance covering risks arising from the payer's liability for damages, as well as from the liability of any private individual who participates in the payer's activity—for the benefit of the payer's activity—covering risks to an extent related to such activity (including restitution).

According to subsection 1a of section 7 of the PIT Act, the insured private individual shall not be considered to have acquired any income at the time of payment of the premium, if the other person paying the premium is entitled to the benefits, without restrictions.

Except if the contract is modified according to the following:

> Subsection 3a of section 9 of PIT Act: If the insurance contract, under the conditions of Subsection 1a of Section 7, is subsequently amended to alter the beneficiary and naming the insured person or another private individual (not the person paying the premium) to receive the benefits (for the purposes of this Act, including the case where the insured person replaces the contracting party), the premium paid up to time of amendment shall be treated in full as taxable insurance premium at that time on the part of the insured private individual, however, if the premium was paid by others, this shall not apply if the private individual repays the amount of the premium to the payer of the premium.

---

490. Subsection 1 of s. 8 of the PIT Act.
491. Under Point 64 of s. 3 of the PIT Act *insurance settlement* shall mean valuable consideration provided by the insurance carrier for which the insurance company is liable at the time an insured event occurs by virtue of the underlying insurance contract.

As a general rule, under subsection 1c of section 7 of the PIT Act, with the exceptions determined in subsection 3a of section 9, the insured private individual shall not be considered to have acquired any income where he takes the place of the policyholder in an insurance contract concluded by another person and fails to reimburse to that policyholder the premiums the policyholder paid previously. From the point of view of the tax law, such a situation cannot be considered the modification of the contract, i.e., the entry of the insured person instead of the contracting party, in particular with the aim of circumventing the personal income tax, is not the modification of the contract according to the law.

443. According to Point a) of subsection 1 of section 7 of the PIT Act, any income that is declared tax exempt under Annex 1 of this Act shall not be taken into account when calculating income.

According to Point 6.3. of Annex 1 of the PIT Act, payments received from insurers are tax-exempt, except otherwise provided by law. Therefore, tax exempt is, for example, the reimbursement of the costs of medical treatment and care according to an accident insurance or sickness insurance. Under certain conditions, a lump-sum payment or a monthly allowance on the basis of pension insurance and annuity insurance is also tax-exempt.

Point 6.6. of Annex 1 of the PIT Act lists the services which have to be considered *taxable income*. These are:

(a) payments for reimbursement for loss of income as part of liability insurance coverage;
(b) payments of benefits received under personal insurance contract[492] that is not qualified as a death benefit under an insurance, pension insurance, annuity insurance,[493] accident insurance, or health insurance policy;
(c) the value of insurance benefits, in respect of which the private individual claimed the insurance premium granting eligibility thereto as a cost.

According to subsection 1 of section 65 of the Act, the above-listed taxable income has to be considered so-called interest income, with the proviso that risk life insurance premium shall not be recognized as premium paid up. The amount of the tax is 15%.

According to Point 6.7. of Annex 1 of the PIT Act, tax-exempt revenues are:

(a) indemnity payments paid to cover the expenses of the aggrieved party, including if such expenses are incurred in connection with the acquisition of income;

492. According to Point 90 of s. 3 of the PIT Act, *personal insurance* shall cover life, accident, and health insurance policies.
493. According to Point 90 of s. 3 of the PIT Act *annuity insurance* shall mean a type of life insurance—including non-degressive, immediate annuity policies—where annuity benefits are provided until the end of the tenth year from the first payment, or until the insured person's death, provided that the benefits are non-degressive and are paid at least annually, or more frequently.

(b) the expense reimbursement portion in respect of a payment, or its lump-sum redemption, that covers damages and is paid in lieu of an expense reimbursement or income.

Part X. Risk Management and Prevention Management[494]

Judit Barta

Chapter 1. Risk Management System

444. Risk management of insurance companies can occur in three areas:

(1) Within the framework of the inner risk management which is ruled by the BIns. and the supplementary legal regulations.
(2) By the obligation stipulated by the BIns., which imposes the regular report obligation, information obligation, and publication of management data.
(3) Through the risk-based supervision of the NBH.

In the event of small insurers, simplified obligations shall be applied with special regard to the smaller risk.

§1. The Inner Risk Management System of the Insurance Company

445. According to section 86 of the BIns., the insurance or reinsurance company shall have in place an effective risk management system necessary to identify, measure, monitor, manage, and report, on a continuous basis, the risks at an individual and at an aggregated level, to which they are or could be exposed, and their

494. EIOPA published the results of the EU-wide insurance stress test on Dec. 15, 2016.
The 2016 survey focused on the low-yield environment. Accordingly, the participants quantified the effects of two theoretical scenarios: In one, yields remain at a persistently low level, while in the other, the decline in yields involves a general decrease of market prices. The survey happened in accordance with the principles of Solvency II, which came into force on Jan. 1, 2016.
In the stress test covering 236 insurers in thirty countries, ten Hungarian insurance companies participated.
According to the results of the stress test, the Hungarian insurers were better than their European partners. In the case of the persistently low-yield scenario, the solvency capital decreases 18% on the European level, and 14% on the Hungarian level. In the case of a "double-blow" scenario which counts on the fall of the prices of market instruments, the average fall of 28.9% of EU insurers would be only 13.2% in Hungarian insurers.
Source: https://mabisz.hu/szemle/?p=6168.

interdependencies. The risk management system is comprised of the necessary strategies, processes, and reporting procedures. The risk management system shall be effective and well integrated into the organizational structure and in the decision-making processes of the insurance or reinsurance company with proper consideration of the activities of executive employees who effectively run the company or have other key functions.

446. The BIns. also defines the areas which shall be covered by the risk management system:[495]

(a) insurance or reinsurance underwriting and reserving;
(b) asset liability management;
(c) investment, in particular derivatives;
(d) liquidity and concentration risk management;
(e) operational risk management;
(f) reinsurance and other risk mitigation techniques;
(g) the risks to be included in the calculation of the solvency capital requirement, as well as the risks which are not fully included in the calculation thereof;
(h) where the matching adjustment or the volatility adjustment is applied, setting up a liquidity plan projecting the incoming and outgoing cash flows in relation to the assets and liabilities subject to those adjustments; and
(i) where the assessments of external credit assessment institutions are used in the calculation of technical provisions and the solvency capital requirement, assessment of the appropriateness of those external credit assessments wherever practicable.

According to subsection 1 of section 88 of the BIns., for the sake of performing the requirements, the insurer defines the detailed rules in a written policy on risk management.

For insurance and reinsurance companies using a partial or full internal model, the risk management function shall cover the following additional tasks:[496]

(a) to design and implement the internal model;
(b) to test and validate the internal model;
(c) to document the internal model and any subsequent changes made to it;
(d) to analyze the performance of the internal model and to produce summary reports thereof;
(e) to inform the management body about the performance of the internal model, suggesting areas needing improvement, and updating that body on the status of efforts to improve previously identified weaknesses.

495. Subsection 1 of s. 87. of the BIns.
496. Subsection 2 of s. 87 of the BIns.

447. As part of its risk management system, every insurance and reinsurance company shall conduct *its own-risk and solvency assessment.*[497]

The own-risk and solvency assessment shall include at least the following:

(a) description of the insurance or reinsurance company's specific risk profile;
(b) the insurance or reinsurance company's underwriting liabilities and its overall solvency needs, taking into account the specific risk profile, approved risk tolerance limits, and the business strategy of the insurance or reinsurance company;
(c) the compliance, on a continuous basis, with the solvency capital requirements, minimum capital requirement, and the requirements regarding technical provisions;
(d) the significance with which the specific risk profile of the insurance or reinsurance company concerned deviates from the assumptions underlying the solvency capital requirement, calculated with the standard formula or with its partial or full internal model; and
(e) where the matching adjustment or the volatility adjustment is applied, the assessment of compliance with the solvency capital requirements and the minimum capital requirement with and without taking into account those adjustments and transitional measures.[498]

As part of its risk and solvency assessment, every insurance and reinsurance company *shall prepare a scheme of operations for at least three years*, complete with the solvency capital requirement covering the entire duration of the plan.[499]

Insurance and reinsurance companies shall perform their own-risk and solvency assessment, prepare the scheme of operations and present the minimum solvency capital requirement *at least once a year* without any delay following any significant change in their risk profile. Insurance and reinsurance companies *shall inform the Authority* by November 30 each year about the results of each own-risk and solvency assessment and the methodologies used for the assessment. Insurance and reinsurance companies shall inform the Authority of the results of own-risk and solvency assessment conducted following any significant change in their risk profile within thirty days.

§2. Performance of the Report and Information Obligation, Publication of Management Data

I. Provisions Relating to Publication Obligation

448. The relevant rules of the BIns. serve compliance with Solvency II. and Article 297 of the Commission Regulation 2015/35, which supplements Solvency II.

497. Subsection 1 of s. 89 of the BIns.
498. Subsection 2 of s. 89 of the BIns.
499. Subsection 4 of s. 89 of the BIns.

Insurance and reinsurance companies are required to produce an annual report covering their financial situation and solvency.[500]

The detailed rules relating to the report can be found in the Government Decree No. 314/2015. (X. 28.).

II. Information Obligation

449. Insurance and reinsurance companies shall inform the NBH within two working days:

(a) if unable to meet their payment obligations due to lack of financial cover;
(b) if their technical provisions—including technical provisions of accountancy—are below the amount required at the time when determined, or if the cover for technical provisions of accountancy is insufficient; furthermore, in the case of insurance or reinsurance companies using the matching adjustment, if they are no longer able to meet the conditions for using the matching adjustment;
(c) if they observe that the solvency capital requirement is no longer complied with—as provided by the BIns.—or where there is a risk of noncompliance in the following three months;
(d) if they observe that the minimum capital requirement is no longer complied with or where there is a risk of noncompliance in the following three months;
(e) if their credit liabilities have exceeded 5% of the subscribed capital;
(f) on transferring eligible own funds available in one class of insurance for covering the solvency capital requirement of the other class of insurance.[501]

450. Insurance and reinsurance companies shall notify the Authority within thirty days:

- the solvency capital requirement is recalculated if the risk profile of the insurance or reinsurance company deviates significantly from the assumptions underlying the last reported solvency capital requirement;
- the reason if the minimum capital requirement is determined by the limit provided for in subsection 1 of section 102 of the BIns.[502]

III. Obligation of Data Reporting

451. Insurance and reinsurance companies shall report to the Authority in accordance with the NBH Act.

Insurance and reinsurance companies shall send to the Authority:

500. Subsection 1 of s. 108 of the BIns.
501. Subsection 1 of s. 267 of the BIns.
502. Subsection 1 of s. 268 of the BIns.

(a) a supervisory report once a year, in addition to the annual account;
(b) a quarterly report concerning the key characteristics of the insurance or reinsurance company's operations, as well as a report covering large exposures and the estimated figures for the solvency margin, own funds, and technical provisions;
(c) the outcome of the calculation of the solvency capital requirement once a year;
(d) the outcome of the calculation of the minimum capital requirement quarterly.[503]

Where the reduction of the matching adjustment or the volatility adjustment to zero would result in noncompliance with the solvency capital requirement, the insurance or reinsurance company *shall also submit to the Authority an analysis of the measures it could apply in such a situation to reestablish the level of eligible own funds* covering the solvency capital requirement or to reduce its risk profile to restore compliance with the solvency capital requirement.[504]

§3. Supervisory Activity

I. Authorization

452. The Authority's authorization shall be required for determining ancillary own-fund items and for the assessment and classification of own-fund items which are not covered by the list established in the Solvency II Directive for the transfer of additional capital if there is a solvency deficit in any class of insurance in the case of insurance companies authorized to conduct both life insurance and non-life insurance business. The authorization is needed for the application of the full or partial internal model, for major changes to an internal model and changes to the policy for changing an internal model, for returning to the standard model, and for the use of specific items within the insurance company's standard model.[505]

II. Supervisory Control

453. According to Points ca) and d) of subsection 2 of section 64 of the NBH Act, the NBH shall carry out a comprehensive supervisory control at insurance and reinsurance companies at least every three years and at small insurance companies at least every five years.

Within the framework of its control procedures, the Authority shall review and evaluate the strategies, processes, and reporting procedures which are established by the insurance and reinsurance companies to comply with the conditions provided by the law or other regulations and administrative provisions adopted relative to insurance activities and in supervisory decisions. That review and evaluation shall comprise the assessment of the qualitative requirements relating to the system of

503. Subsections 1–2 of s. 269 of the BIns.
504. Subsection 5 of s. 87 of the BIns.
505. Subsection 1 of s. 237 of the BIns.

governance, the assessment of the risks which the insurance or reinsurance companies concerned face or may face, and the assessment of the ability of those insurance or reinsurance companies to assess those risks taking into account the environment in which the companies are operating.[506]

454. The Authority shall, in particular, review the own-risk and solvency assessment, technical provisions provided by a separate law, the quality and quantity of own funds, solvency margin requirements, and ongoing compliance with the requirements for full and partial internal models.

The Authority shall assess the adequacy of the methods and practices of the insurance companies designed to identify possible events or future changes in economic conditions that could have adverse effects on the overall financial standing of the company concerned. The Authority shall assess the ability of the insurance companies to withstand those possible negative events or future changes in economic conditions.

III. The Authority's Measures Concerning to Risk Management[507]

455. The BIns. means in the framework of *reorganization measures* any intervention by the supervisory authorities which is intended to preserve or restore the financial situation of an insurance company.

The Authority is entitled to:

- issue a warning to the insurance or reinsurance company and also to its senior executive to comply with the provisions of this Act and other laws and regulations;
- order the cessation of the infringement or prohibit any further infringement;

506. Subsections 1–2 of s. 276 of the BIns.

507. In 2015–2016, there were two occasions, when serious risk management happened. In both cases small mutual associations were affected.

The NBH has assigned a Supervisory Commissioner to the Dimenzió Insurance Association on the basis of its supervisory review. One of its reasons was the insufficient amount of solvency capital.

The financial plan submitted by the insurance association was rejected by the NBH and withdrew the activity license of the insurance association.

Source: https://mabisz.hu/szemle/?p=5642.

https://www.mnb.hu/sajtoszoba/sajtokozlemenyek/2022-evi-sajtokozlemenyek/dimenzio-sikeres-volt-az-allomanyatruhazas-levonul-a-felugyeleti-biztos.

In its final decree the NBH terminated the restriction of the right of disposition relating to the technical provisions and solvency capital of the insurance company, during the supervision at the KÖBE mutual association. This was the last remaining sanction of the bank's successful early precautionary measures. The insurer was placed in a strapped position because of the noncompliant risk management of motor vehicle liability insurance, and a worrying reserve situation emerged. The financial plan submitted by the KÖBE was approved by the NBH.

Source: https://mabisz.hu/szemle/?p=5853.

https://www.jogiforum.hu/hir/2016/08/25/ujabb-korlatozast-oldott-fel-a-kobe-nel-az-mnb-az-atfogo-vizsgalatot-befejezte-a-jegybank/.

- order the insurance or reinsurance company to take measures within the prescribed time limit to ensure compliance with the provisions of laws and regulations governing the pursuit of the business of insurance or reinsurance and to eliminate any deficiencies uncovered;
- order the suspension or prohibition of marketing of certain insurance products;
- establish an obligation for disclosing specific data or information;
- order the insurance or reinsurance company to draw up new internal regulations within the time limit prescribed or to revise or apply the existing regulations along specific guidelines;
- require the insurance or reinsurance company to take measures for the reinforcement of the arrangements, processes, mechanisms, and strategies relating to its internal control mechanism, corporate governance functions, risk management procedures, and internal models for own-risk and solvency assessment;
- advise the insurance or reinsurance company to reduce operating expenses;
- to establish adequate technical provisions or technical provisions of accountancy, to recalculate the solvency margin requirement, and to maintain the solvency margin as appropriate, to preserve or restore its financial situation;
- order the insurance or reinsurance company to submit a finance scheme or a recovery plan;
- impose additional capital requirements upon the insurance or reinsurance company;
- appoint a supervisory commissioner.[508]

456. Where an insurance or reinsurance company does not comply with the Government Decree on the Own Funds and Technical Provisions of Insurance Companies and Reinsurance Companies relating to technical provisions, the Authority may—by means of resolution—prohibit the free disposal of the insurance company's assets.[509]

457. Within two months after the notification, the insurance or reinsurance company concerned shall submit a *recovery plan* for approval by the Authority.

The Authority shall approve the recovery plan if it is suitable to enable the insurance or reinsurance company concerned to achieve, within six months after the notification:

(a) the reestablishment of the level of eligible own funds covering the solvency capital requirement; or
(b) the reduction of its risk profile to ensure compliance with the solvency capital requirement.[510]

458. Within one month after the notification, the insurance or reinsurance company concerned shall submit a finance scheme for approval by the Authority.

508. Subsection 1 of s. 291 of the BIns.
509. Subsection 1 of s. 307 of the BIns.
510. Subsection 1 of s. 309 of the BIns.

The Authority shall approve the scheme if it is suitable to enable the insurance or reinsurance company concerned to achieve, within three months after the notification:

(a) the reestablishment of at least the level of eligible own funds covering the minimum capital requirement; or
(b) the reduction of its risk profile to ensure compliance with the minimum capital requirement.[511]

511. Subsections 1–2 of s. 312 of the BIns.

Selected Bibliography

Banyár, József & NAGY Koppány. *A haláleseti kedvezményezettek védelmének magyarországi helyzetéről* [On the Situation of the Protection of Beneficiaries of Death in Hungary]. Biztosítás és Kockázat, Vol. II/1, 2015.

Banyár, Jozsef & Turi, Petra: *The Evolution of the Insurance Consumer Protection Approach in Hungary.* In *Public Finance Quarterly,* v 2019/2, p. 200. https://unipub.lib.uni-corvinus.hu/4223/1/PSz_Banyar_Turi_2019.pdf.

Christian, von Bar. *Eric* Clive *and Hans Schulte-Nölke: Principles, Definitions and Model Rules of European Private Law. Draft Common Frame of Reference (DCFR) Outline Edition*, Sellier, Munich: European Law Publishers, 2009.

Dr. Barta, Judit. *A biztosító tájékoztatási kötelezettsége a szerződéskötés folyamatában, különös tekintettel az EU vonatkozó irányelveire* [The Notification Obligation of the Insurer During the Conclusion of the Contract with Particular Emphasis on the Relevant EU Directive]. In *Az UNIO-s csatlakozás hatása a letelepedés és a szolgáltatások szabad áramlása körében Tanulmánykötet* [The Effects of the Accession to the EU from the Point of View of the Freedom of Establishment and Services]. Miskolc: Novotni Publisher, 2005, 28–49.

Dr. Barta, Judit & Dr. Dezse Tivadar. *The Hungarian pension system: the present and a possible future.* In *European Integration Studies*, Vol. 12, Number 1, Miskolc University Press, 2016, 87–99.

Dr. Barta, Judit. *The Role and Function of the PAY-AS-YOU-EARN pension system in the Hungarian pension system.* In *European Integration Studies*, Vol. 9, Number 1, Miskolc University Press, 2011, 5–15.

Dr. Barta, Judit. *Visszatérés az egypilléres kötelező nyugdíjrendszerhez* (a 2010. December 13-án elfogadott törvénycsomag értékelése) [Return to the One-Pillar Compulsory Pension System (The Evaluation of the Package of Laws Adopted on December 13, 2010)]. In *Gazdaság és Jog,* 2011/3., 9–15.

Dr. Barta, Judit. *A kiegészítő nyugdíjpillér ezen belül a magánnyugdíjpénztári rendszer aktuális helyzete és értékelése* [The Current State Of The Supplementary Private Pension Fund System From The Aspect Of Contributors]. The Publications of the MultiScience—XXIX. MicroCAD. International Multidisciplinary Scientific Conference University of Miskolc, April 9–10, 2015. ISBN 978-963-358-061-5. http://www.uni-miskolc.hu/~microcad/publikaciok/2015/E2_Barta_Judit.pdf.

Selected Bibliography

Dr. Barta, Judit. *Örökölhetőség, és hozzátartozói ellátás kérdése a magyar kiegészítő nyugdíjpillér egyes intézményeiben* [Issues on Inheritance and Relatives' Care in Certain Institutions of the Hungarian Supplementary Pension Pillar]. In Mélypataki Gábor (ed.), *A szociális jog aktuális kérdései Magyarországon és az Európai Unióban* [Actual Issues on Social Law in Hungary and in the European Union]. Conference volume, February 2, 2016, 22–29.

University of Miskolc, Faculty of law, (ISBN:978-963-358-123-0).

http://fesbp.hu/common/pdf/A_szocialis_jog_aktualis_kerdesei_2017.pdf.

Dr. Barta, Judit. *A pszichés nyomásgyakorlás, mint tisztességtelen kereskedelmi gyakorlat* [Psychological Pressure as an Unfair Commercial Practice]. In Ünnepi tanulmányok Fazekas Judit tiszteletére Keserű Barna Arnold & Szoboszlai-Kiss Katalin (szerk.), 33–49. ISBN 978-615-6491-12-1 DOI: 10.59199/salusvocalis.2023, Kiadó: Universitas-Győr Nonprofit Kft.

Dr. Barta, Judit. *Az EU által meghirdetett digitális forradalom hatása a kereskedelmi jog egyes területein: szerződések, fogyasztóvédelem, gazdasági verseny, gazdasági társaságok* [The Impact of the Digital Revolution Announced by the EU in Certain Areas of Commercial Law: Contracts, Consumer Protection, Economic Competition, Business Companies]. https://www.mjsz.uni-miskolc.hu/files/13820/4_bartajudit_t%C3%B6rdelt.pdf.

Dr. Barta, Judit, *Szakmai felelősségbiztosítás—tervezői felelősségbiztosítás* [Professional Liability Insurance—Designer Liability Insurance]. In Dr. Barta Judit (szerk.). *Biztosítás, több szem-szögéből.* Ünnepi kötet Ujváriné Dr. Antal Edit c. egyetemi docens 65. születésnapja tiszteletére. Novotni Alapítvány-Patrocinium Kiadó, Miskolc-Budapest, 2019, 209–223.

Barta, Judit & Kántor Kinga. *Az öngyilkosság, mint mentesülésre okot adó esemény az életbiztosítási szerződések körében és annak kivételes büntetőjogi szálai. [Suicide as an exempting event in life insurance contracts and its exceptional criminal law implications].* In *Miskolci Jogtudó,* 2019/1, 1–7. https://jogtudo.uni-miskolc.hu/files/4150/MJ2019iss1art1BartaKantor.pdf.

Dr. Barzó, Tímea, *Praxisjog. Aktuális kérdések az egészségügyi alapellátásban* [Praxis Law. Actual Issues on Basic Health-Care Service] Medicina Publisher, 2007, 146–147.

Hugh, Beale. *Digital Content Directive And Rules For Contracts On Continuous Supply.* Journal of Intellectual Property, Information Technology and Electronic Commerce Law Vol. 12, Issue 2, April 2021, 96–111. https://www.jipitec.eu/issues/jipitec-12-2-2021/5286.

Dr. Dénes, Beatrix, et al. *Biztosításfelügyelet változásai az Európai Unióhoz való csatlakozás tükrében* [Charges of the Insurance Supervision in the Light of European Union] Biztosítás és Kockázat, Vol. I/1., 20–32.

Martin, Ebers. *Liability For Artificial Intelligence And EU Consumer Law.* Journal of Intellectual Property, Information Technology and Electronic Commerce Law. Vol. 12, Issue 2, April 2021, 204–220. https://www.jipitec.eu/issues/jipitec-12-2-2021/5289.

Dr. Fazekas, Judit. *Hungarian Contract Law.* International Encylopaedia of Laws, General Editor Prof. Dr. R. Blanpain, Vols. 31, 32, Kluwer Law International Pub. Co., 2003, 372.

Dr. Fazekas, Judit. *Fogyasztóvédelmi jog* [Law of Consumer Protection]. Budapest: Complex Publisher, 2007, 37–90, 137–153.

Dr. Fazekas, Judit. *A fogyasztóvédelmi acquis átvételének jogi és szervezeti kérdései. Csatlakozás-Jogközelítés* [Legal and Organisational Question on the Reception of Consumer Protection Acquis]. Budapest: KJK KERSZÖV Publisher, 2013, 153–193.

Dr. Fazekas, Judit. *General Contract Terms and Unfair Contractual Provisions in Hungarian Civil Law.* In Peter Vojcik & Ján Husár (ed.). *Posobeni práva v. 21. storoci Sukromné právo v. súcastnosti a perspektive. Košice, Univerzita Pavla Jozefa Safárika v. Kosiciach*, 2013, 58–72.

Dr. Fazekas, Judit. *Az általános szerződési feltételek—tisztességtelen kikötések* [Standard Contract Terms—Unfair Terms] In Csehi Zoltán, et al. (ed.). *(L)ex Cathedra et Praxis. Ünnepi kötet Lábady Tamás 70. születésnapja alkalmából* [(L)ex Cathedra et Praxis—Festive Volume on the 70th Anniversary of Lábady Tamás]. Budapest: Pázmány Press, 2014, 269–285.

Dr. Fazekas, Judit. *Fogyasztóvédelmi jog 2.0* [Consumer Protection Law 2.0] Budapest: Gondolat Kiadó, 2022.

Dr. Fazekas, Judit. *Hannibal ante portas! Autonóm járművek—Termékfelelősség—Biztosítás* [Hannibal ante portas! Autonomous Vehicles—Product Liability—Insurance]. In Barta Judit (ed.). *Biztosítás, több szem-szögéből. Ünnepi kötet Ujváriné dr. Antal Edit c. egyetemi docens 65. születésnapja tiszteletére.* Novotni Alapítvány-Patrocinium Kiadó, Miskolc-Budapest, 2019, 139–163.

Dr. Fazekas, Judit. *Az autonóm mobilitás stratégiai és szabályozási keretei az Európai Unióban* [Strategic and Regulatory Frameworks of Autonomous Mobility in the European Union]. In Lévayné, Fazekas Judit & Kecskés Gábor (szerk.). *Az autonóm járművek és intelligens rendszerek jogi vonatkozásai.* Győr, Magyarország: Universitas-Győr Nonprofit Kft. 2020, 348, 221–254.

Dr. Fuglinszky, Ádám. *Kártérítési jog* [Law on Damage Compensation]. Budapest: Hvgorac Publisher, 2015.

Dr. Harsányi, Gyöngyi. *Reflexiók a fogyasztó és a befektető, mint jogi fogalom megjelenéséről a magyar magánjogban* [Reflections on the Appearance of Consumer and Investor as Legal Concepts in Hungarian Private Law]. In *Ünnepi tanulmányok Fazekas Judit tiszteletére Keserű Barna Arnold*, Szoboszlai-Kiss Katalin (szerk.), 227–241. ISBN 978-615-6491-12-1 DOI: 10.59199/ salusvocalis.2023, Kiadó: UNIVERSITAS-Győr Nonprofit Kft.

Dr. Harsányi, Gyöngyi. *A közvetítők szabályozásának speciális vonásai a befektetési ügyletek körében. A biztostásközvetítés és a befektetésközvetítés szabályozásának kapcsolódási pontjai* [Special features of the Regulation of Intermediaries in Investment Transactions. Connection Points of Regulation of Insurance Brokerage and Investment Brokerage]. In Barta Judit (szerk.). *Biztosíltás, több szem-szögéből. Ünnepi kötet Ujváriné dr. Antal Edit c. egyetemi docens 65. születésnapja tiszteletére*, Novotni Alapítvány-Patrocinium Kiadó, Miskolc-Budapest, 2019, 19–30.

Dr. Kiss, Eszter. *A kötelező gépjármű-felelősségbiztosítás rövid története és alapvető jellemzői* [Short History and Basic Features of Compulsory Motor Vehicle Liability Insurance]. Debreceni Jogi Műhely, 2013, 3. szám, 17–36.

Selected Bibliography

Dr. Kovács, Kázmér & Dr. Kovács Szabolcs. *Indemnification and Insurance Contracts* In István Sándor Dr. (ed.). *Business Law in Hungary.* Magister Books, Budapest: Patrocinium Kiadó, 2016, 388–405.

Lencsés, Katalin & PAÁL Zoltán. *Több vagy jobb minőségű tájékoztatás a befektetési termékek piacán? Az Európai PRIIPS szabályozás státusza és kihívásai* [More or Better Information on the Investment Product Market? Status and Challenges of the European PRIIPs Regulation]. Biztosítás és Kockázat, 2015/3., 12–29.

Lencsés, Katalin. *Bevezetés az új európai biztosítási értékesítési (IDD) irányelvbe* [Introduction to the New IDD Directive]. Biztosítás és Kockázat, 2015/3., 16–31.

Lévayné Fazekas, Judit. *A magánjog kihívásai a XXI. században* [The Challenges of Private Law in the XXI. Century]. [online] in Jog-Állam-Politika. *Jog- és politikatudományi folyóirat, 2020, XII. évf. Különszám*, A Széchenyi István Egyetem Deák Ferenc Állam- és Jogtudományi Karának tudományos kiadványa, Győr, 131–144.

https://jap.sze.hu/images/lapsz%C3%A1mok/2020/K%C3%BCl%C3%B6nsz%C3%A1m/JAP_2020_KOLONSZAM.pdf.

Lévayné, Fazekas Judit & Lévay Miklós. *A fogyasztóvédelem alkotmányossági kérdéseiről és a magyar fogyasztóvédelmi intézményrendszer változásairól* [On the Constitutional Issues of Consumer Protection and Changes in the Hungarian Consumer Protection Institutional System]. in Homicskó Árpád Olivér & Szuchy Róbert (szerk.). *De Iuris Peritorum Meritis 11. 60 Studia In Honorem Péter Miskolczi-Bodnár.* KÁroli Gáspár Református Egyetem Állam- és Jogtudományi Kar, Budapest, 2017, 373–389.

Dr. Mádi, Sarolta. *A társadalombiztosítási szerv megtérítési igénye, mint az üzemi balesetek és foglalkozási megbetegedések prevenciójának egyik eszköze* [Compensation Claim of Social Security Institution, as an Instrument of Prevention of Occupational Accidents and Sickness] Miskolci Jogi Szemle, 2013/1., 68–73.

Magnava, Marina. *Hungary: The MNB is Working on a New Concept to Improve Life Insurance.* 5. 12. 2023. (online). https://www.xprimm.com/HUNGARY-The-MNB-is-working-on-a-new-concept-to-improve-life-insurance-articol-19-21167.htm.

Mátyás, Miklós Dániel, et al. *evolúció vagy revolúció—Az etikus életbiztosítási szabályozás előzményei, elemei, hatása, nemzetközi párhuzamok* [Ethical Life Insurance: Evolution or Revolution—Preludes, Elements, Effect and International Parallel of Ethical Life Insurance] In Biztosítás és kockázat, 2016/4. 12., 12–38.

Medve, Flora. *Market Share of Insurance Companies in HUNGARY in 2021, by gross premiums written.* 15. 08. 2023. (online). https://www.statista.com/statistics/1264417/hungary-insurance-companies-market-share-by-gross-premiums-written/.

Dr. Miskolczi, Bodnár Péter & Dr. SÁNDOR István. *A fogyasztóvédelmi jog magyar szabályozása* [Hungarian Regulations on the Law of Consumer Protection]. Budapest: Patrocinium Publisher, 2010, 97–104.

Dr. Miskolczi, Bodnár Péter. *A versenyjog és az új Ptk [*Competition Law and the New CC]. Versenytükör, 2014/1, 73–90.

Dr. Miskolczi, Bodnár Péter. *A vezető tisztségviselők felelőssége és ennek biztosíthatósága* [Liability and Insurability of Executive Officers]. Gazdaság és Jog, 1997/1., 3–16.

Dr. Miskolczi, Bodnár Péter. *Fogyasztói szerződések* [Consumer Contracts], Budapest: Patrocinium, 2015.

Dr. Miskolczi, Bodnár Péter. *A kógens és klaudikálóan kógens fogyasztói szabályok gyökerei* [The Roots of Cogent and Claudically Cogent Consumer Rules]. In *Ünnepi tanulmányok Fazekas Judit tiszteletére Keserű Barna Arnold,* Szoboszlai-Kiss Katalin (szerk.), 523–537. ISBN 978-615-6491-12-1 DOI: 10.59199/salusvocalis.2023, Kiadó: Universitas-Győr Nonprofit Kft.

Dr. Miskolczi, Bodnár Péter. *Biztosítók közötti információcsere kartelljogi megítélése* [Cartel Law Assessment of Information Exchange Between Insurers]. In DR. Barta Judit (szerk.). *Biztosítás, több szem-szögéből. Ünnepi kötet Ujváriné dr. Antal Edit c. egyetemi docens 65. születésnapja tiszteletére*. Novotni Alapítvány-Patrocinium Kiadó, Miskolc-Budapest, 2019, 43–55.

Dr. Novotni, Zoltán. *A biztosítási szerződések joga* [The Law of Insurance Contracts]. Budapest: ELTE Jogi Továbbképző Intézet, 1993, 41.

Dr. Novotni, Zoltán. *A felelősségbiztosítási jogviszony alapkérdései a magyar jogban* [Basic Questions on Liability Insurance Relationship in the Hungarian Law]. Candidate thesis, 1981.

Pandurics Anett & Markó Olga. *Felelősségbiztosítások szerepe, jelene és jövője Magyarországon* [Roles, Present and Future of Liability Insurances in Hungary] Biztosítás és Kockázat, Vol. II/3., 78–94.

Dr. Papp, Tekla. *International Encyclopaedia of Law—Corporations and Partnerships Suppl. 81 Hungary Wolters Kluwer*. Alphen aan den Rijn: Kluwer Law International, 2015; ISBN 978-90-654-4946-7, 139–188.

Pataky, Tibor. *A kötelező gépjármű-felelősségbiztosítás szabályozása és továbbfejlesztésének lehetőségei* [The Regulation of Compulsory Motor Vehicle Liability Insurance and the Possibilities for its Further Development], Budapest: HVG–ORAC, 2019, 236.

Dr. Petrétei, József. *Magyarország alkotmányjoga. 1. köt. Alapvetés, alkotmányos intézmények* [Consitutional Law of Hungary. Vol. 1. Basics, Constitutional Institutions]. Pécs, Kodifikátor Foundation, 2013, 161.

Dr. Pusztahelyi Réka, *Mesterséges intelligencia által okozott károk: A no-fault kártalanítási rendszer bevezetésének előnyei és hátrányai* [Damage Caused by Artificial Intelligence: Pros and Cons of Introducing a No-Fault Compensation System]. *Infokommunikáció és jog* 2020/2., (e-különszám), https://infojog.hu/pusztahelyi-reka-mesterseges-intelligencia-altal-okozott-karok-a-no-fault-kartalanitasi-rendszer-bevezetesenek-elonyei-es-hatranyai-2020-2-75-e-kulonszam/.

Dr. Pusztahelyi, Réka. *Towards a European AI Liability System. Multidiszciplináris Tudományok: A Miskolci Egyetem közleménye* 2021/5., 319–321. https://ojs.uni-miskolc.hu/index.php/multi/article/view/894/648.

Dr.Pusztahelyi, Réka. *A veszélyes üzemi felelősség egyes kérdései az új Ptk. rendszerében* [Certain Issues of Liability for Hazardous Activity in the New Civil Code]. Publicationes Universitatis Miskolcinensis Sectio Juridica et Politica, Tomus XXXIII, 2015, 306–325. http://midra.uni-miskolc.hu/document/22054/16382.pdf.

Selected Bibliography

Dr. Pusztahelyi, Réka. *A veszélyes üzemi felelősség szabályozási környezete* [The Regulatory Environment of Liability for Hazardous Activity]. Nemzeti Közszolgálati Egyetem Budapest, 2018.

https://nkerepo.uni-nke.hu/xmlui/bitstream/handle/123456789/12954/Pusztahelyi_A%20veszelyes_uzemi_felelosseg_szabalyozasi_kornyezete_2018.pdf?sequence=1.

Dr. Szedlák Katalin, Viktória. *A biztosítási tevékenységről szóló 2014. évi LXXXVIII. törvény bemutatása a Szolvencia II. tükrében* [Presentation of Act LXXXVIII of 2014 on Insurance Activity in the Mirror of the Solvency II]. *Biztosítás és Kockázat*, Vol. II/1., 12–19.

Dr. Szedlák Katalin, Viktória & ZÁMBÓ Szilvia. *A biztosítókról és a biztosítási tevékenységről szóló törvény—10 év az EU-ban* [Act on Insurance Companies and on Insurance Activities—10 years in the EU] Biztosítás és Kockázat, Vol. I/1., 32–52.

Tamás, Gábor. *A biztosításügy története Magyarországon a kezdetektől 1857-ig* [History of Insurance in Hungary from the Beginnings to 1857] Sangrey Ltd., Solymár, 2013.

Dr. Tőkey, Balázs. *Kitekintés a magán-egészségbiztosítások legelterjedtebb szabályozási megoldásaira* [Outlook for the Most Common Regulation Models of Private Health Insurances] Biztosítás és kockázat, 2015/4. 12., 48–61.

Ujváriné Dr. Antal, Edit. *Az egységes belső biztosítási piacra vonatkozó közösségi jog átvételének szervezeti és anyagi jogi kérdései* [Organizational and Substantive Legal Issues on the Implementation of Community Law Relating to the Unified Internal Insurance Market]. In *Csatlakozás—jogközelítés. Az acquis communautaire adaptálása a magyar jog és intézményrendszerbe* [Accession—Approximation. Adaptation of Acquis Communautaire into the Hungarian Legal and Institutional Regime]. (further authors: Fazekas Judit, Kalas Tibor, Torma András, Prugberger Tamás, Harsányi Gyöngyi, Miskolczi Bodnár Péter, Csécsy György, Farkas Ákos, Kovács Péter Kjk Kerszöv Jogi és Üzleti Kiadó Kft., Budapest, 2003, 227–285.

Ujváriné Dr. Antal, Edit. *A biztosító részvénytársaság* [The Insurance Private Limited Company] In *Ünnepi tanulmányok Balásházy Mária tiszteletére (Egyes magántársaságok társasági jogi szabályozásának közjogi többletszabályai.* [Festive Volume for the Honor of Balásházy Mária] (Further authors: Kovács István, Barta Judit, Harsányi Gyöngyi), Corvinus University of Budapest, Business Law Institution, Budapest, 2010, 39–48.

Ujváriné Dr. Antal, Edit. *Impact of the European Union Law on Hungarian Insurance Law.* In *Prawo CCLXXII Current Problems of English and European Law and reforms. In Central Europe (Poland, Hungary).* Edited by Konrad Nowachky, Wroclaw, 2000, Wydawnictwo Uniwersytetu Wroclawskiego, 551–563.

Ujváriné Dr. Antal, Edit. *Az új Polgári Törvénykönyv biztosítási szerződéssel kapcsolatos szabályai különös tekintettel a szerződés létrejöttére és hatályosulására a jogharmonizáció tükrében* [Regulation of the New Civil Code Relating to the Insurance Contract, with Particular Emphasis on the Conclusion and the Effectiveness of the Contract in Light of the Legal Harmonization]. In *Miskolci Konferenciák 2010. Kodifikációs Tanulmányok a Polgári jog és a Polgári Eljárásjog témakörében* [Conferences in Miskolc 2010. Codification Studies on Civil Law and Civil Procedure Law]. Miskolc: Novotni Publisher, 2011, 160–179.

Ujváriné Dr. Antal, Edit. *A biztosítási szerződési jog változásai az európai jogfejlődés áramában* [The Changes of the Insurance Contract Law in the Light of the European Legal Development]. In *Európai Tükör* Vol. XV No. 10, 2010.

Ujváriné Dr. Antal, Edit. *A biztosítási szerződési jog sajátosságai és változásai Novotni Zoltán szellemi hagyatékának tükrében* [The Specialities and Changes of the Insurance Contract Law in the Light of the Intellectual Heritage Of Novotni Zoltán]. In *Emlékkönyv—In memoriam Novotni Zoltán* [Memory Book—In Memoriam Novotni Zoltán]. Miskolc: Novotni Publisher, 2003, 235–269.

Ujváriné Dr. Antal, Edit. *Tanulmány "A biztosítási szerződés létrejötte, hatályosulása" (Ptk. Kodifikációs Bizottság "Kártérítés és Biztosítás" Munkabizottság részére készített tanulmány az Igazságügyi Minisztérium Közigazgatási Államtitkárának megbízása alapján) [The conclusion and effectiveness of the insurance contract* (Study for the "Compensation and Insurance" Working Committee of the Civil Code Codification Committee on the mandate of the State Secretary of Public Administration of the Ministry of Justice)], 2000. (Manuscript).

Ujváriné Dr. Antal, Edit. *Biztosítási szerződés* [Insurance Contract] In Majoros Tünde (ed.). *Kereskedelmi szerződések alapvető szabályai* [General Rules on Commercial Contracts]. Budapest: Patrocinium Publisher, 2015, 219–273.

Ujváriné Dr. Antal, Edit. *Közvetítői szerződés* [Agency Contract]. In Majoros Tünde (ed.). *Kereskedelmi szerződések alapvető szabályai* [General Rules on Commercial Contracts]. Budapest: Patrocinium Publisher, 2015, 91–106.

Ujváriné Dr. Antal, Edit. *Felelősségtan* [Law of Liability]. Budapest: Patrocinium Publisher, 2017.

Ujváriné Dr. Antal, Edit. *Approximation of Laws on the Field of Hungarian Insurance Law.* In Sectio Juridica Et Politica Tomus XIV. Miskolc University Press, 1997. 39–51.

Ujváriné Dr. Antal, Edit. *A biztosítási törvény és a polgári jog kapcsolódási pontjai* [Linking Points Between the BIns. and the Civil Law]. In Jogtudományi Közlöny, 1996/6., 236–245.

Ujváriné Dr. Antal, Edit. *Jogharmonizációs törekvések a magyar biztosítási jogban* [Legal Harmonization Efforts in the Hungarian Insurance Law]. Publicationes Universitatis Miscolcinensis.Sectio Juridica et Politice, Tomus 14, 1997, 39–51.

Ujváriné Dr. Antal, Edit. *Az általános szerződési feltételek alkalmazása és a tájékoztatási kötelezettség a biztosítási szerződési jogban* [The Use of Standard Contract Terms and the Notification Obligation in the Insurance Contract Law]. In Sectio Juridica Et Politica Tomus XVI. Miskolc University Press, 1999, 311–322.

Ujváriné Dr. Antal, Edit. *A közvetítői szerződés* [Agency Contract]. In Osztovics András (ed.). *A Polgári Törvénykönyvről szóló 2013. évi V. törvény és a kapcsolódó jogszabályok nagykommentárja. III. kötet* [General Commentary of the Act V of 2013 on the Civil Code and of the Relating Legal Acts—Vol. 3]. Opten Ltd., Budapest, 2014, 729–768.

Ujváriné Dr. Antal, Edit. *A biztosítási szerződéssel összefüggő, tájékoztatási szabályokkal kapcsolatos kárfelelősség, különös tekintettel a közvetítői helyzetekre* [Liability for Damages Related to Information Rules Related to the Insurance

Contract, with Particular Regard to Intermediary Situations]. *Biztosítás és Kockázat* V/2, 48–59.

Ujváriné Dr. Antal, Edit. *Fogyasztóvédelem a biztosított szemüvegén át—különös tekintettel a csoportos biztosításra* [Consumer Protection Through the Lens of the Insured—with Particular Regard to Group Insurance]. In *Ünnepi tanulmányok Fazekas Judit tiszteletére Keserű Barna Arnold*, Szoboszlai-Kiss Katalin (szerk.). 747–767. ISBN 978-615-6491-12-1 DOI: 10.59199/salusvocalis.2023, Kiadó: Universitas-Győr Nonprofit Kft.

Ujváriné Dr. Antal, Edit. *A biztosítási tevékenységet végző szervezet reorganizációja, felszámolása* [Reorganization and Liquidation of the Organization Performing Insurance Activities]. In Barta, Judit (szerk.). *A fizetésképtelenség aktuális jogi problémái nemzetközi kitekintéssel* [Current Legal Problems of Insolvency with an International Perspective.]. Budapest-Miskolc: Patrocinium, 2018, 315–330. http://patrocinium.hu/termek/a-fizeteskeptelenseg-aktualis-jogi-problemai-nemzetkozi-kitekintessel/.

Ujváriné Dr. Antal, Edit. *A kárfelelősségi szabályok sajátosságai a biztosítási jogviszonyban* [The Peculiarities of the Liability Rules in the Insurance Legal Relationship]. In Barta, Judit, Barzó Tímea & Csák Csilla (ed.). *Magyarázat a kártérítési jogról.* Budapest: Wolters Kluwer Kiadó, 2018, Part I, Chapter 6, 218–223.

Ujváriné Dr. Antal, Edit. *Felelősség a szerződésen kívül okozott kárért* [Liability for Damage Caused Outside of the Contract]. In Barta, Judit, Barzó Tímea & Csák Csilla (ed.). *Magyarázat a kártérítési jogról.* Budapest: Wolters Kluwer Kiadó, 2018, Part I, Chapter 3/1, 62–96.

Ujváriné Antal Edit. *Felelősség a szerződésen kívül okozott kárért* [Liability for Damage Caused Outside of the Contract]. In Barzó Tímea & Papp Tekla (ed.), CIVILISZTIKA II. Dologi jog—Felelősségtan Scientia Rerum Politicarum, Dialóg Campus Kiadó, Budapest, 2019, Part II, Ch. II, 261–302. https://nkerepo.uni-nke.hu/xmlui/bitstream/handle/123456789/12659/web_PDF_ATMA_Civilisztika_II.pdf?sequence=1.

Ujváriné Dr. Antal, Edit. *A termékfelelősség* [Product Liability]. In Barzó Tímea & Papp Tekla (ed.). *Civilisztika II. Dologi jog—Felelősségtan*, Scientia Rerum Politicarum, Dialóg Campus Kiadó, Budapest, 2019, Part II, Chapter IV/3., 345–357. https://nkerepo.uni-nke.hu/xmlui/bitstream/handle/123456789/12659/web_PDF_ATMA_Civilisztika_II.pdf?sequence=1.

Ujváriné Dr. Antal, Edit. *Az érvénytelenség különös szabályai a biztosítási jogviszonyban* [Special Rules of Invalidity in the Insurance Relationship]. In DR. Stefán Ibolya PhD hallgató (szerk.) & Dr. Pusztahelyi Réka PhD docens (lektor). *Miskolci konferenciák 2018–2019 in Memoriam Novotni Zoltán. Emlékkönyv Novotni Zoltán professzor halálának 25. évfordulója alkalmából.* Tanulmánykötet, Novotni Alapítvány, Miskolc, 2021, 199–219.

Dr. Varga, Zoltán. *Analysis of the Changes in the Hungarian Pension System in 2011.* XXVI. microCAD International Scientific Conference, 29 March–30 March, Conference Book, University of Miskolc Innovation and Technology Transfer Centre.

Varga, Veronika & Madari, Zoltán. *The Hungarian Insurance Market Structure: An Empirical Analysis.* In Central European Journal of Operations Research (2023)

31:927–940. https://doi.org/10.1007/s10100-023-00842-8, https://link.springer.com/article/10.1007/s10100-023-00842-8.

Dr. Zavodnyik, József. *A biztosítási szerződések* [Insurance Contracts]. In Osztovics András (ed.). *A Polgári Törvénykönyvről szóló 2013. évi V. törvény és a kapcsolódó jogszabályok nagykommentárja III. kötet* [General Commentary of the Act V of 2013 on the Civil Code and of the Relating Legal Acts—Vol. 3]. Opten Ltd., Budapest, 2014, 1106–1270.

Dr. Zavodnyik, József. *A biztosítási szerződési jog alapjai* [Basis of Insurance Contract Law]. BOI, 2004, Budapest.

Dr. Zavodnyik, József. *Jogértelmezés A Biztosítási Piacon. Az Uniós Jogszabályok Értelmezése Az Előzetes döntéshozatali eljárások során* [Legal Interpretation in the Insurance Market. Interpretation of Union laws During Preliminary Rulings]. Biztosítás és Kockázat, Vol. II/4., 28–47.

Online Sources

http://biztositasifeltetelek.hu/?page=3&biztosito=0&modozat=0&ervkezdetmin=&ervkezdetmax=&nyomtatvanyszam=&kereses=hitel&kereses2=&megnevezes=&mutat=50&rendez=0&szerint=erv_kezdete.

https://mabisz.hu/wp-content/uploads/2018/08/tajekoztato-a-szallitassal-kapcsolatos-biztositasokrol-20170413.pdf.

https://en.wikipedia.org/wiki/Ajka_alumina_plant_accident.

https://mabisz.hu/szemle/?p=5850.

https://mabisz.hu/szemle/?p=5850.

https://kkvmagazin.com/v/biztositas-kiberbiztonsag-casco-kotelezo-bizalmi-index/.

https://mabisz.hu/wp-content/uploads/2019/10/biztositas-es-kockazat-6-evf-3-szam-4-cikk.pdf.

https://mabisz.hu/szemle/?p=5728.

https://mabisz.hu/szemle/?p=6085.

https://statisztika.mnb.hu/statistical-topics/supervisory-statistics/iii_-insurance-sector/insurance-intermediaries.

Hungarian Insurers' Yearbook 2022. (Includes data for 2021).

https://mabisz.hu/wp-content/uploads/evkonyv/mabisz-evkonyv-2022-en.pdf.

Hungarian Insurers' Yearbook 2021. (Includes data for 2020).

https://mabisz.hu/wp-content/uploads/evkonyv/mabisz-evkonyv-2021-V6j4-EN.pdf.

https://mabisz.hu/szemle/?p=5617.

https://mabisz.hu/szemle/?p=6166.

https://ado.hu/ado/ev-vegere-meghaladhatja-a-460-ezret-az-adokedvezmenyes-nyugdijbiztositasok-szama/.

https://www.mnb.hu/letoltes/publikalando-jelentes-v4-digitalis.pdf.

http://www.atv.hu/belfold/20150719-ujjlevagas-gyilkossag-karambol-igy-dolgoznak-a-biztositasi-csalok.

http://www.borsonline.hu/aktualis/mindenki-lebukott-az-evszazad-biztositasi-csalasaban/49031.

https://www.ksh.hu/docs/hun/xftp/idoszaki/mo/mo2015.pdf.

http://www.portfolio.hu/finanszirozas/bankok/magyar_banki_rangsor_foldcsusz amlas_az_elen.237133.html.
http://szhisz.hu/a-takarekszovetkezetek-lehetnek-a-legnagyobb-penzpiaci-szolgal tatok/.
https://www.fundamenta.hu/cegtortenet.
https://www.nav.gov.hu/nav/szolgaltatasok/jegybank.
https://mabisz.hu/wp-content/uploads/2018/08/evkonyv-2015-magyar.pdf.
http://www.portfolio.hu/finanszirozas/biztositok_penztarak/letaszitottak_tronjarol_ magyarorszag_legnagyobb_biztositojat.228445.html.
https://www.mnb.hu/bekeltetes/tanulsagok-jotanacsok-jogesetek/jogesetek/joges etek-a-biztositasi-szektorban.
https://www.mnb.hu/letoltes/pbt-2022-hun-eves-jelentes.pdf.
http://kozbeszerzes.hu/ertesito/megtekint/portal_322_2016/.
https://www.bkmkik.hu/attachments/article/5512/Magyarország%20számokban_20 21.pdf.
https://www.portfolio.hu/bank/20220601/itt-a-friss-banki-rangsor-lat-valaki-extra profitot-548293.
https://statisztika.mnb.hu/sw/static/file/hitelintprudencialis-hu-20220902.pdf.
https://view.officeapps.live.com/op/view.aspx?src=https%3A%2F%2Fstatisztika .mnb.hu%2Ftimeseries%2Fhit-int-reszletes-2022-03-31.xls&wdOrigin.
https://www.portfolio.hu/uzlet/20220304/fityiszt-mutattak-a-valsagnak-a-magyar-biztositok-14-eve-nem-szarnyaltak-ennyire-az-eletbiztositasok-531019.
https://www.mnb.hu/letoltes/kocka-zati-jelente-s-2022-hun-0825.pdf.
http://mabisz.hu/wp-content/uploads/2021/09/mabisz-evkonyv-2021-V6j3-HU.pdf.
https://www.mnb.hu/letoltes/pbt-eves-jelentes-2021.pdf.
http://www.fome.hu.
http://fogyasztovedelem-gte.hu/penzugyi-fogyasztovedelmi-tanacsado-irodak/.
http://www.jogsertowebaruhazak.kormany.hu/.
https://issuu.com/jegybank/docs/pbt-2020-eves-jelentes-vegleges/6?ff.
https://www.mnb.hu/letoltes/kocka-zati-jelente-s-2022-hun-0825.pdf.
https://eur-lex.europa.eu/legal-content/hu/TXT/?uri=CELEX:62014CJ0096.
https://www.mnb.hu/letoltes/mfo-vedjegyszabalyzat.pdf.
https://www.mnb.hu/kiadvanyok/jelentesek/biztositasi-penztari-tokepiaci-kockazati -es-fogyasztovedelmi-jelentes/biztositasi-penztari-tokepiaci-kockazati-es-fogya sztovedelmi-jelentes-2022.
https://mabisz.hu/wp-content/uploads/2018/09/T%C3%A1j%C3%A9%C3%A1ko ztat%C3%B3-az-%C3%BCzemsz%C3%BCnet-biztos%C3%ADt%C3%A1sr% C3%B3l-honlapra.pdf.
http://repo.aki.gov.hu/3557/1/Mezőgazdasági%20biztosítások%202019.%20év.pdf.
https://www.parlament.hu/irom41/07930/07930-0001.pdf.
https://mabisz.hu/wp-content/uploads/evkonyv/mabisz-evkonyv-2021-V6j4-HU.pdf.
https://mabisz.hu/wp-content/uploads/2018/09/mabisz-alapszabalya-20171204.pdf.
https://www.mnb.hu/letoltes/kgfb-index-infografika-2022q1.pdf.
https://www.ajbh.hu/documents/10180/3190211/Jelent%C3%A9s+a+k%C3%B6 telez%C5%91+g%C3%A9pj%C3%A1rm%C5%B1-felel%C5%91ss%C3%A9

gbiztos%C3%ADt%C3%A1st+%C3%A9rint%C5%91+szab%C3%A1lyoz%C3%A1ssal+%C3%B6sszef%C3%BCgg%C3%A9sben+39_2020/e7343ce3-fb47-1f56-380d-5515fd599e35?version=1.0.
https://public.mkab.hu/dev/dontesek.nsf/0/165126b4063f0406c1258403004de6d4/$FILE/3293_2019%20AB%20hat%C3%A1rozat.pdf.
https://www.mnb.hu/felugyelet/adatszolgaltatas/biztositok/2018-evre-vonatkozo-adatszolgaltatasok/a-kozponti-kgfb-teteles-adatbazis-kkta-technikai-segedletei.
https://mabisz.hu/dijnavigator/.
https://alk.mnb.hu/data/cms2485099/keksz_25810567.pdf.
https://alk.mnb.hu/fogyasztoknak/tematikus_oldalak/kgfb/dijtarifa.
https://www.mnb.hu/letoltes/fedezetlensegi-dijtablazat-2022.pdf.
https://mabisz.hu/fekete-feher-alapszinnel-bocsatjak-ki-a-jovoben-a-zoldkartyat/.
https://mabisz.hu/fedezetlensegi-dijak-2023/.
https://www.portfolio.hu/gazdasag/20230105/husz-ev-alatt-nyolcszorosara-nott-az-egeszsegbiztositasi-piac-588196.
https://www.ius.uzh.ch/en/research/pricl.html.
https://ado.hu/ado/ev-vegere-meghaladhatja-a-460-ezret-az-adokedvezmenyes-nyugdijbiztositasok-szama/.
https://mabisz.hu/szemle/?p=6168.
https://mabisz.hu/szemle/?p=5642.
https://www.mnb.hu/sajtoszoba/sajtokozlemenyek/2022-evi-sajtokozlemenyek/dimenzio-sikeres-volt-az-allomanyatruhazas-levonul-a-felugyeleti-biztos.
https://mabisz.hu/szemle/?p=5853.
https://www.jogiforum.hu/hir/2016/08/25/ujabb-korlatozast-oldott-fel-a-kobe-nel-az-mnb-az-atfogo-vizsgalatot-befejezte-a-jegybank/.
https://www.jipitec.eu/issues/jipitec-12-2-2021/5286.
https://www.mnb.hu/letoltes/mnb-eves-jelentes-2015.pdf.
https://www.mnb.hu/bekeltetes/tanulsagok-jotanacsok-jogesetek.
https://www.mnb.hu/letoltes/pbt-2022-hun-eves-jelentes.pdf.
https://www.mnb.hu/letoltes/mfo-vedjegyszabalyzat.pdf.
https://www.mnb.hu/letoltes/kocka-zati-jelente-s-2022-hun-0825.pdf.
https://hu.wikipedia.org/wiki/Steinherz_Rudolf-gyilkoss%C3%A1g.
https://telex.hu/eszkombajn/2021/03/27/steinherz-rudolf-gyilkossag-bergyilkos-vonat-cegled-biztositasi-csalas.
https://napitortenelmiforras.blog.hu/2015/12/09/murder_me_a_steinherz_rudolf_gyilkossag.
https://trove.nla.gov.au/newspaper/article/201425687.
https://www.mnb.hu/letoltes/mfo-vedjegyszabalyzat.pdf.
https://www.mnb.hu/letoltes/kocka-zati-jelente-s-2022-hun-0825.pdf.
https://nkerepo.uni-nke.hu/xmlui/bitstream/handle/123456789/12659/web_PDF_ATMA_Civilisztika_II.pdf?sequence=1.
https://nkerepo.uni-nke.hu/xmlui/bitstream/handle/123456789/12659/web_PDF_ATMA_Civilisztika_II.pdf?sequence=1.
https://mabisz.hu/fekete-feher-alapszinnel-bocsatjak-ki-a-jovoben-a-zoldkartyat/.
https://alk.mnb.hu/data/cms2485099/keksz_25810567.pdf.
https://public.mkab.hu/dev/dontesek.nsf/0/165126b4063f0406c1258403004de6d4/$FILE/3293_2019%20AB%20hat%C3%A1rozat.pdf.

Selected Bibliography

https://www.ajbh.hu/documents/10180/3190211/Jelent%C3%A9s+a+k%C3%B6telez%C5%91+g%C3%A9pj%C3%A1rm%C5%B1-felel%C5%91ss%C3%A9gbiztos%C3%ADt%C3%A1st+%C3%A9rint%C5%91+szab%C3%A1lyoz%C3%A1ssal+%C3%B6sszef%C3%BCgg%C3%A9sben+39_2020/e7343ce3-fb47-1f56-380d-5515fd599e35?version=1.0.

https://www.mnb.hu/en/hungarian-financial-arbitration-board/introduction/report-on-the-activities-of-the-hungarian-financial-arbitration-board, https://www.mnb.hu/bekeltetes/bemutatkozas/eves-jelenteseink/jelentes-a-penzugyi-bekelteto-testulet-eves-tevekenysegerol-2022.

Index

The numbers here refer to paragraph numbers.

Index